STUDIES IN THE HISTORY
OF CHRISTIAN MISSIONS

R. E. Frykenberg
Brian Stanley
General Editors

STUDIES IN THE HISTORY OF CHRISTIAN MISSIONS

Alvyn Austin
China's Millions: The China Inland Mission and Late Qing Society, 1832-1905

Michael Bergunder
The South Indian Pentecostal Movement in the Twentieth Century

Judith M. Brown and Robert Eric Frykenberg, *Editors*
Christians, Cultural Interactions, and India's Religious Traditions

Robert Eric Frykenberg
Christians and Missionaries in India:
Cross-Cultural Communication Since 1500

Susan Billington Harper
In the Shadow of the Mahatma: Bishop V. S. Azariah
and the Travails of Christianity in British India

D. Dennis Hudson
Protestant Origins in India: Tamil Evangelical Christians, 1706-1835

Ogbu U. Kalu, *Editor,* and Alaine M. Low, *Associate Editor*
Interpreting Contemporary Christianity:
Global Processes and Local Identities

Donald M. Lewis, *Editor*
Christianity Reborn: The Global Expansion of Evangelicalism
in the Twentieth Century

Jon Miller
Missionary Zeal and Institutional Control: Organizational Contradictions
in the Basel Mission on the Gold Coast, 1828-1917

Andrew Porter, *Editor*
The Imperial Horizons of British Protestant Missions, 1880-1914

Dana L. Robert, *Editor*
Converting Colonialism: Visions and Realities in Mission History, 1709-1914

Wilbert R. Shenk, *Editor*
North American Foreign Missions, 1810-1914: Theology, Theory, and Policy

Brian Stanley, *Editor*
Christian Missions and the Enlightenment

Brian Stanley, *Editor*
Missions, Nationalism, and the End of Empire

Kevin Ward and Brian Stanley, *Editors*
The Church Mission Society and World Christianity, 1799-1999

Interpreting Contemporary Christianity

Global Processes and Local Identities

Edited by

Ogbu U. Kalu

Associate Editor
Alaine M. Low

WILLIAM B. EERDMANS PUBLISHING COMPANY
GRAND RAPIDS, MICHIGAN / CAMBRIDGE, U.K.

Published 2008 by
Wm. B. Eerdmans Publishing Co.
2140 Oak Industrial Drive N.E., Grand Rapids, Michigan 49505 /
P.O. Box 163, Cambridge CB3 9PU U.K.

Printed in the United States of America

13 12 11 10 09 08   7 6 5 4 3 2 1

Library of Congress Cataloging-in-Publication Data

Interpreting contemporary Christianity: global processes and local identities
/ edited by Ogbu U. Kalu; associate editor, Alaine M. Low.
   p.   cm. — (Studies in the history of Christian missions)
Includes bibliographical references and index.
ISBN 978-0-8028-6242-6 (pbk.: alk. paper)
1. Christianity.   I. Kalu, Ogbu.   II. Low, Alaine M.

BR145.3.I57   2008

270.8′3 — dc22

2007040634

www.eerdmans.com

Contents

PART V
CULTURAL AND SOCIO-POLITICAL DIMENSIONS
OF GLOBAL PROCESSES

Preface

Studies of globalization are now legion in the social sciences. Studies of religion in relation to globalization are still relatively few, though becoming more numerous. Studies of the Christian religion and globalization from a primarily historical perspective are, however, virtually nonexistent. This volume seeks to begin to remedy this deficiency.

The chapters in this volume were all originally given as papers at an international conference held at the Hammanskraal campus of the University of Pretoria in July 2001. The conference was the final public event of the Currents in World Christianity Project (formerly the North Atlantic Missiology Project), an international research project coordinated by the University of Cambridge and funded by the Pew Charitable Trusts of Philadelphia. The Project combined an interest in the modern history of Protestant missions with an emphasis on the religious aspects of globalization. The Project, and the Pretoria conference itself, involved historians and theologians, missiologists and social scientists, Christians and non-Christians, southerners and northerners. All participants, however, shared a concern to investigate the complex dynamics shaping the recent expansion of Christianity — and particularly of evangelical and pentecostal variants of Christianity — in the southern hemisphere and parts of Asia. All also shared a dissatisfaction with explanations of this process that appeal simply to monochromatic concepts of globalization as homogenization or the extension of American cultural and economic influence. This book suggests how varied are the intersections of external influence and indigenous appropriation that together make up the pattern of the growth of southern Christianity in the course of the last century.

Gratitude is due in the first place to the Pew Charitable Trusts, without whose visionary initiative and generosity the Currents in World Christianity Project and its conferences would not have taken place. The opinions expressed by the contributors to this volume are solely their own, and do not necessarily represent the views of the Pew Charitable Trusts. The Project was unfailingly supported by the Centre for Advanced Religious and Theological Studies in the Faculty of Divinity at the University of Cambridge, and especially by its Director, Dr. David M. Thompson. The conference itself was made a memorable and pleasant experience through the warm hospitality of the University of Pretoria, and particularly of Professor J. W. "Hoffie" Hofmeyr of the Department of Theology. The efficient labors of Mr. Petrus Maritz of Pretoria and Mrs. Liesl Amos of Cambridge were essential to its success. Finally, I wish to thank Professor Ogbu Kalu, of McCormick Theological Seminary, Chicago, and Dr. Alaine Low of Oxford, for editing these papers so skillfully into their present shape.

Dr. Brian Stanley, *Director*
Currents in World Christianity Project
University of Cambridge
December 2007

Contributors

AFE ADOGAME is Lecturer in World Christianity at the University of Edinburgh. He has previously been an Associate Professor in Comparative Religion at Lagos State University, Lagos, Nigeria, and Senior Research Fellow at the University of Bayreuth and at the Center for the Study of World Religions, Harvard Divinity School. He has published numerous articles and a book on the Celestial Church of Christ (1991).

EDITH BLUMHOFER is Director of the Institute for the Study of American Evangelicals and Professor of History at Wheaton College. Her publications include *The Life and Hymns of Fanny J. Crosby* (2005); *Restoring the Faith: The Assemblies of God, Pentecostalism, and American Culture* (1993); *Aimee Semple Macpherson: Everybody's Sister* (1992); *Pentecost in My Soul: Explorations in the Meaning of Pentecostal Experience in the Assemblies of God* (1989).

JOEL CARPENTER is the Director of the Nagel Institute for the Study of World Christianity at Calvin College, Grand Rapids, Michigan, and a former Religion Officer for the Pew Charitable Trusts (1989-1996). His publications include *Revive Us Again: The Reawakening of American Fundamentalism, 1930-1946* (1997) and *The Changing Face of Christianity: Africa, the West, and the World* (2004).

PAUL FRESTON has been a Professor of Sociology at the Federal University of São Carlos, Brazil, and now holds the Byker Chair of Christian Perspectives on Political, Social, and Economic Thought, Calvin College, Grand Rapids, Michigan. His books include *Evangelicals and Politics in Asia, Africa, and Latin America* (2001) and *Protestant Political Parties: A Global Survey* (2004).

ANTHONY DELA FUENTE researches the interplay between theology and film, and Asian culture and theology. He holds a Doctorate in Theology from Asia Baptist Graduate Theological Seminary, Baguio City, Philippines. He is a senior pastor of Village Baptist Church in the heart of metropolitan Manila.

JEHU J. HANCILES is an Associate Professor of Mission History and Globalization at the School of World Mission, Fuller Theological Seminary. His publications include *Euthanasia of a Mission: African Church Autonomy in a Colonial Context* (2002).

BRIAN M. HOWELL is Associate Professor of Anthropology at Wheaton College where he teaches on global Christianity and anthropological theory. He has published a number of articles including "Practical Belief and Localization of Christianity." His forthcoming book, *At Home in the World,* examines Philippine Baptists' understanding of context as experienced and created in several congregations.

OGBU U. KALU is the Henry Winters Professor of World Christianity and Missions at McCormick Theological Seminary, Chicago. He served on the executive committee of Currents in World Christianity under whose auspices this volume was produced. His publications include *Power, Poverty, and Prayer: The Challenges of Poverty and Pluralism in African Christianity, 1960-1996* (2000); *Clio in a Sacred Garb: Essays on Christian Presence and African Responses, 1900-2000* (2004).

SEBASTIAN C. H. KIM is Professor of Theology and Public Life at York St. John University, England. He was formerly Director of the Christianity in Asia Project, University of Cambridge. His publications include *In Search of Identity: Debates on Religious Conversion in India* (2003).

PHILOMENA MWAURA is a senior lecturer in the Department of Religious Studies, Kenyatta University, Nairobi. She earned the Ph.D. in Gender Studies examining the leadership of women in African Instituted Churches, and has published a number of journal articles. She coordinates the writing projects for the Circle of African Women Theologians for eastern Africa.

JOHN PARRATT was latterly Professor of Third World Theologies at the University of Birmingham. He has lectured at the University of Ife, Nigeria, and the Center for the Study of Christianity in the Non-Western World, Edinburgh. He has published a number of books on African theology and edited *Introduction to Third World Theologies* (2004).

DANA ROBERT is Truman Collins Professor of World Mission at Boston University and directs the Center for Global Christianity and Mission. Her numerous publications include *American Women in Mission* (1997); *Gospel Bearers, Gospel Barriers: Missionary Women in the Twentieth Century* (2002); *Occupy Till I Come: A. T. Pierson and the Evangelization of the World* (2003); *Frontiers of African Christianity: Essays in Honor of Inus Daneel* (2004).

BRIAN STANLEY is Director of the Henry Martyn Centre and a Fellow of St. Edmund's College, University of Cambridge. He was the Director of the Currents in World Christianity Project under whose auspices this volume was produced. His publications include *The Bible and the Flag* (1990); *The History of the Baptist Missionary Society 1792-1992* (1992); *Christian Missions and the Enlightenment* (2001); and *Missions, Nationalism, and the End of Empire* (2003). With Sheridan Gilley he has edited volume 8 (on the nineteenth century) of *The Cambridge History of Christianity* (2006).

DIANE STINTON teaches as a missionary at the Daystar University, Nairobi, Kenya. Her publications include *Jesus of Africa: Voices of Contemporary African Christology* (2004).

FEIYA TAO is a Professor of History at Shanghai University, Shi Jinghuan. His research has focused on Chinese church historiography and Protestant missionary enterprise in China from the nineteenth century. His publications include *Corbett Charles Hodge, 1881-1964* (1999).

KEVIN XIYI YAO received his Th.D. from Boston University and belongs to the Chinese Bible Church of Greater Boston. He has published widely on the history of Christianity in China including *The Fundamentalist Movement Among Protestant Missionaries in China, 1920-1937* (2003).

PART I

The Global and the Local: Rooting Theory into Contexts

Changing Tides: Some Currents in World Christianity at the Opening of the Twenty-First Century

OGBU U. KALU

1. Introduction: Naming the Currents

A powerful archetypal imagery of Christianity is drawn from water to express its inner symbol of salvation and its outward expansion. The imagery of ship, anchor, sail, and tidal waves in describing the changing faces of Christianity and evaluating its shape at the end of the second millennium is, therefore, ancient and significant. It is a religion that emphasizes movement and sharing; the whole inhabited earth is its purview. The only reason for gathering the church is mission. Its evangelists traveled by water. When Islam seized the land routes, the sea and tides were woven into the ecological fabric that determined the fortunes of the movement. When the twentieth century came to a close, the significant character of the tide was its roaring intensity rather than its ebb as predicted by secularist pundits.

Against the background of the declaration that secularism is the new world religion, the apparent numerical growth of Christianity has become obvious. Even more intriguing is its revival in ancient sites that once owed allegiance to other religions. Philip Jenkins has declared that the world is witnessing the making of the next Christendom and the coming of global Christianity.[1] He packaged, in a more popular form, the *rhema* that Andrew F. Walls has been sharing within the academy: that the labors of the missionary movement, and the cross-cultural process in Christian history, have borne fruit and catalyzed a

---

1. Philip Jenkins, *The Next Christendom: The Coming of Global Christianity* (New York: Oxford University Press, 2002).

shift in the center of gravity of Christianity that has immense implications for the theology of the future and for the way we tell its story.[2] Prominent scholars endorsed Jenkins's book, enthusiastically finding it was startling, provocative, disquieting, the voice of a sentinel sounding an alert. As Lamin Sanneh wrote in the blurb to Jenkins's book: "the worldwide resurgence of Christianity is a vigorous movement in our day, and it coincides with the waning of the religion in what is now a post-Christian West — the pace of developments in post-colonial societies shows no sign of slackening."[3]

Alister McGrath, Professor of Historical Theology at the University of Oxford and former principal of Wycliffe Hall, in a trenchant analysis of contemporary Christianity, has argued that the attempt to "modernize" the church in the heady cultural winds of the 1960s set the stage for the growing irrelevance of the mainline churches of the West. It changed the shape of the future that will see the resurgence of the traditional and evangelical forms of the faith; the Christianity of the future will reside with Roman Catholicism, pentecostalism, and evangelicalism as they advance in the Third World.[4] Financial power has disengaged from cultic power. It is not merely a matter of numbers but what David Martin calls a "geological shift in religious identification" — a trend that may be lost on those who still assume that "political and economic spheres are primary realities."[5]

Kwame Bediako may therefore characterize contemporary African Christianity as a non-Western religion.[6] The same could be said of the emergent Christianity in Latin America, Asia, and China. Evangelical resurgence has also been identified in parts of Eastern Europe, notably Romania, and there are still strong voices in the Western academy that privilege externality and the power of the West in the shape of contemporary Christianity.[7] Paul Gifford insists that the dependence on the West is widespread and on the increase, as may be measured in the strength of the missionary influence deployed in the southern hemisphere, in terms of numbers, resources, expertise,

2. Andrew F. Walls, "Theology Is Moving South: Where Christian Growth and Fruitful Questions Are," *Trust* (New Year, 2003): 14-19, presents a synopsis of the argument in his *The Missionary Movement in Christian History* (Maryknoll, NY: Orbis Books, 1996).

3. Lamin Sanneh on Jenkins, *The Next Christendom.*

4. Alister E. McGrath, *The Future of Christianity* (Oxford: Blackwell, 2002).

5. David Martin, "Evangelism and Charismatic Christianity in Latin America," in Karla Poewe, ed., *Charismatic Christianity as a Global Culture* (Columbia: University of South Carolina Press, 1994), p. 73.

6. Kwame Bediako, *Christianity in Africa* (Maryknoll, NY: Orbis Books, 1995).

7. As Paul Gifford's book *African Christianity: Its Public Role* (Bloomington: Indiana University Press, 1998) ably demonstrates.

and power.[8] Rapid growth is occurring mostly in poor regions of the world. This fact raises warning flags over the future of Christianity in the new places. The poverty in these new centers may be important but does not deflect the force and direction of the changing tides. The conversation and competing analyses may confuse the origins of Christianity with the nature of contemporary cultic power. From the perspective of the first, it would be illusionary to perceive twenty-first-century Christianity as a Western religion precisely because many non-Western communities participated in shaping the character of the Jesus movement *before* it flowed into a Europe that then repackaged it with the concept of Christendom. Its contemporary shape compels subtle, interpretative analysis because, argues David Martin, "most recent research recognizes that, whatever the origins of some of these movements in the North Atlantic Protestant world, they are now independent and indigenous in both personnel and finance. In the contemporary world of mass communications and geographical mobility, the missionary is no longer necessary. Missionaries still exist, of course, but even if they did not the evangelical expansion would be much the same, given the capacity of religious messages to pass along lines of personal and familial contact."[9] Besides, these new centers are sending more missionaries into Western and Eastern Europe than has been documented.

Naming the currents in world Christianity has been a major historiographical aspect of the interpretation of the changing tides. The concept of Christendom, for instance, raises the problem of representation of the movement. Embedded in it is more than the expansionist motif in the Christian message and strategy. As the tide of Christianity flowed into Europe, rulers employed it as a cultural signifier and component of national identity. Some posed as *defensores fidei*, situated it in the domain of the state, and exploited it as the compelling rationale for commercial expansion and assertion of national pride. Thus Iberian Catholicism, which initiated the European migration of the fifteenth and sixteenth centuries, incorporated the evangelization of the heathen into the more obvious reasons for the voyages across the Atlantic and into the Indian Ocean. The quest for an alternative sea route to the Far East was a creative European response to the challenges posed by Islam, which had blocked the Levant land route to the sources of spices, seized the breadbasket in the Maghrib, initiated a lucrative trans-Saharan gold trade, and taken over the centers of Christianity. The crusades could not dislodge them, but the discovery of a sea route did, and enabled Europe to regain the upper hand. Christianity be-

8. Gifford, *African Christianity*, p. 17.
9. www.christianitytoday.com/c/2000/001/4.12htm *The People's Church.*

came a social ornament in the nationalist project, and soon conversion of the heathen was overawed by commercial allure. The evangelists found it lucrative to enslave prospective converts. The wind went out of the sails of the movement before the Enlightenment worldview put paid to the Christendom concept.

The significance of the intense European migration and evangelization project between 1875 and 1925 is that it shaped modern Christianity. The Protestant factor predominated, moved by the engine of the abolition of slavery that cleaned up the face of the gospel message. The enlargement in scale of the missionary enterprise created a new vista because of the number of people, organizations, nations, creeds, and races of those who participated. The voluntarist principle changed the strategy and mobilized a greater range of classes into the missionary endeavor. At different times, and as the tides changed with new cultural forces, protagonists have expressed the universal, expansionist thrust of the movement differently. In Chapter 5 Dana Robert explores the ideology of *internationalism* that spurred evangelism through the interwar years to the 1950s. The militaristic language of mission resonated with the temper of the times, redolent with the collusion of altar and throne.

2. The Globalization Discourse

By the 1960s, shifts in material culture had compelled parallel shifts in mental culture. The idea of the "global village" provided a new way of conceptualizing the changing tides of religion and specifically of Christianity. Since the literature has burgeoned, suffice it here to state that globalization is a relational concept to explain the increasing cultural contact that has reduced distances in space and time and brought civilizations and communities into closer degrees of interaction. In the 1960s when Marshall McLuhan talked about the global village, he pointed to the impact of communication on cultures — how, beginning with Gutenberg's invention of the printing press, communication technology had come to "web" the world in such a manner that whatever happens in one part of the globe is immediately known in another part.[10] Since the 1960s, the electronic media in particular have knit together many cultures, societies, and civilizations into unavoidable contact, depriving them of their isolation and threatening their particularity. All humans have been caught up in the integration and differentiation of global societies. This has not only affected the theory of knowledge but has had two

---

10. Marshall McLuhan and B. Powers, *The Global Village: Transformation in World, Life and Media in the Twenty-First Century* (Oxford: Oxford University Press, 1989).

other results: the emergence of a new culture and the intensification of cultural and value clashes. As cultures are juxtaposed the problem of identity looms large.

Some argue that the new culture does not originate from any particular region. Others believe that it is a product and internal requirement of capitalism. Still others fear American dominance and Fukuyama's "end of history." What is certain is that globalism has acquired many characteristics, depending on the lenses used to interpret how certain cultural forces and values (economic, social, and political) have woven the *oikoumene* into a certain order sharing identical values and bound by economic, cultural, and religious forces. These forces are so strong that some inherited values must be surrendered and development trajectories modified or abandoned. This is an emergent global culture using technology, commerce, and monetary power to bind together disparate peoples and cultures. Sometimes the cord is so strong that a tremor at one end causes an earthquake at the other. Sometimes the bounds are so inescapable that even losers cannot extricate themselves.

There has been a shift, however, from the global village concept to one of rather bewildering disintegration and flux. One aspect is the pace and direction of change. The other is that, at the core, globalism is a power concept, bearing the seeds of asymmetrical power relations. There is no guarantee of equality or benefit for all. Globalism is akin to the New Testament concept of *kosmos*, the world order, controlled by an inexplicable, compulsive power, dazzling with allurements or *kosmetikos*. Some wonder whether "friendship" with it is not in fact enmity with God's design because it breeds poverty at the periphery. From this perspective its pursuit of democratic order is designed to create a friendly political and socio-economic environment for the consumer market economy. The embedded concepts of economic interdependence and mutual interest do not diminish the fact that the vulnerability of the Third World is not addressed. The region is the Cinderella in this global dance, and it dreads both homogenization and Americanization. Multinational companies are the vanguards of the New World Order in many nooks of the globe.

On the whole, globalization discourse has taken various routes through cultural and economic terrain to reach its socio-political and geopolitical concerns. Some describe what is happening on the ground while others explain or decipher the impact of what appears to be happening. The weak link, perhaps, is the application of the concept to religion generally and Christianity specifically. A few illustrations on the application of the model in the study of religious systems will suffice to make the point, drawing chronologically on the works of Roland Robertson, Jeff Haynes, Peter Beyer, Karla

Poewe, Mike Featherstone, David Lyon, Rosalind Hackett, Birgit Meyer, and Ruth Marshall-Fratani.[11]

In the early years of the discourse, Robertson drew attention to the worldwide resurgence of religion, contrary to the earlier predictions about the death of religion and ethnicity in the insurgence of modernity. Jeff Haynes analyzed the contrary trend in the Third World, and especially Africa, while Peter Beyer demonstrated the failure of the prophecies on secularism by reference to the insurgence of religious fundamentalism and ecological spirituality in many parts of the globe. It was Karla Poewe who reinterpreted the resurgent, charismatic forms of Christianity as the new global Christianity, contradicting those who imaged these forms as the religion of the disoriented, or locked them into the fundamentalist mold, pigeonholed as a form of American cultural imperialism or, worse, as part of American right-wing insurgence. Rather, she argued, charismatic religiosity reflected the passage of a spiritual flow, with an ancient source, coursing through various impulses into the interior of the globe. As she wrote: "What is global are traditions that reach across national boundaries, take on local color, and move on again."[12] Interest soon shifted to the conjuncture with modernity and postmodernity, probing the impact of the media and technology as they empower religious "crusaders"; the cultural discontinuities that must follow; and how new religious forms become agents in spreading the psychology of modernity: the understanding of the self, the other, and the perception of the past. Does this constitute a Pentecostal attack on communalism in Third World contexts, either by legitimating individualization and the nuclear family, or by liberating members from the burden of the past? These writers explored the religious expression of the cultural discontinuities caused by the globalization process in respect of certain charac-

11. Roland Robertson, *Social Theory and Global Culture* (London: Sage, 1996) and "Globalisation and Societal Modernization: A Note on Japan and Japanese Religion," *Sociological Analysis* 47, no. 8 (1987): 38-39; A. Appadurai, *Modernity at Large: Cultural Dimensions of Globalization* (Minneapolis: University of Minnesota Press, 1996); Peter Beyer, *Religion and Globalisation* (London: Sage, 1994); M. Featherstone et al., *Global Modernities* (London: Sage, 1995); R. Hackett, "Pentecostal Appropriation of Media Technologies in Nigeria," *Journal of Religion in Africa (JRA)* 28, no. 3 (1998): 258-77; Ruth Marshall-Fratani, "Mediating the Global and Local in Nigerian Pentecostalism," *JRA* 28, no. 3 (1998): 278-315; Birgit Meyer, "Make a Complete Break with the Past," *JRA* 28, no. 3 (1998): 350-73; David Lyon, "Wheels within Wheels: Glocalisation and Contemporary Religion," in M. Hutchinson and O. U. Kalu, eds., *A Global Faith* (Sydney: Centre for the Study of Australian Christianity, 1998), pp. 47-68; Jeff Haynes, *Religion and Politics in Africa* (London: Zed Press, 1996); Poewe, ed., *Charismatic Christianity as a Global Culture.*

12. Poewe, ed., *Charismatic Christianity,* p. 17.

teristics: contraction of space; tearing people from received traditions; reorienting them to the wider world; and undermining universal claims and particular identities.

Economists and ecologists meanwhile developed new directions in the globalism discourse that are beyond our purview here. Robertson first applied the concept of "glocalization" to deal with the global/local theme, borrowing from the Japanese *dochakuka,* a micromarketing technique for adapting a global outlook to local conditions. Long before then, "traditionalization" was the favored term that also drew on the example of the Japanese pattern of industrialization which was compatible with traditional mores. For instance, factories operate as families, using the deference system and loyalties derived from traditional ethics.

David Lyon tested the glocalization concept on the Toronto Blessing or Laughter of the early 1990s, a charismatic flow from America into Canada, in which people would be "slain in the spirit" and fall down laughing. This test case was within a culturally homogeneous setting, however, and may have limited value for cross-cultural contexts. Moreover, the glocalization discourse meshed the new religious movements into the "postmodernity project," which might be useful for the West but less so for contexts where modernity is still acquiring tensile roots. The power relationship compels a new discourse because although it allows such communities, and other powerless peoples, to participate in the globalism project, the playing field is not even. The risk is that it prevents Third World peoples from reflecting upon how, and telling the stories of where, the "rain of the gospel" met them. The question should be posed within a new discourse designed to explore the interior dynamics and process of culture contacts in contexts of asymmetrical power relations.

The nature of religious experience and expression contests all images of a globalized religion characterized by increased homogeneity and sameness. Rather, scholarly concern should privilege how transnational cultural forms are appropriated, set in motion, and "domesticated," investigating the way in which local cultural lenses refract the light in global cultural processes. Viewed from several perspectives at the same time, attention should focus on the process between the encoder and the decoder: the interconnectedness of local distinctiveness and global generality. This is akin to Andrew Walls's exposition of the biblical understanding of the interplay between the indigenous and pilgrim principles in Christianity.[13] As Christianity is experienced and translated into other cultural symbols, the indigenous principle blooms.

---

13. Walls, *The Missionary Movement in Christian History,* pp. 53-54.

This inculturating potential cautions against homogeneity because "hearers" interpret employing lenses sourced from their indigenous worldviews. This perspective privileges the initiative and creative responses and character of local actors. Third World contexts are not a *tabula rasa* on which foreign culture-bearers write their scripts with abandon. Hidden scripts abound at the level of infra-politics. By combating the blurring of boundaries and identities in the globalism discourse, it becomes possible to demonstrate how global cultural forms are mediated in the everyday lives of ordinary people in their localities. Finally, the emphasis should be placed on the sense of fluidity and flux in social analysis by restoring the initiative to the underdog. Globalism has usually been defined with the ideological bias of where one is located in the process, but local conditions and cultural patterns do still filter global flows. As Marshall-Fratani puts it, "appropriation of the new occurs in an endless inventive process of cultural bricolage."[14]

All history is interpretation of fragmentary facts. Using rules of evidence as a restraint, the historian reconstructs the events of the past from an articulated bias known as a conceptual scheme or discourse. The perception here is that an explanation of the changing tides of Christianity at the opening of the twenty-first century must trace the indigenous roots while acknowledging the benefits from external interventions and spiritual flows. For instance, an exploration into the growth of pentecostalism in the contemporary period must perforce take into account that many outbreaks of Spirit-type Christianity hit different parts of the world even before the Azusa Street phenomenon of 1906, and that from about the 1970s the pentecostal movement acquired new vibrant forms. The avalanche of spiritual flares in the pre-1970 period sometimes fed into the new forms, as Silas H. Wu demonstrates in his biography: *Dora Yu and Christian Revival in Twentieth-Century China.*[15] Similarly, Edith Blumhofer's account in Chapter 9 of an Indian revival has similarities with the Welsh, Pyongyang, and Seoul phenomena. Many illustrations abound in Africa. These phenomena at the beginning of the twentieth century changed the character of the movement in the 1980s and 1990s. Periodization may betray the fact that the charismatic movement has changed character in each decade until the end of the millennium.

These considerations have led both to the quest for a better representation of the motor that moved Christianity in the twentieth century, and to a shift away from the globalism discourse. Some have canvassed the idea of "trans-

---

14. Marshall-Fratani, "Mediating the Global," p. 280.

15. Silas H. Wu, *Dora Yu and Christian Revival in Twentieth-Century China* (Boston: Pishon River Publishers, 2002), see map on p. xvii.

nationalism" as the movement takes new shapes in different nations. Lamin Sanneh argues:

> "World Christianity" is the movement of Christianity as it takes form and shape in societies that previously were not Christian, societies that had no bureaucratic tradition with which to domesticate the gospel. . . . World Christianity is not one thing, but a variety of indigenous responses through more or less effective idioms, but in any case without necessarily the European Enlightenment frame. "Global Christianity," on the other hand, is the faithful replication of Christian forms and patterns developed in Europe.[16]

Indeed, professorial chairs of World Christianity have now been endowed and installed in many American universities. World Christianity affirms the integrity of all believers in the face of the gospel mandate. It shifts focus from theory to Christianity as a "lived faith" and explains the ferment, varieties, renewals, and plurality of voices in the movement. As the internationalists of the past argued, indigenization is a prerequisite for bonding people across races and nations with the power of the Word. From this matrix, the social activist principle in the gospel and its moral strength would emerge. Many of those protagonists were inspired by ecumenism, a word that struck at the heart of the matter. Its theological usage transformed the ecological dimension by affirming that Jesus is the Lord of all the inhabited earth. Some conservative evangelicals may oppose its broad, liberal articulation but still operate from the same ecumenical map of the universe. Like a creeping plant, the ecumenical ideology entwined the character of Christianity until the end of the last millennium, as witnessed by the number of inter-confessional dialogues and the prominence of dialogues among many faiths in the early twenty-first century.

3. Analyzing the Currents: The Structure

The chapters in this book emerge from a conference that involved Christians from all continents, various confessions, and a variety of disciplines. Exploiting the intellectual environment of the times, contributors applied the global/local discourse in the analyses of the currents, changing tides, and

---

16. Lamin Sanneh, *Whose Religion Is Christianity? The Gospel Beyond the West* (Grand Rapids: Eerdmans, 2003), p. 22.

shape of Christianity at the end of the second millennium. An aspect of this choice of a conceptual scheme is that it perceives the global imperative inherent in Christianity from its very origin. Yet there is a keen awareness of how it has been expressed and appropriated in various world cultures; how it has contributed to increased social, political, and economic interconnectedness, and to intensified global cultural consciousness. The discourse accordingly provides a framework for understanding and appreciating the rich polycentric local expressions of contemporary Christianity.

Most of the authors in this volume are historians and theologians and, therefore, wary of indulging in theorizing on globalism, a discourse that Paul Freston, a sociologist, describes in Chapter 2 as abstract, generalizing, and "tied to First-World religious trends." As he states, "a globalized world need not lead either to a relativistic homogeneity or a clashing fundamentalism." Many of the authors blithely step over the theoretical debates and simply image global processes in terms of encounter of cultural influences: material, mental, and especially religious. In such encounters, new forms emerge whose shapes cannot be predetermined. The problem is how to analyze the changing tides. Some use the anthropological rediscovery of the worldview while others employ conversion motifs as a conceptual scheme.

The chapters are divided into five groups. The first opens with a concern for theory and contests the adequacy of the globalism discourse for understanding the face of contemporary Christianity; it would rather root the Christian experiences in specific local contexts. The second set of chapters, however, demonstrates the innate globalizing impulse within Christianity and the missionary enterprise. A third group pursues the theme of "domestication" or indigenization of the global processes and reinvention in local contexts, with special reference to ministerial formation and issues of theology and social justice. It shows how indigenous factors become increasingly crucial in the process, specifically by exploring four dimensions of the varied patterns of appropriation. First, it shows that a charismatic response to the translated gospel has dominated various forms of indigenous religious initiative; second, that they all use the indigenous map of the universe, colored differently, in their responses to the global Christian influences; and third, that the mass media have influenced the patterns of growth of the new religious movements in Asia and Africa and in the diaspora; and fourth, the impact of global forces on local socio-political processes such as migrations, gender, and social justice.

4. The Global and the Local: Rooting Theory into Contexts

In Chapter 2 Paul Freston underscores the complexity in the literature on globalization, especially as a tool for understanding Christianity. Beyond its abstract nature, theorists have focused on the Western world and failed to explore the data on global religion. Christianity must be set within a context of competing world religions because all religions are growing, either from increase in world populations, or from intensified evangelization, or from spiritual hunger. We are compelled to study other world religions as a means of interpreting contemporary Christianity. Similarly, the contours of state development combine with the tendency towards religious monopoly or theocratic political ideology to constitute constraints on the freedom of religious expression and the pattern of religious change. Freston draws attention to the challenging task of measuring the statistical growth of Christianity worldwide. A number of current sources yield confusing data. Some have queried the sources for the statistics; others the inconsistent typology of Christians; still others have claimed that the figures for the number of Christians in India and China in the *World Christian Encyclopedia* may be exaggerated and differ from the census figures in those countries (although those census figures may have been adjusted downward for political reasons). It would be useful to collate data from different sources and trace the general trend. To obviate the heuristic trend in the globalism discourse, Freston uses the example of evangelicals to illustrate the modern face of Christianity in the non-Western world, stressing the "need to distinguish between 'diasporic and conversionist globalisation.'" More crucial, evangelicalism has engaged the public space in many countries. The political import of the changing religious landscape is therefore important.

The next two authors appear to have heeded Freston's advice by using the Philippines and Africa to illustrate the intricacies of conversion and religious expression. The anthropologists Brian Howell and Anthony dela Fuente show that in the Philippines the films that attract popular interest also represent how people integrate the traditional and the modern, the gospel and primal religion in their psychological matrices. Films share congruence as outward symbols of inner conversion stories. Developing the localization theory from anthropological perspectives, they show that conversion narratives suggest the nature of the relationship between the wider social context, as seen in film, and the experience of Christianity as offered by converts. People, they argue, redeploy the global in locally meaningful ways. A certain twist in the globalization discourse is illustrated by Jehu Hanciles (Chapter 4) using an African case study to show that beyond numerical growth, the shift in the center of gravity has not become fully manifest because of culture lag. Many non-Western contexts are not fully implicated in the global cultural processes. Theory might be running ahead of reality. For instance, curricula in the academy still reflect Western intellectual influence, power, and money. The new face of contemporary Christianity may be discerned, however, through missionary migration from the old periphery (which has turned into new centers) to old centers that may become the new periphery. The currents in contemporary Christianity transform old receptors into new initiators. The story must perforce be told with a new historiography that privileges indigenous agency.

5. The Globalizing Impulse in Christianity

The innate globalizing impulse within Christianity and its practice in the missionary movement could be illustrated with many of the missionary slogans, policies, and strategies through time. Each century crafted a new driving ideology, and these slogans tended to betray the regnant spirit of the nations. Thus the internationalism that emerged during the period from 1900 to 1945 bore an exuberant American imprint. Germans were chagrined because their role in founding the Protestant missionary impulse went unacknowledged as the American tide deluged the enterprise. They perceived the slogan of "the evangelization of the world in this generation" as a confusion of human efforts with God's initiatives. For the leading German missiologist, Bruno Gutmann, the *volkskirche* ideal was the bastion for protecting local identities from global processes. Primal cultures served as points of contact, containers, and the ground in which the Spirit of God works. Primal ties must be redeemed but not destroyed, replaced, or ignored; those ties should be converted and received into the new reality of Christ's body. The irony is that even when policies clashed, as happened when the Germans accused the Americans of westernizing the mission field, they shared the mandate to globalize their perception of the task. The Germans were installing a folk ideology that was native to their own soil, as later became clear in the support by German missionary bodies for the National Socialist cause. Admittedly, Gutmann was not a Nazi but his ideas were hijacked.

In Part Two Dana Robert explores the contours of internationalism as an emotive globalizing impulse in the interwar years. In spite of its richness and patterns, Christianity faced the challenge of the resilient strength of other religions and how it was experienced in other cultures. Sebastian Kim illustrates these clashes with the debates at the conference of the International Missionary Council held at Tambaram, Madras, in 1938. This conference was to have taken place in China but was moved because of the Sino-Japanese war. It remains very important for Third World Christians for a number of reasons. It was held in Asia, and within a context of a strong Hindu religion and Hindu-dominated politics. The backdrop consisted of both the insurgent nationalism of India and the use of Christianity as a liberating force by the lower castes. The organizers created the opportunity for voices that had not been heard: a large contingent of Third World people. Africans, who had been absent at the 1910 World Missionary Conference in Edinburgh, participated.[17] Moreover the Tambaram conference re-examined the place of the church in evangelism and how missionaries should respond to other faiths. Europe itself was reeling from the effects of strong geo-political conflicts, including the emergence of National Socialism in Germany. The conference not only continued the rancorous debate between Barthians and non-Barthians over the relationship of nature and grace but also discussed the lordship of Christ in the new cultural contexts and the use of indigenous structures for building national churches. It was stunned by the new voice of a Madras group that submitted a counter-proposal: *Rethinking Christianity in India.* This anti-structural document was the harbinger of Third World Theology. It raised the problem of becoming a Christian without social dislocation and the need for flexibility and sensitivity to context in globalizing the gospel.

Twentieth-century missionary enterprise was not univocal. The voluntarist principle had created a problem, as for example, between the Church Missionary Society and the Anglican church hierarchy. Quarrels at the home bases of mission tended to reverberate into the mission field as witnessed in the divided Anglicanism of South Africa. Further, the ecumenical spirit evident among Protestants in the 1960s was replaced by the refurbished denominational identities in the next decade. The propagation of the concept of the worldwide Anglican communion is only one example; other bodies such as the Lutheran World Federation sought to bind their adherents into a global ecclesial entity. In spite of this, new forms of ecumenism, such as interfaith discussions, blossomed at the end of the second millennium. In the United States a new organization emerged: Churches Working Together, which was designed to ensure that Roman Catholics worked with Protestants. Mariology is winning a hearing outside the Roman Catholic fold as the Apocrypha is being printed and read by evangelicals.

Why is everyone tired of the denominational battles of the past? Some

17. Frieder Ludwig, "Tambaram: The West African Experience," *JRA* 31, no. 1 (2001): 49-91.

conjecture the impact of globalism; others point to the need for a bulwark against eroding secularism that knows no faith boundaries. It may be the result of years of ecumenical discussions within Faith and Order committees that have thrashed out the doctrinal divides, or perhaps a feeling of shallowness that compels a search for roots. The friendship among the new breed of church leaders may have conjured the spirit of comity. The character of these inter-faith talks matters. Leaders are not talking about visible unity anymore but are picking up on the resonance in their faith confessions as a prelude to cooperation and a healthy relationship. Inclusivism has become the order of the day.

6. Domestication, Tooling, and Reinvention:
Education and Ministerial Formation

Education was the strongest instrument employed in the missionary enterprise to domesticate or indigenize Christianity. It was the globalizing ligament that, through the modes of ministerial formation, catechism, and theological education curricula, bonded the periphery to the center. However, the recruitment, training, and status of indigenous peoples betrayed the regnant ideology within the missionary enterprise. Enlargement of scale and other exigencies forced an increased use of indigenous "resources," but there was still an unwillingness to ordain and promote indigenous people. The racist ideology of the period, the control and monopoly of religion, countered the imperatives of the local contexts. Bishop Shanahan of the Irish Holy Ghost Fathers was quoted as saying that it took decades to make one convert out of the neophytes. The Roman Catholics were possibly slower in indigenizing the enterprise until rudely awakened by the bugle call of political independence in Africa. The openness of the enterprise that invited indigenes was blocked by a cultural ideology that monopolized the religion, kept the indigenes from decision-making roles and stultified the indigenization of Christianity. All of that changed in the latter part of the twentieth century as the space for the indigenes widened.

By the end of the second millennium the rise of nationalism and political independence in many nations had caused Christians to lose control of education. Recently churches have reasserted their participation in education by leapfrogging into the tertiary sector. Joel Carpenter's seminal analysis (Chapter 7) of the emergence of university institutions in Third World Christianity moves the story forward into the late twentieth century and shows how local imperatives continued to produce the currents in Christianity. In the last two decades, Christian groups in Asia, Latin America, Eastern Europe, and Africa ventured into the challenging area of tertiary education, exactly the zone that missionary organizations had feared to tread. Missionary education had focused on primary schooling, and teachers' programs, and sometimes into technical and secondary levels. Education was an investment and not a consumer good. School was a means of evangelization. As independent states came into being in the period from 1948 to 1965, many established universities under state control; there were only a few Christian colleges. State control was seen as an index of freedom from the colonial past. Thus, missionary reticence and various forms of nationalism determined the fortunes of tertiary education, and in the early years there were few Christian colleges, but in the 1980s and 1990s many Christian groups established universities. The numbers are growing so rapidly that statistics soon become obsolete. In mid-2004 West Africa sported thirty-four institutions (one each in Cameroon, Republic of Benin, and Senegal; eleven in Ghana and twenty in Nigeria). The Roman Catholic Church, the Roman Catholic charismatic movement, the Anglican communion, the Methodist Church in Nigeria, the Presbyterian Church in Ghana, the Seventh Day Adventists in Ghana and Nigeria, the Evangelical Church of West Africa, and pentecostal churches have all founded Christian universities. Muslims have recently followed by founding seven Islamic universities in Nigeria where, apart from the universities, there are also Christian theological colleges that have obtained affiliate status (under Decree 17 of 1979) and prepare students for degrees awarded by government-owned universities.

Education, the tested and reliable instrument for domesticating Christian principles, has been reinvented and deployed (in part to contest the debased morality emanating from government-controlled universities). Explanations for the growth of these institutions, therefore, include the process of deregulation linked to a shift from the state ideology that sustained state monopoly of education, and the burgeoning of populations with a large component of young people who want more education at the technical and tertiary level than is currently available. In addition, the collapse of state economies means that they can no longer sustain the financial burdens of tertiary education; while agency by Christian groups, and competition between Muslims and Christians, as well as among Christians, are contributing factors. Governments have been forced to privatize tertiary education as young people seek relevant education for new times.

Evangelical spirituality has matured to compete and offer a new leadership for the nations, a leadership that could fight corruption and the collapse of the salient morality in the public arena. The growth of Christianity has intensified the need for an educated population as old and new churches try to regain the ascendancy that churches had enjoyed in the field of education during the colonial period. Even politicians indulge in a rhetoric that blames the collapse of public morals on the takeover of schools from missions by nationalist governments.

The emergent institutions provide a high profile for Christianity, constitute a form of social activism and engagement, and will probably eventually challenge other power nodes in the public space. This is agency of indigenous people who seize the high ground and deliberately link themselves to international or global cultural forms such as academia. When the Roman Catholics established the Catholic Higher Institutes in the 1980s, their motives were, first, as a cost-saving device, because the cost of training one priest in Europe was so astronomical that three priests could be trained in Africa for the same sum; and second, to obviate the mis-formation of priests who were not familiar with the indigenous terrain or, to provide leadership for the inculturation project following Vatican II. Such higher institutions were established in Dakar, Port Harcourt, and Nairobi. The problem of relevant curricula has remained endemic in Christian education. A flipside of the coin is that the universities soon became a source of rivalry among the pentecostal churches, as a measure of the size and importance of a particular Christian group.

In Chapter 8 Kevin Yao illustrates this theme in relation to indigenous Protestants through a case study of the North China Theological Seminary (NCTS), 1919-1950. The indigenous church participated effectively in the "three-self" principle, when given the opportunity, and the ministerial vocation was so attractive that theological institutions flourished. Only geopolitical developments beyond its control forced the closure of the NCTS. It merged with the seminary in Nanjing that is still the biggest of the eighteen seminaries in contemporary China. The study reveals another dimension to the globalizing enterprise: how certain doctrinal stances were transmitted from the West and absorbed in local contexts. It also leaves a puzzle, namely, what elements in Chinese primal culture reinforced and reinvented fundamentalist theology? It illustrates the growing tensions within the missionary enterprise in the twentieth century between conservative and liberal wings. In the U.S., the Layman's Foreign Missions Inquiry (1930-1932) revealed that this problem had shifted from the home base to the foreign fields. In Britain, the Bible Churchmen's Missionary Society split from the Church Missionary Society in 1922 over the differing views of the Bible and its authority. In China, the China Inland Mission disengaged from the National Christian Council of China, and the disagreement reverberated into ministerial formation. In America, the conservatives perceived the NCTS in China as their overseas shop window.

7. Charismatic and Pentecostal Transformation of the Religious Landscape

Philip Jenkins characterized Southern Christianity at the end of the twentieth century as conservative, with a strong supernatural orientation, interested in personal salvation and radical politics, privileging deep personal faith, communal orthodoxy, mysticism, and puritan spirituality and founded on clear scriptural authority. Its adherents, in his words,

> preach messages that, to a Westerner, appear simplistically charismatic, visionary, and apocalyptic. In this thought-world, prophecy is an everyday reality, while faith-healing, exorcism, and dream-visions are basic components of religious sensibility. For better or worse, the dominant churches of the future could have much in common with those of medieval or early modern European times.[18]

As indicated earlier, there is no aspect of the globalization discourse that has attracted more attention than the analyses of charismatic pentecostal spirituality in the Third World. Soon attention may shift to Eastern Europe, which has reopened to global interactions and become a new mission field for pentecostal groups. In Russia pentecostal groups are violently attacked, yet many continue to meet in homes. The competition with the revival of monasteries and spiritual retreat centers is in full swing in Hungary and Poland. Some see the pentecostal phenomenon as having flowed, like molten lava, from America — that it is as American as apple pie — and the churches in other parts of the world are extensions of the American electronic church.

This perception of American influence is contested in the case studies in this book. Rather the authors explore indigenous agency in the making of charismatic revivals. Two studies from Asia reveal different facets of the process. In the Indian case study, as Edith Blumhofer shows in Chapter 9, the character and development of the revival at Mukti (Liberty) remained inexplicable, indigenous, unconnected with Azusa Street, and different in its trajectory. It did not share the Azusa Street concern for globalizing the "latter rain" around the parched earth, rather the contrary. The study points to a recovery of the miraculous in telling the story of gospel-people encounters. The biography of Pandita Ramabai, her conversion from Hinduism, passion for saving oppressed women, and her walk with the Lord dominate the story and put an indigenous stamp on the character of the revival that occurred between 1905 and 1907.

---

18. Jenkins, *The Next Christendom*, p. 8.

Equally intriguing is Feiya Tao's story from China (Chapter 10). It focuses on Jing Dianying's Jesus Movement, a proletarian, utopian pentecostal movement that operated in northeast and northwest China from the late 1920s to about 1952. Admittedly, Jing was influenced by reading the American Methodist missionary E. Stanley Jones, and was apprenticed under the Assemblies of God structures, but his career was determined by his personal experiences, agency, and determination to respond to the challenges of rural poverty (in times of unsettled political and ideological forces): the scourges of flood, plague of insects, and exploitation by corrupt officials. These conditions resonated with his poor, orphaned background. His dalliance with Taoism may have steeled him and yet left him sensitive to fellow sufferers. Contact with charismatic Christianity provided the spiritual energy for constructing a redemptive solution that wove some apocalyptic biblical resources into indigenous knowledge and culture. His theology bobbed like a cork in the changing political currents. Caught in communist currents of the 1950s, his all-weather church ran aground.

Blumhofer's and Tao's studies focus on the colonial era. In the post-1970 period also, the Assemblies of God catalyzed charismatic revivals. These were noteworthy in contexts as different as South Korea, Ghana, and Kenya, and raise the problem of numbers or quantitative growth. The impact of technology and modernization on religion force the need for balancing institutionalization and charisma, modernity and transcendence. Social science models continue to bedevil the study of Third World pentecostalism,[19] gyrating between allegations of shamanism and being overawed by global forces explicable only by applying market economy models. In this discourse, the purely religious dimension may be lost as votaries are alleged to file into pews for modernity's resources.

Why does prosperity theology thrive among non-Western communities? Some give the reasons as poverty and the collapse of economies. This may not explain its salience in an industrialized nation such as the United States, or why it gained currency within the oil boom period in Nigeria. The rise of postmodernist theories of knowledge may have opened new possibilities for interpreting the world in Western nations. In Africa, prosperity theology tapped into fertile ground already watered by the traditional concept of pros-

19. On this see Joop Vernooij, "Winti in Suriname," *Mission Studies* 20, no. 1 (2003): 140-59; Cephas N. Omenyo, *Pentecost Outside Pentecostalism: A Study of the Development of Charismatic Renewal in the Mainline Churches in Ghana* (Zoetermeer: Boekencentrum, 2002). He examines six mainline churches. See also Ogbu U. Kalu, "Preserving a Worldview: Pentecostalism in the African Maps of the Universe," *Pneuma* 24, no. 2 (Fall 2002): 110-37.

perity, which is understood as wealth, longevity, and fertility or procreativity. The attraction of pentecostalism could be explained by three factors. First, the cultural: the resonance with African maps of the universe.[20] In Chapter 11 Diane Stinton's study of local portraits of Jesus in Ghana underscores the process of renaming Jesus with indigenous chieftaincy and kingship titles. The music, choruses, and dance in liturgy are choreographed as the entry and presence of the king among his people. Jesus is showered with heroic praise names as the one who leads to war; the one who holds the knife and the yam and so dispenses goodness as he sees fit; who succors those who run to him for refuge; whose mouth pronounces the final and just judgment because, as a king, his tongue is as sharp as the tiger's. He is the needle that unravels the most troublesome knot — the paramount ruler of rulers. Some titles are derived from the Bible, as when believers remind themselves that Christ owns the cattle upon a thousand hills and is the ruler of the whole inhabited earth. The most intriguing aspect is the charismatization of the mainline churches, as this pattern of renaming Jesus, or "Pentecost outside Pentecostalism," is now widely practiced.[21]

A second line of explanation of pentecostalist success notes the use of instrumentalist discourse — the deployment of socio-economic discourse to stress the salience of hardship as collapsing soft states force people to return to hot religious sources of empowerment. All religious forms are growing. It also points to the impact of demographic shifts and competition, akin to that of the market economy, on religious allegiance.

Third, a specifically religious discourse argues that this charismatic brand of Christianity has something intrinsic in its spirituality, especially its self-integrative demand for a closer walk with God, that attracts. Yet, as Philomena Mwaura demonstrates in Chapter 12, it exploits modern facilities such as the media in order to gain wider acceptance. Indeed, the urban-based ministries tend to grow faster than rural and other low-technological ones. Two key themes in Mwaura's contribution are: the gender dimension and the competition posed by the new pentecostals to the older African Indigenous Churches. The African Independent Church forms that "made waves" in the mid-1920s — Zionists in Southern Africa, Arathi in Eastern Africa, and Aladura in West Africa — are still important but have lost prestige because of the new pentecostal forces of the post-1970s. Both groups, however, enlarged the space for female leadership and participation, a tendency that has challenged the patriarchal models in some of the mainline churches. Mwaura

---

20. Kalu, "Preserving a Worldview."
21. Omenyo, *Pentecost Outside Pentecostalism.*

takes a case study of each type, both led by women in contemporary Nairobi, to show their relative importance for women as a coping mechanism and as examples of feminist agency. Pentecostal use of the media has attracted much scholarship, often skewed, to illustrate the quest for modernity and the flow of global cultural forces.[22] Here, by contrast, the focus is on the capacity of women to witness and succor other women amid feminized poverty.

In Chapter 13 Afe Adogame deals with a scholarly interest that is itself a fruit of globalization, namely, how the charismatic Christian forms have invaded Europe, and the import of migrations and diasporic Christianity. There is a "reverse flow" or "feedback loop" as the former recipients of missionary evangelism are now bearing the gospel to the former centers. A number of reasons are adduced: the decline of Christianity in the West because of secularization; the growing wealth that draws people from poorer environments; the liberalization of immigration laws; and the compelling force of the gospel demand to evangelize. Additional factors include: the prestige and competition among the new churches that use international connections as a signifier of their relative status; the mutual demand in the religious market to create broad partnerships between indigenous preachers and Western ministries; and the acute need for "soul care" of immigrant communities that are well established and use religious culture as a mark of identity and group coherence in the face of the threat from secular cultures.

8. Cultural and Socio-Political Dimensions of Global Processes

Many of the reflections above privilege the non-Western world, but the linkage between religion and population shift is an old one. Indeed it reshaped the religious landscape of Europe many centuries ago with the migration of populations both within Europe and beyond it to the transatlantic world caused by religious conflicts and despotic royal hegemonies in Europe. Population shifts "scrambled" the old political orders that were sustained by religious homogeneity. They created secularism, the culture of religious diversity without religious freedom, separation of church and state, privatization of religion, and the new socio-political order that precipitated the decline of Christianity. There are four crucial trends: the effects of the Reformation and Counter-Reformation; nineteenth-century industrialization; the Enlightenment worldview; and the new wave of migration into Europe from Africa and Asia. Many commentators have observed that the complex result is that as

22. See the articles in *JRA* 28, no. 3 (1998).

Europeans attempt to create a new unity, concentrating on economic dimensions and neglecting religious ones, new immigrants bring various religious traditions that clash violently. For the immigrants, the exilic or diasporic experience compels people to sharpen their racial identities and legitimate these with religion. Globalization has fueled the dysfunctional religious forces that surfaced in the sixteenth century and intensified in the nineteenth century, as colonialism involved population redistribution while missionaries participated in, stood aside from, or actively resisted those essentially demographic processes, according to how they saw them in relation to their religious work. Again, Christianity is implicated in a major global trend and yet, in the long run, global processes are multi-directional cultural flows that bedevil easy analysis. Europe has gained from the religious flows from outside its borders. Among American evangelicals, this explains the rise of the so-called Third Wave led by people such as Peter Wagner, which seeks to apply to the West spiritual lessons drawn from non-Western experience.

In much of the book, the authors locate the key dynamics of change in the internal processes and the initiatives of indigenous players. Protagonists in various contexts appropriate global forces to serve the indigenous interests. A balanced perspective should, however, show that externality or the impact of global forces has remained crucial to the development of Third World contexts. In Zimbabwe, for example, Christianity became important in the independence struggle in the guise of the Justice and Peace Commission, the World Council of Churches, and the Vatican. In a concluding chapter, John Parratt provides the balancing perspective that externality or the intervention of global forces has remained crucial to the development of Third World religious contexts. Parratt bewails the low level of external concern for the oppression of the Christian enclave in northeast India, where nationalist struggle is buttressed with geography, history, ethnicity, language, and religion. Indeed, one of the crucial marks of contemporary Christianity is the high level of intolerance and violence against its practitioners. In Nigeria, Pakistan, India, and the Philippines, to name but a few examples, Christians have been victimized and subjected to violence. It would appear that the growth of the movement in the new century will be at a great price because other religions have become aware of the changing tides and are increasingly hostile, and because the pursuit of social justice enrages dictatorial governments. Ironically the lack of religious freedom is the characteristic of a new world suffused with the rhetoric of freedom. Christianity remains at the center of the swirl.

CHAPTER 2

Globalization, Religion, and Evangelical Christianity: A Sociological Meditation from the Third World

PAUL FRESTON

This chapter is a critique of the way religion has been examined under the rubric of globalization, especially with regard to macro-trends in the Third World. It suggests certain emphases that would help to make studies of globalization and religion either less abstract or less tied to First World religious trends. These emphases include a greater use of data on religion globally; attention to global constraints on religion as choice; a renewed emphasis on the study of the world religions; awareness of the distinction between fundamentalism and evangelical Christianity, and between diasporic globalization and conversionist globalization; and greater priority to the study of global conversion and of Third World evangelical mission activity. The chapter concludes by looking at the worldwide prospects for evangelical Christianity in a globalizing world, in the context of other forms of Christianity and of other religions.

1. Religion in the Context of Globalization

This section is concerned not only with globalization theory *strictu sensu,* but also with works on religion in relation to a particular global theme (such as "religion and global order"), as well as works by sociologists of religion who look at contemporary trends in religion globally.

Religion under globalization (when not neglected altogether, as in Appadurai's list of global cultural scapes)[1] is often studied either in an overly

1. Arjun Appadurai, "Disjuncture and Difference in the Global Cultural Economy," in Mike Featherstone, ed., *Global Culture* (London: Sage, 1990), pp. 295-310.

24

abstract and generalizing fashion or with empirical examples limited to the developed world. Even when other parts of the world are contemplated, the remit is often too limited (Islamic "fundamentalism" and liberation theology being the usual candidates).[2] David Martin's question to a theologian who, in the 1960s, was enthusiastic about "modern secular man" ("How many examples are there extant?")[3] might well be asked of some globalization theorists whose work on global religion suffers from the same lack of empirical knowledge of people's actual religiosity. As Woodhead and Heelas comment, much more research is needed to specify the particular circumstances under which particular forms of religion are waxing or waning worldwide.[4]

Globalization studies could justify paying little attention to grassroots religious trends in the Third World only on "modernization theory" grounds (i.e., that what happens in the developed West is more important since it represents everybody's future). If, however, the West is not paradigmatic for the whole world with a time-lag, then an epistemological equalization of the whole globe and some degree of worldwide empirical knowledge are vital. Of course, global religious trends have to be interpreted in terms of the major tendencies of globalization, but not in a "delayed reaction" paradigm. If scholars of globalization are not disguised modernization theorists, then one of the key requisites would seem to be some knowledge of what is actually happening around the globe in one's particular theme. Developed Western trends are not necessarily more indicative of our global religious future than trends anywhere else.

One of the most serious limitations of current discussions of religion under globalization is the lack of attention to global realities regarding religious freedom and effective choice (see section 2 below). Another limitation is insufficient discussion of the internal organizational and social characteristics of the major religious candidates for globalization. A consequence of this is lack of awareness of the major shift in Christianity from being overwhelmingly Western to largely Third World. This shift has happened in the twentieth century, and especially in the post-colonial period. Some scholars have difficulty seeing the reality of post-colonial Christian expansion, or else explain it away as American fundamentalist neo-imperialism. It is important

2. E.g., Peter Beyer, *Religion and Globalization* (London: Sage, 1994).

3. Quoted in Christie Davies, "David Martin: Sociologist of Religion and Humorist," in A. Walker and M. Percy, eds., *Restoring the Image* (Sheffield: Sheffield Academic Press, 2001), p. 56.

4. Linda Woodhead and Paul Heelas, eds., *Religion in Modern Times* (Oxford: Blackwell, 2000), p. 431.

that globalization theory does not treat Christianity as *par excellence* the religion of the developed Western world.

Global evangelicalism, more than Catholicism, has especially suffered from this "invisibility." Spreading from "below," rarely associated with violence, and largely independent of Western initiative, it is often overlooked. For example, a recent book on religion and global order has chapters on Catholicism and Islam but not on evangelicalism.[5] Casanova's chapter on Catholicism in a volume on transnational religion and fading states makes an explicit comparison with Islam but no mention of evangelicalism.[6] Woodhead and Heelas's anthology on religion in modern times, despite its breadth, does not take global evangelicalism much into account, partly because it only has readings from works published in English and partly because it relies on James Hunter, an undisputed expert on American evangelicalism, as its guide to the supposedly unfavorable picture worldwide.[7] Simon Coleman's *The Globalisation of Charismatic Christianity,* despite its title, turns out to be about the Swedish Word of Life church founded by a Swede who had studied in the United States. The reader is obviously supposed to be impressed by the fact that Swedish pentecostalism is "relatively large" (90,000, or 1 percent of the population), that the Swedish neo-charismatic Faith movement involves around 8,000 members, and that Word of Life has some 2,000 members after only fifteen years and is probably the largest charismatic church in Europe.[8] The reader familiar with Third World evangelicalism, on the other hand, is impressed with the *smallness* of the phenomenon treated under the title of "the globalization of charismatic Christianity." In size, media penetration, and international expansion, it is inexpressive compared to many Brazilian phenomena.

Besides limited knowledge, the literature on globalization and religion often suffers from the same tendency to introduce false dilemmas as did classical secularization studies. This is a reworking of what Evans-Pritchard called the "if I were a horse" mentality: if I were a Third World person, I would feel such-and-such a dilemma due to globalization and my religiosity would be affected in such-and-such a way. This approach is valid for formu-

5. John Esposito and Michael Watson, eds., *Religion and Global Order* (Cardiff: University of Wales Press, 2000).

6. José Casanova, "Globalizing Catholicism and the Return to a 'Universal Church,'" in Susanne Rudolph and James Piscatori, eds., *Transnational Religion and Fading States* (Boulder, CO: Westview Press, 1997), pp. 121-43.

7. Woodhead and Heelas, eds., *Religion in Modern Times*, p. 320.

8. Simon Coleman, *The Globalisation of Charismatic Christianity* (Cambridge: Cambridge University Press, 2000), pp. 8, 92, 97.

lating initial research questions, but is inexcusable when so much information is available about what is actually happening. One example is Juergensmeyer's statement, in the context of a discussion of religious nationalism, that "one can foresee the emergence of a united religious bloc stretching from Central and South Asia through the Middle East to Africa,"[9] a prediction even more unlikely than Samuel Huntington's civilizational blocs. Although Juergensmeyer later concedes that this might not happen, the mere raising of the possibility reflects an extraordinary view of the world: the idea of "religion" as a category that makes any empirical, as opposed to analytical, sense (excepting militantly atheistic states), as if the common denominators of "religious people" were more important than their differences, *vis-à-vis* the existence of "secular" people. It also imagines that "religion" can be a basis for unity against "the secular," as if all religions had the same attitude towards the secular. We can ask, however, whether increased global expansion of evangelicalism, for example, would mean more *sacralization* or more *secularization*.

For many students of globalization, it seems as though a world must either lead to religious relativism or to clashing fundamentalisms, despite the fact that these are not the only logical or empirical options. These seem to be religious equivalents of the contrast between Francis Fukuyama's global triumph of liberal capitalist ideology versus Huntington's clash of civilizations. For Waters, the options seem to boil down to ecumenical or fundamentalist alternatives.[10] Similarly, Beyer sees two options for religion if it desires to have any public influence: the "liberal" option, ecumenical and tolerant and making few really religious demands; and the "conservative" option that reasserts the religious tradition "in spite of modernity" and champions the cultural distinctiveness of a particular region of the globe, such as the New Christian Right and Islamist movements.[11]

Italian sociologist Enzo Pace, in a text published in a major work on religion and globalization in Brazil, says globalization weakens the symbolic limits of belief systems, which leads to openness to cultural miscegenation. The rigid symbolic frontiers between religious fields disappear, as do the frontiers between religion and magic, and between religion and the new secular self-help beliefs. Globalization favors loss of memory of the traditions. Believers desert the religious institutions. Religion is freed from institutional control

9. Mark Juergensmeyer, *The New Cold War? Religious Nationalism Confronts the Secular State* (Berkeley: University of California Press, 1993), p. 201.

10. Malcolm Waters, *Globalization* (London: Routledge, 1995), pp. 127-33.

11. Peter Beyer, "Privatization and the Public Influence of Religion in Global Society," in Featherstone, ed., *Global Culture*, pp. 385-93.

and returned to individual free enterprise.[12] I would say that for most of the Third World this is unrealistic. Huge numbers still look to religion to provide community. An overemphasis on individualization and bricolage in religion seems too parochial when viewed from the Third World. What seems much more likely is that one or a few of the world religions will expand and become really global. Of course, they will undergo transformations, but will still be recognizably part of those traditions as we know them. Sometimes discussions of the effect of globalization on the "religious traditions" give the impression that the latter had never been subject to change before. An antidote to that, as far as Christianity is concerned, is Andrew Walls's work. He contrasts the serial expansion of Christianity with the progressive expansion of Islam. Whereas the latter has spread from a constant heartland, Christianity has had periodic shifts in its demographic and geographical center of gravity, resulting in the immense diversity of cultural expressions, theological emphases, and ritual and social practices of each "heartland" of the faith throughout history.[13]

Just as some existing religions may be viable combinations of the universal and particular and hence well suited to globalizing times, there is also no need to resurrect the false dilemma raised by secularization theory and supposedly aggravated by globalization, regarding the alleged agonies of choice under pluralism. Religious pluralism is said to make plausibility precarious. But, as Riis says, this early Bergerian view of dark anomic threats behind pluralism neglects the possibility that confrontation of worldviews may lead to clarification of their differences rather than to relativism.[14] And as Lyon points out, today's religious choices may reflect a seriousness of faith that did not exist in ascribed identities — a respite from the Disneyfied trivialization of choice, rather than from choice itself.[15] Choice may not be as agonizing as some academics imagine it to be. The idea of cognitive minorities hanging on for grim death, always on the verge of defecting, ignores much evidence to the contrary.

This is one of many critiques that can be made regarding Huntington's "clash of civilizations." He does not seem to understand the logic of being a minority; many people take pride in conjugating a majority cultural or na-

12. Enzo Pace, "Religião e Globalização," in Pedro Ari Oro and Carlos Alberto Steil, eds., *Globalização e Religião* (Petrópolis: Vozes, 1997), pp. 25-42.

13. Andrew F. Walls, *The Missionary Movement in Christian History* (Edinburgh: T. & T. Clark, 1996), pp. 16-25.

14. Ole Riis, "Modes of Religious Pluralism Under Conditions of Globalisation," *Journal on Multicultural Societies* 1, no. 1 (1999), pp. 21-34.

15. David Lyon, *Jesus in Disneyland* (Cambridge: Polity Press, 2000), p. 40.

tional identity with a minority religious identity. Although his work takes religion seriously (perhaps too seriously) as a "central defining characteristic of civilizations," many of which he calls by religious names, his world does not exist.[16] This is just as well for the future of evangelical Christianity, which would be hamstrung in a "clash of civilizations" world; a world of fluid deterritorializing globalization is much more congenial for it. It is interesting that Huntington virtually ignores the Catholic-Protestant divide, even though only one hundred years ago it might have appeared that the great divide was between Protestant "civilization" and all the others. In addition, Islam's "progressive expansion" lends itself to a "civilizational" analysis in a way that Christianity's "serial expansion" does not.

We thus have a situation in which much writing on globalization is unrealistic about global religious trends, while many specialists in religion "see" global Catholicism and global Islam but not global evangelicalism. Yet others talk of small religions and exaggerate the import of their supposed "globalization," without knowledge of the totally different scale of global evangelicalism. The following sections suggest some ways for overcoming these limitations.

2. The Need for Greater Use of Global Data on Religion

Statistical data are always, of course, ambiguous, but greater (though always critical) attention to available data is important for advancing the study of religion under globalization.

Sources such as the *Encyclopaedia Britannica* place Christianity at around one-third of the world population, of which Catholicism accounts for 19 percent and Protestantism about 17 percent. Two common impressions jostle in the literature: that Christianity is declining, and that it is expanding! In fact, in the twentieth century Christianity overall did not expand and did not lose ground. After growth in the nineteenth century, it stabilized in the twentieth. This, however, masks a vital change in its composition that affects projections for the twenty-first century.

Christianity is now much more global. It was 81 percent white (i.e., European and North American) in 1900; but by 2000 that figure was down to 40 percent.[17] On the one hand, this is due to lower birth rates, by which the

---

16. Samuel Huntington, *The Clash of Civilizations and the Remaking of World Order* (London: Touchstone, 1998), p. 47.

17. David Barrett and Todd Johnson, "Annual Statistical Table on Global Mission," *International Bulletin of Missionary Research* 23, no. 1 (Jan. 1999): 24-25.

Western percentage of world population fell dramatically from 30 percent to 13 percent; and to the decline of Christianity in the West. On the other hand, it reflects impressive Christian expansion outside the West, and the high birth rates of those regions. The result is that Christianity has become a predominantly non-Western religion and indeed probably the leading non-Western religion (only Islam could possibly rival it). It would thus seem to have a better springboard for expansion than it had in 1900. For the first time since the seventh century, the majority of Christians are not of European origin; Christianity is finally breaking out of the "Western" mold imposed on it by Islam. Until about the year 600, Christian expansion was multi-directional. The rise of Islam affected this multi-directional expansion; and although it was not immediately catastrophic for Asian Christianity (in the thirteenth century there were still more Christians in Asia than Europe), in the long run the effect was devastating. Between 1350 and 1500, there was a dramatic decline in the Christian population of Asia, giving Christianity the aspect of a "European religion."[18] Attempts to expand outside of Europe soon became intertwined with European state expansionism after 1500. Only in the second half of the twentieth century was the impulse of the first centuries effectively resumed, i.e., a multi-directional spreading with a high degree of distance from the flows of world political and economic power.

Catholicism grew impressively in the twentieth century, although it has declined as a percentage of world Christianity in the last forty years, especially as the result of difficulties in retaining its traditional hold in Latin America which has opened up to religious choice. Of the 2.3 million Christian congregations in the world 79 percent are Protestant,[19] which may not bode well for Catholic retention in the twenty-first century. Within Protestantism, liberalism's decline and evangelicalism's rise (especially in its pentecostal form) are well known. Non-Catholic pentecostals are cautiously estimated by David Martin at a quarter of a billion, or 4 percent of world population.[20] The *World Christian Encyclopedia* talks of evangelicals as 3.5 percent of global population based on a very restricted institutional definition of evangelical.[21] On the other hand, Barrett's combined categories of "pentecostal/charismatic and neo-charismatic-independent" come to 8.7 percent. If any confidence can be placed in these numbers (the Brazil ones are too high, and all sorts of method-

18. Philip Jenkins, *The Next Christendom* (New York: Oxford University Press, 2001), pp. 23-27.

19. *Quadrant* (Christian Research Association, March 1997).

20. David Martin, *Pentecostalism: The World Their Parish* (Oxford: Blackwell, 2001).

21. David B. Barrett, George T. Kurian, and Todd M. Johnson, eds., *World Christian Encyclopedia*, 2nd ed. (Oxford: Oxford University Press, 2001), vol. 1, p. 4.

ological questions have to be asked), one could place worldwide evangelicalism at somewhere between the first figure and a combination of the two figures (minus Catholic charismatics and repeated entries). Allowing for methodological doubts, I would opt for an estimate nearer the lower end of the scale, say at around 5 percent. This is fairly consistent with the Angus Reid World Poll of 1997, which surveyed thirty-three countries.[22] (Only twelve of these were in the Third World and in some only the urban elite was surveyed.) Of these thirty-three, the most evangelical nations in percentage terms are the United States and South Africa (28 percent), followed at some distance by Brazil, South Korea, and the Philippines on 10 percent (a surprisingly low estimate for the first two of these). Without wanting to give too much credence to these figures, they do show the range of countries that have to be taken into account in any analysis of evangelical religion under globalization.

3. The Need for Greater Attention to Global Constraints on Religious Choice

Globalization studies regarding religion need to pay more attention to global limitations on religious freedom, to avoid an exaggerated emphasis on the extent of religion as choice. The standard portrayal of religion in modern times can be exemplified by Lyon's affirmation that the religious marketplace has become extremely deregulated, with the result that signs circulate freely and personal choice rather than traditional authority determines how they are appropriated;[23] or Wuthnow's statement that "religious expression is becoming increasingly the product of individual biographies."[24] Rarely does one see such statements being qualified by a mention of awareness of limits to choice. Religious diversity in a society does not automatically translate into real choice at the individual level. A large part of the world is characterized by optionless plurality; in some areas, even that does not exist.

Freedom of religion operates at diverse levels, including freedoms for individuals and religious organizations, as well as general human rights as applied to such organizations and individuals. Its dimensions include not only the right to worship and organize but also to propagate and convert. Restrictions on religious freedom are equally varied in nature. There are innumerable legal restrictions used around the globe (including, at the more "moder-

---

22. Angus Reid Group, "Faith in the Modern World" (Jan. 1998).

23. Lyon, *Jesus in Disneyland*, p. 56.

24. Robert Wuthnow, *The Struggle for America's Soul* (Grand Rapids: Eerdmans, 1989), p. 116; cited in Lyon, *Jesus in Disneyland*, p. 51.

ate" end, restrictive registration laws or official lists of "dangerous sects" in some Western European countries); but there is also the problem of discriminatory implementation of otherwise good laws and of reservations policies, as well as social and cultural pressures and terrorist violence. Marshall affirms that the overall trend in religious freedom around the world has been negative. Notwithstanding, there are relatively free countries in every continent and at every level of economic development, giving the lie to assertions that religious freedom is a peculiarly "Western" concern or a luxury for the rich. However, many countries score lower on religious freedom than they do on civil liberties in general, showing the sensitivity of religious questions.[25]

A few examples from different parts of the globe will suffice. In Armenia, legislation has become increasingly restrictive, state-inspired attacks have proliferated, and minority religions in general have become virtually synonymous with foreign influence. In Austria, the two-tier system (recognized churches versus recognized associations, with differential privileges) was further divided into three tiers in 1997, apart from a fourth category of "dangerous cults" (including some evangelical groups) denied legal status altogether. In Burma, state promotion of Buddhism includes cases of forced conversion of Christians in ethnic minorities and targeting of clerics. In Egypt, all mosques must be licensed, nonconformist Muslims face state-run heresy trials, Coptic Christians have suffered discrimination and terrorist threats, Muslim converts to Christianity have been imprisoned even though the law does not prohibit proselytizing, and the Bahai religion is outlawed. In Mexico, despite liberalized religious laws since 1992, religious bodies may still not own radio stations or support candidates in elections; clergy may not criticize the government or run for office; and in Chiapas some 30,000 indigenous evangelicals have been expelled from their lands by the Catholic *caciques* over the last thirty years.[26]

Religion as personal choice thus has to be seriously qualified at a global level. In India, besides social limitations, the reservation (i.e., affirmative action) laws place a strong disincentive for untouchables to convert to Christianity, and some states actually prohibit conversion. China and the remaining communist countries still present limitations on freedom of religion, and the Muslim world is overwhelmingly restrictive, even sometimes of dissident forms of Islam. Thus, religion as choice is limited to, at best, half of the world's popu-

25. Paul Marshall, ed., *Religious Freedom in the World* (Nashville: Broadman and Holman, 2000).

26. Examples taken from Marshall, ed., *Religious Freedom;* Paul Freston, *Evangelicals and Politics in Asia, Africa and Latin America* (Cambridge: Cambridge University Press, 2001).

lation. It may, of course, be alleged that globalization is going to change all of this, but the more it does so, the more it will favor voluntary conversionist religion rather than the relativistic or fundamentalistic options often touted.

4. The Need for Renewed Study of the World Religions

Awareness of globalization makes study of the "world religions" more important than ever, that is, the study of whole traditions and of the interaction between these great traditions.

It may be that the very concept of "world religions" will in the end be contested (whether as too Western, or as too elitist and scripturalist); or perhaps the concept will be expanded through the birth of new "world religions" just as the process of Western expansion "produced" Hinduism and Buddhism. Hamilton rightly laments that the sociology of the world religions is still largely tied to Max Weber; while studies of secularization and sectarianism have flourished, the world religions have been studied more at the ethnographic level and studies of whole traditions remain rare.[27] This may explain why even Hamilton's own book is sparse on the current reality of each world religion.

Weber himself was open-minded about the possibility of re-secularization led by some of the world religions. After portraying the disenchantment of the world and the development of the iron cage of capitalist and bureaucratic modernity, he comments wistfully: "no-one knows whether at the end of this tremendous development entirely new prophets will arise, or there will be a great rebirth of old ideals, or, if neither, mechanized petrification."[28] In the West today, it may seem that the first rather than second possibility is the greater challenge to the iron cage. But this situation may be only temporary even in the West (Martin talks of a cyclical swing between the rise of universal narratives, which he calls the "big idea" of human history, and the assertion of difference);[29] and globally it makes more sense to see Islam, Catholicism, and evangelicalism as the main candidates for "global religion," which in Weberian terms represents the triumph of the religions of the "west" (i.e., Middle East) over those of the "east," the opposite of the much-discussed "orientalization" of current Western religiosity.

27. Malcolm Hamilton, *Sociology and the World's Religions* (New York: St. Martin's Press, 1998), p. 54.

28. Max Weber, *The Protestant Ethic and the Spirit of Capitalism* (London: Unwin, 1985), pp. 181-82.

29. David Martin, "The Idea of Unity as the Big Idea," in Woodhead and Heelas, eds., *Religion in Modern Times*, pp. 299-300.

5. The Need to Distinguish Fundamentalism from Evangelicalism in Relation to Globalization

Evangelicalism and fundamentalism have a complex relationship. While there is overlap (some evangelicals are fundamentalists), evangelicalism is an older and broader tendency within Protestantism, while the "fundamentalist" label has been extended in another direction to include phenomena from other religions. Fundamentalism and evangelicalism relate differently to globalization, the former being more properly a reactive phenomenon within globalization whereas the latter predates and possibly contributes to it.

The *Fundamentalism Project* illustrates this. The introduction to the volume on the state defines fundamentalism as embracing "movements of religiously inspired reaction to aspects of global processes of modernization and secularization . . . the struggle to assert or reassert the norms and beliefs of 'traditional religion' in the public order."[30] But evangelicalism is far from traditional in most of the Third World.

The dynamic of conversion places evangelicalism in a very different relationship to global cultural processes from either pan-religious ecumenism (tending to global homogeneity) or fundamentalism (tending to irreducible pockets of anti-pluralism). As generally a non-traditional religion (in local terms) spreading by conversion, its interests are usually the opposite of those of a reactive fundamentalism. For evangelicalism, pluralism and cultural diffuseness would seem to be advantageous, whereas non-Christian fundamentalisms constitute one of its most serious barriers. It may be that evangelicalism flourishes best in a world that is tranquilly religious, rather than one that is either secularized or defensively religious. As Waters says, "a globalized culture is chaotic rather than orderly. . . . The absolute globalization of culture would involve the creation of a common but hyperdifferentiated field of value, taste and style opportunities, accessible by each individual without constraint. . . . Islam would not be linked to particular territorially based communities . . . , but would be universally available."[31] The spread of evangelicalism through conversion fits this picture of hyperdifferentiation, pluralism, and de-territorialization.

It is tempting to say that, when in doubt about how evangelicalism relates to globalization in any specific aspect, as a rule of thumb one can take whatever is said about fundamentalism and invert it. Besides having different po-

---

30. Martin E. Marty and R. Scott Appleby, eds., *Fundamentalisms and the State* (Chicago: University of Chicago Press, 1993), pp. 2, 5.

31. Waters, *Globalization*, pp. 125-26.

litical implications from Islamic fundamentalism (autonomous space versus comprehensive systems), pentecostalism is more about the democratic avail-ability of spiritual gifts than a conservative understanding of the Bible. In ad-dition, fundamentalists are not usually conversionist, or when they attempt to be they are not usually very successful. Evangelicals convert, and Sufis con-vert, but fundamentalists rarely change religious percentages; rather, they re-trench and revive nominals.

What about the "Americanization thesis" regarding evangelical growth in the Third World, as exemplified in the Brouwer, Gifford, and Rose volume: that it is "contributing mightily to the Americanisation of global culture" and that "the social product that [evangelicals] distribute so successfully around the world is clearly stamped 'Made in USA'"?[32] In Latin America this is some-times styled the "invasion of the sects" theory.

Aside from the complicating factor that we live in a world in which, as Roland Robertson says, the cult of the local is globally sustained and ques-tions of authenticity have become largely redundant,[33] the "invasion of the sects" theory obviously builds on certain facts. Latin American Protestantism has many foreign contacts; the question is how important they are. In person-nel and money, both Catholicism and historical Protestantism are far more foreign than pentecostalism. As for the Assemblies of God, the flow of bene-fits is mainly to, not from, the United States; the American church retains an almost symbolic presence in Brazil, for example, because it helps fund-raising in the United States to say they collaborate with the Brazilian Assemblies, the largest in the world. In much of Latin America, the foreign presence is most noticeable in the media, whose efficacy for growth is doubtful. In Brazil, on the other hand, the large evangelical media presence is totally national. A third of foreign missionaries in Brazil work with the Indians, a mere 0.5 per-cent of the population, while pentecostals make little use of foreign person-nel. International contacts often do not indicate dependence at all, but rather a source of symbolic legitimacy for fighting local battles. David Maxwell has demonstrated Zimbabwean pentecostals' ability to use, but not be swamped by, First World global operators.[34]

32. Steve Brouwer, Paul Gifford, and Susan D. Rose, *Exporting the American Gospel: Global Christian Fundamentalism* (London: Routledge, 1996), pp. 271, 11.

33. Roland Robertson, *Globalization: Social Theory and Global Culture* (London: Sage, 1996), pp. 66-68.

34. David Maxwell, "Christianity Without Frontiers: Shona Missionaries and Transna-tional Pentecostalism in Africa," in David Maxwell, ed., with Ingrid Lawrie, *Christianity and the African Imagination: Essays in Honour of Adrian Hastings* (Leiden: Brill, 2002), pp. 295-332.

American influence has to be demonstrated rather than presumed, and certainly should not be read off from the well-publicized claims of the American operators themselves. While Brouwer *et al.* concentrate on religious globalization from above, it is the simultaneous globalization from below that is far more widespread and determinant. American power (and will) to package and diffuse messages is undisputed. But "glocalization" (micromarketing, adaptation of the global to local conditions) is always necessary if any sort of resonance is to be achieved; and even then, the actual effects are dubious. In addition, transnational evangelicalism is more and more initiated within the Third World itself (see section 6 below). The "hard" (orchestrated) Americanization thesis is hard to defend as an account, not of American religious actors' intentions but of global evangelical growth. The "soft" (emulationist) version of this thesis is still plausible, but close examination of evangelical networks tends more towards a "complex global flows" explanation.

"Glocalization" strategies are, of course, in a sense homogenizing, making particularity only a strategy. But most evangelicalism is not in the hands of global operators, whether American or whatever, but in the hands of autonomous locals for whom particularity is the only option open. "Glocalization" is a strategy of global operators, and therefore it is misleading if applied to most of evangelicalism.

Thus, although Huntington says that "soft" power follows hard power,[35] and the Brazilian anthropologist Segato claims imported religious goods carry the prestige of their materially wealthy source country,[36] most proselytizing today (transcultural or not) is done by the relatively powerless of the world. The sociology of the world religions prepares us for just this. As Weber said, new religious conceptions generally emerge on the periphery of great civilizations and not at the center. People on the periphery retain "the capacity to be astonished about the course of events," a prerequisite for "questioning the meaning of the world."[37] With the shift in the center of evangelicalism (in numerical predominance and in worldwide expansionist impulse), conversion is now flowing again, as it did in the primitive church, from the periphery of world power to the center, rather than vice versa.

35. Huntington, *Clash of Civilizations*, p. 109.

36. Rita Laura Segato, "Formações de diversidade: nação e opções religiosas no contexto da globalização," in Oro and Steil, eds., *Globalização e Religião*, p. 228.

37. Max Weber, *Ancient Judaism* (New York: Free Press, 1952), p. 207.

6. The Need to Distinguish Diasporic and Conversionist Globalization: The Importance of the Theme of Conversion

It has become common to talk about the "globalization" of many religions, and it is true that current trends allow many religions to become globalized, but evangelicalism is different in scale and in nature. We must distinguish between diasporic and conversionist globalization, since their sociological implications are quite different. When researchers consider global religious flows at all, however, they often seem to think only of diasporas.

Diasporas have increased in importance and have resulted in the visible presence of religions hitherto associated only with other parts of the world, such as Hinduism in Britain. The effects on Hinduism are great, but the globalization of Hinduism remains diasporic. Even for a traditionally missionary religion such as Islam, diasporic globalization is clearly more important than conversionist globalization. Ahmed and Donnan, for example, when discussing transnational Islam, mention that Islam now has some one billion adherents in "about 50 countries," and proceed to talk only about diasporic connections.[38] The case of Christianity, however, and above all of evangelicalism, is different not only in *scale* (well over fifty countries) but also in *type*. There is, evidently, a diasporic evangelicalism (Latin Americans in the United States, West Africans in Europe, Chinese in Malaysia, etc.) and its study is important; but its conversionist globalization is even more vital. In fact, since diasporas go largely to traditionally Christian areas of the globe, their overall effect on Christianity is not so important (although it may be for particular types of Christianity, and on its overall intensification). However, evangelicalism today is practically everywhere that it is politically permitted to be. This means its relationship to globalization cannot be read off from discussions of Hinduism or even of Islam. While the study of diasporic religion is important, it is also vital to study the very different dynamics and implications of global missionary activity and of conversion.

If the de-territorialization and voluntarism usually associated with globalization really do expand, then religious conversion will become a major phenomenon of the twenty-first century, with profound cultural, social, and political implications. *Pace* many scholars of globalization, a globalized world need not lead either to a relativistic homogeneity or to clashing fundamentalisms. Conversion, the main route of evangelical growth in the Third World, is another alternative, with quite different cultural and political implications.

---

38. Akbar Ahmed and Hastings Donnan, "Islam in the Age of Postmodernity," in A. Ahmed, ed., *Islam, Globalization and Postmodernity* (London: Routledge, 1992), pp. 1-20.

Globalization studies, however, usually fail to discuss the dynamics and results of actual shifts between religions. This can be exemplified from the excellent anthology edited by Woodhead and Heelas. It contains very little on the growth or decline of particular religions at the macro level, that is, the changing balance *between* religions. The sociology of religion has largely neglected the theme, perhaps not wishing to seem tributary to religious agendas. Yet the decline of secularization theory would seem to open space for greater investigation. On two occasions the theme of conversion is broached by Woodhead and Heelas (when discussing "universalisation" and "sacralisation"), only to be quickly discarded. It seems that only conversions from secularity to religion are deemed important, whereas conversion in the sense of switching religions, even if it also (as very often) involves intensification (since the previous commitment was weak or nominal), is not. This is another example of the disproportionate weight given to the "religion versus secularity" dichotomy.

Recognition of the importance of conversion has many implications. For example, works on religion and politics at the global level often seem to suppose a stable situation in terms of religious identities, varying only in the degree of political mobilization of such identities, whereas in fact switching of religion may be rife and may be creating both new conflicts as well as new bases for social cohesion. For example, there is need for greater research into the effect of evangelical expansion on some normative conflicts, such as the place of Sarawak within the Malaysian Federation, the delicate equilibrium of Nigeria, and the armed struggles in the Sudan, Northeast India, and Burma. As far as globalization is concerned, two key themes raised by Roland Robertson are nostalgia and relativization. Globalization, he says, has been a primary root of the rise of willful nostalgia and the urge to invent traditions.[39] Evidently, Third World evangelicalism goes in a very different direction, and it may be fruitful to explore the idea of nostalgia (the invention of tradition) and conversion to biblical Christianity (the adoption of an alien tradition via the Hebrew scriptures) as alternative responses to the relativization of personal, ethnic, and national identities. As to relativization, characterized by Robertson as "perhaps the central sociological and anthropological phenomenon of the globalization process,"[40] we should stress that evangelicalism, which is proselytistic, depends for its lifeblood on relativization (not relativism). Converts to pentecostalism in Brazil, for example, are well aware of relativization; the convert has inevita-

39. Robertson, *Globalization*, p. 155.
40. Robertson, *Globalization*, p. 61.

bly relativized his original religious affiliation, so he cannot fail to be aware of the possibility of doing the same again with his new one. But this seems to be less threatening than many academics think it must be for poor Third World people. It may also be that the main impact of globalization is *within* each religious tradition, as each one is impelled with new force to seek a universal formulation of the tradition, rather than in relativizing the inter-action *between* traditions.

Why has conversion to evangelical religion, especially in pentecostal forms, become so widespread in many parts of the Third World? According to Waters, a globalized world would have a single society and culture, probably not harmoni-ously integrated, and with high multi-centricity.[41] Pentecostalism's foundation document, the biblical narrative regarding the descent of the Holy Spirit on the day of Pentecost, in which each person in the cosmopolitan crowd heard "the wonders of God in their own tongue," is the basis for its current polycentric globalization. In fact, without much numerical impact, pentecostalism quickly reached the four corners of the earth through missionary and immigrant net-works that intersected with the starting-points in American popular Protestant-ism. (In fact, there are stories from many parts of the world about pentecostal phenomena *before* the Azusa Street revival in Los Angeles in 1906, even though the latter is clearly a historical turning-point. It would seem the novelty of Azusa was not the *phenomenon*, but the *networks* that allowed this particular eruption of the phenomenon to have global repercussions. It is only in this sense that we can say that pentecostalism is "American.") Born amongst the poor, blacks, and women, on the underside of American society, pentecostalism was exported at virtually no cost, often by non-Americans. It is this popular, counter-establishment Western Christianity that has become one of the most globalized religious phenomena. A recent survey of evangelical institutions in Greater Rio de Janeiro discovered that, of the fifty-two largest denominations in the city, thirty-seven were of Brazilian origin, virtually all Pentecostal.[42]

7. The Need to Study Third World Mission Activity as a Key Theme for Religion and Globalization

Protestantism has been important in sociology because of its two concepts of "calling." The Reformational concept of calling in a profession took ascet-

41. Waters, *Globalization*, p. 3.
42. Rubem César Fernandes, *Censo Institucional Evangélico CIN 1992: Primeiros Comentarios* (Rio de Janeiro: ISER, 1992).

icism out of the monastery and into the world, leading in the end to the "Protestant ethic" which contributed to the "iron cage" of bureaucratic rationality and global capitalism.[43] The pietist concept of calling, on the other hand, led to modern Protestant missions independent of the state and essentially "from below," which in the end meant that the popular voluntaristic Protestantism of the West could become globalized. Most sociological discussions of the spread of Protestantism have concentrated on the "Protestant ethic" concept of calling, asking to what extent it has been transmitted and what socio-economic effects it might have in other regions. Such inquiries may be very relevant to current economic globalization. A century ago it seemed to Weber that the capitalist workplace, whose development had owed a lot to the Puritan ethic of duty and frugality, no longer needed any internalized support. Control was exerted by the "mechanized petrifaction" of the "iron cage" rather than by "character." Today, however, with the demise of the Fordist-Taylorist model, some form of self-discipline may once again be necessary, whether to stay employed or to succeed as self-employed.

Our main concern here, however, is with the second concept of calling. There has been little sociological study of this pietist concept as it has spread around the globe: a calling that is essentially independent of institutional confirmation, autonomous of the state, and little concerned about educational or social qualifications, creating genuinely popular social movements and with inherently pluralist consequences in religious and political terms. (The link with principled pluralism in relation to the state is not historically inevitable but is logically close; if mission is in the domain of civil society, then the state cannot be regarded as having a "Christian nation" role, since the principle applied to foreign mission will soon be applied also to evangelization at home.)

Andrew Walls suggests that the "voluntary society" which arose out of this concept of calling depends on a certain type of economy and polity (characterized by freedom of association, individual consciousness, well-distributed economic surpluses, and freedom of capital movement) and that therefore we should not expect a general burgeoning of Third World "overseas mission" societies.[44] While Walls's conditions obviously apply (though less so to a "tiger" such as Korea or an "emerging" economy such as Brazil), they may be offset somewhat by other factors. In the evangelization of Europe, dependence on mass volunteerism in mission was undermined by the Constantinian model, leading to a shallow conversion of the European

43. Weber, *Protestant Ethic.*
44. Walls, *Missionary Movement,* p. 259.

masses.[45] African mass Christianity, constituted through volunteerism, may thus turn out to be even more fecund of "callings," although within the economic and political constraints mentioned. It is also possible to regard the Latin American masses as only now being effectively Christianized via pentecostalism as well as Catholic phenomena such as the Base Communities and the Charismatic Renewal, creating another solid base for voluntaristic mission.

In line with globalization theories regarding the complexity of global cultural flows, globalized evangelicalism is characterized by "a multisource diffusion of parallel developments."[46] Expansion often follows diasporas, but there is also a Third World missionary effort that goes way beyond diasporas. The British diaspora and Anglo-Saxon missions responsible for much worldwide expansion of Protestantism since the eighteenth century have now been overtaken by other diasporas (African, Caribbean, Latin-American, Chinese, and Korean) and by other missions. We need to study the key missionary centers of world evangelicalism and the key diasporic flows, in order to map out the characteristic channels of contemporary evangelicalism's multilateral networks. Leaving aside the already well-studied routes, I would propose looking at Swedes and Italians (especially for their importance in earlier decades of the twentieth century), and at Nigerians, Ghanaians, Koreans, Chinese, and Brazilians (for their contemporary importance).

Whilst the Third World mission movement can sometimes reflect tendencies in secular labor markets (cheap labor for Western-controlled missionary enterprises), it is mostly better studied as an autonomous Third World social movement, which may soon be larger than its First World equivalent. Third World missions are an important part of the current transformations of religion in an era of globalization. South Korea has produced the strongest evangelical foreign missions movement, rising from only ninety-three missionaries in 1979 to 5,804 in 1998, distributed over 152 countries. South Africa has some 600 in over fifty countries. Other African countries are handicapped by the limitations Walls mentions, but even so by 1992 there were about 250 Nigerian missionaries abroad under the auspices of Nigerian-based agencies. However, migration for economic reasons, rather than sending by mission agencies, has been the prevailing mode by which West African evangelicals

45. Rodney Stark, "Efforts to Christianize Europe, 400-2000," *Journal of Contemporary Religion* 16, no. 1 (2001): 105-23.

46. Irving Hexham and Karla Poewe, "Charismatic Churches in South Africa: A Critique of Criticisms and Problems of Bias," in Poewe, ed., *Charismatic Christianity as a Global Culture* (Columbia: University of South Carolina Press, 1994), p. 61.

have exported their faith (the above data are from the *Evangelical Dictionary of World Missions*).[47]

We shall illustrate at greater length with the case of Brazil. In 1997 the news magazine *Veja* reported that there were 1,700 Brazilian missionaries abroad, twice as many as in 1990, of whom 500 were from the Universal Church of the Kingdom of God (UCKG).[48] Another source gives data for the year 2000: it talks of 1,494 missionaries sent by forty-five sending agencies, of which only thirteen were Brazilian branches of foreign agencies.[49] If we include some large pentecostal denominations whose mission work is not counted in the survey, we can estimate a total of some 2,000 Brazilian evangelical missionaries, nearly 90 percent of whom are sent by missionary societies resulting from Brazilian initiative. The receiving countries (sixty-nine in all) cover all the continents. Latin America receives 41 percent, Africa 19 percent, and Europe also 19 percent (a significant inversion of historic flows). If we include the UCKG, there are probably nearly one hundred Brazilian missionaries in the United Kingdom today. Asia receives 12 percent and North America 9 percent.

Approximately 79 percent of all these missionaries are working among Portuguese- or Spanish-speaking people. However, the total of fifteen missionaries in Albania (down from twenty-three in 1997) is noteworthy, perhaps indicating another logic in choice of destination, i.e., the strong emotive and symbolic value of proselytizing in a country that until recently was a by-word for the most complete communist effort to eradicate religion.

The above data are certainly incomplete, however, since they ignore not only the UCKG but also the God Is Love Church (which in 1991 claimed to be present in seventeen countries with 413 workers, many of whom were presumably Brazilian), the Christian Congregation (which in 1996 was in thirty countries), and *Renascer em Cristo*. Although the true size of the Brazilian evangelical missionary effort can only be estimated at around 2,000 missionaries, its significance can be gauged by a comparison with the United States. The latter has about four times as many practicing evangelicals as Brazil, with a per capita income perhaps eight times higher, but it does not export thirty-two times as many long-term missionaries (the 1996 figure was 40,000).[50]

47. A. Scott Moreau, ed., *Evangelical Dictionary of World Missions* (Grand Rapids: Baker, 2000), pp. 546, 692, 898.

48. *Veja*, 23 April 1997.

49. Ted Limpic, "Organizações Missionárias Ibero-americanas País: Brasil," www.comibam.org/catalogo/por/consulta/bra/index/htm, 2000.

50. Jo Siewert and E. Valdez, eds., *Mission Handbook 1998-2000* (Monrovia: MARC, 1997).

The main Brazilian church in this process is the *Igreja Universal do Reino de Deus* (Universal Church of the Kingdom of God — UCKG). Founded in a poor suburb of Rio de Janeiro in 1977, it is now present in some sixty countries. Its social composition in Brazil is markedly lower class. This lower-class base is linked with enormous institutional power due to strongly hierarchical organization, political strength (seventeen members in the Brazilian Congress), financial wealth (thirty-fourth largest private enterprise in the country), and media empire (daily newspaper, over thirty radio stations, and above all the third largest television network in Brazil). While seeing itself as part of the Protestant community and heir to the evangelical tradition, the UCKG also has links with traditional Brazilian religiosity. In the phrase of one leader, "We do not follow a European or American evangelical tradition; we start from the religious practice of the people." It is also (thanks to constant methodological innovation facilitated by centralized control) a bricolage of practices from diverse sources, well adapted to times of globalization. The UCKG is typical: liturgy is "glocalized" by, for example, talking about *sangomas* rather than *orixs* in South Africa, and by tuning in to specific problems in each country (AIDS in Africa, family disintegration in the UK, and so on).

The UCKG invests heavily in foreign expansion. Three cultural blocs account for well over 90 percent of the UCKG churches abroad: (i) the Latin American bloc, which includes Hispanics in the United States; (ii) the Portuguese-speaking countries; and (iii) African countries and the African diaspora in Europe. The Lusophone, Latin American, and African worlds, with which the Brazilian UCKG has cultural and/or linguistic links, provide the vast majority of the worldwide membership. In South Africa, perhaps its greatest success outside Brazil, it is the first major example of a new phenomenon: a church that is neither First World nor African in origin, but part of the globalization of Third World evangelical religion. However, the non-Iberian white world, Asia, and the politically inaccessible Middle East remain a challenge.[51]

The UCKG may be unique because, unlike other Third World pentecostal groups, it has the political power and economic strength to guarantee some visibility even in the developed world. By the late 1990s, Asia was viewed by the church as its next great challenge; it will certainly be the greatest test yet of the Universal Church's ability to live up to its name in contexts that are both

51. Paul Freston, "The Transnationalisation of Brazilian Pentecostalism: The Universal Church of the Kingdom of God," in A. Corten and R. Fratani, eds., *Between Babel and Pentecost: Transnational Pentecostalism in Africa and Latin America* (London: Hurst, 2000), pp. 196-215.

non-Christian and have few cultural affinities with the Brazilian cauldron in which it emerged.

Conclusion: The Future of Evangelical Christianity Under Globalization in the Context of Other Religions

Roland Robertson stresses that the globalization of religion could have happened in different ways, one of which would have been the global triumph of a particular form of organized religion.[52] We can add that all religions now have to live with the fact that that did not happen, even though there were moments in Christian and Muslim history when such an outcome seemed on the cards. But, as Robertson adds, the shape of the global field is still "up for grabs"[53] and religious interpretations and responses to it can play an important part.

We can surmise that any globally successful religion will have to be able to survive under pluralism, without state support, and to meet the needs of people caught up in the traumas of globalization, while at the same time being serviceable for ethnic and "anti-globalizing" uses. The right mixture of universalism and particularism is essential for globalization as a mass religion. Elite religions are easily globalized but remain small, while some mass religions are too culturally specific. It may be that the particularism of a truly global religion has to be based on historicity rather than anything else; and the story told has to have universal applicability, which means respect for cultural particularities. Religions with a fairly harmonious resolution to the tension between the universal and the particular will do well. It may be that characteristics relating to its mode of expansion are important, such as decentralization, flexibility, mobility, and lay initiative. It would seem at the moment that the only real candidates for global religions (there could be more than one) are from what we know as the world religions, but that not all of them are equally viable.

Woodhead and Heelas conclude that global religious "winners" will be those that put people in touch with a God beyond self, make a difference, sustain supportive and affective communities, emphasize experience, have a political or economic job to do, and empower people. They are especially sanguine about the chances for "experiential religions of difference" (which include pentecostal and charismatic Christianity), and (though less strongly) for "religions

52. Robertson, *Globalization*, p. 54.
53. Robertson, *Globalization*, p. 62.

of heightened difference" (fundamentalist). As for "spiritualities of life," they recognize that worldwide they are less prevalent, and that in the West, while the "turn to self" will continue, such "formless" self-centered religiosity may be short-lived.[54] We can add that the current moment of pulverized experimentation with the new or the locally newly available from afar may be a passing phase rather than a linear trend. In the medium run, the newly available that is tried and tested elsewhere in the world, especially in competitive religious conditions, will do better than other newly available options.

It is noteworthy that virtually all Woodhead and Heelas's predictions presuppose that people have the power to choose; they do not take questions of power and degree of religious freedom into account. Surely, however, the fate of religion under globalization will depend a lot on how this develops. While much in globalization theory seems to envisage a trend to greater openness, not all visions of the global future do (Huntington's being one such exception), and many processes that may in the end be invincible may take decades or centuries to work themselves through. If the global future is really still "up for grabs," then surely this whole question cannot be neglected in studies of global religion.

While Hinduism may be going through a process of "semitification,"[55] it has yet to show that it can be successful in mission, and its globalization remains basically diasporic. Buddhism, on the other hand, is one of the great missionary religions. Originally elitist, with a strong distinction between monks and laity, it is "Protestantizing" and producing strong voluntary associations, but has yet to attain mass success outside its traditional Asian strongholds.

Islam is often touted as the fastest-growing religion in the world, and its "fundamentalist" wing is the most discussed in relation to globalization. Dreams of revolution waned in the 1990s and interest shifted more to the Islamization of society. The close association of religion and law in Islam would seem to be a disadvantage in a globalizing world, in comparison with the greater Christian flexibility derived from the fact that Christ gave no law. In any case, Islamic growth among new populations has been largely through the more culturally flexible Sufism. If fundamentalism means more cultural conversion, it may end up producing a "Java" situation,[56] in which erstwhile

---

54. Woodhead and Heelas, eds., *Religion in Modern Times*, pp. 431, 439.

55. Richard King, *Orientalism and Religion* (London: Routledge, 1999), p. 104.

56. Robert Hefner, "Of Faith and Commitment: Christian Conversion in Muslim Java," in Robert W. Hefner, ed., *Conversion to Christianity: Historical and Anthropological Perspectives on a Great Transformation* (Berkeley: University of California Press, 1993), p. 109.

Muslims decide that if they are to be classed as "bad" Muslims they would rather not be Muslims at all.

Long-term prospects for Muslim growth are not so good if it cannot break out of its "progressive expansion" mode related to territoriality plus diaspora. Current good performance has been assisted by three factors: state suppression of freedom of religion for Muslims, petrodollars, and high population growth. The last two will not last. It is, of course, important to recognize the internal diversity of Islam and the possibility of change; but the most likely scenario, while distant from Huntington's pessimistic essentialism, is also distant from those who exaggerate the chances of "liberal Islam."

Ruthven's prediction is that the globalization of culture must lead to secularization in Muslim societies because of increasing choice. The Muslim diaspora educated in the West will be significant, and the Muslim world will develop along the lines of the post-Christian West. The faith will become private and voluntary.[57] Against Ruthven, one can argue that maybe the choice is not between the current situation and imitation of the West. The Islamic world may not secularize, but it may be exposed to religious pluralism one day. It would, of course, be capable of adapting to that new challenge; but it would probably suffer some heavy initial losses (just as previously monopolistic Catholicism has recently in Latin America) until it learnt to maintain its traditional populations against competition. While neither Islam nor Christianity has so far had much success amongst each other's traditional populations in modern times, there has been a crucial difference with regard to religious freedom. We can already say that Islam is unlikely to grow appreciably in traditionally Christian areas, even with religious freedom, but vice versa may not be true.

The alternative scenario is that Islam will retain the image of a besieged religion that needs political protection, neglecting to develop in other ways (as protected monopoly religions tend to do). Akbar Ahmed says the threat to Islam today is not so much Jesus as Madonna,[58] i.e., not so much conversion as secularization; but this is because conversion is easier to legislate against. Islamic human rights schemes, says Mayer, fudge the question of religious freedom. The Arabic version of the Islamic Declaration of Human Rights states: "it is not permitted to . . . disseminate that which involves encouraging . . . forsaking the Islamic community." One of the many motives for retaining

---

57. Malise Ruthven, *Islam: A Very Short Introduction* (Oxford: Oxford University Press, 1997), p. 138.

58. Akbar S. Ahmed, ed., *Islam, Globalization and Postmodernity* (London: Routledge, 1992), p. 206.

the sharia ban on apostasy is, as a government memorandum on a Kuwaiti law puts it, because "the devil makes the route of apostasy attractive to the Muslim woman so she can break a conjugal tie."[59] Any effective loosening of this ban, as some Muslims advocate, would have momentous consequences for the future of religion globally.

Christianity's relationship to globalization, abstractly considered, can be introduced in the words of St. John Chrysostom: "Though he be neither relation nor friend, yet he is a man, who shares the same nature with thee. And if besides he partakes of the same faith, behold he hath also become a member of thee"[60] — universal humanity plus limited brotherhood, the latter being not a substitute for the former but rather a model for it. It is the hope of obliterating this division that motivates Christian globalism. Rather than abstract enunciation, it is limited incarnation of a universal ideal that is the model. Universalism, according to Christianity, starts as particularism somewhere. Christianity grew out of Judaism, an ethnically enfleshed religion but one that possessed, not a concept of generation by the deity (a racial-descent concept difficult to universalize), but one of adoption by the deity (a potentially universalizable concept).

The relationship between the universal and the particular, says Robertson, must be central to our comprehension of globalization processes.[61] Walls points to two characteristic Christian dimensions of this: on the one hand, all Christians are landed with an adopted biblical past, "several millennia of someone else's history," a particularity which, since it is shared by all believers, becomes universal. On the other hand, says Walls, no conversion is complete without the conversion of the past.[62] Thus the globalization of Christianity involves bringing particular pasts in, albeit re-read pasts; not a past-less global uniformity, but a global community incorporating local pasts, on the basis of the incorporation of the local past of the scriptural "people of God." The alternative is Hannah Arendt's warning, that "a global present without a common past threatens to render all traditions and all particular past histories irrelevant."[63]

Within Christianity, there have been different approaches to effectuating this basic thrust. Russian Orthodoxy developed the idea of the "third Rome": all previous Christian empires had fallen but this one would not. Catholicism,

---

59. Ann Elizabeth Mayer, *Islam and Human Rights* (Boulder, CO: Westview Press, 1999), pp. 139-74.
60. In Chrysostom's XV Homily on St. John's Gospel.
61. Robertson, *Globalization*, p. 96.
62. Walls, *Missionary Movement*, pp. 9, 53.
63. Quoted in Robertson, *Globalization*, p. 49.

of course, retained the first Rome. The Russian Orthodox idea of the "third (and last) Rome" is at a low ebb, but the Catholic idea of the "eternal Rome" is alive and well and is one of the main contenders for global religion. Global evangelicalism, often interpreted as resulting from an American version of the "third Rome" idea, is in fact a completely different phenomenon with no "Rome" at all, or perhaps an enormous and fluctuating plurality of "Romes" (organizational centers) and indeed "Meccas" (centers of pilgrimage and sentiment).

As Christianity becomes more and more non-Western the process of distinguishing the "Christian" from the "Western" will proceed apace, perhaps with unexpected results. While post-colonial nationalism presented a challenge to "indigenize" the churches on the nationalist mold, globalization challenges the churches to rethink the meaning of "indigenization." Since some of the main divisions in Christendom were the result of processes of de-globalization, it is possible that the new global reality of the church may implode these and produce entirely new major forms, especially if Christianity at last achieves a mass base in South and East Asia.

Catholicism's future is portrayed ambiguously in recent analyses. On the one hand, Berryman talks of Catholic reliance on Fordist-Keynesian forms of organization being challenged by evangelicals' "network" style in tune with global changes.[64] On the other hand, Walsh speaks of the recent global effectiveness of the papacy,[65] while Casanova describes how globalization offers a transnational religious regime like Catholicism (which never felt really at home in a system of sovereign nation-states) the chance to expand and even have a role in shaping global reality. Since the 1960s, the papacy has been globalized, and the pope has gained visibility as the high priest of a new universal civil religion of humanity. Once Vatican II had assumed the modern doctrine of human rights, the concern with *libertas ecclesiae* was transformed into *libertas personae,* and the pope was transformed from being the Holy Father of all Catholics to the common father of God's children. However, Casanova maintains that this role as first citizen of a global society, made possible by the globalization of the mass media and the centralization and homogenization of Catholicism by Vatican II, is often in tension with the pope's official role as infallible head of the Catholic Church. There are also tensions between the simultaneous processes of Roman centralization and the formation of na-

64. Phillip Berryman, "Churches as Winners and Losers in the Network Society," *Journal of Interamerican Studies and World Affairs* 41, no. 4 (1999): 21-34.

65. Michael Walsh, "Catholicism and International Relations: Papal Interventionism," in J. Esposito and M. Watson, eds., *Religion and Global Order* (Cardiff: University of Wales Press, 2000), p. 100.

tional conferences of bishops. Casanova concludes that the Church will have to learn to let all the faithful participate in the constant elaboration of its normative teachings.[66] This may become ever harder as the Church hierarchy becomes more and more international. As Walsh predicted in 2000, it remains an open question whether the new pope, Benedict XVI, will share John Paul II's enthusiasm for his global role, or will turn instead to the growing internal divisions.[67]

Catholicism's size and centralized structure make possible some global roles that would be difficult for evangelical Christianity however much it grows. A key challenge for global evangelicalism will be to combine its voluntarism and fissiparity with some viable means of organization for social and political impact at national and global levels. While form may still be up for grabs, it is unlikely that global evangelicalism's impact will be rapid at this level, especially as its Third World manifestations are too divided, poor, often educationally deprived, and institutionally under-endowed.

If de-territorialization, pluralism, and voluntarism expand their global reach in the twenty-first century, conversion will become a major phenomenon. The best-equipped and most experienced religions in this respect are Islam, Catholicism, and evangelicalism. Institutional flexibility and lay initiative may give Islam and evangelicalism an advantage, by facilitating a "weaker" rather than a "stronger" form of globalization. (In Friedman's terms, the "weak" form merely requires a global field of reference, global access to "the same set of expressions or representations," whereas the "strong," more homogenizing, form also requires that "we all understand in the same way the objects and representations that circulate" globally.)[68] Experience in coping with religious pluralism may further favor evangelicalism over Islam. Evangelicalism also seems well equipped to flourish in many places due to its capacity to combine expressive individualism with moral obligation and community loyalty.

Although many trends in globalization seem positive for evangelicalism, its effective growth will also depend on less favorable scenarios losing their current hold on large parts of the globe (especially with regard to religious freedom). But freedom of religion is just the cords around the ring. For large-scale conversion, there must be incentives to change religion, a positive public image for evangelicalism, and concrete local supply. However, it may be that

66. Casanova, "Globalizing Catholicism."
67. Walsh, "Catholicism and International Relations," p. 116.
68. Jonathan Friedman, *Cultural Identity and Global Process* (London: Sage, 1994), p. 203.

evangelicalism is successful in a first moment of globalization, but later encounters resistance, either from revitalization and imitation on the part of other religions, or through non-Christian religious nationalism that mobilizes to exclude it, or even because it "blows its own chance" by staining its public image through association with corrupt and self-serving political postures or unscrupulous monetary practices.

These problems aside, continued appreciable growth of evangelicalism is possible and even likely among "animist," Orthodox, and Confucian populations, and also among Hindu Dalits ("Untouchables") if the disincentives of the reservation system are removed. (The greater the success of Hindu fundamentalism, the greater may be the chances for Christian conversion.) Prospects are also good among nominal Catholics in Latin America, Latinos in the United States, and (depending on the religious policies of governments) in the currently communist countries. The Muslim and Hindu worlds will probably remain extremely difficult for the foreseeable future, with Buddhist areas somewhat less so.

China already has probably the second- or third-largest evangelical community in the world, although the price of the isolation that has allowed an indigenous Christianity to flourish is that, if and when an opening-up occurs, much of the Chinese church will appear excessively "local" (i.e., heretical and sectarian). In interaction with the diaspora, Chinese Christianity may come to have great global influence. If the Chinese world can get up to Latin American or African percentages of evangelicals, its human and material resources will form the first ever non-Western power center within evangelicalism.

China shows that communism in traditionally non-Christian (and non-Muslim) lands can open up space for Christianity by secularizing and disenchanting society and by weakening traditional religions, and then leaving an ideological and spiritual vacuum. The effects of "post-communism" on religion in a globalizing world will be interesting to see. In terms of population, most of the communist world has not yet entered post-communism. We do not yet know what post-communism will lead to in non-Christian countries (over 20 percent of the world's population). There are already signs of notable Christian growth in China and Vietnam; as for North Korea, it was the center of Korean Protestantism before division.

In Latin America, the probable future is of an evangelical peak, followed by a Catholic revival (including "evangelical" forms) and then a settling to a long-term religious pluralism. Guatemalan and Korean stagnation at "20 something" percent evangelical may lend credence to the idea of a built-in decelerator to the evangelical symbolic "protest." But the great variety of forms and creativity in crossing social frontiers counsel caution in predicting a ceiling. The Catholic Church is being slowly transformed, under the weight of its territorial structure that makes it hard to follow demographic changes, and of the clericalism that inhibits lay initiatives and creates cognitive distance from the masses.

It is worth asking whether Third World evangelicalism can play a role in opposing existing market-driven globalization. While militant Islam does so in its own way, can evangelicalism adopt a stance that is neither subordinate to neo-liberalism nor hostile to the Western (and heavily Christian) heritage of democracy and human rights? Critiques of IMF-recommended policies do exist, but they are occasional and piecemeal rather than systematic and self-aware. Perhaps the increasingly "social" discourse of prosperity teachers such as the Universal Church in Brazil and Mensah Otabil in Ghana may in the future find common ground with movements of the "evangelical left."[69]

As Bauman says, globalization for some means localization for others, as well as the removal of public spaces from local life. Localities lose their meaning-generating capacity, and the "agoras" in which local opinion leaders processed messages from the outside are removed.[70] In this context, one can ask about the possible role of evangelicalism as more and more a religion of the "localized" rest. The local rootedness and continuity of the churches can help re-create spaces where alternative cultural norms can predominate. Church leaders still have access to localized agoras. However, evangelicalism's advantage in combating exclusionary globalization at the local level is offset by disadvantages at other levels. Not only does globalization create weak states, but evangelicalism creates "weak" churches, besides weakening the "strong" Catholic Church in many areas.

69. Freston, *Evangelicals and Politics*, p. 315.
70. Zygmunt Bauman, *Globalization: The Human Consequences* (Cambridge: Polity Press, 1998), pp. 2-3, 24-26.

CHAPTER 3

Redemption and Progress: Analogies of Protestantism and Popular Culture in the Philippines

BRIAN M. HOWELL AND ANTHONY DELA FUENTE

If history has taught us anything, it is that change is constant. This is, of course, no less true of a historically rooted religious movement such as Christianity as it is of the most contemporary aspects of popular culture. In attempting to interpret the local and global dynamics of evangelicalism, we believe it is in this realm of popular culture that a profound insight into an interpretation of Protestant Christianity can be found. This case study is drawn from the Philippines, although the conceptual framework should have broader appeal and application. Specifically, this chapter draws on the medium of film as a window into the contemporary ethos of Philippine spirituality and thought, and applies that insight to an analysis of ethnographic data on the Philippine evangelical (in this case, Baptist) church. Through a close analysis of conversion narratives as shared with us, it is possible to offer analogies to the messages of popular culture and the streams of thought they represent. We argue that this illuminates both a theoretical perspective (localization theory) and a methodology that is enormously fruitful in interpreting contemporary Christianity.

Although evangelical Christianity in the Philippines, like its counterpart in many other parts of the world, is experiencing its most dynamic growth in pentecostal and charismatic forms, denominational forms such as Baptists, Methodists, and United Church of Christ of the Philippines (UCCP) have continued to grow and enjoy a high profile in Philippine life.[1] Yet even (or

1. This was particularly true after the election of Fidel Ramos in 1992, the first Protestant (UCCP) President of the Philippines, who continues to be an enormously popular political figure.

perhaps, especially) among Filipino theologians and scholars of church history, there is a concern that these denominations continue to exhibit a colonial form of their faith. Practices and teachings, the argument goes, continue to reflect their Western (virtually always American) origins.

A cursory observation of many of these denominations would suggest this is the case. Services conducted entirely in English, hymns taken from the United States hymnody, Sunday school curricula published in Waco, Texas, and sermons drawing on the writings of Charles Swindoll are frequently the daily fare of these congregations. In the case of the Baptists, the church has elected to retain the name "Southern Baptists of the Philippines," so reflecting their missionary heritage in spite of the financial and ecclesial independence they have enjoyed for over thirty years.

The conclusion that this necessarily represents a blinding hegemony of imperial legacy, however, does not match our experience in speaking with members of these congregations. Nor does it take into account the social context in which Spanish, Chinese, and other cultural streams, along with North American culture, have become part of Philippine life. To understand more than just what people do, to interpret how they think about these practices, it is important to bear in mind this larger social matrix. It is in this context that it is possible to see how contemporary Filipino cultural idioms construct their own cultural traditions, the place of religion and spirituality, and how change can maintain a constant, rather than representing imposition or disruption. Using two contemporary commercial films as illustrative of these cultural idioms, we consider the expressions of faith of the Baptist Christians. Drawing on their conversion stories, we argue that the major cultural change involved in conversion, in spite of the Western forms and heritage of the new commitments, is not interpreted as a rejection of "Filipino tradition," but is analogous to the representation of tradition expressed in the films. In other words, these local Baptists, for all their U.S. "trappings," are reflecting the larger Philippine social matrix in which tradition can be reinterpreted to include the sorts of changes present in their lives.

The first part of this chapter sets out the theoretical perspective and places the study in a broader context of Christian scholarship, particularly within cultural anthropology. We adopt localization theory as the approach that provides a conceptual framework for the study. The next section explores the films themselves, giving narrative details and literary content, with a particular focus on aspects we feel are most salient for our discussion here. Finally we present the ethnographic data of Philippine Baptist Protestantism, in which we employ several conversion narratives to suggest the relationship between the wider social context as seen in the films, and the experience of Christianity offered by our informants. By bringing together two seemingly disparate sources of data, it is possible to present a new conceptual framework for interpreting contemporary Christianity.

1. Traditions in Recent Scholarship of Christianity

A great deal of the recent scholarship on Christianity, particularly within anthropology, has focused on the relationship between so-called Western elements of Christianity and the non-Western societies into which it enters. These studies have taken the form of inquiry into the colonial relations of missionaries and the powers they "represented," how the practices of those foreign missionaries related to the social changes they occasioned and the incentives, advantages, disadvantages, and consequences of conversion among the early converts to Christianity of a given area.[2] In their interpretations of this process of change, scholars have provided important conceptual tools for understanding Christianity outside the West. Although their arguments are invariably subtler than a simple categorization can capture, their perspectives usually fall into one of three theoretical perspectives.

Although the term "syncretism" has fallen out of favor in anthropology and religious studies, many academic studies have focused on the "blending" or "marriage" of Christianity with indigenous systems. These works often focus on the so-called pre-Christian religions as the local, while Christianity is the "global" cultural force coming from the outside. At times the religious system is parsed into discrete elements that can be identified as "Christian" or "traditional," while some scholars emphasize how traditional categories and worldviews exist beneath the surface of seemingly Christian forms, but the general theory is one of conflicting and identifiably separate systems.

The second perspective is that of politics, perhaps best represented through the theories of resistance offered by scholars such as John and Jean Comaroff.[3] This view stresses the degree to which local people "use" the new

2. Regarding colonialism see John Bowen, "Islamic Transformations: From Sufi Doctrine to Ritual Practice in Gayo Culture," in Rita Smith Kipp and Susan Rodgers, eds., *Indonesian Religions in Transition* (Tucson: University of Arizona Press, 1987), pp. 113-35; T. O. Beidelman, *Colonial Evangelism* (Bloomington: Indiana University Press, 1982).

3. Jean Comaroff and John Comaroff, *Of Revelation and Revolution: Christianity, Colonialism, and Consciousness in South Africa* (Chicago: University of Chicago Press, 1991, 1997). On conversion see Nicholas Tapp, "The Impact of Missionary Christianity upon Marginalized Ethnic Minorities: The Case of the Hmong," *Journal of Southeast Asian Studies* 20 (1989): 70-95; C. A. Kammerer, "Customs and Christian Conversion Among

religion, often in subversive ways, to deal with the political and economic changes wrought by colonialism. Religion, and Christianity in particular, is often seen less in explicitly religious terms and more in a political-economic role. Responses to and the practice of Christianity, then, are often phrased in political terms (e.g., the "colonization of consciousness"). One must beware of caricaturing these approaches, however, even in their most richly detailed forms; neither of these positions captures the dynamics found among the relatively autonomous, often second- and third-generation Christian communities such as those found in the Philippines.

The third position represented in the literature comes closest to our own theoretical perspective. "Translation," as seen in the work of such scholars as Lamin Sanneh and Vicente Rafael, looks at the ways in which people understand (or, in the case of Rafael, misunderstand) Christianity through their unique social and cultural lens.[4] The instant the Christian message arrives in a new context, the people of that context must translate it into the categories and cultural idioms of their lives. This position is quite similar to the more general cultural theories of Marshall Sahlins and Frederik Barth, who have likewise explored the intersection of local and global (or, at least, non-local) systems of thought and practice.[5] We agree with this approach for its general affirmation of religion as something more than either the politics, or self-contained system of symbols, it presents, but we argue for a different understanding of the process.

Perhaps best understood by the name localization theory, this third perspective is rooted in the work of scholars such as Arjun Appadurai and Homi Bhabha. It includes both the instantaneous application of local understandings to global or outside systems of thought, as well as the active and reflexive process in which the given meanings of various cultural flows are grasped and redeployed in self-conscious ways but with often unintended meanings as a result.[6] What is required here is a nuanced understanding of the context as it

---

Akha Highlanders of Burma and Thailand," *American Ethnologist (AE)* 17, no. 2 (1990): 277-91. For social change see Richard Elphick, *Christianity in South Africa: A Political, Social, and Cultural History* (Berkeley: University of California Press, 1997); Mary Margaret Steedly, "The Importance of Proper Names: Language and 'National' Identity in Colonial Karoland," *AE* 23, no. 3 (1996): 447-76.

4. Lamin Sanneh, *Encountering the West: Christianity and the Global Cultural Process* (Maryknoll, NY: Orbis Books, 1993); Vicente Rafael, *Contracting Colonialism: Translation and Christian Conversion in Tagalog Society Under Spanish Colonial Rule* (Durham, NC: Duke University Press, 1993).

5. Fredrik Barth, *Balinese Worlds* (Chicago: University of Chicago Press, 1993).

6. Arjun Appadurai, *Modernity at Large: Cultural Dimensions of Globalization* (Minne-

is understood and re-created in the lives of the people themselves. Unlike "contextualization" or "indigenization" (terms most popular among Christian scholars of non-Western Christianity), the context is not taken as a social given, but rather as a social construct that is lived and re-created in the lives of individuals and communities through daily practice.[7] Nevertheless, rather like Marx's making of history, this constructed context is never wholly of any one individual's choosing. Larger social forces are at work on the understanding and conceptualization of individuals. In this chapter we show how contemporary Filipino film is a powerful instrument for understanding the broader social context as it is understood in a wider arena. Our argument is not that the particular films under discussion were especially notable vehicles for disseminating a social message, or that film in general is the engine driving social context, but rather that there are cultural themes found in the national (or, at least, non-local) life of a people that can be seen in these films.

Film is a particularly powerful medium for understanding contemporary cultural thought, since film-makers are often culturally literate people who have great commercial, if not artistic, motivation to find themes and images that resonate with the greatest number of people possible. The two films considered here were, in fact, both critical and commercial successes. They were widely considered to be two of the best films released by the prolific Philippine film industry in the year 1997. What these films offer is an insight into the social context as it was understood by Filipinos. This throws light on how another aspect of social life, that is evangelical Christianity, is being interpreted by those in that context.

2. Redemption and Tradition: Themes of Filipino Film

A prostitute wants to buy her way out of her situation and she longs for a man who will treat her as if she has never been "dirty." A fisherman seeks for a way home as he drifts aimlessly into the wide expanse of the ocean and into the maze of his own soul. These are the basic storylines of two successful films that the Philippine movie-going audience has seen in recent years.[8] The two

---

apolis: University of Minnesota Press, 1996); Homi Bhabha, *The Location of Culture* (London and New York: Routledge, 1994).

7. Although both terms have been debated and redefined for decades, they remain stock in trade for most Christian scholars of non-Western Christianity and Christian missiologists. See, for example, Charles Van Engen et al., *The Good News of the Kingdom: Mission Theology for the Third Millennium* (Maryknoll, NY: Orbis Books, 1993).

8. Joel David, *The National Pastime: Contemporary Cinema* (Pasig City, Philippines:

films significantly won the hearts and the minds of Filipinos, who are known for their avid film-watching habits.[9]

Gordon Matties said, "Film is powerful in that it not only reflects worldviews but it also shapes them. It embodies the commitments, virtues and values of a society and serves as an expression of religious vision."[10] Film as an artistic medium is especially significant in that it "shows us ourselves, and is a mirror both of our achievements and our strivings; we make meaning in all we do, whether this is done in order to illuminate our path or to search for the infinite. In learning to read film, we become fluent in interpreting the language of life."[11] Film is not only a form of entertainment, it can be a powerful vehicle for communicating stories, meanings, and values to a mass audience and it offers us a window through which to observe the deeper meanings and spirituality of a people. We explore the medium as a source for learning about a particular people's psyche and beliefs.

The two films deal with divergent issues, yet they hold common themes, motifs, and concerns. Both films evoke the theme of redemption and progress, of liberation and escape. The two films meditate on the idea of becoming a better person, of overcoming circumstances and emerging as someone else: a new person. Ian Maher describes that sort of progress as one that is "essentially concerned with overcoming all that prevents a person from becoming fully human. Both the oppressed and oppressor need to be liberated from actions, attitudes and ideologies that are life-diminishing. This often involves radical, if not revolutionary change in the lives of individuals, institutions and structures that are responsible for the oppression."[12] This quest for liberation, redemption, and progress becomes the centerpiece not only with these two particular Filipino films, but has become an important motif in many other media in popular Filipino culture. Although the films invoked many traditional images of religion, economy, machismo, gender relations, and so forth, these films are really not about the rejection of these traditions as something irrelevant or something that must be discarded in order to become "modern" or "developed." What these films are trying to communicate

---

Anvil Publishing Inc., 1990). It is said that the *Guinness Book of Records* once listed the Philippines as the country where people watch the most number of movies in a year.

9. George Matties, "Religion and Films: Capturing the Imagination," *Religion and Film* 2, no. 3 (1998): 156-88.

10. Matties, "Religion and Films: Capturing the Imagination."

11. David Browne, "Film, Movies and Meanings," in Clive Marsh and Gaye Ortiz, eds., *Explorations in Theology and Film* (Oxford: Blackwell, 1997), pp. 33-58.

12. Ian Maher, "Liberation in *Awakenings*," in Marsh and Ortiz, *Explorations in Theology and Film*, pp. 40-41.

is that redemption can be achieved through building on these traditions, in the re-appropriation of an essence, in holding to the core values of these traditional elements. The films meditate on the characters, who overcome their limiting circumstances through ways and methods that transcend the boundaries of traditional Filipino social tradition.

Ligaya Ang Itawag Mo Sa Akin (They Call Me Joy) is about a feisty and determined woman who does not want to spend the rest of her life as a prostitute.[13] Ligaya finds temporary reprieve from her life as a prostitute when a seemingly innocent farmer takes her out of the brothel and marries her. She ends up deeply disappointed, for an escape from her past life was not as easy as she first envisioned it. Her past haunts her. Wholeness, cleanness, and redemption are the central foci of the film.

Muro-ami (The Reef Hunters) is about a man's quest for peace and wholeness as he grapples with his past pains. Fredo, a fisherman and ship owner, is a man haunted by the loss of his wife and child, and he is in desperate need of healing, not only for his physical wounds, but for his emotional and spiritual ones that could cause his death, as a healer tells him. It is also a film about Fredo's enigmatic relationship with the sea and his coming to terms with his anger and unresolved conflict with the sea.[14] Fredo holds the sea responsible for the death of his family. *Muro-ami* is about the need to break through from the confines of one's situation, of psychologically and physically overcoming the bondage that shackles the characters.

Religion and its accompanying traditions play an important role in the quest for redemption. The Filipino, whose religion is predominantly Roman Catholic, examines and questions the relevance of the Church and its role as its people seek for a better life, and redemption from their current situation. In one particularly vivid scene, Ligaya, usually portrayed as a strong character, is seen begging one of her regular patrons to take her out of the brothel. Not typical of her usual behavior, there is desperation as she pleads to be re-

---

13. Initially banned from exhibition in the Philippines because of its adult theme and graphic sex scenes, this film has caught the attention of critics and film enthusiasts because of its sensitive portrayal of the life of a prostitute. Exhibited in various international film festivals, it has received favorable reviews.

14. *Muro-ami* took thirteen awards at the 1999 Metro Manila Film Festival in the Philippines, including the awards for "Best Director" and "Best Picture." The film was also the film festival's top earner with takings of almost 10 million pesos on the opening day of the film. The film also won accolades at the Benodet Film Festival in Benodet, France in 2000, where it was selected as one of the Jury's Choice nominees and was the Public's Choice winner for "Best Picture." The "Best Actor" trophy was given to the lead star, Cesar Montano. Such accolades have sealed the critical as well as economic success of the film.

deemed by that man. He spits at her and repeatedly calls her a whore, humiliating and degrading her. The man turns out to be the parish priest of their town. This scene and subsequent images of the Roman Catholic Church in the film are significant in various ways. First, it is a candid portrayal and commentary on the fallibility and corruptibility of the priests, who are usually seen as the channels of grace and atonement by the Filipino.[15] Second, the portrayal of the inability of the church ultimately to help the people liberate themselves suggests that, as an institution, the church is openly criticized and often considered inadequate. The traditional church is not able to become the liberator of her people in their earthly concerns. In seeking redemption and progress, one cannot find it in the corrupt, crumbling edifice of the traditional church. Instead of finding redemption, Ligaya is humiliated and condemned by the church.

At the same time, however, the film continues to recognize the strong influence of the church in the lives of the people and their aspirations for a better or moral life. A church wedding and a white wedding dress seem to make Ligaya ecstatic. After meeting the man she believes will be her husband and savior, and moving into a humble house with him, Ligaya is seen repeatedly fingering the fabric of the wedding dress she has purchased and hidden away in anticipation of her church wedding. These become important symbols of her redemption. They mark the departure from her old life, and the beginning of the new. The Roman Catholic rituals and sacraments remain a significant element in the Filipino's quest for wholeness and liberation. Ligaya, as a prelude to her church wedding, finds it necessary to go to confession (although this is cut short by the unfortunate discovery that the parish priest is her regular patron). The town mayor, a hypocrite who has ravished a novice prostitute, appears to show piety and righteousness by making a daily trip to the church to advertise to the public his "clean and upright" person.

The portrayal of the Roman Catholic Church in the film is a hodgepodge of conflicting images. While Filipinos may see the Roman Catholic Church as a corrupt, flawed institution, they are continually drawn to its embrace as they see the church as the channel and dispenser of the better life. The role of the Catholic Church remains a significant theme in Filipino religious consciousness. What is important for the Filipinos is what this institution represents: it is not just some antiquated, ineffective structure but remains the center of Filipino spirituality — offering sanctuary, grace, and life abundant that can be experienced within, or in spite of, the apparent flaws of the religion.

15. Melba A. Maggay, *Filipino Religious Consciousness* (Quezon City: Institute for Studies in Asian Church and Culture, 1999), p. 24.

The presence of God, or recognition of the mystical, remains important in the hope for change and redemption. Although there is no direct allusion to God or deity in the traditional Christian sense and understanding of God (as a personal God who is Father), *Muro-ami* contains rich and repeated allusions to the divine. As Fredo consults the healer to tend the wound he received from a mishap, the healer diagnoses his problem to have a deeper nature. "Your wound goes deeper than your physical wound. You need to rest from your labors. I can no longer treat you in the old ways for as the new millennium approaches, all things we used to do are being erased. They are no longer effective." With such pronouncements, the healer implies that something is in control of their situation, something totally Other. At the same time, though the healer's words suggest the inefficacy of tradition, his place in the film as the source of wisdom and insight affirms the importance of traditional Filipino mysticism as a source of knowledge and wisdom. Likewise, Fredo's father repeatedly asks Fredo to make peace with the ocean and to listen to its guidance.[16] The ocean is seen as a mystical, god-like element that somehow has control of the lives of those that are "trespassing" her domain.[17] The role of the father, the importance of the sea to Filipino spiritual and social life, and the mystification of nature all suggest Filipino traditions and become instrumental in Fredo's ultimate renewal, even as he seems to break away from the traditions of his life that are constraining him.

At the beginning of their expedition in the high seas, Dado, Fredo's father, portrayed as the prophet figure, offers to the sea a blood offering. "The sea is generous, she gives abundantly and yet there is a limit to her generosity, and

16. In an interview the director, Marilou Diaz-Abaya, said of the plot and development of the film, "There's little plot to the movie because I wanted to deal with its less event-oriented aspects. It's more about the enigma of the sea. It's so powerful, it's all around us. The fishing ship's voyage itself is a metaphor. Getting lost between ports. . . . Since we have toned down the plot, we could concentrate on experiencing an alien environment, the sea. In that environment, people are forced to confront questions, like what is good, or bad, what is right or wrong. . . . Fredo wants to subdue the sea (because it took his wife and child years ago). But after everything that happens to him, and to his ship in the movie, he begins to accept that he will never conquer it." Nestor Torre, "Marilou Diaz-Abaya and the Sea," *Philippine Daily Inquirer,* 18 December 1999.

17. Mircea Eliade states that "every contact with water implies regeneration; first because dissolution is succeeded by a 'new birth,' and then because immersion fertilizes, increases the potential of life and of creation. In initiation rituals, water confers a 'new birth,' in magic rituals, it heals, and in funeral rites it assures rebirth after death. Because it incorporates in itself all potentiality, water becomes a symbol of life ('living water')." Mircea Eliade, *Patterns in Comparative Religion* (New York: World Publishing Company, 1968), p. 188.

you need to respect it," Dado explains.[18] Reverence, submission, and fear must mark one's attitude with regards to the sea. One of the turning-points in the development of Fredo's character is when he recognizes his anger with the sea, traced back to the loss of his wife and child through drowning. In anguish he cries out, "Why did the sea do this to me?" He recognizes that he cannot ignore the enigmatic authority of the sea over his life. It is a turning point in the development of the story, and more importantly, in Fredo's quest for wholeness and development. In the end, Fredo plunges into the sea, wrapped in the shroud of a fishing net, sinking to certain death. In the depth of the sea, however, he has a vision of his wife and child in a grotto, their souls reaching back to give him hope and new life. Fredo emerges from the net and the sea, reborn to a life no longer tormented by the loss of his family and estrangement from the sea/God/the divine. Thus, from images of the sea as the foreboding Other, to a healer prophesying that the end of the millennium will usher in renewal and change, God/the divine is clearly the source of hope, redemption, and change.

Both Fredo and Ligaya have to contend with seemingly overwhelming obstacles as they face the challenge to become a better if not a new person. They want to break through the traditional roles and conventions. Both are trapped by circumstances and their respective stations in life. The repeated phrase in *Ligaya* is "a woman who is destined to be a whore will in fact become a whore and will remain a whore until she dies." This traditional Filipino fatalism runs against her hope for redemption through the institutions of the church (the wedding) and society (traditional Filipino domesticity). In the end, the failure of these institutions to offer any real hope of redemption stands out starkly against what the film-maker suggests is the real source of such possible redemption: love.

In a similar way, Fredo plays a tough, dominating figure as he commands his ship. His role as the *maestro-pescador* and as the captain of the ship dictates a Filipino machismo and emotional constraint. He must remain strong, relentless, and impassive despite the pain and the wounds of body and mind and his growing affection towards a child on his ship. Both Fredo and Ligaya struggle and long to transcend constricting demands of society, of their situation, and of life in general.

Ultimately, it is not just through overcoming (or seeking to overcome)

---

18. The translation is rough, since the pronoun used for the sea implies a person or for this matter, a being. The Tagalog "siya" is a neutral third person personal pronoun akin to "him" or "her," thus building on the notion that the sea is seen as something that possesses a personality.

these social obstacles that these characters find the possibility or actualization of redemption: it is in the wrestling and coming to terms with what they have and who they are. In each film, the hope for redemption does not involve the casting off of traditional roles, morals, or cultural worlds, but in the reformation of those traditions through what can be seen as a surprisingly evangelical vision of an individual's relationship with the divine. For Fredo, it is in harmonizing his discordant self that he emerges as a new being. The healer whom Fredo consults advises him to take a rest, to stop all his activities; the healer says his wounds are "the wounds from deep within." Failure to rest could be the death of Fredo. In the climactic scene mentioned above, his deliverance out of a cocoon-like, womb-like cover (the fishing net) symbolizes the emergence of a new person. The allusion to a rebirth is palpable as he emerges out of this watery grave as a new being transcending the barriers to his selfhood, his past resolved, and his personal demons slain. Thus, for this film, it is in the individual, personal encounter with the divine that Fredo comes to realize the truth he has heard from those around him. In that moment he does not reject the Filipino world and his relationship with it, but redefines his masculinity and occupation not as dominance and control but harmony and submission to the divine. He gains hope in his spiritual enlightenment.

For Ligaya, the way to redemption proves to be somewhat problematic as she seeks it through playing the traditional woman's role of farmer's wife but fails. Her inability to cook, her accustomed ways and vocabulary are complete giveaways that she is different from the mainstream society and cannot achieve the longed-for respectability. Again, traditional roles and values are not discarded or denigrated, but flawed or constricting in the quest for personal progress and freedom. Traditional life is not to be destroyed, but reformed. Her ultimate submission to the social world of prostitution does not mean that the film portrays a hopelessness for the plight of the oppressed, but there is a clear indication that the social world could never be the source of her salvation.

These two films look at the traditional methods, modes, and motifs of redemption and prescribe new ways of becoming human and achieving dignity as persons. Tradition is not dismissed as wholly irrelevant in the process of redemption and moral progress. In fact, the repeated allusions and invocation to these traditional motifs underscore their importance and continuing role in the Filipino minds. The traditional elements or what they represent are held out as critically important, though in the end, it is through redefining how these values are experienced that the characters realize the sort of redemption they seek. Filipinos, then, do not simply dismiss traditions and traditional institutions as backward and unimportant, but emphasize the need to transcend the institutions through the hope of spiritual and moral progress.

This insight is informative for understanding many facets of contemporary Philippine society, including the development of the Protestant church. Although a distinct minority religion (10-15 percent of the population), Protestants, by and large, have personal religious roots in the Roman Catholic Church. All, of course, live in a national context that is profoundly shaped by Roman Catholicism and church institutions. There are those, of course, who characterize Protestants as having rejected both Catholicism and Filipino cultural tradition in the most profound manner imaginable by leaving the Church.[19] We argue that a proper understanding of Philippine Protestantism should not conclude too easily that converts are rejecting a previous and deeply ingrained tradition. In the cultural messages seen in these films we find the key to interpreting how many Filipino converts view their own religious change.

In the second part of this chapter, we will use the insights from these films to place contemporary Philippine Baptists within this larger cultural matrix. The correspondence, we argue, is not genetic or causal, but reflective of the dual local/global nature of both Philippine Protestant Christianity and Philippine society generally. A superficial or isolated examination of Philippine Protestantism would give the impression that it is merely imitative and "Western," an extreme rejection of Catholicism, Catholic tradition, and perhaps, the culture with which it is so closely associated. We suggest that, on the contrary, the practice of Protestantism is very much a part of the local Philippine moral landscape as it is developing in the early twenty-first century.

3. Philippine Sunday

Sunday morning at Urban Baptist Church, in Baguio City, finds a congregation of between eighty and one hundred people gathering in their church building in a working-class neighborhood. Seated on movable wooden benches, the congregation begins to settle in as the worship team, a group with electric guitar, bass, drums, and piano, begin to sing English worship songs that would be familiar to evangelical Christians in many parts of the world. The order of the service follows a pattern that would be familiar to

19. Ruben F. Trinidad, "Nicolas Zamora and the IEMELEF Church," in Anne C. Kwantes, *Chapters in Philippine Church History* (Colorado Springs: International Academic Publishers, Ltd., 2002), pp. 203-24.

American, European, Australian, and even other Asian evangelicals: singing, collection of the offering, special music, sermon, and announcements. As many who have studied both historic and contemporary non-Western Christianity have noted, however, the mere presence of so-called foreign elements does not indicate the passive acceptance of a whole cultural system.[20] In the case of these Philippine Baptists, they are not merely aping a foreign religion, abandoning their local setting for a non-local identity. Rather, behind the forms and discourses, we find the themes identified in our discussion of Filipino film being experienced in very locally appropriate ways.

Our research of Philippine Protestantism followed an anthropological track by exploring the meanings and uses to which religious understandings are put. Following Weber, Parsons, Geertz, and many others, we would suggest that culture, religious or otherwise, is an essentially contested process of meaning-making. This process is not isolated from prior cultural messages, of course, and the larger social context is taken into account. From our ethnographic study we looked at the conversion narratives of individual members, a sampling of sermons and the teachings of Sunday school, prayer meetings, and Bible studies in the congregations of our field site. In each case the themes of progress and redemption were expressed and/or experienced in ways analogous to the film versions, even while they often indexed obviously Western (generally American) frames of reference. Here we will focus on one aspect of this data: the conversion narrative.

Conversion and conversion narratives have become a hot topic among anthropologists, bringing competing theoretical perspectives and leading scholars from many disciplines into academic dialogue.[21] Although we originally thought that our research on these more established congregations of second- and third-generation Christians would have relatively little to do with conversion, in the Baptist scenario, even those raised in church-going families experienced a moment in which they decided to become Christians

20. See, for example, Lamin Sanneh, *Translating the Message: The Missionary Impact on Culture* (Maryknoll, NY: Orbis Books, 1989); Andrew Walls, *The Missionary Movement in Christian History: Studies in the Transmission of Faith* (Maryknoll, NY: Orbis Books, 1996).

21. In anthropology see Susan Harding, "Convicted by the Holy Spirit: The Rhetoric of Fundamental Baptist Conversion," *AE* 14, no. 1 (1987): 126-81; Peter Stromberg, *Language and Self-Transformation: The Study of Christian Conversion Narrative* (New York: Cambridge University Press, 1993); Rita Smith Kipp, "Conversion by Affiliation: The History of the Karo Batak Protestant Church," *AE* 22, no. 4 (1995): 868-82; Bronwen Douglas, "From Invisible Christians to Gothic Theatre: The Romance of the Millennial in Melanesian Anthropology," *Current Anthropology* 42, no. 5 (2001): 615-50. For an important contribution from a post-colonial literary scholar see Gauri Viswanathan, *Outside the Fold: Conversion, Modernity, and Belief* (Princeton: Princeton University Press, 1998).

"for themselves" and accept baptism. For every member of the congregation, being able to "give a testimony" was an important aspect of their Christian identity.[22] As we collected these testimonies from new and long-time Christians an intriguing theme emerged. Regardless of whether their religious background was in Catholicism, *Iglesia ni Kristo,* or Methodism, "conversion" as it was portrayed in the conversion narrative was not about a wholesale rejection of previous beliefs, affiliations, or doctrinal positions. Rather, conversion was conceived in terms of progress and the discovery of a "better way" of knowing God, being a Christian, or worshiping. Previous beliefs were rarely characterized as theologically or doctrinally wrong, but beliefs and behaviors were simply deficient when compared to the experience and teachings of the new affiliation, in this case, Baptist Christianity.

Rosa Canales, a member of La Trinidad Baptist Church (TBC), had a very familiar story in which she encountered a group of evangelical Christians who befriended her and invited her to an informal Bible study in one of the members' homes. Her family, particularly her mother, proffered staunch opposition to her conversion from Roman Catholicism, cutting off virtually all contact for over a year. Rosa persevered, however, and when asked what convinced her that this change was worth such family strife she replied:

[For] me? It's like I was just convicted and because of that I started worshiping together with the people here before — before where we were still at Camp Dangwa [the first location of the group which would eventually become TBC]. We worshiped the Lord together but there were times — there were Sundays when I would go to the Catholic Church and then — it was like I saw the difference of — as if when I was there in the Catholic Church my worship is sort of mechanical. It's like it's choreographed like that. But when I was there . . . together with my Bible study companions, it's as if I can begin . . . oh . . . nothing . . . automatic in your worship. If what you are feeling is like that. And then it is as if the Word of the Lord says to you, "Follow me, come follow me," like that. And suddenly I thought about the Bible . . . like that . . . you forget yourself. . . . You feel renewed. I said, "How will I follow Christ really? If I follow you?" So that was what convicted me: to follow Him . . . really through and through, come what may, through thick and thin. Yes.

22. Harding, "Convicted by the Holy Spirit," makes a similar point in her discussion of conversion narratives among U.S. fundamentalist Baptists. Although her focus is on the relationship of the listener to the speaker and the role of the narrative in reconstructing the identity of the speaker vis-à-vis the listener, her argument turns on the importance of testimony for Christians themselves.

Praise God, I am victorious. Because even when I was a new Christian it was as if I still had downfalls, but God was there to support me. And now I am stronger. . . . I believe![23]

Her testimony contains a number of elements familiar to others who have examined these narratives: renewal, commitment, a personal encounter with the divine. What is absent, however, is a sense of rejection of the former life in a very strict sense. Her complaint with the Catholic Church is neither doctrinal nor relational. She does not suggest that she came to a truth she previously did not possess in any form. Rather, she says that the worship of the Catholic Church was "mechanical" and "choreographed" and ultimately unfulfilling for her. Her conversion, though dramatic and in clear contrast to her life prior to her decision to join the evangelicals, is not one of rejection and enlightenment but of improvement and progression.

For Irene Bulasao, the issue of joining the Baptists turned not on the efficacy of worship so much as on the general commitment level of Catholics and United Church of Christ members. Although she herself was nominally Catholic prior to joining the Baptist group, other members of her family had previously joined the UCCP. Thus she was familiar with Protestantism, and her decision to join another church was not taken as a rejection of Filipino culture in the way Rosa's had been. For Irene, however, the doctrinal distinctions of Catholics and UCCP Christians were irrelevant. Rather it was her perception of commitment levels that led her to take a new path:

I was sometimes a Roman Catholic. Actually my parents [were] mixed; my father was a Catholic and my mother was UCCP. But I just go [to the Baptist group]. Because there were a lot of Bible studies, there were many books and leaflets back then. I could see that they were given by the [American] missionaries because they were printed in the United States. Beautiful, with pictures. There were Bible courses and the like.

[Before that did you attend the UCCP Church?]

Hmmmm . . . from time to time . . . it was like there was no real/correct direction. No commitment. It's as if . . . just to go because it's Sunday. Still there was no deep commitment . . . no relationship . . . we thought it was just enough to go to church. Then after that we were discipled in depth to grow, and understanding.

23. This, like all subsequent passages, was translated from "Taglish," the common mixture of Tagalog and English used by a majority of Filipinos in everyday life.

In talking about her family, who also considered themselves Christian (including a brother who was a pastor with the UCCP), she often returned to the theme of commitment and her perception of these other traditions as lacking an emphasis on personal commitment and relationship to the divine. Doctrinal issues only came into the discussion in terms of those practices (worship of saints) that struck her as going against this kind of commitment/relationship.

A similar theme was invoked by Velorio Sag-dan, a leader and long-time member of Trinidad Baptist Church. His "conversion" story was somewhat different in that he described attending the church after his children became involved in the summer Vacation Bible School.

> It was the children who started [going to TBC]. I believe it is good. . . .
> They go and say, "come with us." For me, it is no problem. I am already
> Christian. So it is no problem, I just go. I like this church and it is better
> I go with the children so later I think I can join.

Like Irene, his background was with the United Church of Christ in the Philippines (UCCP) although he did not have family members who also held Catholic membership. For him, becoming a member of the Baptist church was less problematic, since both are Protestant denominations and there would likely be little or no resistance from family members or those in the community, as is often the case with Catholic converts. In terms of his own interpretation of why he would leave the UCCP for the Baptists, it is essentially no different from Rosa's decision to convert from Catholicism. Doctrinally he does not distinguish UCCP and Baptists; he calls both "Christians." But he finds in the Baptist church a superior form of Christianity that is free of the empty ritualism with which he characterizes the UCCP. "[The Christianity] there is dead," he suggested. "Here I learn to love God and His Spirit." When pressed to elaborate he explained, "They are always working. Trying to do good works. They do not trust and believe like at TBC. It is better to just trust, you know?" Later, when asked to identify who, among other Christian groups, were "really Christians" in terms of doctrine, he elaborated: "I do not know who is just going to heaven only. But they are too much for works. It is not the Bible. They have the same Bible. But they are trying only to work, and not trusting."

There were those among the congregations who expressed stronger differences with Catholics and other Christian groups in terms of doctrine, but they were very much in the minority and more likely to be those raised in Baptist homes rather than converts from other religions. Even among sermons, in over seventy sermons and messages noted, fewer than 10 percent made reference to Catholics at all with only a small number of those making doctrinal comparisons or references that could be interpreted as oppositional statements.

As seen in the reaction of Rosa's family to her conversion, the interpretation of many Catholic Filipinos is that conversion represents a rejection of Catholicism and the tradition it is thought to convey. Even among Filipino scholars, the growth of evangelical Christianity and the increasing visibility of other "American" cultural forms suggest the further degradation of "authentic" Philippine culture. In looking at the conversion narratives here, we find no themes of rejection and rupture, in which the new affiliation is seen as a break from a personal or cultural past. Rather, the new affiliation with Baptist Christianity is the improvement and progression of spirituality and religion. This interpretation is not explicit, but is foregrounded by an understanding of a larger social context as seen in the films; finding a "new" spiritual path does not entail the rejection of the old, but is seen as providing a continuation and improvement of prior commitments.

4. Conclusion

Philippine culture generally has often been a slippery topic for researchers, as Filipinos themselves have frequently decried their society as an amalgam of traits from their colonial oppressors.[24] Many Filipinos today continue to refer to Jaime Bulatao's famous declaration of the Philippines as "damaged culture" to call for a more "authentic" expression of their heritage and spirituality.[25] Other than the numerous studies of the relatively less-assimilated upland minorities, many scholars have accepted this description of lowland Philippine culture and, among anthropologists and theologians, have devoted relatively less attention to lowland society.[26] Fenella Cannell's recent work challenges this view by taking the locus of culture to be the relationships and power dynamics of interpersonal society, rather than the festivals, rituals, and public culture of conventional anthropological study.[27] Without

24. This was a common theme heard among scholars of Philippine Christianity, particularly from those within the Philippine evangelical church.

25. Jaime Bulatao, *Split-Level Christianity* (Quezon City: Ateneo de Manila University Press, 1966); see also Maggay, *Filipino Religious Consciousness*.

26. Susan Russell and Clark Cunningham, eds., *Changing Lives, Changing Rites: Ritual and Social Dynamics in Philippine and Indonesian Uplands* (Ann Arbor: University of Michigan Press, 1989).

27. Fenella Cannell, *Power and Intimacy in the Christian Philippines* (Manila: Ateneo de Manila University Press, 1999).

detailing her well-crafted argument here, one of her conclusions relevant to our discussion is the degree to which an ability to replicate and participate in "foreign," particularly American, activities becomes an important source of social power. To the extent, however, that this replication is firmly rooted in the local relationships of importance, it is not an attempt to "be American" but is very much about being Filipino. Furthermore, when understood in light of the films and the manner in which they present the Filipino relationship to the traditional and institutions at the heart of "Filipino Culture," it becomes increasingly clear that in the mind of many, the hope of reform, change, and "progress" is not to degrade those institutions but to bring them to their original purpose and rescue the value they are purported to embody.

There is no doubt that Filipinos can identify those practices and elements within their social world that originated outside the Philippines, but are those elements necessarily replacing, hiding, or challenging locally produced identity, religious or otherwise? Does a departure from traditional forms suggest that the ideals, values, or legacy of those traditions is being left behind as well? We would suggest not. The modern capitalistic notions of progress currently on display in Protestant meanings of conversion, spiritual improvement, and psychological health are also part of the larger Philippine social context and woven into expressions of popular culture. Filipinos do not draw strong lines between being "with" the Catholic Church in terms of their membership and the spirituality and faith it represents; the former can be abandoned while the latter are embraced.

In the same way, "local" and "global" are no longer satisfactory categories where locality is found as the global is redeployed in locally meaningful ways. The practice of a very Western form of Christianity allows individuals to place themselves within a flow of Philippine history that is unbroken from earlier times. Their membership in either the Catholic Church or Protestant movements is recast as a form of their current faith — a flawed or imperfect form — but one that led to their current faith and practice. This is not to say that interpretations of conversion are uniform across Protestant believers.[28] There are some (perhaps through their internalization of dichotomies created in other contexts) who hold to a very clear division between Protestant life and faith and the Catholic Church they or others have left behind. Yet this is not an intrinsic feature of Protestant conversion. In a very non-local medium of artistic expression, we find evidence that understandings of traditions and practices held to be intrinsic to definitions of Filipino culture can

28. See Brian Howell, "At Home in the World: Philippine Baptists and the Creation of Context" (unpublished Ph.D. thesis, Washington University, St. Louis, 2002).

be both cherished and suspect at the same time. In the same way, so-called foreign elements so prominent in Philippine Protestantism and Philippine society can be seen as intimately connected to local traditions, as logical extensions of the faith with which Filipinos are so familiar. Recast as meaningfully local, even a seemingly United States–style Protestantism can become a source of redemption and fulfillment for Filipinos who find traditional religious expressions lacking. For Ligaya, it was to reinterpret her experience as a prostitute; for Fredo, it was his relationship to the sea; for these Filipino Protestants, it is their understanding of how to serve, worship, or relate to God; but for all of these, the traditions of the past, whose forms are left behind, nevertheless continue in their progress and redemption.

CHAPTER 4

African Christianity, Globalization, and Mission: Marginalizing the Center

JEHU J. HANCILES

In 1899 the Commissioner of the United States Office of Patents recommended that his office be abolished, on the grounds that "everything that can be invented has been invented."[1] While this astonishing declaration bore significant testimony to the spectacular wave of technological innovation and scientific invention that had characterized the late nineteenth century,[2] its foolhardiness is startling. History, however, is littered with imprudent predictions about technology and its consequences, the lesson being that such analysis is to be avoided if at all possible or undertaken with utmost caution. This chapter is not about technology *per se;* yet the foregoing caveat is supremely relevant to the study of globalization (a phenomenon that embodies and amplifies some of the most spectacular advances in technology in recent decades), to which we now turn our attention.

The term "globalization" has been in fashion for over two decades, and its immensely complex dimensions are the focus of a burgeoning literature with no end in sight. It has become a frame of reference for groups as diverse as politicians, historians, geographers, businessmen, management consultants, economists, literary critics, and so on. Yet few concepts today generate as much confusion and contention. The proliferation of definitions in the literature amply testifies to the concept's complexity and unwieldiness. Precisely

1. "A Survey of the New Economy: Untangling E-conomics," *The Economist,* 23 Sept. 2000, insert on p. 6.

2. Such innovations included the invention of the telephone (1876), the first bicycle (1878), the discovery of the malarial parasite (1880), the invention of the wireless telegraph (1891), and of the first car (1891).

because it "conveys a widespread sense of transformation of the world" the concept can mean all things to all people, in a manner reminiscent of the way in which the twelve blind men asked to describe an elephant ascribed to the whole animal the qualities of the individual features they touched. Probably the safest conclusion that can be drawn from the plethora of studies on the phenomenon is that reality is more complicated than theory. In short, anyone looking for a golden, one-size-fits-all, theoretical model is more than likely to be disappointed. As Thomas Friedman has observed, it is "too complex a system to be explained by grand theories alone."[3]

Here, our main concern is to map out its most easily recognizable contours, with non-Western perspectives forming a primary focus. In this regard it is important to stress that globalization is not an all-encompassing phenomenon. Not only is it experienced unevenly throughout the world but also its dynamic involves marginalization and exclusion. As James Mittelman notes, "There are many phenomena, especially on a local level, that are either outside globalization or mingle only indirectly with global processes."[4]

1. Aspects of the Non-Western Experience

Partly because popular understanding of the concept is laden with notions of American (or Western) hegemony and global capitalist expansion, many Third World observers see globalization as a dark force that "contributes to greed, the desire for control, materialism, consumerism and the promotion of a global culture or lifestyle that destroys values, customs and traditions in local communities."[5] A 1998 meeting attended by thirty-seven church leaders from India, Pakistan, and Sri Lanka concluded that the open-market system and multinational corporations have increased the misery of the poor in developing Asian nations, and it called on churches "to fight globalization."[6]

---

3. Thomas L. Friedman, *The Lexus and the Olive Tree: Understanding Globalization* (New York: Farrar, Straus and Giroux, 1999), p. 22.

4. James H. Mittelman, *The Globalization Syndrome: Transformation and Resistance* (Princeton: Princeton University Press, 2000), p. 226.

5. Cf. D. Mukarji, "Gospel and the Search for Identity and Community," *International Review of Mission (IRM)* 85, no. 336 (Jan. 1996): 25-34, especially p. 26. For a more wide-ranging treatment see Martin Khor, "Global Economy and the Third World," in J. Mander and E. Goldsmith, eds., *The Case Against the Global Economy and for a Turn towards the Local* (San Francisco: Sierra Book Clubs, 1996), pp. 47-59.

6. The meeting was organized by the Association of Christian Institutes for Social Concern in Asia and the Urban Rural Mission of the National Council of Churches in

Given common assumptions about, and perceptions of, the phenomenon, such reactions are understandable. They also point, however, to the need for theoretical analysis of globalization from a non-Western perspective that would also address its multi-dimensionality, limitations, and inherent contradictions. Mittelman's *The Globalization Syndrome: Transformation and Resistance* attempts such a treatment and sheds important light on the non-Western experience of globalization.

Mittelman argues that globalization is best seen as "a syndrome of processes and activities" rather than "a single unified phenomenon."[7] He observes that for the majority of the world's peoples, the poor and powerless in particular, "the dominant form of globalization is experienced as a historical transformation of a collectivity's [community's?] livelihoods and modes of existence, a lessening of political control, and a devaluation of its cultural achievements and perceptions of them."[8] His anatomy of globalization depicts it as a triangulated structure comprising first, the global division of labor and power; second, new regionalism; and third, resistance. What follows is a simplified presentation of the relevant points in his rather complex analysis, which is then used as a springboard for broader discussion.

What Mittelman refers to as the global division of labor and power is essentially a restructuring of the familiar core, semi-periphery, and periphery thesis by combining vertically integrated regional divisions of labor with horizontally diversified networks across neighboring countries. This construct significantly highlights the incompleteness and contradictory nature of globalization: how it intensifies as well as undermines interactions among nation-states; how it frequently acts as both a homogenizing force and an agent of diversity; how it incorporates hegemonic power and resistance in a cause-and-effect dynamic.[9]

Using Mozambique as a case study, Mittelman demonstrates the strong links between globalization and marginalization. He reasons that for poorer countries severe economic underdevelopment engenders a donor-driven response to globalization by which they are "integrated into the world political economy on someone else's terms."[10] And since they are forced to yield to the demands of more powerful states and international institutions they are es-

---

Asia. See Teresa Malcolm, "Meeting Deplores Globalization," *National Catholic Reporter* 34, no. 24 (April 1998), p. 9.

7. Mittelman, *Globalization Syndrome*, p. 4.

8. Mittelman, *Globalization Syndrome*, p. 225.

9. Mittelman, *Globalization Syndrome*, p. 56. He notes that "hegemony is not a stable condition; it is always being created and undermined," p. 128.

10. Mittelman, *Globalization Syndrome*, p. 99.

sentially excluded from "playing a central role in the growth mechanisms of the world economy and achieving meaningful participation in decision making (to the extent that political control is being exercised at all)." Consequently, under globalization, "entire zones of the global political economy, except for their dominant strata, and pockets in the developed world are left out."[11] Most significantly, sub-Saharan Africa's estimated 800 million people are confronted with the paradox of inhabiting the most marginalized region in the global system yet having economies that are the most dependent on the global economy for their growth.[12]

The data on the marginalizing effect of globalization are as overwhelming as the analysis is varied. Using a "core-periphery" analysis, Ankie Hoogvelt advances the thought-provoking argument that under the impact of globalization, the relationship between the developed nations (the "core") and Third World countries has declined (since the colonial era) from one of structural exploitation to one of structural irrelevance.[13] Even more recently, Hernando de Soto has taken aim at the "culture" thesis, which stipulates culture as a key element in accounting for lack of economic progress,[14] and posited that what keeps huge masses in Asia, Africa, the Middle East, and Latin America mired in poverty is not (culturally conditioned) lack of enterprise or ingenuity but an inability to convert poorly documented assets into capital.[15]

Undeniably, economic globalization creates winners and losers, or at best divides the world into rabbits and snails. "Participation in global economic policymaking," lamented the Human Development Report 2000, "is embedded in a world of grossly unequal economic power." Intensified global competition has not only deepened economic inequality within countries (concentrating capital rewards in a few hands) but also continues to widen the

11. Mittelman, *Globalization Syndrome,* p. 241.

12. Mittelman, *Globalization Syndrome,* p. 63. For a similar point, see Kidane Mengisteab, *Globalization and Autocentricity in Africa's Development in the 21st Century* (Lawrenceville, NJ: Africa World Press, Inc., 1996), p. 17; also J. S. Saul and C. Leys, "Sub-Saharan Africa in Global Capitalism," *Monthly Review* 51, no. 3 (July/Aug. 1999): 13-30. Home to over 10 percent of the world's population, sub-Saharan Africa has just 3 percent of its trade and only 1 percent of its GDP.

13. A. Hoogvelt, *Globalization and the Postcolonial World: The New Political Economy of Development* (Baltimore: Johns Hopkins University Press, 1997), ch. 4.

14. See, among others, David S. Landes, *The Wealth and Poverty of Nations: Why Some Are So Rich and Some So Poor* (New York: W. W. Norton & Company, 1999); Richard Lynn and Tatu Vanhanen, *IQ and the Wealth of Nations* (Westport, CT, and London: Praeger, 2002).

15. Hernando de Soto, *The Mystery of Capital: Why Capitalism Triumphs in the West and Fails Everywhere Else* (New York: Basic Books, 2000).

gap between rich and poor countries. Much quoted statistical representation of this reality include the following: the rich countries (comprising 15 percent of the world population) account for about 60 percent of the world GDP;[16] in today's market-driven economy, 20 percent of the world's people receive 83 percent of the world's income;[17] the combined wealth of the world's 200 richest people reached $1 trillion in 1999 while the combined incomes of the 582 million people living in the forty-three least developed countries is $146 billion.[18]

The second dimension of globalization in Mittelman's analysis is a new regionalism, by which he means "concentrations of political and economic power competing in the global economy, with multiple interregional and intraregional flows."[19] What makes this type of regionalism "new" is that unlike the pattern of the Cold War era, it is spontaneous (not driven by superpowers) and fashioned in a multi-polar context. Also, while states often emerge as the main actors, civil society — voluntary associations distinct from the economy — outside the direct control of the state also provide impetus from below. Configurations vary from the highly institutionalized European Union model to the more amorphous Southern African Development Community (SADC) or the newly emergent New Partnership for Africa's Development (NEPAD). For Mittelman regionalism exposes one of globalization's more evident paradoxes, for while it functions as a hegemonic project for [countries like] the United States, it may also provide space for a variety of counter-hegemonic projects. Regionalism is thus not only a component and reflection of globalization, but also acts as a modifying response to it.[20]

The third dimension in Mittelman's framework is resistance to globalization. The activities of anti-globalization protesters periodically dominate the news, especially as these relate to major summits or to issues of the environment. But such public organized protests on a world stage can obscure what is sometimes called "soft protest" — latent, often culturally conditioned, and perhaps more sustained, forms of resistance mounted by those "whose modes of existence are threatened by globalization." Depending on the context, Mittelman argues, everyday activities, such as what one wears, buys, or consumes, may constitute "undeclared forms of resistance conducted individu-

16. Bruce Scott, "The Great Divide in the Global Village," *Foreign Affairs* 80, no. 1 (Jan./Feb. 2001): 160-77, esp. p. 163.

17. Ronald J. Sider, *Rich Christians in an Age of Hunger: Moving from Affluence to Generosity* (Nashville: Word Publishing, 1997), p. 142.

18. *Human Development Report 2000*, p. 82.

19. Mittelman, *Globalization Syndrome*, p. 112.

20. Mittelman, *Globalization Syndrome*, p. 145.

ally and collectively in submerged networks."[21] In many developed countries "supermarket" or "consumer activism" has increased in popularity and increasingly represents a potent form of political expression — albeit one limited to the middle class or relatively well-off.[22] Some have also argued that globalization naturally stipulates or necessitates the formation of "transnational civil society" groups (including religious associations) which address issues that transcend the interests of any one nation-state.[23]

The above summary hardly begins to do justice to Mittelman's extensive and sophisticated analysis. Often poorly articulated in the relevant discourse, globalization's ambiguities and paradoxes — how it incorporates both movement and counter-movement, forces from above as well as from below, hegemony and resistance — are thoroughly explored in his treatment. In this dynamic, I would argue, "center" and "margin" are potentially transformed into fluid, relative, even overlapping, constructs. Understanding these elements of multi-directionality and indeterminacy yields tremendous insights into the many intricate ways in which non-Western forces can become powerful agents of change within the globalization process. There are few spheres of existence in which this is more powerfully demonstrated than within contemporary global Christianity, as non-Western forms and movements increasingly inform and define its shape and significance . . . and perhaps none more so than African Christianity.

2. African Christianity and the New Global Order

Christianity is the most missionary and expansionist of world religions; and by the end of the last century profound and complex shifts on a global level had rendered the centuries-old association of Christianity with Western societies absolutely redundant. Quite simply, more people are joining the church (or renewing their commitment to Christianity) in Latin America, Africa, and the Pacific than anywhere else, as powerful charismatic movements and indigenous forms of Christianity thrive in the face of acute socio-economic crises. In fact, so radically have the contours of global Christianity shifted in the last ten decades that the standard representation of Christianity as a West-

21. Mittelman, *Globalization Syndrome,* p. 176.

22. See Noreena Hertz, *The Silent Takeover: Global Capitalism and the Death of Democracy* (New York: The Free Press, 2001), pp. 109-31, quotation at p. 151.

23. Cf. Ann M. Florini, ed., *The Third Force: The Rise of Transnational Civil Society* (Washington, DC: Carnegie Endowment for International Peace, 2000). Cf. J. A. Siewert and E. G. Valdez, eds., *Mission Handbook* (Monrovia, CA: MARC Publications, 1997), p. 34.

ern religion has all but lost credence — providing grounds for the assertion that being church in the third millennium will be largely defined and influenced by developments within Third World Christianity. This shift is most strikingly demonstrated by sub-Saharan Africa, an area arguably "experiencing the fastest church growth of any region" in the world.[24]

The statistical evidence used to buttress these claims is now all too familiar, and increasingly appears in the most unexpected places. In early 2000, an article in *Time* magazine's international edition noted that "adherents to the world's largest religion are increasing at 3.5% a year in Africa, compared with 2.55 in Latin America and Asia, and less than 1% in Europe and North America."[25] A year later, an article in *Newsweek* declared that in "the world's second largest continent, Christianity is spreading faster than at any other time or place in the last 2,000 years."[26] Similarly, a February 2002 article in the *Atlantic Monthly*, titled "Oh, Gods!," proclaimed the noteworthiness of African Christianity as a significant component of the recent dramatic shift in global Christianity's center of gravity.[27] A more conventional source documents that African Christians currently represent some 8.9 percent of the world's population (up from 0.6 percent in 1900) and are increasing at a rate of 23,000 new Christians a day (or 8.5 million a year).[28] In sharp contrast, the church in Europe and North America loses an estimated 6,000 church members a day.[29]

3. Structures of Dependency

These indicators deserve attention, but less well noticed is the fact that the much-celebrated shifts in global Christianity have had little impact on the privileged position of the Western tradition within the theological curriculum. In the West, with few exceptions, courses in which the non-Western

24. Siewert and Valdez, eds., *Mission Handbook*, p. 34.

25. Simon Robinson, "The Lord's Business," *Time* (Europe) 155 (7 Feb. 2000); see online reference, www.time.com/time/europe/magazine/2000/27/christian.

26. Kenneth L. Woodward, "The Changing Face of the Church: How the Explosion of Christianity in Developing Nations Is Transforming the World's Largest Religion," *Newsweek* (16 April 2001), pp. 46-52, quotation at p. 48.

27. Toby Lester, "Oh, Gods!," *Atlantic Monthly* (Feb. 2002): 37-45, esp. pp. 37, 44. Lester noted that African Christianity had grown from less than 10 million in 1900 to an excess of 360 million by 2000.

28. D. B. Barrett, G. T. Kurian, and T. M. Johnson, eds., *World Christian Encyclopedia: A Comprehensive Survey of Churches and Religions in the Modern World*, 2nd ed. (New York: Oxford University Press, 2001), vol. 1, p. 5.

29. Barrett, Kurian, and Johnson, eds., *World Christian Encyclopedia*, vol. 1, p. 5.

Christian experience receive significant attention are usually surplus to requirements and taught as the special interest of a faculty member. Even then exotic appeal often has to take a backseat to cash value, since economic (or market) considerations dictate syllabus structure in many Western theological institutions.

Andrew Walls, who has consistently drawn attention to the historical significance of African Christianity for three decades, has argued that "the global transformation of Christianity requires nothing less than the complete rethinking of the church history syllabus."[30] Elsewhere he insists that "anyone who wishes to undertake serious study of Christianity these days needs to know something of Africa."[31] But possibly his most provocative observation is that, given recent global shifts, "African Christianity must be seen as a major component of contemporary representative Christianity, the standard Christianity of the present age, a demonstration model of its character. That is, we may need to look at Africa today, in order to understand Christianity itself."[32]

Walls's arguments stand out because, unlike other commentators, his analysis takes in the full history of African Christianity and does not focus exclusively on the over-analyzed African Initiated Churches. His has not been an isolated voice, however. In his ground-breaking 1968 study, *Schism and Renewal in Africa,* David Barrett declared that "African independency represents something quite new and unprecedented in the entire history of the expansion of Christianity." Never before, he averred, have "strong and complex traditional societies, mass conversions of whole peoples from among those societies, the destructive approach by missions, and widespread circulation of vernacular scriptures" combined together on the extent and scale found in contemporary Africa.[33]

Alluding to the same phenomena, Harold Turner asserted in the early 1970s that "Western studies of Christianity remain distorted in so far as they

30. Andrew F. Walls, *The Missionary Movement in Christian History: Studies in the Transmission of the Faith* (New York: Orbis Books, 1996), p. 145.

31. Andrew F. Walls, "Eusebius Tries Again: Reconceiving the Study of Christian History," *International Bulletin of Missionary Research (IBMR)* 24, no. 3 (July 2000): 105-11, quotation at p. 106. Walls reasoned at the same time that "the problem is not so much that [the traditional Western church history syllabus] does not contain African or Asian church history, but that it provides no framework in which either can be considered as a part of the whole Christian story," p. 108.

32. Andrew F. Walls, "African Christianity in the History of Religions," *Studies in World Christianity* 2 (1996): 183-203, quotation at p. 186.

33. For the full argument and discussion, see David Barrett, *Schism and Renewal in Africa: An Analysis of Six Thousand Contemporary Religious Movements* (Nairobi: Oxford University Press, 1968), pp. 190-93.

take little account of Christian forms in non-Western cultures and of local and contemporary forms of all cultures."[34] He proceeded to explain that in the non-Western areas of the Christian world the Christian historian "can often find living forms that come very close to a recapitulation of parts of the biblical and Christian centuries," and "especially in the multitudinous African phenomena he will find many parallels to the earlier stages in the history of the people of God."[35] Recently also, Dana Robert has affirmed that "the days are gone when the history of Christianity could be taught as the development of Western doctrine and institutions" and that "the challenge for historians lies in seeing beyond an extension of Western categories and into the hearts, minds, and contexts of Christ's living peoples in Asia, Africa, and Latin America."[36]

The scholarly consensus could hardly be more significant; yet it would appear that these are voices crying in the wilderness. For the most part, studies of the church and much theological reflection within theological institutions (in both the North and the South) are dominated by the body of knowledge associated with the Western phase of Christian expansion. The uncritical assumption being that the Western Christian experience remains dominant and that its reflections and preoccupations set the agenda for the rest of the world.

Kwame Bediako responds that "it is perhaps too much to expect that the significance of modern African Christianity should readily find general acceptance, given the history of the interpretation of Africa in Western scholarship and the standpoint of Western missionary expectations."[37] Maybe so. It could also be argued that Africa's emergence as a major center of world Christianity is hostage to its marginalization in the new global order — academic marginalization being a corollary of economic insignificance. The mushrooming of Korean Studies programs in Western theological institutions underscores the validity of this point.

Already by the mid-1970s dependency theories were being adapted to explain the continuing institutional and theoretical dependence of Third World academics upon their counterparts in the First World. Priscilla Weeks has

34. Harold Turner, "The Contribution of Studies on Religion in Africa to Western Religious Studies," in M. E. Glasswell and E. W. Fasholé-Luke, eds., *New Testament Christianity for Africa and the World* (London: SPCK, 1974), pp. 169-78, quotation at p. 170.

35. Turner, "Contribution of Studies on Religion in Africa," p. 172.

36. Dana Robert, "Shifting Southward: Global Christianity Since 1945," *IBMR* 24, no. 2 (April 2000): 50-58, esp. pp. 56-57.

37. Kwame Bediako, "Africa and Christianity on the Threshold of the Third Millennium: The Religious Dimension," *African Affairs* 99 (2000): 303-23, quotation at p. 306.

highlighted specific conditions that reinforce what she terms "structures of academic dependency." Included among these are "the disproportionate amount of research and development controlled by the 'core' [i.e., Western] institutions"; the control by the Western academy of scholarly journals and organizations through which the bulk of information is disseminated; the fact that "prestige accrues to those who are members of international organisations and publish in [First World] journals"; and "the political and ideological 'contamination' of social theory and its consequent political use."[38]

This state of affairs takes on added significance if one accepts that globalization engenders new forms of hegemonic relationships that build on the old structures of dominance. The American sociologist Peter Berger provides a helpful perspective when he identifies "the Faculty Club International" as one of the four faces of global culture.[39] This community, he argues, lends itself quite well to neo-Marxist dependency theory because it involves "overwhelming 'dependency'" with an indigenous "comprador class" (on the margins) carrying out the agendas devised in the cultural centers of the "metropolis."[40] Given this scenario, the very possibility of imagining new (or alternative) "centers" is thus undermined, limiting the possibility of the sort of re-conceptualization that Andrew Walls calls for. To acknowledge this is not to deny the value and enduring relevance of the Western intellectual discourse for academic development, but rather to suggest that the dynamics of contemporary globalization help to obscure distortions in the study of Christianity by perpetuating the marginalization of the center.

In the case of African Christianity the structures of dependency apply not only to its place in the Christian history curriculum but also to its relationship with other global forms of Christianity that are associated with these same "cultural centers." In particular, troublesome questions have been raised about whether African Christianity — in particular its neo-pentecostal dimensions — is a genuine African construct (a product of the creativity and

---

38. Priscilla Weeks, "Post-Colonial Challenges to Grand Theory," *Human Organization* 49, no. 3 (1990): 236-44, esp. pp. 237ff. She notes that in 1981 an estimated 90 percent of worldwide research funds were spent on research projects controlled by First World institutions. She points out, for example, that what often passed for "neutral" social science was often a Western one.

39. Peter Berger, "Four Faces of Globalization," in P. O'Meara et al., eds., *Globalization and the Challenges of a New Century: A Reader* (Indianapolis: Indiana University Press, 2000), pp. 419-27. He describes this as a community that represents the internationalization of the values, ideologies, and concerns of the Western intelligentsia as well as the conflicts in which this intelligentsia has been engaged in home territories.

40. Berger, "Four Faces of Globalization," p. 423.

genius of Africans) or essentially the purveyor of a product made in America and exported around the world in the form of a "new Christian fundamentalism." The mechanisms intrinsic to the globalization process lie at the heart of this issue; and the two opposing views might conveniently be termed externalist and internalist.

4. The Externalist View

Paul Gifford, perhaps the most outspoken proponent of this perspective, insists that "externality has always been a factor in African Christianity" and that, as Africa experiences acute marginalization within the new global order, its burgeoning Christianity has become a vital means of linking Africans to global networks.[41] He explains that Africa's massive economic and social collapse has created a state of dependency that makes Africans "vulnerable to resourceful outside interests that radiate success, professionalism, and enthusiasm."[42] Hordes of missionaries, he writes, mostly "sent from independent, charismatic churches in North America," have flooded the continent where in addition to establishing "countless ministries, fellowships, and churches of their own kind," they have "profoundly influenced existing churches." He identifies this external influence with a new global fundamentalism that is spreading across the globe via powerful and sophisticated networks.[43] This American-derived and -driven movement has become so significant and pervasive on the African subcontinent that "it may be exerting an influence every bit as great as colonial Christianity of the last century."[44]

Gifford admits that the term "fundamentalism" typically applied to the American phenomenon has limited applicability to Africa's new breed of

41. Paul Gifford, *African Christianity: Its Public Role* (Bloomington: Indiana University Press, 1998), pp. 318, 320.

42. S. Brouwer, P. Gifford, and S. D. Rose, *Exporting the American Gospel: Global Christian Fundamentalism* (New York: Routledge, 1996), p. 151. For the full discussion on Africa, see ch. 8, which contains the shell of arguments that are presented in Gifford's later book, *African Christianity*.

43. The common attributes associated with this new global phenomenon include a personal "born again" experience that forms the basis for global evangelism; a literal understanding of the biblical text; strict moral standards in everyday life underpinned by the belief that "personal belief and piety are necessary for salvation," a view of the world that includes expectations about the miraculous and "God-centred interpretations of history" linked to millennialist and dispensationalist beliefs; cf. Brouwer et al., *Exporting the American Gospel*, p. 4.

44. Brouwer et al., *Exporting the American Gospel*, p. 178.

churches: in part because "in Africa the appeal is to a primal 'imagination' without an attendant repudiation of Enlightenment rationality."[45] He also concedes that such external links "are quite compatible with a considerable creativity on the part of African Christians," as in the stress on deliverance.[46] He is insistent, however, that "this creativity should not be so emphasized that it glosses over the West's cultural significance."[47] Even if the faith gospel so prevalent in Africa can be rationalized within an African religious worldview notoriously preoccupied with material benefits, it was not, insists Gifford, devised in Africa — not least because the prosperity motif that forms its centerpiece does not reflect the common experiences of most African Christians.[48] Ultimately, "the format of Africa's crusades and services, the music, the use of the Bible and even the selection of the texts continually suggest particular origins and betray particular roots."[49] He asserts: "Africa is not reacting to globalization by revitalizing African traditional religion. . . . Africa is responding to globalization by opting into exotic religions . . . [and] much of Africa's mushrooming Christianity is closely linked with a particular religious expression in the United States."[50]

5. The Internalist View

Externality arguments, such as those espoused by Gifford, have been met with robust criticism from other scholars who share Gifford's basic assumption that understanding the role of Christianity in Africa is crucial for any serious study of Africa. The Ghanaian theologian, Kwame Bediako, takes issue with Gifford's suggestion that "theology" or reflective thought (so central within Western Christianity) plays an insignificant role in African Christianity, making it a consumer of external forms. Arguing that this observation is essentially a corollary of Gifford's assertion that Christianity is a Western cultural product, he condemns it as reflecting "the Eurocentrism of the past" which prevents the recognition that "a new, possibly irreversible, trend has occurred, providing a new outlook on the relative positions of Christians from the West and Africa, and indicating, to an increasing degree, a new self-

---

45. Gifford, *African Christianity*, pp. 333ff.
46. Gifford, *African Christianity*, p. 339. Though even this stress is found within American Pentecostalism.
47. Gifford, *African Christianity*, pp. 321ff.
48. Gifford, *African Christianity*, p. 337.
49. Gifford, *African Christianity*, p. 322.
50. Gifford, *African Christianity*, p. 321.

reflection on the part of African Christianity."[51] Pointing to the growing importance of the African element in the worldwide Anglican Communion, Bediako insists that "the significance of the African 'Christian factor' in world Christianity . . . could well be a reverse process to the prevailing Western-driven globalization."[52]

The Nigerian church historian Ogbu Kalu has also taken exception to Gifford's thesis. In his review of Gifford's *African Christianity* (1998), he comments that Gifford's "method fails to produce an accurate image of a lived faith and the *over-emphasis on extraversion* is jarring" (italics mine).[53] Elsewhere, he defends the peculiarity and independence of African pentecostalism, stipulating that while there is "foreign influence in the proliferation of Pentecostalism in Africa" such foreign contacts served a limited material purpose; moreover that South-South relationships were equally significant in the ministerial formation of African pastors.[54] He is adamant that African pentecostalism "has a certain uniqueness which could best be understood from its *fit in* [an] *African primal worldview*. It is a strand in the element of continuity between African traditional religion and Christianity. Its problematics and idiom are sourced from the interior of African spirituality and the resolutions are a reconstruction of that source from Christian and biblical perspectives. This gives the end product its peculiarity" (italics his).[55]

In a thorough review of Gifford's 1998 work, David Maxwell commends his original research but attributes his conclusions to "an inadequate methodology and an inattentiveness to the sheer complexity of the culture and the history of African religion."[56] Maxwell points out that Gifford's interpretation is heavily skewed towards "the faith of the clerical elite" among whom the "external" influence is most manifest, and fails to move beyond the megachurches to the townships and rural locations where "the faith gospel has a different meaning."[57] He censures "Gifford's tendency towards 'totalizing explanations' of contemporary African Christianity" that ignore its peculiarities and internal impulses, and he counsels that "the challenge is

---

51. Bediako, "Africa and Christianity on the Threshold," p. 310.

52. Bediako, "Africa and Christianity on the Threshold," p. 314.

53. Ogbu U. Kalu, "Review of *African Christianity: Its Public Role*," *IBMR* 24, no. 1 (Jan. 2000): 36.

54. Cf. Ogbu U. Kalu, *Power, Poverty and Prayer: The Challenges of Poverty and Pluralism in African Christianity, 1960-1996* (New York: Peter Lang, 2000), p. 113.

55. Kalu, *Power, Poverty and Prayer*, p. 104.

56. David Maxwell, "In Defence of African Creativity," *Journal of Religion in Africa (JRA)* 30, no. 4 (2000): 468-81, quotation at p. 474.

57. Maxwell, "In Defence of African Creativity," pp. 474-75.

surely not to label things African or Western but to trace the processes by which ideas and objects move from imitations to appropriations."[58] Most importantly, he makes the point (on which I expand below) that the West's cultural project looks far less hegemonic when the westward transatlantic flows of African movements are taken into consideration.[59]

6. The Future Through the Rear-View Mirror

Gifford's analysis strongly coheres with cultural homogenization arguments in the broader globalization discourse that impute a one-directional American (at least Western) dominated process underpinned by economic hegemony. This much is given away by his claim that "whatever else it is, Christianity is a cultural product, honed in the West over centuries."[60] As John Tomlinson points out, however, and Gifford's own detractors imply, the view that cultural forms or products can transfer in a unilinear way — so that a particular model invented and prepackaged in Los Angeles is exported and unwrapped in innocent minds — is quite unsound.[61] And while Gifford's analysis provides many crucial insights about African Christianity, he insinuates too strong a correlation between economic collapse in African societies, the flooding by American missionaries, and the flowering of African pentecostalism.

Gifford's analysis suffers from a lack of attentiveness to historical details. From a historical point-of-view the comparison he draws between an American-devised global fundamentalism and colonial Christianity is instructive for reasons that undermine his core arguments. Throughout its history African Christianity has continually displayed a remarkable capacity to adapt and readjust to shifting socio-political contexts, constantly reshaping its religious maps to achieve congruence between physical realities and spiritual need within situations of powerlessness. First and foremost, the cultural imperialism associated with the colonial Christianity yielded quite unexpected results. True, under colonialism (certainly by the turn of the twentieth century) African microcosms suffered massive collapse, foreign missionaries grew thicker on the ground than ever before, and the vastly superior technological resources of the invader were painfully manifest. Yet the same period also witnessed the growth of movements of protest and resistance, like

58. Maxwell, "In Defence of African Creativity," p. 478.
59. Maxwell, "In Defence of African Creativity," p. 476.
60. Gifford, *African Christianity*, p. 322.
61. Cf. John Tomlinson, *Globalization and Culture* (Chicago: University of Chicago Press, 1999), p. 84.

Ethiopianism, that focused on independence and identity, and in many ways provided the seed plot for the African-initiated movements that radically transformed the African Christian landscape within half a century.

African responses to externality, in other words, have tended to be profoundly shaped by African instincts and self-consciousness. If the pentecostal movement has flourished so remarkably on this continent it is arguably because of its "capacity to absorb pre-Christian and extra-Christian practices into an explicitly Christian vehicle."[62] In other words, pentecostalism has generated a global culture precisely because it "has been the quintessential indigenous religion, adapting easily to a variety of [local] cultures."[63] It is also worth pointing out that American domination of media and marketing networks can obscure the origin of religious experiences — as in the case of the "Toronto Blessing," which David Lyon traces to the separate ministries of an Argentine and a South African minister.[64]

Undeniably, American missionaries, media resources, sponsored evangelistic campaigns, funding, and Bible schools are having a massive impact on the African Christian landscape, often in ways that are only made possible by profound economic decline. Mission schools burgeoned in earlier decades for not-dissimilar reasons: reflecting as much a desire for material and social progress as openness to new religious ideas that provide alternative keys to meaning in a globalized context. Then too, Christianity benefited not only from its association with modernization and technological advancement but also from a global image that contrasted sharply with the localized framework of African religions. To fully understand this process, however, requires greater, not less, attention to local factors. Quite simply, the desire for miracles and instant transformation are greatly amplified in contexts of social upheaval.

In Africa's overpopulated cities — with all the attendant problems of joblessness, social insecurity, and bone-racking poverty — a well-funded crusade preserves the association between material prosperity and new forms of Christianity. Often, any miracle would do, which helps to account for the pro-

---

62. Harvey Cox, *Fire from Heaven: The Rise of Pentecostal Spirituality and the Reshaping of Religion in the Twenty-First Century* (Boston: Perseus Books, 1995), p. 255.

63. Byron D. Klaus, "Pentecostalism as a Global Culture: An Introductory Overview," in M. W. Dempster et al., eds., *The Globalization of Pentecostalism: A Religion Made to Travel* (Irvine, CA: Regnum Books International, 1999), pp. 127-30, quotation at p. 127. This otherwise excellent volume lacks a chapter on Africa.

64. David Lyon, "Wheels Within Wheels: Glocalization and Contemporary Religion," in M. Hutchinson and O. Kalu, eds., *A Global Faith: Essays on Evangelicalism and Globalization* (Sydney: Centre for the Study of Australian Christianity, 1998), pp. 47-68, esp. p. 47.

liferation of "deliverance" ministries and "new breed" churches in many parts of Africa (including war-torn Monrovia) as well as the irrationality of giant tabernacles being erected at huge cost while those they hope to reach languish in abject poverty. Christian ministries boom because they are big business; and even when the promises of prosperity fail, the disappointed often simply move on to another ministry with even more exaggerated claims. There are few other voices of hope.

The long-term impact on African Christianity of what Ruth Marshall-Fratani has aptly described as "morally controlled materialism" is yet to be seen.[65] Ultimately, however, whether exalting their religious heritage in an effort to wrest the gospel from the possessive clutches of a dominant culture or demonizing traditional religion in a bid to appropriate modernizing spiritual principles, Africa's Christians have always taken the engagement with traditional culture very seriously indeed. Pentecostalism thrives because it taps into an innate African spirituality; and its phenomenal success on the African continent raises the question whether Africa needs American ministries as much as American initiatives need Africa.

7. African Christianity and Missions

Arguments that favor American (or Western) dominance in the mosaic of processes that constitute globalization are prone to overlook the inherent paradoxes of a phenomenon that allows for counter-movements: a convergence of globalization from above as well as from below. This applies as much to Christianity as to other global movements. The shift in global Christianity's center of gravity has important missiological implications. For the first time in over a millennium the global church displays the most explosive growth and increasing missionary vitality precisely in those areas that are marginalized and impoverished.[66] While this means that the new heartlands of Christianity lack the kind of resources associated with the Western missionary movement, it does indicate the possibility of a counter-flow. Clearly also, the new face of global Christianity is one of relative poverty and powerlessness. It is the faith of the marginalized, of a majority geographically centered in areas of the new global economic and political context that may be

65. Ruth Marshall-Fratani, "Mediating the Global and Local in Nigerian Pentecostalism," *JRA* 28, no. 3 (1998): 278-315, quotation at p. 282.

66. An exception to this is South Korea which, as well as experiencing rising prosperity (until the late 1990s) and decreasing population growth, is currently touted the greatest missionary-sending nation.

considered insignificant, or even structurally irrelevant. This makes for a very complex relationship between global Christianity and more dominant forms of globalization.

The fact that pentecostals are preponderant outside North America[67] and that there are, for instance, seven times as many Anglicans in Nigeria[68] as there are Episcopalians in the entire United States does beg the question about American leadership. Generally speaking, however, the tacit assumption that global mission initiative is a Western privilege (by virtue of wealth, education, and expertise) remains strong, particularly in North America. Andrew Kirk comments on the "incipient paternalism, not to say racism [of the Church in the West], towards other Churches, often manifest in the surprise expressed at the vitality, spiritual maturity and intellectual strength of the Church elsewhere."[69] For many Christians in the North the South is still "the" mission field. This understanding, which is informed by outmoded, one-directional, geographical, us-them categories, continues to find ample expression in short-term missions.

The dominance of the United States in many other global aspects means, however, that many American Christians, if they are aware of it at all, struggle with the notion that the West is now a vast mission field that must reckon with the missionary outpouring from the non-Western world. They struggle to accept that far from being mere products or objects of missionary labor, non-Western churches are self-acting agents of change and a major force for the worldwide propagation of the gospel. In a sharp and candid critique of modern missionary structures, Engel and Dyrness observe that "the door is slowly but steadily swinging shut on North Americans who are reluctant to recognize that the Two-Thirds World and its churches now lie at the very centre of world missions influence and initiative. The need now is to come alongside in a spirit of *partnership and submission,* participating where we can in an enabling and facilitating manner to help increase the impact of all that God is doing in this era" (italics mine).[70]

As Christians from the Third (or Fourth World) become the largest segment of the Protestant missionary force, it is time to reflect on what this non-

67. Cf. Everett A. Wilson, "They Crossed the Red Sea, Didn't They? Critical History and Pentecostal Beginnings," in Dempster et al., eds., *The Globalization of Pentecostalism,* p. 109.

68. Woodward, "Changing Face," p. 48.

69. Andrew Kirk, *What Is Mission? Theological Explorations* (Minneapolis: Fortress Press, 1999), p. 194.

70. J. F. Engel and W. A. Dyrness, *Changing the Mind of Missions: Where Have We Gone Wrong?* (Downers Grove, IL: InterVarsity Press, 2000), p. 21.

Western missionary movement looks like and what strategies will help it overcome the formidable obstacles in its way. Crucially, this movement boasts neither the educational, economic, nor technological advantages of the Western missionary movement nor the protection of strong economic and military powers that the latter enjoyed. In acute contrast it comes not from the centers of political power and economic wealth but from the periphery. Its models and strategies must perforce be radically different; more akin to the biblical model in fact.[71] It is arguably more church-based; and some suggest it may be modeled on "the kenotic Christ," on the "Jesus who carried on his mission from a position of powerlessness," or on the Apostle Peter who proclaimed, "Silver and gold have I none; but such as I have I give you" (Acts 3:6).

It is too early to say how this movement will evolve, but one dimension stands out: namely, migration. Christianity is a migratory religion and, throughout the centuries, migration movements have been a functional element in Christian expansion.[72] This fact takes on added significance in the present global context. Migration and extensive people movement are a major factor of globalization. A recent survey puts the number of migrants — defined as people who have lived outside their homeland for one year or more — at 150 million.[73] Most international migration is said to take place within, not between, regions; but economic divergences caused by global restructuring of production have accentuated South to North migration movements.

With more migrants and a faster demographic growth than any other continent, Africa remains a critical source of migrant flows, including South to North movement. From the 1980s the volume of African migrants to Europe has risen dramatically as, convulsed by escalating conflicts and crises, the continent spewed out a steady flow of economic refugees and asylum seekers. The developed nations, to be sure, have erected ever higher barriers to stem this flow, transforming the world less into a global village than a "gated community."[74] The migration movement has become an unstoppable tide. Robert Kaplan, an award-winning American journalist, speculates that "the political and strategic impact of surging populations . . . will be the core foreign-policy challenge from which most others will ultimately emanate."[75]

---

71. Engel and Dyrness, *Changing the Mind*, pp. 40-43, is suggestive on this point.

72. For a similar point, see Samuel Escobar, "The Global Scenario at the Turn of the Century," in W. Taylor, ed., *Global Missiology for the 21st Century: The Iguassu Dialogue* (Grand Rapids: Baker Academic, 2000), pp. 23-46, esp. p. 34.

73. Cf. Special Report, "The Longest Journey: A Survey of Migration," *The Economist*, Nov. 2, 2002, p. 5.

74. Bruce Scott, "Great Divide in the Global Village," pp. 160-77, esp. p. 160.

75. Robert Kaplan, "The Coming Anarchy," in Patrick O'Meara et al., eds., *Globaliza-*

Contemporary international migration is complex and multifarious, but it is clearly anchored in historical processes, in particular Western colonial expansion and is a manifestation of worldwide transformations associated with globalization.[76] Most important, the volume and velocity of population transfers have profound implications for the spread of religious ideas and will conceivably transform the contours of major world religions. The link between migration, missionary expansion, and globalization is indubitable and, within the current global context, spotlights the great significance of African Christianity.[77]

It is not possible to stipulate with any certainty the percentage of African migrants who are Christian. Studies indicate that the earliest migrants tend to be the relatively well educated, skilled, productive, and highly motivated. The emphasis on basic levels of skill and education for legal immigration to many Western nations also fosters this prevalence. Undoubtedly, a good proportion of African Christians fall into this category, not least because Christian agencies have historically played a significant role in Africa's educational development. According to one estimate there are over 3 million African Christians living in Europe.[78] In addition, in the wake of the 1965 Immigration Reform Act ethnic diversity in the United States has also increased markedly, reflecting greater immigration from the southern continents. This has included a growing percentage of Africans;[79] and if the growing number of African immigrant churches is any indication, the ratio of Christians may be fairly high.[80]

In major U.S. cities, immigrant churches are among the most dynamic, as Africans and Latin American migrant Christians act as agents of new spiritual vitality and help initiate effective forms of outreach to multi-ethnic com-

---

tion and the Challenges of a New Century: A Reader (Indianapolis: Indiana University Press, 2000), pp. 34-60, quotation at p. 42.

76. For more on this, see S. Castles and M. J. Miller, *The Age of Migration: International Population Movements in the Modern World* (New York: Guilford Press, 1998) (1st ed., 1993).

77. I develop this thesis further elsewhere. See "Migration and Mission: Some Implications for the Twenty-First-Century Church," *IBMR* 27, no. 4 (Oct. 2003): 144-53.

78. Report of the Council of African Christian Communities in Europe (CACCE) at the 1999 meeting in Belgium, quoted in Roswith Gerloff, "Religion, Culture and Resistance: The Significance of African Christian Communities in Europe," *Exchange* 3, no. 3 (2001): 276-89, esp. p. 277.

79. For a recent study, see John A. Arthur, *Invisible Sojourners: African Immigrant Diaspora in the United States* (Westport, CT: Praeger, 2000).

80. The Nigerian-based Redeemed Christian Church of God (RCCG) alone has 82 parishes in the U.S.

munities.[81] Woodward confirms that "evangelists from Latin America and Africa now hold crusades in cities like London and Berlin."[82] On 1 July 2000 an article in the London *Sunday Times* (provocatively titled "Missionaries arrive to save 'heathen' Britain") proclaimed that "missionaries from South America and Africa are heading to Britain to save our souls in a reversal of traditional roles." In a fascinating scholarly survey, the Dutch scholar Gerrie ter Haar describes the deliberately missionary enterprise of African-initiated churches that are mushrooming throughout Europe.[83] She explains that "every one of these new churches sees itself charged with the task of bringing the Gospel back to Europe from where they once received it."[84]

The long-term significance and impact of these new missionary movements remain to be seen and need to be more thoroughly researched from a global perspective. Much about the impact of globalization still remains poorly analyzed and poorly understood, and this crucially applies to its implications for global Christian witness. The church in the West is liable to fall into the self-deception of the U.S. Commissioner who concluded that "everything that can be invented has been invented." As Gerrie ter Haar reports, "The concept of African missionaries in Europe is still new to many Christians in the West, but will become more and more familiar as African Christian communities spread throughout Western Europe." This movement, she continues, "provides a new outlook on the relative positions of Christians from Europe and Africa, reflecting the changed relations and the beginning of what seems to be an irreversible trend."[85] The complexities of globalization make prognostications inadvisable, but there is much to suggest that "Africa may present us with a picture of the future, not of the past."[86]

81. See Andrew P. Davey, "Globalisation as Challenge and Opportunity in Urban Mission," *IRM* 88, no. 351 (Oct. 1999): 381-89; also, Samuel Escobar, "Global Scenario at the Conclusion of a Century," paper presented at the World Evangelical Fellowship International Missiological Consultation, Iguazu, Brazil, October 1999.

82. Woodward, "Changing Face," p. 49.

83. Gerrie ter Haar, "Strangers in the Promised Land: African Christians in Europe," *Exchange* 24, no. 1 (Feb. 1995): 1-33. Her research findings were subsequently published as a book entitled *Halfway to Paradise: African Christians in Europe* (Cardiff: Cardiff Academic Press, 1998).

84. Ter Haar, "Strangers," p. 30; also her *Halfway to Paradise*, p. 92.

85. Ter Haar, "Strangers," p. 30.

86. Cox, *Fire from Heaven*, p. 258.

PART II

The Globalizing Impulse in Christianity

CHAPTER 5

The First Globalization? The Internationalization of the Protestant Missionary Movement Between the World Wars

DANA L. ROBERT

The global vision intrinsic to Christianity — that of one world, one kingdom of God under Jesus Christ — has been both the motive and purpose behind much missionary fervor. Yet the mission of the church has been conducted within rather than above human history: Protestant missions emerged in the context of the Enlightenment, the industrial revolution, and the subsequent expansion of capitalism and modernization. With its internal logic of universalism, or catholicity,[1] Christian mission of necessity finds itself in dialogue with the secular globalizing tendency of the historical moment whether that be European expansionism, Western capitalism, or the World Wide Web.[2]

The Anglo-American Protestant missionary movement of the 1920s and 1930s functioned within the globalizing discourse of "internationalism," a moral vision of one world that emerged after the horrors of the First World War, and stemmed from the idealism of Woodrow Wilson's Fourteen Points.

1. Robert Schreiter suggests that catholicity is "the theological equivalent of globalization." See Richard Bliese, in K. Muller, T. Sundermeier, S. Bevans, R. Bliese, eds., "Globalization," in *Dictionary of Mission. Theology, History, Perspectives* (Maryknoll, NY: Orbis Books, 1998), p. 176.

2. While mission scholars would not equate Christian missions with globalization itself, there is a theoretical and practical problem of how to relate to secular globalization, how to influence it, and how to avoid being so closely identified with it that when globalization's time has passed, the mission of the church does not get washed away with the ebbing tide of popular support.

An earlier abridged version of this chapter appeared by permission in *International Bulletin of Missionary Research (IBMR)* 26, no. 2 (April 2002): 50-66.

Internationalism launched a massive pacifist movement, brought into being the League of Nations and the Permanent Court of International Justice (World Court), and established the idea of the rights of self-determination for all peoples.[3] Not only did sectors of the missionary movement embrace internationalism but, to a far greater extent than with the current business and technology-oriented definitions of globalization, the missionary movement helped to shape it, participated in it, and both defended and critiqued it at a grassroots level. In their most optimistic phase during the 1920s, mission advocates were accused of confusing internationalism with the kingdom of God. In North American mainline churches, in particular, it became hard to distinguish internationalism from the mission impulse itself.

While internationalism was central to mainline Protestant missions in the 1920s and 1930s, recent scholarship has not used it as an interpretive framework for the missionary issues of the era. It has preferred to interpret the interwar period in light of the Kraemer-Hocking debate, or the tension between evangelistic and social gospel approaches to missions. This chapter is a preliminary effort to explore the relationship between internationalism and indigenization in the mission movement between the world wars, with primary reference to a North American conversation. It aims to demonstrate that internationalism and indigenization were two sides of the same coin. The globalizing vision of one world stood in tension with the cultural particularities that emerged in relationship to the global context itself. Internationalism demonstrated all the complexity that bedevils globalization in the early twenty-first century: a shifting set of both secular and religious definitions, and assumptions of universality both challenged and affirmed by nationalistic or particular ethnic identities. In this study, the mission thought of the 1920s and 1930s is placed in the larger context of internationalism, and the chapter explores briefly the parallels with globalization today.[4]

1. Missions and the Development of Christian Internationalism

The internationalist agenda emerged quickly among young adults, many of them university students, whose generational cohorts died by the millions in

3. For a discussion of the internationalist movement in the United States and its opposition to isolationism, see William Kuehl and Lynne K. Dunn, *Keeping the Covenant: American Internationalists and the League of Nations, 1920-1939* (Kent, OH: Kent State University Press, 1997). On the pacifist aspect of internationalism, see Charles Chatfield, *For Peace and Justice: Pacifism in America, 1914-1941* (Knoxville: University of Tennessee Press, 1971).

4. This chapter is a foray into a larger research project into the relationship between so-called older and younger churches after World War I.

the trenches of Europe from 1914 to 1918. On 8 January 1918, President Woodrow Wilson of the United States put forth the "Fourteen Points" as a basis for ending the war. Among the points was the idea of the self-determination of minority peoples, the end of the Ottoman Empire, the return of European territory under imperial control, and the founding of a League of Nations as a forum for resolving international disputes. In May 1919, the terms of the actual peace treaty became public, revealing that instead of reconciliation among nations, there would be economic punishment of the defeated states so severe that a new basis for continued conflict was created. Then the U.S. Senate refused to ratify the treaty founding the League of Nations. The conditions of the Treaty of Versailles, coupled with the failure of the United States to ratify it, set in motion a widespread internationalist movement among young adults determined to achieve lasting peace based upon Wilson's Fourteen Points.

Before the First World War, international student Christian movements such as the Young Men's Christian Association (YMCA) and the World's Student Christian Federation (WSCF) had already spread throughout the Christian colleges of Europe, Asia, South Africa, and the United States. From 1889 to 1892, Luther Wishard of the World Committee of the YMCA toured Japan, China, India, and parts of Africa to organize student associations. He visited 216 mission stations in twenty countries. Missionaries considered the YMCA a partner in youth work and were its strongest supporters in so-called mission lands. The YMCA was also the sponsor of the Student Volunteer Movement for Foreign Missions, founded in 1888. In 1889, the first YMCA foreign secretaries arrived in Japan and China, the first of nearly 600 Western men who had planted organized youth work in Christian colleges in mission lands by the early 1940s.[5] With its focus on developing indigenous leadership, the YMCA quickly developed a partnership model whereby foreign secretaries worked alongside, and then under, indigenous student leaders. The WSCF, founded in 1895, "piggybacked" on the YMCA and to some extent was an extension of it. Archbishop Nathan Söderblom of Sweden, leader of the ecumenical Faith-and-Order and Life-and-Work movements during the 1920s, reminisced that it was the YMCA, beginning with his attendance at the Northfield Conference for college students in 1890 which was organized by the evangelist Dwight Moody, that gave him his "world-wide vision of ecumenical Christianity."[6]

---

5. Sherwood Eddy, *A Century with Youth. A History of the Y.M.C.A. from 1844 to 1944* (New York: Association Press, 1944), pp. 88-91.

6. Eddy, *Century with Youth*, p. 106.

Given the missionary focus and international connections of the student Christian movements before the First World War, it was a logical, though not uncontested, step for the younger generation to merge the missionary agenda into the internationalism of the post-war period. Already the Christian students had sustained a Christian vision for world unity, and the WSCF maintained its formal unity across the battle lines during the war. As Christian students and church leaders reestablished friendships across national boundaries after the end of hostilities, the internationalist agenda of pacifism and international unity created a new rationale for missionary commitment that seemed progressive and modern. Internationalism provided a new discourse, a new way of talking about missions, for well-educated mainline Protestants.

The transformation of mission organizations into internationalist ones occurred across the board in mainline Protestant colleges and student movements in the United Kingdom and the United States during the 1920s. Although there are numerous examples of this process, a few will have to suffice. In his history of the British Student Christian Movement, Tissington Tatlow, an Anglican student volunteer who was its general secretary, eloquently described the transformation of his own consciousness into internationalism. In 1925, 1,600 people from twenty-nine countries attended the Manchester Quadrennial Conference of the British student movement. In addition to fellowship, worship, and singing, the most memorable speaker who addressed the students was T. Z. Koo, head of student work for the YMCA in China. Speaking on "The New China," Koo described the work of social reconstruction being undertaken under the Nationalist government. Remaining in England for a few weeks after the conference, Koo addressed different gatherings of students. After he witnessed a meeting between Koo and the Archbishops of Canterbury and York, Tissington Tatlow recalled, "He stood, a slender figure in his Chinese dress of blue, with an archbishop at each side of him. . . . And as each archbishop shook hands to say good-bye, each thanked him warmly and simply for what he had done during his visit to help English Christians. I was deeply moved by the scene. Behind the trio there rose for me a vision of men of every kindred and tribe and race in one fellowship worshipping God."[7]

In 1919 the British Student Christian Movement (SCM) issued a "Call to Battle" that stressed the unity among Christian students of all races and nations. It stated: "We are convinced that this unity is the only sure hope of peace and of the true development of nations. . . . There is a desire that is of-

---

7. Tissington Tatlow, *The Story of the Student Christian Movement of Great Britain and Ireland* (London: Student Christian Movement Press, 1933), p. 673.

ten passionate to find some new way of international life, to see new principles applied and a real stand made for a better world."[8] By 1920 the Student
Christian Movement held a meeting to mobilize students in support of the
League of Nations. Tatlow interpreted the move into internationalism as a
logical progression on the part of the student movement. All of their pre-war
meetings had concerned missions, and over 2,300 British students had become missionaries before the war. The post-war decision to focus on international relations, and on building friendships across national and racial lines,
was for Tatlow an outgrowth of the missionary focus. He spent the 1920s networking to establish a student movement committed to peace and inter-racial
unity. A representative from the Indian Student Christian Movement joined
the British staff as a visible sign of unity across colonial boundaries. With the
Dutch student movement providing a neutral meeting ground, Tatlow and
his group met the representatives of the German student movement to seek
reconciliation. Other forces behind the internationalist focus in the 1920s
were the increasing numbers of international students attending British universities after the war, and the needs of stranded and destitute students
throughout Europe.

In the United States, the agenda of internationalism swept through the
YMCA, YWCA, Student Volunteer Movement, and other student mission
groups.[9] While the failure of the United States to ratify the League of Nations
was a disappointment for mission-minded college students, the passage of the
Oriental Exclusion Act in 1924 gave more immediacy to internationalist concerns. Missionaries largely opposed the passage of the law that kept Chinese,
Japanese, and other "Orientals" out of the United States, for why would Asians
become Christians if a so-called Christian country was refusing them admit-
tance? The post-war American mission focus on "world friendship" represented a combination of pacifism, inter-racial reconciliation, and vision of

8. Quoted in Tatlow, *Student Christian Movement,* p. 685.

9. See, for example, John Mott's promotion of a new social order and "Christianizing
international relations" through the work of the World's Student Christian Federation.
John R. Mott, *The World's Student Christian Federation: Origin, Achievements, Forecast*
(London: WSCF, 1920), pp. 76-87. See also Milton T. Stauffer, ed., *Christian Students and
World Problems: Report of the Ninth International Convention of the Student Volunteer
Movement for Foreign Missions* (Indianapolis, 28 Dec. 1923 to 1 Jan. 1924) (New York: Stu-
dent Volunteer Movement for Foreign Missions, 1924). The agenda of internationalism
was apparent especially in the exhibits, pp. 445-50. Michael Parker, *The Kingdom of Char-
acter: The Student Volunteer Movement for Foreign Missions (1886-1926)* (Lanham, MD:
ASM and University Press of America, 1998), pp. 155-63; Nathan D. Showalter, *The End of a
Crusade: The Student Volunteer Movement for Foreign Missions and the Great War*
(Lanham, MD: Scarecrow Press, 1998).

global unity that emerged from mission ideals. The history of the student missionary movement at Mount Holyoke College is a concrete example of the evolution into internationalism. The preeminent training school for Congregationalist missionary women in the mid-1800s, Mount Holyoke developed into the first women's college in the United States. In 1878, students founded the Mount Holyoke Missionary Association. With the founding of the Student Volunteer Movement a decade later, and its co-sponsorship by the YWCA, the Mount Holyoke Missionary Association became the Missionary Literature Committee of the campus YWCA. At the beginning of the twentieth century, the YWCA spearheaded missionary interest on campus, holding mission study classes and missionary meetings. In 1925 the Missionary Department of the YWCA changed its name to the World Fellowship Department. The words applied to similar developments at Carleton College (another stronghold of missionary Congregationalism) held equally true for Mount Holyoke after the First World War: "the spirit of evangelical missions and of a more secular internationalism fused and became almost indistinguishable."[10]

While internationalism blossomed quickly among the younger generation after the war, the middle-aged missionary movement also "hitched its wagon" to the vision of a peaceful, united world. Major church conferences in the mid-1920s shared a focus on internationalism, with the most optimistic Americans merging it into their visions of the kingdom of God.[11] In their dissatisfaction at the decision of the International Missionary Council not to hold an international meeting until 1928, the North American mission societies held their own "Foreign Missions Convention" in Washington, D.C., in 1925. Eighty-five mission organizations, eleven missionary training schools, and 3,419 delegates attended the convention. President Calvin Coolidge opened the meeting with an address urging missionaries to counteract the evils of Western civilization by carrying the best of Christianity to other cultures, and by bringing back to America the best of other cultures. Internationalism suffused the proceedings. Papers on the "present world situation" reviewed the position of missions in different parts of the world. A number of the distinguished missionary speakers addressed aspects of internationalism.

One of the most explicit of the missionary speakers was Charles Brent. He

10. Quoted in Dana L. Robert, *American Women in Mission: A Social History of Their Thought and Practice* (Macon, GA: Mercer University Press, 1997), pp. 273-74.

11. As late as 1944, the missionary statesman and pacifist socialist Sherwood Eddy indicated the ecumenical movement's hope for a "Christian world order" and the "coming of the Kingdom of God on earth." Eddy, *Century with Youth*, p. 109. For a biography of Eddy, see Rick L. Nutt, *The Whole Gospel for the Whole World: Sherwood Eddy and American Protestant Mission* (Macon, GA: Mercer University Press, 1997).

had been the Episcopal bishop of the Philippines for sixteen years before becoming senior chaplain of the American Expeditionary Forces during the
war, and then Bishop of Western New York. Appealing for the conversion of
those in so-called "Christian nations," Brent noted that the shrinking distance
between East and West meant that Christians would only be made in the East,
if Easterners saw Christian behavior in the West. To be truly of service to the
world, and to reach the East, Western civilization needed to become more
meditative and worshipful, "more empowered to use silence."[12] The greatest
opportunity for Western Christians, according to Brent, however, lay with the
League of Nations, and could be established by an international treaty binding on all nations. Both the League of Nations and the proposed Court of International Justice were "Christian in their aim and in their possibilities. . . .
The Christian Church has got to say in no uncertain voice whether it accepts
war as an evil necessity and will support war when it arises, or whether it believes that it is a barbarous atrocity, that there is a substitute for it, and that we
must discover and use that substitute."[13] In a statement of his own "passion,"
made more moving by his ill health, Brent declared, "I see but two things to
live for: one of them is the unity of the church of God; the other is the good
will among the nations that will forever banish war."[14]

A section of the Foreign Missions Convention of 1925 was devoted to the
relationship of the missionary movement to "peace and good will among nations." Speaking on international relations, one speaker indicated that a major problem of the day was in harmonizing nationalism with the Christian
ideal of worldwide unity. Others spoke of the need for prayer and humility,
and for Christian cooperation to counter the divisiveness between peoples. As
John R. Mott, chairman of the International Missionary Council (IMC), said
"Christian missions are indeed the great and the true internationalism. Our
29,000 missionaries are ambassadors, interpreters, and mediators in the most
vital aspects of international and inter-racial relationships."[15] Speaking for
the woman's missionary movement was Evelyn Nicholson, president of the
Woman's Foreign Missionary Society of the Methodist Episcopal Church,

12. Charles H. Brent, "The Situation at Home," in Fennell P. Turner and Frank Knight
Sanders, eds., *The Foreign Missions Convention at Washington 1925* (New York: Foreign
Missions Conference of North America, Fleming H. Revell, 1925), p. 30.

13. Brent, "Situation at Home," p. 33.

14. Brent, "Situation at Home," p. 5.

15. John R. Mott, "New Forces Released by Cooperation," in Turner and Sanders, eds.,
Foreign Missions Convention, p. 209. For a biography of Mott that traces his work in build-
ing the global Christian movement, see C. Howard Hopkins, *John R. Mott, 1865-1955*
(Grand Rapids: Eerdmans, 1979).

member of the IMC, and author of the first book on peace education to be published by the Methodist Church after the war. Stressing the importance of the church for creating world peace, Mrs. Nicholson argued that the teachings of Christ commissioned the church to teach interdependence, peace, and mutual respect. The church "is in itself a League of Nations functioning now, through its representatives, in every land. It is a recognized educational agency, training not only the intellect but the will and spirit."[16] Through its schools, missions were teaching that people had rights. According to Nicholson, the promotion of friendship among people of different races and nationalities was a unique responsibility of mission agencies.

Another important church meeting that took place in 1925 was the Stockholm Conference on Life and Work. While the mission convention in Washington demonstrated agreement among the British and American speakers that internationalism was an essential part of the missionary agenda, the international Stockholm Conference revealed a chasm between the former Allies and the German delegates over the issue. Although the Anglo-Americans and French seemed to agree that the League of Nations should be supported as part of creating a new world order, the German delegation accused them of confusing a temporal program with the kingdom of God. Invoking Luther's "two kingdom" theory, the Germans insisted that their suffering under the terms of the peace treaty made them wary of identifying a human program with the divine will.[17] Dr. Klingemann, superintendent of the Rhine Province, protested: "Now remember that disarmed we live in an armed world. We wait for the promised general disarmament to be able to believe in peace."[18]

The protest of the Germans that the internationalist agenda looked suspiciously like a hijacking of the kingdom of God by a particular political program was the same objection raised by German students to the optimism of Tissington Tatlow. Of what good was an idealistic movement for world peace, when economic disparities loomed between national winners and losers? The German objections raised not only the theological question of confusing internationalism with the kingdom of God, but they implied that the movement for world peace was a political ploy of the victorious Allies. In short, the

---

16. Mrs. Thomas Nicholson, "Educating for Peace and Goodwill," in Turner and Sanders, eds., *Foreign Missions Convention*, p. 177. On Nicholson's role in the missionary movement, see Robert, *American Women in Mission*, pp. 277-87.

17. G. K. A. Bell, *The Stockholm Conference 1925* (London: Oxford University Press, 1926), p. 451.

18. Bell, *Stockholm Conference*, p. 452.

internationalist agenda was being promoted by those nations who held all the power in the post-war world.[19]

Although the Stockholm Conference launched the Life and Work movement (one of the streams leading to the formation of the World Council of Churches) it was not strictly speaking a missionary gathering as was the North American conference. Viewing it with the Washington Conference, and with the Manchester Quadrennial of the British Student Christian Movement in the same year, shows just how widely some form of the internationalist agenda had spread throughout the leadership of Western Protestantism by the mid-1920s. The adoption of Christian internationalism by a large group of missionaries and mission leaders was an important factor in the growing rift with fundamentalist mission leaders who, like some Europeans, distrusted the idea that the internationalist agenda was somehow connected with an emerging kingdom of God. For more conservative missionaries, world unity would be a result of the establishment of God's heavenly kingdom, not a step in its development on earth.[20]

On the part of self-identified liberal Protestants in the 1920s, the emergence of internationalism replaced a traditional, more narrowly evangelistic view of missions: it dealt with Christianizing the relationships between nations, rather than conversion of individuals. While the internationalist liberals of the day usually retained a focus on individual commitment, they broadened the missionary agenda to emphasize Christianizing the social realm.

An extremely interesting example of this process occurred within the Fosdick family. These Baptists from upstate New York played major roles in the development of internationalism within liberal Christianity. Harry Emerson Fosdick was the most famous preacher in America between the wars. He recalled in his autobiography, *The Living of These Days,* that his childhood decision to be baptized was because he wanted to become a missionary: "The wide, wide world was called to our attention mainly as a mission field. It grew vivid to us when missionaries pictured it in all its heathen need. When I graduated from high school in 1895 the Turks had just been massacring the Armenians, and my 'oration' was an appeal for that decimated peo-

19. Such arguments are similar to those of anti-globalization, anti–free trade protesters today, to whom economic globalization looks like the agenda of the rich countries.

20. On the missionary aspects of the Fundamentalist-Modernist controversy, see Bradley J. Longfield, *The Presbyterian Controversy: Fundamentalists, Modernists, and Moderates* (New York: Oxford University Press, 1991); Kevin Xiyi Yao, *The Fundamentalist Movement Among Protestant Missionaries in China, 1920-1937* (Lanham, MD: University Press of America, 2003).

ple."[21] Through his theological training at Colgate Seminary, and his field work in the Bowery in New York City, Fosdick's theological views became modernistic. He became Professor of Practical Theology at Union Theological Seminary, as well as sharpening his homiletical skills as a preacher in many churches. Through his many books on spirituality and preaching, especially *The Manhood of the Master*, Fosdick's ideas had a wide readership among missionaries and indigenous Christian leaders. In 1921 he went to China to hold conferences among missionaries, and experienced firsthand the split opening within the missionary community between fundamentalism and modernism.

In 1922 Fosdick, after his return from China, delivered his controversial sermon "Shall the Fundamentalists Win?" which became a lightning rod for the fundamentalist movement in Presbyterianism. The controversy over that sermon was one of the major events in the fundamentalist-modernist controversy in the 1920s. In response to the uproar, the Baptist and millionaire businessman John D. Rockefeller, Jr., called Fosdick to be pastor of his church. On the upper east side of multi-cultural Manhattan next to the Union Theological Seminary, Rockefeller constructed the nonsectarian Riverside Church, which under Fosdick's leadership embodied the internationalist movement. Fosdick's stated goals for Riverside Church were to help youngsters discover their divine vocations and say "Here I am, send me." "If wherever soldiers of the common good are fighting for a more decent international life and a juster industry, they should feel behind them the support of this church which . . . has kept its conviction clear that a major part of Christianity is the application of the principles of Jesus to the social life, and that no industrial or international question is ever settled until it is settled Christianly, that would be wonderful."[22]

Many missionaries on furlough and international students attended Union Seminary while Fosdick taught there, and the Riverside Church became their "home away from home." In its mission giving, Fosdick noted that typical causes supported by the congregation included a rural project under the Kyodan (Japanese Protestant Church), the education of girls in an Arab refugee camp, Korean refugees, an American Indian college in Oklahoma, the International Christian University in Japan, the Vellore Medical College in India, the School of Social Work in Delhi, the YMCAs in Mozambique and Senegal, a settlement house in Tokyo, work among migrants under the Home

21. Harry Emerson Fosdick, *The Living of These Days: An Autobiography* (New York: Harper and Brothers, 1956), p. 24.

22. Fosdick, *Living of These Days*, p. 194.

Missions Council, an agricultural missionary in China, Union Seminary in Tokyo, the radio ministry of the Philippine Christian Council, the Agricultural Missions Foundation, ecumenical work in Santo Domingo, and various projects in New York City.[23] While he never became a missionary in the narrow sense, Harry Emerson Fosdick's internationalism was an outgrowth of that earlier interest. Describing internationalism as an "idea that has used me," he wrote, "The idea that mankind is inevitably becoming 'one world,' so far as the conquest of distance and the intensifying of economic interdependence can make us one, has had a major influence on my thinking and preaching."[24]

The Fosdick involvement in internationalism becomes even more fascinating when one realizes that Harry's younger brother Raymond was the first Undersecretary of the League of Nations. Having studied under Woodrow Wilson at Princeton for both his bachelor and master's degrees, and then worked in New York City as a reformer rooting out corruption, Raymond Fosdick was selected as the first Undersecretary by President Wilson before the U.S. Senate voted on the League of Nations. Harry Fosdick preached a pacifist sermon in Geneva at the opening ceremony of the League of Nations in 1925. After retiring from the League, Raymond Fosdick became a lawyer, and John D. Rockefeller, Jr., became his first client. Spending more and more time on the various organizations funded by the Rockefeller family, and as senior advisor to John D. Rockefeller, Jr., Raymond eventually became head of the Rockefeller Foundation.[25]

Rockefeller was a liberal Baptist whose faith strongly shaped his philanthropy. The line between missions and internationalism becomes even more blurred when one realizes that John D. Rockefeller erected YMCA buildings around the world, funded the China Medical Board and the Institute for Social and Religious Research, paid for some of John R. Mott's projects, and initiated and bankrolled the *Laymen's Missionary Inquiry* (led by philosopher W. Ernest Hocking and published in 1932 as *Re-thinking Missions*). He also donated the land for the site of the United Nations, and the Interchurch Center on Riverside Drive.[26] Laura Spelman Rockefeller, his pious Baptist mother, had provided the matching funds for the ecumenical American Woman's

23. Fosdick, *Living of These Days*, p. 198.
24. Fosdick, *Living of These Days*, p. 304.
25. See Raymond B. Fosdick's autobiography, *Chronicles of a Generation* (New York: Harper and Brothers, 1958).
26. On John D. Rockefeller, Jr.'s internationalism, relationship to Fosdick, and support for many liberal non-denominational projects, see John Ensor Harr and Peter J. Johnson, *The Rockefeller Century* (New York: Charles Scribner's Sons, 1988), pp. 153-80.

Missionary Movement drive to fund seven union women's colleges in Asia in the 1920s.[27]

The Fosdick commitment to internationalism was embodied in Raymond Fosdick's twin sister, Edith, who spent her life abroad as a teacher in various mission-founded colleges. After graduating from Vassar and becoming a social worker at a settlement house in New York City, she spent the First World War in Italy as a canteen worker under the YMCA. She taught English literature at Kobe College in Japan, Ginling College in China, the American College for Girls in Greece, and the American College for Girls in Istanbul. In a telephone interview with Dr. Elinor Downs, the daughter of Harry Emerson Fosdick, Downs insisted that her aunt Edith never considered herself a missionary.[28] Downs herself worked in Geneva for the World Health Organization, and then became Dean of Public Health at Columbia University. Her sister Dorothy became a foreign policy expert who helped craft the United Nations, the Marshall Plan, and NATO in the 1940s.

The commitments of the Fosdick family show how, during the 1920s and 1930s, the span of Christian internationalism ranged from the ministry-centered focus of Harry, to the politicized Christian civilization model of Raymond, and to the hands-on international service of Edith. The embrace of internationalism by the mission-minded among liberal Protestants after the First World War may have set into motion a secularizing trend that ultimately rejected its missionary origins. Or did it? To what extent did the Protestant missionary movement make a distinctive contribution to internationalism? While the overlap between missions and internationalism was substantial, not all internationalist Christians came to repudiate the term "missionary." It was as missionaries themselves that a network of internationalists had a profound impact on the shape of Christian internationalism.

Christian missions were, from a religious perspective, the generative impulse behind the internationalist movement. The vision of one world, united by peace, economic capitalism, and what is now called "human rights," was essentially a product of the "civilizing" aspect of Protestant missions that became increasingly more secular and more widely shared after the First World War. Wilson's Fourteen Points were a Christian vision, produced by the son, grandson, and son-in-law of Presbyterian ministers, who was the president of a Presbyterian-founded college before going into politics. At some level, conservative suspicions of the conflation of the League of Nations with the king-

---

27. On the ecumenical campaign to fund women's colleges, see Robert, *American Women in Mission*, pp. 269-70.

28. Telephone interview with Dr. Elinor Downs, May 7, 2001, Newton, MA.

dom of God were correct, inasmuch as the supporters of internationalism represented the "mission" of Anglo-Americanism writ large: a movement into the global arena of the same kind of impulse that had inspired the Puritan settlers to prophesy they would be a "city on a hill," radiating light to the rest of the world. Although not all internationalists were missionaries and mission leaders, the literature of the interwar period shows that mission thought had a profound impact on the religious dimensions of internationalism.

2. Missionary Indigenization Within the Internationalist Paradigm

In the remainder of this chapter, the focus is on one aspect of missionary internationalism that was particularly significant in the 1920s and 1930s, namely the movement toward cultural indigenization. A primary missionary contribution to Christian internationalism was the active promotion of indigenization in non-Western Christianity: the vision of the church as a worldwide panoply of different cultures and heritages. Paradoxically, it was those mission leaders who were the most visible internationalists who were at the cutting edge of promoting indigenous cultures within Christian expression. They believed that having a truly global church meant appreciating the individual cultures within it. The self-determination of peoples meant encouraging their individual contributions to the world church, and liberating church life — including its history, art, architecture, literature, and worship — from domination by Western traditions.

Separation of Christ from Western Culture

At the theological center of missionary internationalism was the separation of Christ from Western culture. The horrors of the First World War not only provoked a widespread search for ways to prevent war, but caused a revulsion against the easy association of Christianity with Western culture: it was so-called Christian nations that had fought the most devastating war in human history. The shift in tone in American missionary literature was immediate. For example, before the war, the annual women's study books by the Central Committee on the United Study of Foreign Missions often took a condescending view toward the cultures of the world.[29] Starting with Caroline

---

29. Robert, *American Women in Mission,* pp. 260-85.

Atwater Mason's book on *World Missions and World Peace* in 1916, the study books of the women's series, as well as those produced by the Missionary Education Movement of the United States and Canada, took a positive view toward non-Western cultures and criticized even more loudly the non-Christian aspects of Western culture. The key shift from late nineteenth-century theology to that of the 1920s was the ability to separate Christ from Western culture, and to see him embodied in other cultures.[30]

To illustrate the theological and missiological dynamics of the separation of Christ from culture, a handful of ground-breaking works that appeared around 1925 will be examined. By 1925 the post-war shift in missionary thinking was clearly expressed not only in the conferences already discussed, but in publications by experienced missionaries that had a wide impact on both missionary and popular thinking.[31] Among North Americans, E. Stanley Jones was undoubtedly the most popular and visible figure among those missionaries self-consciously associated with internationalism and its twin, indigenization. He was widely influential in pacifist circles. He was an early and prominent supporter of Indian independence, and he shaped the thinking of the 1920s generation of seminarians and young church leaders in the United States. The author of twenty-eight books, Jones's missiological and spiritual writings influenced both evangelical and liberal missionaries all over the world into the 1960s.[32] Designated in 1938 by *Time* magazine as the

30. The attempt to separate Christianity from Western culture had been a goal of nineteenth-century "three-self" mission theory, but Western cultural assumptions were not widely criticized until after the First World War. For an overview of Western mission thought, see Timothy Yates, *Christian Mission in the Twentieth Century* (New York: Cambridge University Press, 1994).

31. The foremost among these books was E. Stanley Jones, *The Christ of the Indian Road*. My copy was printed in Nov. 1926, and indicated that after its first issuance in Sept. 1925, it had been reprinted monthly. I do not know how many times it was reprinted, but it must have sold hundreds of thousands of copies.

32. For a short biography of Jones, see Richard W. Taylor, "E. Stanley Jones, 1884-1973: Following the Christ of the Indian Road," in G. Anderson, R. Coote, N. Horner, J. Phillips, eds., *Mission Legacies: Biographical Studies of Leaders of the Modern Missionary Movement* (Maryknoll, NY: Orbis Books, 1994), pp. 339-47. Jones's name appears widely in meetings, publications, and causes associated with Christian internationalism. His influence was greater than that of any missionary. His ideas deeply impressed the Methodist Walter Muelder, a seminarian in the 1920s who became the leading social ethicist, ecumenist, and seminary dean of mid-century Methodism. Telephone interview with Muelder, Dec. 2000, Newton, MA. References to Jones are jotted in the papers of South African, American, and British missionaries. On Jones's importance in Protestant pacifist circles, see Patricia Appelbaum, "The Legions of Good Will: The Religious Culture of Protestant Pacifism, 1918-1963" (unpublished Ph.D. diss., Boston University, 2001).

"world's greatest missionary," Jones first went to India as a Methodist missionary in 1907. Coming from a pietistic grounding in holiness theology, Jones believed that religious experience through a personal relationship with Jesus Christ was the foundation of Christian living.

As Jones immersed himself in Indian culture in attempts to reach Hindus and Muslims, he realized that their association of Christianity with Western culture left them unable to relate to Jesus Christ, who seemed to them a metaphor for British imperialism. Jones began giving public lectures on Jesus Christ, followed by fatiguing question-and-answer sessions with the indigenous intelligentsia. By stripping away the trappings of Western Christianity from Jesus Christ, Jones proved able to get thousands of Hindus and Muslims to stand and acknowledge their allegiance to Jesus Christ — not to a system of doctrines, but to a person. Jones's description of his work did not include an Indian interpretation of Christ, something he felt would be better left to Indians themselves. Rather, *The Christ of the Indian Road* described the process of how Christ was "becoming naturalized" in India.[33] By giving a straightforward presentation of Jesus Christ, Jones refused to become embroiled in defenses of Christianity as a religious or cultural system. He argued that the absoluteness of Christ permitted a generous view of non-Christian systems.[34] A friend of Gandhi, Jones believed that the Hindu reformer pointed to Jesus, who was Life and Truth itself. In his optimism, Jones felt that the spiritual atmosphere in India was permeated with Christ, and belief in him would soon burst from the heavy clouds like a rainstorm.

Jones's theology of mission was a form of fulfillment theology. "Just as he [Jesus] gathered up in his own life and person everything that was fine and beautiful in Jewish teaching and past and gave it a new radiant expression, so he may do the same with India." Although Jesus' words "I came not to destroy but to fulfill" were "locally applied to the Law and the Prophets," they were "capable of a wider application to truth found anywhere."[35] In the paper he gave on "The Aim and Motive of Foreign Missions" in 1925 at the Foreign Missions Convention in Washington, Jones described the development of his radical methodology as a means of separating Christ from the view that missionaries were creed-mongers, forerunners of imperialism and capitalism, and supporters of domineering ecclesiasticism. By separating Christ from Western culture, Jones experienced a breakthrough with the Hindus and

33. E. Stanley Jones, *The Christ of the Indian Road* (New York: Abingdon Press, 1925), p. 1.

34. Jones, *Christ of the Indian Road*, p. 49.

35. Jones, *Christ of the Indian Road*, p. 170.

Muslims who opposed him. At the heart of Jones's fulfillment theory was a theology of the cosmic Christ: "If we go deep enough into religion, we must stand face to face with Jesus, who is religion itself in its final expression."[36] In relation to the East, Jesus Christ was the way: the way — the *karm marg,* "the way of life"; the truth — the *gyan marg,* "the way of knowledge"; and the life — the *bhakti marg,* "the way of devotion."[37]

To E. Stanley Jones, one of the wonders of the age was the new revelation that Christianity was breaking out beyond the borders of the church, and into non-Western societies. *The Christ of the Indian Road* was the Christ of service, moving among the people in his flowing garments, touching and healing them, and announcing the kingdom of God.[38] In accordance with his desire to "naturalize" Christ in the Indian context, in 1930 Jones opened his first Christian *ashram,* the beginning of a series of live-in communities in which religious seekers ate and prayed together. He initiated Round Table conferences among Hindus, Muslims, and Christians, an early attempt at interreligious dialogue based on sharing religious experiences. The very term "round table" mirrored meetings in the political realm held between the British and Indian nationalists, and consultations to support attempts to solve the world's problems through negotiation and peaceful means. In 1928 his book *The Christ of the Round Table* played a role in the acceptance of interreligious dialogue as a feature of mainline Protestant missions.

A second ground-breaking book of 1925 did not reach the popular audience that E. Stanley Jones did, but Daniel Fleming's *Whither Bound in Missions* put Jones's anecdotal insights into a more systematic form and laid out a program for missions that was widely influential among practicing missionaries. A former Presbyterian missionary to India, Fleming was Professor of Missions at Union Theological Seminary from 1918 to 1944.[39] A professor along with Harry Emerson Fosdick at Union, he and Fosdick lived in the same building for decades and their families were friends. Fleming attracted a

36. E. Stanley Jones, "The Aim and Motive of Foreign Missions," *Foreign Missions Convention,* p. 54.

37. Jones, "Aim and Motive," p. 54.

38. Jones, "Aim and Motive," p. 56.

39. I greatly admire William R. Hutchison's pioneering history of American mission theory: *Errand to the World: American Protestant Thought and Foreign Missions* (Chicago: University of Chicago Press, 1987), pp. 150-56, but he misinterprets the interwar period by treating Fleming as an isolated, prophetic figure whose ideas were not widely distributed until reaching their fulfillment in Hocking's *Laymen's Missionary Inquiry* in 1932. Despite Fleming's heavy reliance on Jones in *Whither Bound in Missions* (1925), Hutchison makes no reference to Jones in his book. Fleming did not stand alone, but was part of a network of progressive mission thinkers and internationalists.

wide range of international students, missionaries on furlough, and "missionary kids," including Timothy T. Lew, Y. T. Wu, Frank Laubach, and Charles Forman. Since many of Fleming's twenty-three books were published by the international student movement, they reached a wide audience of YMCA workers, missionaries, and indigenous Christian leaders around the world.[40]

In *Whither Bound in Missions,* Fleming distinguished between Christ and Western Christianity and predicted that the "storm center of Christian controversy" would soon pass to the "oriental seminaries" as they adjusted Christian thought to their ancient heritages. The context for the new mutuality in mission, and interpretation from West to East and back again, was an "organic conception of a world society, where independence gives way to interdependence, and where competition is superseded by cooperation. Fully to realize this co-relationship as members one of another constitutes a great part of growth in spirituality."[41] Like Jones, Fleming emphasized that Jesus was handicapped by his association with the West. Given that the goal of missions was to communicate Christ, it was necessary for missions to separate Christ from a culture of racism and Western self-righteousness. Fleming dwelled on the need for friendship with those of other religions, on international issues that affected the church, on indigenization in worship, and on devolving control of missions to the indigenous churches. He devoted an entire chapter on developing "Christian world-mindedness": ideas of the universal brotherhood of all people; the rights of smaller groups to pursue their own ways of doing things; and the need of worldwide cooperation in common tasks, including the League of Nations and the International Court. Mission education must emphasize "the universal brotherhood of children of God and purposeful, constructive endeavor for world ends," part of what Jesus meant by the kingdom of God.[42] Developing the "international mind," including "world consciousness, world outlook, world background, world fellowship, and world objective" should be the subject of mission education for students. Fleming advised that the "Christian internationalist" will read foreign papers, study foreign languages and cultures, and be concerned with international relations.

One of the missionaries whom Daniel Fleming influenced was Frank Laubach, a Congregational missionary in the Philippines who took his fur-

---

40. My copy of *Whither Bound in Missions,* for example, was owned in 1926 by M. Searle Bates, the Sinologist and missionary who taught for thirty years at the University of Nanking before filling Fleming's old post at Union Seminary in 1950.

41. Daniel J. Fleming, *Whither Bound in Missions* (New York: Association Press, 1925), p. 45.

42. Fleming, *Whither Bound,* p. 199.

lough at Union Theological Seminary between 1919 and 1922. Deeply influenced by Daniel Fleming's vision that missions should be concerned with the total welfare of peoples, Laubach realized through reading Fleming's book, *The Mark of the World Christian,* that two-thirds of the world were illiterate.[43] After returning from America and working among the Muslim Moros in the Philippines, Laubach pioneered the "each one, teach one" method, and the use of a basic set of words by which adults could learn to read in as short a time as a few hours.[44] In addition to being "Mr. Literacy," Laubach was widely recognized as a Christian internationalist, pacifist, and mystic. The author of forty-three books, he was a completely ecumenical figure who could not believe that one part of the church had a monopoly on truth. As he delved deeper into mysticism, influenced by the faith of the Muslim Moros, he came to the spiritual truth that he was a member of all denominations, and even of all faiths. Eager to soak up the riches of diverse devotional traditions, he applied the same idea to the nations: "I have become an internationalist so much that patriotism means the Lord's Prayer for the whole world, and especially for those who are being forgotten or oppressed."[45]

Daniel Fleming wrote the Foreword for Laubach's *People of the Philippines: Their Religious Progress and Preparation for Spiritual Leadership in the Far East.* In his comprehensive history of religion in the Philippines, Laubach started with its pre-Christian and then Muslim heritage, and worked through the history of Christian missions. The aim of his book was "to discover the footprints of God across the history of the Philippines."[46] Published at a time when the United States, under the influence of the Fourteen Points, was debating whether to handle the "problem of the Philippines" (a United States colony) by giving in to its right to self-determination, Laubach pursued an internationalist agenda through the historical method, and argued for the independence of the islands. Americans had been given a distorted picture of Philippine culture by the expeditionary forces and disgruntled Spanish priests; rather than barbaric cannibals, Filipinos were

43. David E. Mason, *Frank C. Laubach, Teacher of Millions* (Minneapolis: T. S. Denison & Co., 1967), p. 59.

44. Laubach's later work as the apostle of literacy training lies beyond the scope of this chapter. For a short summary of Laubach's life and work, see Peter G. Gowing, "Frank Charles Laubach, 1884-1970: Apostle to the Silent Billion," in Anderson et al., eds., *Mission Legacies,* pp. 500-507.

45. Quoted in Mason, *Laubach,* p. 130.

46. Frank Laubach, *The People of the Philippines: Their Religious Progress and Preparation for Spiritual Leadership in the Far East,* with a Foreword by Daniel Johnson Fleming (New York: George H. Doran Co., 1925), p. vii.

meek, gentle, hospitable people, he argued. Their deep religious insights, drawn from their rich heritage, meant that they were progressing toward the kingdom of God, and were set to exert spiritual leadership throughout Asia. In his history, he focused less on Western missionaries than on Filipino leadership in the mission of the church, including the founding of nineteen different indigenous denominations from 1909 to 1921.

To Laubach, the Philippines bore deep insights into Indian, Chinese, Eastern, and Western cultures, and so were in a position to reconcile Eastern and Western civilizations. In the words of a Filipino educator, the Filipinos were internationalists, located in a strategic position to precipitate "new world relations."[47] Laubach prophesied that the Filipinos would "re-orientalize" Christianity and free it from the "slough of theological despond" into which rationalistic Western minds had led it.[48] Filipinos were going to "work out for the Far East a simplified, beautified conception of the spirit of Jesus Christ . . . they will help the Kingdom of God to throw off its European garb, and take upon itself once more the Oriental dress in which it began its career."[49] As beacons of Christianity and of democracy — the only Asian Christian nation — the Philippines were poised to teach these things to Asia. If the Philippines failed in their task, it might be that Asia would turn away from both democracy and Christianity. "She would then learn from the Occident only science, militarism, hatred, and vengeance."[50]

The last missionary book to be considered here was one that pushed missionary internationalism in an important direction: *A Straight Way Toward Tomorrow* by Mary Schauffler Platt. A member of the famous German-American, American Board missionary dynasty, Mary Schauffler also married a missionary. She wrote several books that were distributed to hundreds of thousands of American women gathered in denominational mission study groups in American Protestant churches. Published in 1926, *A Straight Way Toward Tomorrow* represented the application of Christian internationalism to the distinctive concerns of missionary women: child welfare, the Christian home, and religious education. It culminated in a call for "Worldwide Friendship," which became the keynote of the interdenominational woman's missionary movement in the interwar period. In "World Friendship," American women endorsed a Christian internationalism that stressed world peace, inter-racial harmony, and building personal bridges between women of dif-

---

47. Laubach, *People of the Philippines*, p. 456.
48. Laubach, *People of the Philippines*, p. 461.
49. Laubach, *People of the Philippines*, p. 462.
50. Laubach, *People of the Philippines*, p. 464.

ferent cultures.[51] In the foreword to Platt's book the Central Committee for the United Study of Foreign Missions expressed its plan for breaking national barriers through united mission study among Christian women around the world: "We are coming together into a spiritual federation of the Christian Women of the world for which we have longed and prayed."[52] The Committee expressed optimism that Christian women would unite on a spiritual basis before governments would "agree on political plans" for world unity.

Among the many fascinating emphases in Platt's book are the child-centered aspects of internationalism, including the founding of the Save the Children Fund in 1919, and the Geneva Declaration on the Rights of the Child, endorsed by the League of Nations in 1924, the aims of which she declared were biblical. Like Jones, Fleming, and Laubach, she believed that the future of mission lay in the hands of indigenous Christians. "The evangelization of Africa lies with the African of the future."[53] Speaking of Christian women of the world, Platt indicated that "What they have done and can do for their own people, is far beyond the possibilities of foreigners who come to their shores, learn their language more or less imperfectly, and try to think their thoughts and understand their racial feelings. Our Christian sisters of China, Japan, India and Africa are those on whom Christ chiefly depends for leading the women and little children of their own people into the Straight Way Toward Tomorrow . . . they will always need our prayers, sympathy and love; but they must increase and we must decrease in influence, in leadership, in interpretation of the message of Christ to the women of their own lands."[54]

In the final chapter of her book, Platt underscored the women's basis for World Friendship: true love as the means to end war. She drew attention to the giant women's peace rally held in London in 1926; to the founding of the Institute of Pacific Relations in 1925 as "an adventure in friendship"; to the missionary movement's attempt to end the unjust treaties imposed upon China and to revoke the Japanese Exclusion Act; and to the World Conference of Education in 1926 that was inspired by the idea that in order to end war, children must be educated for peace. Platt praised the international movement of Boy Scouts and Girl Reserves, youth movements that were teaching the youth to resolve conflicts by means other than war. In its final pages, *A*

51. On the missiology of World Friendship, see Robert, *American Women in Mission*, ch. 6.

52. Foreword to Mary Schauffler Platt, *A Straight Way Toward Tomorrow* (Cambridge, MA: Central Committee on the United Study of Foreign Missions, 1926), p. v.

53. Platt, *Straight Way*, p. 124.

54. Platt, *Straight Way*, p. 129.

Straight Way Toward Tomorrow evoked the idea of a Cosmic Christ, who illumined the pathway to Life in all cultures: "He is the same Christ yesterday, today, and on through the days to come; the 'Christ of the Andes' who stands as the emblem of peace between two great countries; 'The Christ of the Indian Road' whom Eastern mystics can worship and crave as their Companion; the 'Christ of the Trackless Desert' to guide the wandering Arab; the Christ of Order and the Law of Love for nations that are struggling to find themselves in the seething world of today; the Christ of Unselfish Service for those who know him and would follow in his steps."[55] The Christian women of every race and country would thus walk in "happy fellowship" with Christ and each other on the straight way "unto the perfect day."[56]

In the works of Jones, Fleming, Laubach, and Platt, all of them experienced missionaries, we see the full development of a missionary internationalism by 1926. Although they wrote in different genres of personal narrative, missiological treatise, history, and mission study book, each expressed deep confidence in the ability of Jesus Christ to be fully represented in non-Western cultures. Each looked forward to the development of indigenous theologies, and to what we would today call the full contextualization of Christianity. Their vision of a new world order, of Christian internationalism — including peace, democracy, and the political and religious self-determination of peoples — provided the framework for the indigenization of Christianity throughout the world. From a theological perspective, while they supported personal evangelism, they perceived Christ embodied in all cultures. In the case of Jones and Laubach, both ardent and activistic pacifists, although they maintained the absoluteness of Jesus Christ, they saw the Spirit of Christ operating within other religions as well.[57]

Missionary Indigenization

Having briefly explored the synergism between internationalism and indigenization in the mission thought of a few leading missionaries in the mid-1920s, the discussion now turns to specific attempts at indigenization on

55. Platt, *Straight Way,* p. 222.
56. Platt, *Straight Way,* p. 222.
57. The Cosmic Christ was a common theme adopted by twentieth-century missionaries who experienced good in other cultures, and even in other religions. The idea of the Cosmic Christ was a correlative of "fulfillment theory" — on the prominence of the latter see Kenneth Cracknell, *Justice, Courtesy, and Love: Theologians and Missionaries Encountering World Religions, 1846-1914* (London: Epworth Press, 1995).

the part of missionaries in the interwar period. All of the leaders whose books were examined above stated clearly that interpreting Jesus Christ according to each culture was a vital task for indigenous Christians. It was not something that Western missionaries could do on their behalf. While stopping short of claiming to develop truly indigenous theologies, missionary internationalists in the 1920s and 1930s encouraged the inculturation process in many different ways. As the years passed, deliberate attempts at promoting indigenization increased, especially after the publication of the proceedings of the Jerusalem Conference of 1928, which contained an extensive report on the indigenization process. The third volume of Conference Reports, on "Younger and Older Churches," contains discussion of indigenization testimonies from China, Japan, India, Burma, and the West. The concluding definition of the "indigenous church" included the following: "when its interpretation of Christ and its expression in worship and service, in customs and in art and architecture, incorporate the worthy characteristics of the people, while conserving at the same time the heritage of the Church in all lands and in all ages."[58]

As with the mission books considered above, the discussion of indigenous churches by the International Missionary Council was set in an internationalist framework of cooperation for world peace, and the need to "Christianize" nationalism. Words from the Indian Methodist Conference of 1926 exemplified the relationship between indigenization and Christian internationalism: "There will always be a need of some missionaries to come to India with the best Christian culture from the West, just as there will always be a need of Indian Christian missionaries to take the best of Christian culture from the East to the West. In this fusion of the Christian culture of Occident and Orient will arise a new and international consciousness of Christ which will help to solve so many of the problems of nation and race and color, the great unsolved problems of this age."[59]

Ironically, the promotion of indigenous culture in the younger churches could be seen as a "top-down" imposition by outsiders: a part of the liberal, North Atlantic agenda. For by the 1930s missionaries from mainline churches were working among people who, in many cases, had been Christians for several generations, and whose traditions had been handed down by those who had seen Western Christianity as part of a necessary critique of their own

58. *The Jerusalem Meeting of the International Missionary Council, March 24–April 8 1928* (New York: International Missionary Council, 1928), vol. 3, *The Relation between the Younger and the Older Churches*, p. 166.

59. *Relation between the Younger and the Older Churches*, p. 53. See Timothy Yates's excellent summary of the internationalist themes at Jerusalem 1928, *Christian Mission*, pp. 65-70.

non-Western cultures. The resistance to indigenization could be just as strong by "native Christians" as it was by theologically conservative missionaries. Both groups worried that indigenization would invite paganism into the church through the back door. The movement toward indigenization was part of a liberal agenda to create a world church that was a mosaic of different cultures. Indigenizing internationalists frequently commented on the resistance to their work by conservative native Christians.[60]

The longest sustained attempt at missionary support for inculturation was sponsored by the Committee on Christian Literature for Women and Children in Mission Fields (CCLWCMF), founded in 1912. It was one of the three joint programs of the women's mission boards in North America and lasted until 1989. During the 1920s the program received the collections taken by women on the World Day of Prayer, supported by missionary women around the world. Its goal was to sponsor Christian literature for women and children, who after becoming Christian needed reading material and artwork appropriate to their own cultures. In its first fifty years, the CCLWCMF sponsored twenty-seven magazines in different languages. Some of the magazines were not labeled as Christian and so gained widespread acceptance as children's literature in other religious contexts. The magazine *The Treasure Chest,* for example, in 1922 featured stories, plays, poems, and articles. It carried a regular section, "The Friendly League," on social service. Children wrote letters to the editor, and enjoyed sections on the flora and fauna of India, biographies of famous people in Indian history, and travelogues. In the late 1930s the National Christian Council of India endorsed *The Treasure Chest,* which by 1938 was being published in English, Urdu, Malayalam, Telugu, Hindi, Tamil, Marathi, Burmese, Gujarati, and Bengali editions.[61] Most of the magazines supported

60. Interview with Charles Forman, 6 Dec. 2000, New Haven, CT. Forman (b. India) trained at Union Seminary and was a missionary in India; he was later Professor of Missions at Yale and Chairman of the Foundation for Theological Education Southeast Asia, 1970-1989. A promoter of indigenous music and liturgy, he learned that although the Indian church had had to accept the Western culture brought by the first missionaries, they would not let young missionaries tell them what was indigenous or not. Clearly missionaries' attitudes to indigenization could be seen as missionary paternalism. See entry for Forman in Gerald H. Anderson, ed., *Biographical Dictionary of Christian Missions* (New York: Macmillan Reference, 1998), p. 218.

61. See pamphlets in the Archives of the Committee on Christian Literature for Women and Children, Record Group 90, Special Collections, Yale Divinity School, New Haven, CT. Ruth Robinson, "The Treasure Chest" (n.d.); Clementina Butler, "A Quarter Century of Service to the Christian Home" (CCLWCMF, 1939), RG 90, Box 7, File 124. From the 1950s through the 1970s, the CCLWCMF conducted writing workshops for indigenous women around the world.

by the project worked in vernacular languages under indigenous editors, and encouraged children to contribute stories. The American chairman of the project hoped that their work would not only help sustain "Christian homes," but would teach the ideals of peace. In 1939 Clementina Butler, the Chair of the Committee and one of its original founders, quoted support of the program from missionary leaders who considered it helpful "in education for world understanding, cooperation and peace."[62] Whenever possible, the CCLWCMF cooperated with the newer Christian literature committees, such as the International Committee on Christian Literature for Africa, a subcommittee of the International Missionary Council founded in 1929. By the early 1940s the CCLWCMF was planning to translate some of its magazines into romanized characters for use by Frank Laubach in his literacy work.

One of the most interesting aspects of the work of the CCLWCMF was its sponsorship of native Christian art, the first mission organization to do so in a systematic way. Concerned that converts in India only had cheap pictures of Hindu gods with which to decorate their homes, Clementina Butler, who had grown up in India in a missionary family, began commissioning Christian pictures in Indian styles in the 1930s. Sold at cost for two cents a piece, response to the first ten pictures was immediate. "The Good Shepherd" sold 27,000 copies in the first year, and later E. Stanley Jones's ashram in Lucknow sent 2,600 copies as Christmas presents to workers among the poor. The CCLWCMF held annual contests for the best indigenous Christian art in India.[63] In China, in addition to its magazines, the Committee sponsored a *Pictorial Life of Our Saviour* in five volumes. The first volume sold 23,000 copies in the first eighteen months. A missionary made filmstrips of the series which was watched by thousands, who accompanied it by sung rhymes.[64] At a time when most mission literature was still using pictures of blonde and blue-eyed Madonnas, the CCLWCMF was commissioning native art for the covers of its magazines and books.

Some of the art commissioned by the CCLWCMF was introduced to a Western audience by its inclusion in a series of three books edited by Daniel

---

62. Quoted by Clementina Butler, "Report of the Committee on Christian Literature for Women and Children in Mission Fields, Inc." (Nov. 1939), 9, CCLWCMF Archives, RG 90, Box 4, File 65.

63. Butler, "A Quarter Century of Service to the Christian Home," ff. 8-10.

64. Butler, "Report," f. 4. The filmstrip of the Life of Christ used to evangelize the Chinese was a forerunner of the phenomenally successful "Jesus Film," seen in 665 languages by over 4 billion people as of 31 May 2001. See www.jesusfilm.org/index.html. The trend to the globalization of Christianity during the twentieth century was evident in the history of multimedia as well.

Fleming on non-Western Christian art and architecture, *Heritage of Beauty* (1937), *Each With His Own Brush* (1938), and *Christian Symbols in a World Community* (1940). They were published by Friendship Press, itself a product of missionary internationalism, representing the merger of the publishing arms of interdenominational North American mission education programs. In Fleming's introduction to the first of the three books, he explored the relationship between the Christian vision of a "world community," and the indigenization process in the younger churches. Referring to the world community, he stated that "doubtless the greatest influence making for its fullest realization, is the Christian world fellowship — a fellowship which is no political federation of the world, no mere brotherhood of man, transcending all differences of race and nationality, but a community which progressively embodies the Christian faith, renewed distinctively by worship of God through Jesus Christ."[65] The Christian world fellowship should become a "conscious reality" in the Christian's life. Achievement of the world fellowship required becoming aware of "cultural embodiments of Christianity other than our own." He continued:

> We are not satisfied to think of ourselves as belonging merely to an American, a British, a Japanese or an Indian group of Christians; but are striving to attain a loyalty and an attitude of mind that consciously and unconsciously will reveal that we are citizens of a universal kingdom. We realize that, for Christians, the word community should have a universal, a catholic, an ecumenical connotation. Any objective approach, therefore, which helps us to gain a sense of the wide diffusion of the church and to acquire more understanding of its truly multi-national, multi-racial character should be of help.[66]

One of the significant aspects of Fleming's thought in the late 1930s, as compared to his ideas in the early 1920s, was the shifting of his international vision from the world to the church itself. Fleming raised the knotty problems of indigenization: the relationship of culture to religion; the question of how far forms should be adjusted to the cultural backgrounds of the people; and how to separate the essential features of Christianity from its host cultures. Having lost some of his easy optimism of the early 1920s, Fleming admitted that these issues were difficult, and it would take centuries to develop a

---

65. Daniel Johnson Fleming, *Heritage of Beauty* (New York: Friendship Press, 1937), p. 9.

66. Fleming, *Heritage*, p. 10.

common world culture, but in the 1930s, to recognize cultural differences was "to affirm the catholic character of the Christian church."[67] The main hope for missions was "that an indigenous church may develop — church that smacks of the soil, that grows naturally, that feels itself to be native and not exotic."[68] One of the difficulties in encouraging indigenous art was the resistance of Asians themselves, who assumed that indigenous art was pagan. The amount of locally produced Christian art was very small. "Certain interested Western representatives, therefore, take the initiative in producing model experiments in adaptation in order to overcome the initial attachment to alien forms to which second and third generation Christians have become accustomed."[69] Most of the buildings that Fleming pictured in *Heritage of Beauty* were produced in the 1920s and 1930s, demonstrating the recent nature of movements toward indigenization in architecture.

In the second book of the series, *Each With His Own Brush*, Fleming noted that Christian art was in its infancy, partly because the poverty of most Christians prevented them from sponsoring high-quality work. He had received statements from all over the world indicating that indigenous Christian art did not yet exist. Yet he managed to put together a book of paintings, much of it commissioned by missionaries and by the CCLWCMF. He judged that Christian art was in its most advanced phase in China, where the Episcopal priest, and later bishop, T. K. Shen had begun sponsoring the creation of Christian art in 1926 under the name St. Luke's Studio. Catholics connected with the Catholic University of Peking had also begun to sponsor Christian art in the 1920s and had held several exhibitions.[70] In his third book on Christian symbols, Fleming quoted from missionaries who had tried to introduce indigenous symbols in India, only to be opposed by the Indian people for fear of paganism entering the church. The prophetic voice of indigenizers like Bishop Azariah aside, the inculturation process was not an easy road.[71]

In early 1938 the Committee preparing for the International Missionary Council (IMC) meeting in Madras, India, began receiving suggestions that they sponsor an international exhibition of Christian literature to join a

67. Fleming, *Heritage*, p. 11.

68. Fleming, *Heritage*, p. 12.

69. Fleming, *Heritage*, p. 15.

70. Daniel Johnson Fleming, *Each With His Own Brush* (New York: Friendship Press, 1938), pp. 2, 11-12.

71. On Azariah, the first Indian bishop of the Anglican Church, and indigenization of his churches, see Susan Billington Harper, *In the Shadow of the Mahatma: Bishop V. S. Azariah and the Travails of Christianity in British India* (Grand Rapids: Eerdmans; Richmond, U.K.: Curzon, 2000), pp. 261-62.

planned exhibition of Christian art.[72] On 1 June, the IMC secretary, A. L. Warnshuis, sent a letter to the secretaries of National Christian Councils requesting that they send materials for exhibits on Christian literature, art, and architecture. Materials requested included pictures, sculptures, tapestries or needlework, photographs of church buildings, sketches, and models. The purposes of the exhibits included to "demonstrate the long history and universality of Christianity and the contributions which different ages and different lands are making to the enrichment of Christian art and architecture." The artwork itself would be a unifying factor in a conference set to accommodate the widest geographic range of delegates who had ever attended an ecumenical conference.[73]

In February 1938 Mr. J. Prip-Moller wrote to the International Missionary Council requesting that they consider the subject of Christian architecture at the forthcoming meeting. The brother of a former medical missionary in Syria, Prip-Moller had worked for five years in Manchuria in cooperation with the Danish Mission Society, Scottish and Irish Presbyterians, and the YMCA. An architect and author of a work, *Chinese Buddhist Monasteries,* Prip-Moller had designed the YMCA building in Moukden to follow the structure of the typical Chinese family house. He also designed and built schools, hospitals, and churches. Probably his most important work, however, had been as the friend for eighteen years to the Reverend Karl Reichelt, a Norwegian missionary operating a unique mission to Buddhist monks in Hong Kong. Like E. Stanley Jones, Reichelt was a long-term missionary who believed in fulfillment theory: that Mahayana Buddhism found its fulfillment in Jesus Christ. He opened a mission to Buddhists under the Norwegian Lutherans that was destroyed in the civil war in 1927 in Nanking. Becoming a Buddhist monk to attract monks, as a freelance missionary Reichelt developed a liturgy based on Buddhism, and in 1931 dedicated a complex of buildings called "Tao Fong Shan," a Christian community closely modeled on the Buddhist monastery. It was Prip-Moller who was Reichelt's architect at Tao Fong Shan.[74]

72. "Notes of Discussion on International Exhibit of Christian Literature," 1 March 1938. International Missionary Council Archives 1910-1961, World Council of Churches, Geneva (IDC, 1987). Fiche 262005, #4, Madras 1938, "Exhibits."

73. A. L. Warnshuis to Secretaries of National Christian Councils and Conferences, 1 June 1938. International Missionary Council Archives, Fiche 262005, #2, Madras 1938, "Exhibits."

74. See Letter J. Prip-Moller to David Paton, 12 Feb. 1938, IMC Archives, Fiche 262005, #1, Madras 1938, "Exhibits." On the life and work of Karl Reichelt, see Notto R. Thelle, "Karl Ludvig Reichelt, 1877-1952: Christian Pilgrim of Tao Fong Shan," in Anderson et al., eds., *Mission Legacies,* pp. 216-24.

In *Heritage of Beauty*, Daniel Fleming discussed how Reichelt adapted Buddhist symbols to Christianity in his Brotherhood of Religious Friends near Nanking. In particular, he used the emblem of a cross rising out of a lotus. The chapel contained an altar finished in red lacquer, candles in the form of white cranes, and ample use of varied symbols such as the fish, fire, and sun. Liturgical adaptations included the use of red candles and incense at the beginning of services.[75] In the third book of the series on indigenous art, *Christian Symbols in a World Community*, Fleming included photographs of the church and altar at the Tao Fong Shan Christian Institute. In an interesting domestic example of liberal Protestant internationalism, he also featured a photograph of the front door of Harry Fosdick's Riverside Church in New York City, with its sculptures of Moses, Confucius, Buddha, and Mohammed, along with the missionaries William Carey and David Livingstone.

Prip-Moller felt that architecture was usually neglected by missions because of concerns about expense, even at the cost of making Christianity seem like a foreign religion, as well as a prejudice by Protestants against aesthetical concerns. He believed missionaries were inconsistent in teaching people that their culture was a gift of God, while excluding their buildings as if God only gave architecture to the West.[76] In an article for *The Chinese Recorder*, "Christian Architecture in New-Christian Communities," Prip-Moller argued for the Christianizing of local architecture by adapting it to the new Christian ideas, so that harmony was obtained "and the soul and spirit of the old architectural forms retained."[77] The spirit of Christian internationalism shone through as Prip-Moller's rationale for indigenous architecture when he wrote: "In the world today we need more than ever a strong Christian church which in the spirit of Christ cannot merely balance but lift up to a higher plane the nationalism, which in some places tends to draw man away from God."[78] Stating that Western-style churches were just as nationalistic and non-universal as non-Western styles, Prip-Moller urged that Christ's "supernationality" would become apparent only when his children could "sing His praise in their own tongue."[79]

The building momentum in the missionary movement toward indigenization in the 1920s and 1930s culminated in the meeting of the International

---

75. Daniel Johnson Fleming, *Christian Symbols in a World Community* (New York: Friendship Press, 1940), pp. 92-93.

76. Prip-Moller to Paton, f. 3.

77. J. Prip-Moller, "Christian Architecture in New-Christian Communities," *Chinese Recorder* (July 1939), reprint ed., pp. 3-4. IMC Archives, Fiche 262005, #2.

78. Prip-Moller, "Christian Architecture," p. 6.

79. Prip-Moller, "Christian Architecture," p. 6.

Missionary Council in Madras, India, in 1938. The exhibits on indigenous Christian literature, art, and architecture were well received. Many different discussions took place on various aspects of indigenization in the "younger churches," including liturgy and worship, the Christian home, indigenous hymnody, poetry, Christian festivals, and religious art. Delegates concluded that each nation should be encouraged to offer its own cultural forms to Christ. In the section on Worship, it was recommended that National Christian Councils collect cultural adaptations of liturgy and keep them in a library for future reference. The recent writings of Daniel Fleming on indigenous art, as well as the reflections of Prip-Moller on indigenizing architecture were mentioned.[80] The official findings of the conference expressed the consensus on inculturation:

> When churches grow up in the environment of non-Christian religions and cultures, it is necessary that they should become firmly rooted in the Christian heritage and fellowship of the Church Universal. They have their place in the great Christian brotherhood of all ages and races. But they should also be rooted in the soil of their own country. Therefore we strongly affirm that the Gospel should be expressed and interpreted in indigenous forms, and that in methods of worship, institutions, literature, architecture, etc., the spiritual heritage of the nation and country should be taken into use. The Gospel is not necessarily bound up with forms and methods brought in from the older churches. The endeavor to give Christ His rightful place in the heart of people who have not previously known Him so that He will neither be a foreigner, nor be distorted by pre-Christian patterns of thought "is a great and exacting spiritual task in the fulfilling of which a young church can bring a rich contribution of her own to the Church Universal."[81]

At the same time, the conference kept before the churches the vision of Christian internationalism. While acknowledging that the missionary must "identify himself with the best aspirations and interests of the people he serves," the findings of the section on Church and State cautioned that the missionary must at the same time "be ever mindful of the world-wide fellowship he represents, and of the common citizenship of all Christians in the Kingdom of God."[82] Despite the concerns of the delegates over militant na-

---

80. IMC, *The Life of the Church*, The Tambaram Madras Series, vol. 4 (New York: IMC, 1939), pp. 5-6.

81. IMC, *The Authority of the Faith*, The Tambaram Madras Series, vol. 1, pp. 185-86.

82. IMC, *The Church and the State*, The Tambaram Madras Series, vol. 6, p. 256.

tionalism, the Sino-Japanese War, and the rise of Nazism, they still affirmed that "in the missionary enterprise the Christian movement makes an indispensable contribution to the international order. . . . Here international and inter-racial contact may reach its highest level. The true missionary comes as a friend. . . . The wall and partition between nations and races is broken down in the ever-widening fellowship of the ecumenical Church."[83]

Although a full analysis of the relationship between internationalism and indigenization at the Madras meeting of the IMC is not possible here, it is safe to say that the 1938 meeting represented how they had grown together since the First World War.[84] The 1938 meeting had the highest proportional representation from the non-Western world of any mission gathering to date. With so many indigenous Christians from diverse parts of the world, the main topic of the conference was the "younger churches." The vision of Christianity as a worldwide community and force for unity, peace, and justice in the world was visibly evident in the global fellowship gathered there. At the same time, the conference called for the deepening of the Christian life in each national context through the adaptation of Christianity into different cultures. While faith in moving toward the kingdom of God on earth had receded since the more optimistic 1920s, the international vision had not died. Rather, in mission circles it had become more focused as the principle of indigenization within a global church, rather than confidence in the Christian nature of government policies such as the Fourteen Points, the League of Nations, the Geneva Protocols against weapons of mass destruction, and so forth. In other words, by the late 1930s, the locus of Christian internationalism had become re-centered in the church itself, rather than in the ability of the church to effect a new world order.[85]

83. IMC, *The Church and the State*, The Tambaram Madras Series, vol. 6, p. 255.

84. "Internationalists" were not the only mission advocates interested in indigeneity in the 1930s. Internationalist discourse emanated from the "liberal" wing of the missionary movement. Continental missiologists like Hendrik Kraemer and Bruno Gutmann were also interested in indigeneity, but did not share the theological framework or rhetoric of internationalism. They tended toward a "bottom-up" method of promoting indigeneity rather than the "top-down" one of the internationalists. On Continental criticisms of the "crusading" idealism of North American mission advocates, see Jan A. B. Jongeneel, "European-Continental Perceptions and Critiques of British and American Protestant Missions," *Exchange* 30, no. 2 (April 2001): 117-18.

85. Church-centric mission was what the German and other Continental missionary advocates had been supporting all along. On the German insistence on church-centric mission between the wars, see Yates, *Christian Mission* and Jongeneel, "European-Continental Perceptions."

World Friendship and Ambassadors from the Younger Churches

The stance of separating Christ from Western culture and supporting cultural indigenization formed part of the missionary contribution to Christian internationalism in the interwar period. Neither would have been effective without the substantial participation of non-Western Christians in communicating a universal vision to the Western church. In the eyes of Westerners, the most effective witness to world fellowship in God's kingdom was an actual living, breathing, English-speaking Christian from a so-called "mission land." With "World Friendship" as the mission slogan of the era, the 1920s and 1930s marked the beginning of the widespread use of indigenous Christians as ambassadors, or "reverse" missionaries, to the West. If one peruses missionary magazines of the period, one is struck at how the actual voices of non-Western Christians are being heard by the 1930s. While a story written about a Chinese or African Bible woman in a missionary magazine would be in the Western missionary's voice in earlier years, by 1930 the story would be from the perspective of the indigenous Christian herself. Not only had years of missionary higher education produced literate non-Western leaders, but the missionaries realized that the voice of a so-called "native Christian" was far more effective in promoting an internationalist agenda than that of a missionary.

Starting in the 1920s, student Christian movements and mission organizations began sponsoring the publications in English of writings by non-Western Christians, especially of those who had been educated in the West and who shared the internationalist perspectives of their sponsors. The international Christian student movement provided leadership in this area, and the indigenous officers of various YMCA, YWCA, and World's Student Christian Federation branches became popular speakers among Western university students and international friendship groups, as the experiences of Tissington Tatlow testified.[86] A cursory examination of this literature as produced in the West indicates a strong focus on Chinese and Japanese Christian perspectives in the 1920s. As missionaries sought to counteract the negative publicity of the anti-Christian movement in China in 1922, to create support for renegotiating the unjust treaties, and to build opposition to the Oriental Exclusion Act of 1924, they tried to humanize and individualize the Chinese and Japanese in the minds of Westerners. Among the ground-breaking attempts in this regard were the two series of essays titled *China To-Day through Chinese Eyes,* published in 1922 and 1926 by the Student Christian Movement

86. While the indigenous Christians considered had their own perspectives, here they are considered in the context of facilitating the Western missionary agenda.

of Great Britain. The list of authors reads like a "who's who" of Chinese Christian intellectuals and YMCA leaders, including T. C. Chao, David Z. T. Yui, Timothy Tingfang Lew, and T. Z. Koo. While exploring the various aspects of the Christian movement in China, the authors endorsed the internationalist agenda, as did the Christian Church in China in 1922, when it called for "international world brotherhood" and "international friendship" as Christian obligations. The newly founded Christian Church in China called for the Christianization of "the rapidly developing national consciousness" that was growing in China.[87] Writing on intellectual movements in China, P. C. Hsu, Professor of Philosophy at Yenching University, indicated that the Christian contribution to the rising tide of nationalism was to supplement it "by the spirit of Christian Internationalism," the doctrine of human brotherhood that would make possible a warless world.[88]

An article by Timothy Tingfang Lew, former student of Fosdick and Fleming at Union Seminary and Dean of Theology at Yenching University, discussed the mixture of science, democracy, nationalism, and spiritual quest pursued by Chinese intellectuals in the New Culture Movement. A noted hymn writer, Lew later received praise at the 1938 IMC meeting for having produced an experimental series of indigenous liturgies and devotional materials. In 1927 Lew became the first non-Western Professor of Missions in the United States when he taught for a year at the Boston University School of Theology.

Among supporters of women's missions in the United States, none had the stature of the Japanese educator Michi Kawai, a former Bryn Mawr student, founder of a Christian girls' school in Japan, and co-founder and head of the Japanese YWCA. Kawai was a devout internationalist who maintained a network of friends in the United States, Great Britain, and China. Her first speaking trip to the United States was for six months in 1910 on behalf of the YWCA. She returned in 1926 to get help in supporting her Christian school, and to create momentum against the exclusion of Japanese from the United States. In one interesting meeting, Mrs. John D. Rockefeller and the former missionary in Japan, Sydney L. Gulick, took her to a church meeting where they spoke in favor of Japanese citizenship and the repeal of the exclusion acts. Kawai recorded in her autobiography that her trip in 1926 affirmed her desire to make "international study" a feature of her school, and to encourage her pupils to "usher in a new world order, with peace and goodwill prevail-

87. Cited in Platt, *A Straight Way,* p. 206.
88. P. C. Hsu, "Intellectual Movements," in *China To-day through Chinese Eyes,* 2nd series, 3rd ed. (London: Student Christian Movement, 1927), pp. 29-30.

ing."[89] In 1934 she wrote the mission study-book *Japanese Women Speak,* sponsored by the Central Committee on the United Study of Foreign Missions. This book explored the themes of education, internationalism, pacifism, and world friendship being promoted by Japanese Christian women against the rising tide of militarism.[90] Having previously brought two speakers from China the year before, the women's mission boards of North America sponsored a speaking tour by Kawai in 1934.

As one of the Japanese delegates to the International Missionary Council meeting in 1938, Kawai summarized the significance of the conference for Christian education: "It exhorts us to treasure each national or racial heritage and demands that we put into it the rich Christian blood which revives and invigorates the old indigenous culture." She believed that evangelism was the foundation for "ushering in the Kingdom of God on earth," and that teachers were co-workers with God.[91] Kawai and other Japanese Christian women suffered for their pacifism and international outlook during the Second World War. American readers were able to sympathize with her struggles by reading her two autobiographies printed in English, *My Lantern* (1939) and *Sliding Doors* (1950).[92]

The impact of non-Western "reverse missionaries" on the shape of an internationalist missionary agenda between the world wars is a topic that deserves further research, but a few brief examples follow. In 1923 Miss Helen Kim, a recent graduate of Ewha Woman's College, was in the United States doing graduate work. Kim was founding president of the Korean YWCA and later became long-term president of Ewha. In 1923 she attended the executive committee meeting of the Woman's Foreign Missionary Society of the Methodist Episcopal Church, the largest women's mission organization at that time. Kim gave a speech advocating the unification of women in a worldwide organization as an alternative to the League of Nations, which she considered a male organization. The proposed organization would promote world peace and fellowship, encourage the professionalization of women's work, protect women and children, train women to be world citizens, and establish justice and righteousness everywhere. Kim's proposal was presented by a Japanese

---

89. Michi Kawai, *My Lantern* (Japan: privately printed, 1939), p. 170.

90. Kawai and Ochimi Kubushiro, *Japanese Women Speak* (Boston: Central Committee on the United Study of Foreign Missions, 1934). Other books by the same publisher promoted "World Friendship" by making heard the voices of non-Western Christian women. Of particular interest is *Women and the Way: Christ and the World's Womanhood* (New York: Friendship Press, 1938).

91. Kawai, *My Lantern*, pp. 227-28.

92. Kawai, *Sliding Doors* (Tokyo: Keisen-Jo-Gaku-En, 1950).

and a Chinese Christian woman to the entire Federation of Woman's Boards of Foreign Missions. In 1929 the Methodist women's missionary society tried to change its name to the Women's International Missionary Society to reflect that the world church was a sisterhood of equals. Then in 1939 women from twenty-seven countries formed the World Federation of Methodist Women. With its symbol the tree of life, suggested by Lucy Wang, president of Hwa Nan College in China, the Federation supported the following "fruits" in each country: evangelism, education, medical work, literature, youth, childhood, world peace, temperance, rural education, home life, interracial relationships, and economic justice. The leaves of the tree symbolized the healing of the nations, as Methodist women of different nationalities together sought to build a "Christian world order."[93]

The International Missionary Conference meeting in Madras, 1938, was noteworthy for having seventy women in attendance. This remarkable event came about partly through sustained pressure by Western women's mission organizations that pushed the various Christian Councils to appoint women to their delegations. A Chinese woman, Dr. Wu Yi-fang, even headed the Chinese delegation — the first woman to head any delegation at an international conference. A graduate of mission schools, Wu held a Ph.D. in biology from the University of Michigan, and was the first Chinese president of Ginling College in 1927, the only inter-denominational woman's college in China.[94]

One of the international women at the IMC was a delegate from South Africa, the first African woman delegate to an international missionary conference. Her attendance came about when the long-time missionary Clara Bridgman, the only woman on the nominating committee of the newly founded National Christian Council of South Africa, insisted that a woman be chosen as part of the African delegation. Mina Soga, a teacher and social worker, was the only woman among the twelve black Africans to attend the conference. She made a big impression on the gathering with her singing, and with her plea that Christianity be put into African form, in the culture of Africans. Ruth Seabury, who later wrote Soga's biography, recalled: "As we listened to her words some of us began for the first time to see the possibilities of the Christian message expressed in African terms."[95] The conference greatly impressed Mina Soga too: she experienced true inter-racial fellowship

93. Rosemary Keller, gen. ed., *Methodist Women, a World Sisterhood. A History of the World Federation of Methodist Women 1923-1986* (n.p.: The World Federation of Methodist Women, n.d.), pp. 3-12.

94. On Wu, see Sherwood Eddy, *Pathfinders of the World Missionary Crusade* (New York: Abingdon-Cokesbury Press, 1945), pp. 220-27.

95. Ruth Isabel Seabury, *Daughter of Africa* (Boston: Pilgrim Press, 1945), p. 79.

for the first time, and felt a solidarity with other delegates from the developing nations. As she recalled, "My journey out of Africa turned me from a South African into an African. Madras made me a world Christian."[96] After the conference, with the American delegation making her arrangements, Mina Soga and a few other international delegates sailed to the United States to share their experiences of world fellowship at Madras with mission circles, youth meetings, and church groups. Soga spoke in twenty-four American cities over a six-month period. The racial segregation in the United States meant that Saga's presence and her message about the situation in South Africa, as well as the vision of international Christian fellowship, were very timely and inspiring to both black and white Christians struggling to affirm racial reconciliation in the segregated United States.

The most notable "reverse missionary" in the United States between the world wars was the Japanese evangelist, social worker, socialist, and pacifist Toyohiko Kagawa. Although some had been aware of his work earlier, the biography of Kagawa published in 1932 by the long-term Japan missionary William Axling, brought Kagawa to the eye of the Western churches.[97] With another missionary, Helen Topping of the Kobe YWCA, acting as his "right hand man," Kagawa wrote several books in English, including poetry, spiritual reflections, and an autobiography. Kagawa was one of the chief representatives of Christian internationalism, and he was sought after by mission groups, Japanese American groups, and pacifist organizations to share the spirit of Japanese Christianity with Americans in a time of hostility and distrust between the two nations.

I cannot close this cursory glance at ambassadors of Christian internationalism without mentioning the effect of Hindu reformer Mohandas Gandhi on Christian internationalists throughout the West. Although the impact of Gandhi is much too complicated to consider here, it should be noted that he had a number of missionary partners who introduced his nonviolent campaigns to a Western audience, including E. Stanley Jones and C. F. Andrews. One early and extremely thoughtful biography that introduced Gandhi to a Western audience was published in 1932, the same year as Axling's Kagawa biography, with the odd title *That Strange Little Brown Man Gandhi*. It was written by Frederick Fisher, supporter of Indian independence and former Methodist missionary bishop of India, who had retired from the bishopric to make way for the first Indian Methodist bishop. Fisher's study of Gandhi was a scathing indictment of white racism, Western imperialism, and capitalism. In it, Fisher called

96. Quoted in Seabury, *Daughter of Africa*, p. 77.
97. William Axling, *Kagawa* (New York: Harper & Brothers, 1932).

for the self-determination of all peoples, and for Christian methods as the only adequate means to fulfill the Christian ideals of human brotherhood.[98]

While the non-Western Christians who spent so much of their time between the world wars being ambassadors of "World Friendship" and Christian internationalism had motives of their own for their work as "reverse missionaries," what is clear from the historical record is that the development of an international Christian consciousness between the wars was a deliberate partnership between Western missionaries and English-speaking, well-educated non-Western Christian leaders. Returned missionaries such as Fred Fisher and "native" Christians like Toyohiko Kagawa shared an international vision, even if their backgrounds and motives differed.

3. Conclusion

This short treatment of internationalist discourse within the missionary movement in the 1920s and 1930s shows that the global vision of a cooperative, worldwide, peaceful community of different races and cultures required deliberate attention to deepen the meaning of Christianity in each culture. While internationalism was a broader movement than the missionary movement in the period under review, missionaries made a distinctive contribution to it by envisioning a Christian internationalism in which indigenization of Christianity in each culture was a central feature. As the 1920s gave way to the 1930s, optimism about the achievement of secular internationalism faded with the power of Italian, German, and Japanese fascism, Soviet communism, and nationalist movements among colonized peoples. A church-centered internationalism thrived, however, as the growing world church deepened its emphasis on indigenization. It was not a coincidence that the most prominent missionary spokespersons for internationalism of the period were also the same people who were the most committed to indigenization and devolution in mission practice. As mission practitioners, they were open to the spirit of Christ taking form in diverse cultures, and sometimes even in diverse religions, and in secular movements such as the nationalist struggle in India.

This chapter has focused on three steps taken by the missionary movement to encourage Christian internationalism and its twin, indigenization. First was

---

98. Frederick B. Fisher, *That Strange Little Brown Man Gandhi* (New York: Ray Long & Richard R. Smith, 1932), pp. 231-33. After Fisher's death, his widow Welthy Honsinger Fisher, a former missionary in China and leading speaker on internationalism, opened Literacy House in Allahabad at the request of Gandhi before he was assassinated.

the willingness to separate Christ from Western culture and to see him incarnated in varied ethnic and national contexts. While missionaries did not develop fully fledged indigenous theologies, they saw such development to be an unfolding major task for the so-called "younger churches." Second, mission groups entered into specific experiments in indigenization, including the sponsoring of indigenous Christian literature, art, architecture, liturgy, and the like. Still couched in the "liberal" internationalist discourse, it is no surprise that such experiments were accused of syncretism by both Western fundamentalists and indigenous conservative Christians. Karl Reichelt, for example, whose *Ritual Book of the Christian Church among the Friends of the Tao* was praised at the 1938 IMC meeting for its adaptation to Chinese culture, was criticized for his Cosmic Christ theology by Hendrik Kraemer.[99] If indigenizers went outside the Christian context for their points of reference, they were seen as going too far by both missionaries and nationals. With Christian internationalism the underlying reference point for indigenization projects, the day was not yet come for pluralistic, contextual theologies. Third, the missionaries worked in partnership with a group of highly educated, articulate Christian nationals who, for their own reasons, became ambassadors of internationalism and indigenization to the West.

How does the Christian internationalism of the interwar period compare with the emphasis on global Christianity in our own day? On the surface, cynics could consider both to be religious manifestations of larger movements for world unity spearheaded by materially successful, capitalist nations. Both the global agendas of the interwar period and the end of the twentieth century were driven by worldwide educated elites in partnership. While internationalism was a program for political unity, globalization has pursued a capitalistic, technological vision of world unity. A second similarity between internationalization and globalization is the tension between "top down" visions of world unity and opposing forces of nationalism or ethnic resurgence that draw strength from the global context. Militant nationalism marks both periods of history, and in both situations the Christian missionary has taken on a role as symbolic villain for anti-Western forces. As much as Christian mission organizations like to think of themselves as apolitical, they are caught inevitably in the web of human history that paints them as representatives of Western capitalism and political power.

99. See Reichelt's speech on the *Logos spermatikos*, the Cosmic Christ idea that underlay points of contact between Christianity and Buddhism. As a result of his missionary experience, Reichelt saw continuity between religions. Karl Reichelt, "The Johannine Approach," in IMC, *Authority of the Faith*, pp. 83-93.

In terms of Christian mission, the major similarity between internationalism and globalization is the strong emphasis on the indigenization of Christianity. The excitement today about the local forms of Christianity within a world church parallels that of the 1930s.[100] While missionary leaders of the interwar period lamented the lack of non-Western art and theology, by the late twentieth century non-Western theology was a thriving enterprise, though in many cases published by Western presses. Just as missionaries promoted non-Western art and literature between the wars, today Western Christian publishers sponsor non-Western theology. Although the internationalists tended to be theological moderates or liberals, today's advocates of globalization can be found in both liberal and conservative theological camps. Liberals tend to be interested in contextual theologies, while conservative evangelicals point to the global spread of evangelical Christianity into cultures all over the world. The World Council of Churches is today seen by many conservatives as a relic of a bankrupt, outdated liberal idealism. Yet as globalizing entities historically embedded in Western culture and capitalism, it may be that liberals and new conservative evangelical "world Christians" have more in common than they would like to admit.

100. Ironically, a focus on indigenization, or multi-culturalism in the church, is a critique of Western hegemony sponsored by segments of the Western church itself. In both the 1930s and the 1990s, American foundations established by rich tycoons funded research into Christianity as a global religion. Comparison of the research funded by the (liberal) Rockefeller Foundation in the 1920s and 1930s with that of the (conservative) Pew Charitable Trusts in the 1990s would be of interest.

CHAPTER 6

The Kingdom of God versus the Church:
The Debate at the Conference of the International
Missionary Council, Tambaram, 1938

SEBASTIAN C. H. KIM

Tambaram is known to many Indians because of the presence of the presti-gious Madras Christian College, the *alma mater* of many prominent Indian thinkers and theologians, and also, for those interested in mission studies, the place where the third conference of the International Missionary Council (IMC) took place in 1938. Paul Devanandan, who participated in the conference as a lay leader, commented that it was the outcome of a combina-tion of "continental theology" "tempered by American pragmatism" and "the British genius for effecting compromises." Or, as one of the Latin American participants reportedly said, "At Tambaram, the United States provided the financial machinery, the continent furnished the brains and the Great Britain claimed prestige"![1] This may be so as the main players were John Mott, the American chairman of the IMC, H. Kraemer, the Dutch theologian, and Wil-liam Paton, the British secretary of the IMC. But the unique historical context of the meeting place of India, with its religious complexity and political cli-mate of the time, produced at the conference far more diverse perspectives than the organizers initially anticipated.

The Tambaram conference is regarded as a continuation of the discus-sions of the issue of Christianity and non-Christian religions in a changing context of secularism and religious pluralism, which had already been raised at the Jerusalem conference in 1928 and in the *Laymen's Enquiry* in 1932. After

---

1. Paul Devanandan, *Guardian,* 26 January 1939.

Jerusalem, there was a growing desire among Christians involved in mission to clarify the Christian position on these issues, and as a result Hendrik Kraemer's famous book, *The Christian Message in a Non-Christian World*, was commissioned and circulated to the participants of the conference. This book understandably appears to have dominated the Tambaram conference; it was even called "Kraemer's conference" or viewed as a continuation of the Hocking-Kraemer debate of Jerusalem (a debate between liberal and neo-orthodox Barthian theologians). Consequently there have been many articles and books written from this perspective, and this is generally how it is viewed in the numerous quotations on the conference in mission studies texts.[2]

This chapter takes a somewhat different perspective. Timothy Yates rightly points out that there were two key issues at Tambaram:[3] the Christian relation to non-Christian faiths, in sections I and V,[4] and the place of the church in evangelism, in sections III and IV.[5] On consideration of these themes, it appears that the two issues are not divorced, but are bound up in the discussions at the conference. These two themes need to be viewed in a more integral way, examining one in the light of the other. This chapter will show that, though there were intensive discussions on the problem of the relationship between Christianity and other religions, this problem was treated in the light of concerns raised by the ecclesiological problem of the mission situation in the younger churches and that this was largely prompted by the problems of the churches in India. The major concerns were: the place of the church in the wider community; the problem of conversion and proselytism; and the question of the goal of mission. These were raised by the Indian dele-

---

2. See Carl F. Hallencreutz, *Kraemer Toward Tambaram: A Study in Hendrik Kraemer's Missionary Approach* (Uppsala: Gleerup, 1966); *The Ecumenical Review* 41, no. 1 (Jan. 1989); *International Review of Mission* 78, no. 307 (July 1988); Origen V. Jathanna, *The Decisiveness of the Christ-Event and the Universality of Christianity in a World of Religious Plurality: With Special Reference to Hendrik Kraemer and Alfred George Hogg as Well as to William Ernest Hocking and Pandipeddi Chenchiah* (Bern: Peter Lang, 1981); Wesley Ariarajah, *Hindus and Christians: A Century of Protestant Ecumenical Thought* (Grand Rapids: Eerdmans, 1991).

3. Timothy Yates, *Christian Mission in the Twentieth Century* (Cambridge: Cambridge University Press, 1994), pp. 117-24.

4. Section I, "The Faith by Which the Church Lives" and Section V, "The Witness of the Church in Relation to the Non-Christian Religions, Etc.," in International Missionary Council (IMC), *The Authority of the Faith*, Tambaram Madras Series, vol. 1 (London: Oxford University Press, 1939).

5. Section III, "The Unfinished Evangelistic Task," and section IV, "The Place of the Church in Evangelism," in IMC, *Evangelism*, Tambaram Madras Series, vol. 3 (London: Oxford University Press, 1939).

gates and missionaries in India and resulted in debate about the kingdom of God and the church. The situation in India demanded that the participants examine the practical problem from the perspectives of Christians in younger churches. As John Mott, in his opening speech, said, "India to-day presents the world's most instructive laboratory of Christian experience, method and adventure."[6]

1. The Emerging Politics of the Nationalist Movement and Mass Conversions of the Depressed Classes in the 1930s

In India in the twentieth century, the idea of the common religious identity of Hindus was promoted by the nationalist movement. Those who wished to integrate the politics of the nationalist movement and Hindu religion in their struggle for India's independence faced a serious challenge, however, in the conversion of increasing numbers of the depressed classes to Christianity. "Mass conversion" along the lines of caste group or community was a general pattern in the history of Christianity in India.[7] These conversions from the depressed classes in the late nineteenth century and the early twentieth century gave rise to various problems: First, conversions of the depressed classes undermined Hindu claims to religious supremacy, or at least "equal" rank with other religions, especially Christianity; therefore they were a challenge to the basis of the political framework with which the nationalists were opposing British rule. Second, both Hindu leaders and the leaders of the depressed classes saw the political potential of conversion, especially as the British Government moved in 1932 to provide a separate electorate for these people.[8] Third, despite considerable evidence to the contrary, mass conversions were seen as caused by "outsider intervention" by the missionaries for "ulterior motives," which raised strong suspicions among Hindus.

The Indian Christian leaders were initially cautious of association with the mass conversion movements because of their political sensitivity. Never-

6. John Mott, "The Possibilities of the Tambaram Meeting" in IMC, *Addresses and Other Records,* Tambaram Madras Series, vol. 7 (London: Oxford University Press, 1939), p. 6.

7. See J. Waskom Pickett, *Christian Mass Movements in India* (New York: Abingdon Press, 1933), pp. 36-57; John C. B. Webster, *The Dalit Christians: A History* (Delhi: ISPCK, 1992), pp. 33-76.

8. See Susan B. Harper, "The Politics of Conversion: The Azariah-Gandhi Controversy over Christian Mission to the Depressed Classes in the 1930's," *Indo-British Review* 15, no. 1 (1988): 147-75.

theless, some of the writings of Christian leaders show that their attitude to mass conversion was not unfavorable, and Bishop Azariah, the chairman of the (Indian) National Council of the Churches, believed that in spite of the problems there was a spiritual dimension to mass conversions that was the sovereign work of God.[9] The most significant forum for cooperative evangelism among the Protestant churches in India was the "All-India Forward Movement in Evangelism" in 1932, which was initiated by the National Council of Churches. It was very much a church-centered mission, emphasizing that the church is the "divine instrument" and that the convert should join the church to share in its privileges and responsibilities. The Council issued a series of "Calls to the Church," beginning in August 1933, to mobilize its members for evangelism. A nation-wide Protestant Christian movement developed, which was supported by churches and mission organizations.[10]

In October 1935, B. R. Ambedkar, leader of the All-India Scheduled Castes Federation and a renowned lawyer, made the unprecedented declaration that he and his followers would leave Hinduism. Indian Christian leaders, cautious about the political nature of Ambedkar's move, did not, it seems, immediately make a direct approach to him to persuade him to become a Christian.[11] It was in this context, however, that Bishop Azariah, in his third "Call to the Church" issued in January 1936, saw fit to challenge the churches in India to make a "concentrated and definite advance in evangelism." In 1936 and 1937 Gandhi's polemic against conversion became more forceful: he denounced it as the "deadliest poison that ever sapped the fountain of truth"[12] and "an error which is perhaps the greatest impediment to the world's progress toward peace."[13] The active mobilization of mass movements among the depressed classes by Indian Christian leaders created tension with Hindu leaders, and the relationship between Azariah and Gandhi especially was soured.[14]

Around the time of the Tambaran conference, there was a growing fear among Indian Christian leaders and missionaries that Hindus would use po-

---

9. "Living Forces Behind Mass Movements," *International Review of Mission (IRM)* 18, no. 72 (Oct. 1929): 509-17.

10. See J. Z. Hodge, "The Forward Movement in Evangelism," in IMC, *Evangelism*, Tambaram Madras Series, vol. 3 (London: Oxford University Press, 1939), pp. 86-115.

11. See Webster, *Dalit Christians*, pp. 109-12.

12. *Harijan*, 16 Jan. 1937.

13. *Harijan*, 30 Jan. 1937.

14. See *Harijan*, 17 April 1937. See also Susan B. Harper, *In the Shadow of the Mahatma: Bishop V. S. Azariah and the Travails of Christianity in British India* (Grand Rapids and Richmond: Eerdmans and Curzon Press, 2000), pp. 318-38.

litical means to halt conversion, as Gandhi had openly threatened more than once in his arguments against conversion.[15] In fact, in the princely state of Raigarh, the Conversion Act of 1936 required that a person seeking conversion needed to obtain a certificate of conversion from the authorities, and it disallowed preaching for the purpose of conversion. Other similar acts were to be passed by princely states in the following years.[16]

The Hindu objections to Christian conversion prompted two opposite responses from Indian Christians and missionaries. One section of the Christian community, represented by the "Rethinking Group" of Madras, saw the problem of the politicization of mass conversion and raised concern over the Christian community being confined to the church, which they saw as a Western product. They regarded the traditional missionaries' emphasis on conversion to the Christian community — and therefore change of religious affiliation by joining the church — as the root cause of the problem in Christian mission. They insisted that there must be an alternative model and goal for Christian mission: either creating an Indian church, radically different from the traditional church structure, or seeking the kingdom of God and rejecting any form of church. The other group, represented by Bishop Azariah, saw the church as the focal point of Christian living and community life and resented some Indian attempts to integrate Christian thought with Hindu religious traditions, which were the very reason for many of the lower castes' decision to convert to the Christian faith. They regarded the church, with all its weaknesses, as the Body of Christ, not simply a Western product, but a place where believers share their religious experience and grow in maturity. The church was, for them, primarily a spiritual community, which in turn would represent the kingdom of God and would be a base for witnessing to the Hindu community. These sharp differences on the church and the kingdom of God were evident in the discussions around the conference and the dominant concern for many of the participants.

---

15. *Young India*, 23 April 1931; *Harijan*, 11 May 1935.

16. See K. F. Weller, "Religious Liberty in Some Indian States," *National Christian Council Review* 66, no. 3 (March 1946): 80-81; Dhirendra K. Srivastava, *Religious Freedom in India: A Historical and Constitutional Study* (New Delhi: Deep & Deep Publications, 1982), p. 161; Donald E. Smith, *India as a Secular State* (Princeton: Princeton University Press, 1963), pp. 176-81; Rajah B. Manikam, "The Effect of the War on the Missionary Task of the Church in India," *IRM* 37, no. 142 (April 1947): 175-90.

2. The Church-Centered Mission Advocated by Hendrik Kraemer, John Mott, and V. S. Azariah

One cannot do justice to the Tambaram conference without looking at Kraemer's book, a unique preparatory work, in terms of its scope and impact, for an international conference of this nature. Responses to the book differed widely: C. F. Andrews was reported to have "unceremoniously dumped" his copy of Kraemer's book into a wastepaper basket,[17] whereas William Temple highly praised it as "the classical treatment of its theme." While Wesley Ariarajah criticizes Kraemer for "ignoring or totally rejecting the theological struggle" of the people in the mission fields,[18] Lesslie Newbigin saw the challenge Kraemer brought to the conference as marking a "turning point in the history of the Christian world mission."[19] These views clearly reflect differing perspectives on the Christian attitude to non-Christian faiths.

Kraemer's book, however, needs to be examined more closely in view of his intention in writing. The tendency in reading Kraemer's book as a textbook for a systematic theology of religions is to ignore the fact that it was written for the missionary conference as a response to growing uncertainty in the Western world about the missionary endeavor, especially as presented in the findings of the *Laymen's Report*. Kraemer was responding to more than one issue here: the liberal challenge to the validity of traditional Christian missionary approaches; the theological relationship between Christian faith and other religions; and the question of the nature of the church. In other words, his book was designed to respond to what Kraemer and many others saw as the "crisis" of mission in three ways: defining the missionary imperative (mandate, motif); asserting the clear message of Christian mission to the non-Christian world; and affirming the role and place of the church in Christian mission. Consequently, the book is an apology for mission rather than a systematic theology of religions.

As Visser 't Hooft commented, Kraemer was "the most lucid expositor of the dialectical tension of a genuine missionary approach."[20] Kraemer was eager to reaffirm the missionary mandate of the Christian church in the midst

---

17. M. Hunter Harrison, "The Study of the Relation Between Christianity and Other Religious Faiths: The Contribution of Eric J. Sharpe," in D. J. Ambalavanar, *The Gospel in the World: Essays in Honour of Bishop Kulandran* (Madras: Christian Literature Society, 1985).

18. Ariarajah, *Hindus and Christians*, p. 86.

19. Lesslie Newbigin, "A Sermon Preached at the Thanksgiving Service for the Fiftieth Anniversary of the Tambaram Conference of the International Missionary Council," *IRM* 78, no. 307 (July 1988): 328.

20. In Emilio Castro, "Editorial," *Ecumenical Review* 41, no. 1 (Jan. 1989): 1-3.

of what he saw as the contemporary challenges of religions and secularism. This emphasis on the missionary mandate of the church was explicit when Kraemer, in his concluding chapter, emphasized the purpose of the book, as to affirm (a) the fundamental position of the church as the "witness-bearing body," and (b) its missionary approach "to the great non-Christian faiths."[21] He regarded the missionary endeavor and the church as integral; therefore "apostolic consciousness" was vital in understanding the essential nature and obligation of the church toward God and the world,[22] and he insisted that missionary rethinking should aim at "re-discovering the true missionary motive and purpose."[23] He further argued that, because of this "apostolic theocentric apprehension" from God himself, the church "not only has the right but also the duty to take conversion and evangelization as prime necessities for mankind."[24] Kraemer envisaged Christian mission as mandatory for Christians and as especially applicable in the face of the contemporary challenge of secularism and religious pluralism because of his understanding that God's revelation in Christ was meant for all without distinction.[25] For this reason, he sought to establish the uniqueness of the relevance of the Christian message in the context of the pluralist world.

Kraemer's approach to people of other faiths can be summarized in his own phrase, "radical humility and downright intrepidity."[26] Bert Hoedemaker sympathetically characterized Kraemer's writings as giving the "distinct identity of the Christian mission in an age of uncertainty" and saw that there is "no contradiction between his emphasis on the uniqueness and superiority of the biblical revelation, and positive attitude toward the people of other religions."[27] Kraemer saw non-Christian religions as not merely sets of ideas about the destiny of man but as "inclusive systems and theories of life."[28] He discussed some limitations and the problem of general revelation and natural theology[29] and asserted that "every religion is a living, individual unity" and every part of it is vitally related to the whole.[30] Therefore he saw the relation-

---

21. Hendrik Kraemer, *The Christian Message in a Non-Christian World* (London: Edinburgh House Press, 1938), p. 405.
22. Kraemer, *Christian Message*, p. 33.
23. Kraemer, *Christian Message*, p. 59.
24. Kraemer, *Christian Message*, p. 294.
25. Kraemer, *Christian Message*, p. 445.
26. Kraemer, *Christian Message*, p. 128.
27. "Kraemer Reassessed," *Ecumenical Review* 41, no. 1 (Jan. 1989): 41-49.
28. Kraemer, *Christian Message*, p. 102.
29. Kraemer, *Christian Message*, pp. 103, 115.
30. Kraemer, *Christian Message*, p. 135.

ships between Christianity and other religions as fundamentally discontinuous, and regarded the only point of contact as missionaries themselves.[31] The basis of Kraemer's argument was the revelation of Christ, which he regarded as the "ultimate standard of reference" applicable to non-Christian religions as well as empirical Christianity. He made it clear that, at least for Christians, the "most fruitful and legitimate way to analyse and evaluate all religions is to investigate them in the light of the revelation of Christ" since he believed revelation consists in "fundamental conditions and relations between God, man and the world."[32]

Kraemer disputed the view that non-Christian religions are full of darkness and error and also insisted that empirical, historical Christianity itself needs to be examined in the light of Christ.[33] But when it comes to the question of "does God — and if so, how and where does God — reveal Himself in the religious life as present in the non-Christian religions?," his answer was negative. This was because of what he believed was the unique revelation in Christian religion, which means that the "universal religious consciousness" in other religions does not express this revelation in such "unmistakable and consistent terms" as Christianity.[34] This radical discontinuity not only made a theological distinction between revelation in Christ and religious experience in other religions, but also between the Christian community — the church — and other religious communities. This approach implied the missionary imperative of the church: that the only way forward for Christian mission is to expand the Christian community by presenting Christ. This is particularly in evidence in Kraemer's defense of the nature and the role of the church in Christian mission, and as we shall see, this was a key issue around which the debate of the conference focused.

In his section on missionary approaches, Kraemer made it clear that the church is vital in Christian mission to carry the message of revelation in Christ, and he insisted that the aim of missionary work is witnessing to Christian truth and building up "living Christian communities."[35] He thought that, though the kingdom of God is the "underlying and infallible hope of the Christian and a reality that works already, . . . it can never be the direct object and achievement of our labors, because it is in the hand of the Father."[36] Instead, Kraemer presented his strong support for the church and

---

31. Kraemer, *Christian Message*, pp. 136-40.
32. Kraemer, *Christian Message*, p. 110.
33. Kraemer, *Christian Message*, pp. 284-86.
34. Kraemer, *Christian Message*, pp. 111-13.
35. Kraemer, *Christian Message*, p. 287.
36. Kraemer, *Christian Message*, p. 48.

went so far as to say that the "future progress of Christianity in the non-Christian world lies in the strength and vitality of the indigenous Churches." The Christian church, he insisted, is a community *sui generis* since it is governed by Christ, the "ultimate King and Lord," and it is a "fellowship that finds its origin and ends in God's redemptive Will for the world."[37]

Kraemer's emphasis — on the missionary mandate of the church, the clear and uncompromising nature of the Christian message based on the unique revelation in Christian gospel, and church-centered mission — was also echoed by others in the conference. As Newbigin observed, Kraemer's concern was the "integrity of the Christian message" in the context of changing theological trends in the West, but more significantly, he was looking at the theological justification for Christian mission, for its motive, its contents, and its means, and relating it to the church. Therefore Kraemer's position was not that of an "unpopular minority,"[38] but rather it was in line with many who understood that Christian mission and the church were integral. Among them, John Mott and Azariah were the representatives of this church-centered mission, though they drew different implications from Kraemer's theological framework.

John Mott, the chairman of IMC and strong advocate of the missionary mandate of the church, asserted that the Tambaram meeting rested on two convictions based on two passages: "I am the Way, the Truth, and the Life" and "I, if I be lifted up, will draw all men unto me." He saw the central objective for the conference as the "building up of the Church" and "spreading of the Christian religion."[39] In the same vein, J. Z. Hodge, the secretary of the National Christian Council of India, Burma, and Ceylon, presented the report of the "Forward Movement," in which he reiterated that the church is the "divine instrument" in evangelism and that the National Christian Council "has never swerved from the conviction that in any forward movement in evangelism the Church is, and must remain, central."[40]

It was Azariah, however, who most forcefully asserted the integral nature of the church and mission and, as Carl Hallencreutz points out, Azariah's church-centered mission was reinforced by Kraemer. Azariah wanted to use this international platform for asserting his views on mass conversion, and indeed in his plenary speech he made it clear that "the Church is the divine society created by

---

37. Kraemer, *Christian Message*, p. 33.

38. See Harper, *Shadow of the Mahatma*, pp. 412-18.

39. John Mott, "The Significance of the Symposium," in John Mott, *Evangelism for the World Today: As Interpreted by Christian Leaders Throughout the World* (New York: Harper & Brothers, 1938), p. 4.

40. Hodge, "The Forward Movement in Evangelism," in IMC, *Evangelism*, pp. 117-18.

God for the continuation in the world of the work that Jesus Christ began."[41] Azariah continued to argue that, based on the "Great Commission" in the four gospels, evangelization was the divine commission and that this was given to the church just as Christ was commissioned by God: "Jesus came to save men; the Church exists to save men too"; therefore the church is the "divine instrument" of evangelism to the world.[42] In Azariah's view the Christian mission should aim at creating a mature Christian community — the local church — which itself becomes a witness. Azariah's confidence in the church was pragmatic. He saw the preaching of the gospel as the divine task of Christians and that Christ had created the Christian community — the church — for that purpose.

This identification of the church with Christ in terms of its role in the world was based on the ideal manifestation of the church rather than on the reality of the Christian community. As we will see, the emphasis at the conference on church-centered mission faced fierce criticism mainly from the Rethinking Group of Indian Christians and also from some missionaries. They believed Christian mission desperately needed an alternative model from the contemporary form of the church, which was Western, hierarchical, colonial, and a stumbling block to Indian converts.

3. The Kingdom-Centered Mission Promoted by the Rethinking Group and Missionaries

In the context of mass conversion to the Christian church and the reaction from Hindu leaders to Christian missionary approaches, there was strong disapproval of this church-centered mission. This was especially prominent when the "Rethinking Group" of Madras produced a book, *Rethinking Christianity in India*.[43] The book was interpreted by many authors as a response to Kraemer's understanding of the theology of religions, but careful examination of the book informs us differently. It appears that the authors' concern was not necessarily the theology of religions, but the practical problems of the Indian church in relation to the current debate on mass conversion: the problem of proselytism; the need for integration of the Hindu and Christian communities; the problem of Christian communalism; and the search for an alternative model for Christian mission.[44]

41. V. S. Azariah, "The Place of the Church in Evangelism," in IMC, *Evangelism*, p. 32.
42. Azariah, "Place of the Church," pp. 33-42.
43. D. M. Devasahayam and A. N. Sunarisanam, eds., *Rethinking Christianity in India* (Madras: Hogarth Press, 1938).
44. When we read the whole book, the articles are heavily concentrated on the church;

In his article "The Church and the Indian Christian," Pandipeddi Chenchiah questioned the choice of the church as the central theme of the conference. He asked openly, "By what right has Christendom all but jettisoned the kingdom of God which occupies so central a place in the message of Jesus and substituted in its place the Church of which the Master said so little?"[45] Furthermore, in his article "Jesus and Non-Christian Faiths," he raised the question, "Why should Hindu converts join the Church?" He criticized the missionaries' dogmatic view and insisted on the necessity of continuity in the life of Indian Christians in a Hindu context.[46] He went on to discuss the questions that Kraemer addressed concerning the church, the message, and the missionary mandate. First, on the issue of the church, Chenchiah saw that the problem of the church in India was that it had become "the centre of influence, the source of salvation, the object of loyalty," and it was "identified with the core and acquired as it were the same value as the original nucleus." He rejected institutional Christianity by separating Christ from Christianity, and seeking what he called the "Raw Fact of Christ."[47] His strongest criticism was that "the Church with all its claims cannot lead us to the Christ,"[48] "the Church distracts our attention from the central fact," "the Church has never been the cradle of new life,"[49] but instead "accommodator to the dominant forces of the old life."[50] In the church's place, he insisted, Indian Christianity needs "Christ, the Holy Spirit, the Kingdom of God."[51]

Second, on the Christian message to people of other faiths, Chenchiah in his critique of Kraemer's book said that the issue of inter-religious relations is not merely theological or intellectual, but "a matter of life and death," and furthermore, the Christian in India "can never understand Jesus till he understands the drama of God's dealing with man in and through the other religions of the world."[52] For this, "Indian Christians naturally look to Indian

---

out of thirteen articles, over seven deal with the church or the Christian community in India.

45. P. Chenchiah, "The Church and the Indian Christian," in Devasahayam and Sunarisanam, eds., *Rethinking*, pp. 81-2.

46. P. Chenchiah, "Jesus and Non-Christian Faiths," in Devasahayam and Sunarisanam, eds., *Rethinking*, pp. 47-49.

47. Chenchiah, "Jesus and Non-Christian Faiths," p. 53.

48. Chenchiah, "Jesus and Non-Christian Faiths," p. 53.

49. Chenchiah, "Jesus and Non-Christian Faiths," p. 55.

50. Chenchiah, "Jesus and Non-Christian Faiths," p. 60.

51. Chenchiah, "Church and the Indian Christian," p. 99.

52. Chenchiah, "The Christian Message in a Non-Christian World: A Review of Dr. Kraemer's Book," in Devasahayam and Sunarisanam, eds., *Rethinking*, pp. 1-2.

philosophy for guidance."[53] He criticized Kraemer's dogmatic approach, what he called "juridical theology," and instead emphasized the importance of faith and the Holy Spirit.[54] Agreeing with Kraemer, however, he rejected the fulfillment theory of religions since he believed that Hinduism is "not only longing but also provides satisfaction to its adherents."

Third, regarding the missionary mandate, Chenchiah argued that there are two obstacles to mission in India. One was communalism and the church, the other intolerance, and he hoped that eventually the "social intolerance of the Hindu and excessive zeal of the missionary may disappear in India."[55] In order to achieve this, he argued that conversion should be separated from church membership. That is, he saw conversion as a change of life without insisting on affiliation to the church because he viewed mission as a "movement in the Hindu social fold" rather than the creation of "a solid society outside."[56] He strongly objected to either individual or mass conversion to the Christian church, but supported a Christian mission in India that was "prepared to see the gradual infusion of Hinduism by Christian ideals and above all Christian life" by creating "a powerful Christian atmosphere within Hinduism." He saw the heart of Christian mission as the creation of "new life" as demonstrated in the life of Jesus, which he believed was able to fulfill the "unrealised longing for a life here" of the Hindus.[57]

In similar vein, Vengal Chakkarai, another key figure in the Rethinking Group, asserted that the church had arisen out of the historical setting of Western Christianity and that Indian Christians are not obliged to follow its pattern. Whatever the positive elements of the church might be, they cannot be included in the "revelation of Christ Himself" since they are not eternal and not of "divine essence." Therefore the church should be inspiration, not institution, and the institutionalized church, for Chakkarai, is "the tents put up by our Western friends; but they can never be our permanent habitation." Instead, he emphasized that Indian Christians should seek the kingdom of God which the Lord "announced and for which He gave His life."[58]

The rejection of the institutionalized church and mass conversion to the church was a common feature of the Rethinking Group, and this was supported by some missionaries. These were C. F. Andrews, E. Stanley Jones, and

---

53. Chenchiah, "Christian Message," p. 10.
54. Chenchiah, "Christian Message," pp. 20-22.
55. Chenchiah, "Christian Message," p. 44.
56. Chenchiah, "Christian Message," p. 44.
57. Chenchiah, "Christian Message," pp. 50-52.
58. Quoted by Chenchiah, "Christian Message," pp. 119-23.

A. G. Hogg, each of whom attended the conference and tried to respond to the problem of mass conversion and its political implications in India. Although their approaches and theologies are quite different, the solution they came to was seeking the kingdom of God, in the sense of promoting Christian values in Indian society.

During the conference, the most vocal opponent to Kraemer was A. G. Hogg, who had just retired as principal of Madras Christian College, and who challenged Kraemer's notions of discontinuity, Christian revelation, and the Christian attitude to people of other religions. Hogg distinguished faith, which he regarded as the religious life in other religions, from faiths, which are complexes of spiritual, ethical, intellectual, and social elements of religions. He insisted that the religious life, faith, is "hid in God" in people of other religions; therefore the missionary attitude toward non-Christian faiths should not be only "respect or admiration" but a "religious reverence," believing that this faith is the holy ground of communion between God and man. Just as Kraemer separated the revelation of Christ from empirical Christianity, Hogg opposed the idea of identifying faith (the divine initiative of self-disclosure) with its empirical forms, since he was convinced that there must be a divine response to human seeking.[59]

The greatest difference between Kraemer and Hogg was that Hogg believed "God reveals Himself," not ready-made truths about himself, in both Christian and non-Christian faiths.[60] He asserted that Christianity is unique not because of unique occurrence of revelation but because of the unique content (Christ) of revelation. In other words, it is Christ that matters, and whether he was revealed in Christianity or non-Christian religions is secondary. Responding to Kraemer, however, Hogg used the philosophical analysis of separating faith and faiths, just as Kraemer separated Christ from Christianity. They both tried to present Christ in the non-Christian context but in different ways. The question is not whether one is arrogant and the other is not — they both struggled to find appropriate means to present the gospel with respect to people of other faiths. Kraemer saw that by acknowledging the differences and discontinuity, Christians could respect the separate integrity of other religions, and that the only way to present Christ was through proclaiming the gospel and incorporating converts into the body of Christ, the church. Hogg, however, understood that there was clear continuity in terms of faith (singular) and in that Christ was somehow present himself in the

---

59. A. G. Hogg, "The Christian Attitude to Non-Christian Faith," in IMC, *The Authority of the Faith*, pp. 102-25.

60. Hogg, "Christian Attitude," p. 108.

Hindu context, without the aid of the church or missionaries, so he held that Hinduism was capable of bearing God's revelation directly, the content of which is Christ. Both Hogg and Kraemer were missionaries and their concern was to understand other faiths and how to approach them; therefore O. V. Jathanna's observation that Kraemer and Hogg were basically in agreement was not unjustified perception.[61]

4. The Church Versus the Kingdom of God in Christian Mission

As a result of two-and-a-half weeks of intensive discussions and reflections, the participants of each section drew up their findings. The findings of sections III and IV affirmed the conference's strong position that the church and mission are inseparable; the church "must so present Christ Jesus to the world . . . that men shall come to put their trust in God through Him their Saviour and serve Him as their Lord in the fellowship of His Church."[62] Moreover, even in the findings of sections I and V, we find strong support for the church and mission. It was stated that although the church should "only be obedient to the will of the Good Shepherd" and "proclaim the Kingdom of God," it should also "call men of all faiths by word and deed into the one life of the Beloved Community," that is, the church. Regarding the goal of missionary work, it rejected the "permeation" of the gospel as the goal of Christian mission but found that the "end and aim of our evangelistic work is not achieved until all men everywhere are brought to a knowledge of God in Jesus Christ and to a saving faith in Him."

Furthermore, although members affirmed that other religions do contain values resulting from deep religious experience and great moral achievement, the findings stated, "yet we are bold enough to call men out from them to the feet of Christ. We do so because we believe that in Him alone is the full salvation which man needs."[63]

Reporting the Tambaram conference, William Paton, the secretary of IMC, rightly pointed out that, although there were clear differences in understanding of the Christian attitude to non-Christian religions, "there was no shadow of difference in their sense of the overpowering obligation to make known the Gospel to all mankind, nor upon the uniqueness both of the Per-

61. Jathanna, *The Decisiveness of the Christ-Event*, pp. 291-99.

62. *The World Mission of the Church* (London: IMC, 1939), pp. 32-46.

63. *The World Mission of the Church*, pp. 46-55. See the response from E. Stanley Jones in the *Guardian*, 9 March 1939. Jones had been a strong voice among missionaries who emphasized the importance of the kingdom of God over against the church.

son of the redeemer and of His saving work."[64] In other words, the theological differences were evident in the question of where and how God is revealed in non-Christian religions and in what degree the non-Christian religions, as total systems of thought and life, manifest God's revelation, but the imperative of presenting Christ to the people of other faiths was not in question, at least among the participants of the conference. As Devanandan rightly observed, the missionary mandate during the conference was so dominant that the question of the relationship between Christianity and other faiths became secondary.[65] Therefore the criticism of Ariarajah that Kraemer himself was in "total discontinuity" from what had been achieved in Edinburgh and Jerusalem in terms of Christian relations to non-Christian faiths does not really reflect what went on at the conference.[66] As we have seen in the debate, the participants in the conference were in agreement about the necessity of presenting Christ to people of other faiths, though their approaches were different according to their theological orientation. The idea of inter-religious dialogue was not ready to take root in the Tambaram conference; there was still a one-way approach of presenting Christ to non-Christians, and the differences were in terms of how to do so, whether through individual or mass conversion or through permeation of Christian values in society, whether through the church, the visible community, or the kingdom of God.

The theological question of the kingdom of God and the church is important when it comes to missionary endeavor because it relates to the practical life of the converts in their relationship with their past religious experiences and the wider community. The Rethinking Group represented Christians of a higher-caste background who regarded the Hindu tradition as part of their heritage, and did not wish to be excluded from the wider Hindu society. They also saw themselves as sharing a common identity with Hindus in their search for the welfare of India and its people in a time of national struggle against colonial rule. These approaches are recurring themes of Indian theologians, and they arise out of their sincere attempt to solve the problems of communalism and proselytism, for which they saw the church in its Western pattern and theology as responsible. Their arguments, however, need to be examined in the light of the critique from the Christians of a lower-caste background. Just before the Tambaram conference, the Christians of the Scheduled Castes issued a statement addressed to the conference

64. "The Meeting of the International Missionary Conference at Tambaram, Madras," *IRM* 28, no. 110 (April 1939): 168.
65. *Guardian*, 27 Jan. 1939.
66. See Ariarajah, *Hindus and Christians*, p. 87.

that strongly accused the church of caste discrimination, saying that "untouchability, and even inapproachability is still practiced against us by the 'advanced castes' still within the Church even after we have been thoroughly Christianized."[67] The problem seen by these Christians was not the Western form of the church, but that the Christian community tolerated the Indian problem of caste discrimination, which they saw as contradictory to the gospel of Christ. The solution to the problem, for them, did not lie in creating an Indian church separate from wider Christian traditions, nor in seeking the alternative model of the kingdom of God, but rather they wished to see the kingdom values of equality and dignity manifested within the existing Indian churches.

The group represented by Bishop Azariah addressed the concerns of people of lower-caste background, and saw the value of the manifested Christian community in its ideal outcome. As J. W. Pickett and Azariah made clear in their presentations in the conference, they were very much encouraged by the transformed life of the converts in the church.[68] However, Kraemer and Azariah were on weak ground when they argued that the kingdom cannot be the goal of mission because it can never be identified with any social, economic, political, and cultural order because this was, in Kraemer's words, making a relative absolute.[69] The kingdom is not confined to a spiritual realm of life but represents the whole spectrum of human experience, just as the church is not only a human institution, as Kraemer and others argued. Furthermore, there was a tendency to regard the church as the goal of mission, as we saw in Azariah's writing. The main problem that Kraemer's exclusive claim of Christian revelation and Azariah's church-centered mission faced in the Indian context is that they led logically to the Christian community becoming an exclusive society separated from the wider community. As a result, rather than presenting Christ to the people of other faiths, as they claimed, their exclusive claims resulted in the isolation of the Christian community from the wider Hindu community. There was no point of contact or common ground for Hindus and Christians to meet in this context. The only option was for Hindus to be shifted (converted) into the Christian community. The concept of the kingdom of God gives theological and sociological space for those who wish to follow Christ and share kingdom values, but yet find it hard to fit into the structured church, and this is possible because of the fact

---

67. *Indian Social Reformer*, 24 December 1938.

68. See J. W. Pickett in "Recent evangelistic work in India," in IMC, *Evangelism*, pp. 63-86; Azariah, "Place of the Church," pp. 32-47.

69. Kraemer, *Christian Message*, pp. 77, 430.

that Christ is not bound by the church. It is also possible because the work of the Holy Spirit, as Chenchiah pointed out, transcends and is not limited to the church.[70]

The debate at Tambaram was the result of a painstaking search to answer the question of what it means to be Christian and to follow Christ, who preached the kingdom of God and also shared his life with the community of believers. What is the place of the church and the kingdom of God in Christian mission? The Christian church, in spite of its weaknesses, or rather because of them, can bear witness to Christ and continue to be a place for worship and sharing. The church as a visible community, rather than a hindrance, can make an impact on the wider community; and more importantly, the Christian community need not be understood merely in a functional way, but as the body of Christ and therefore of the essence of the gospel. On the other hand, the church constantly needs to be shaped and challenged by the kingdom perspective that there is a hope in Christ beyond the boundaries of the exclusive visible community of believers. The kingdom of God is not limited by historical and cultural traditions of religious affiliation, but open to the possibilities in Christ who has called believers to be part of his ongoing "new creation."

As we have seen, one group insisted on the radical discontinuity between Christianity and Hinduism, holding the notion of continuity between the wider Christian church and the Indian church, whereas the other group asserted the continuity between the two religious traditions but argued that there should be clear discontinuity between the two church traditions. In the case of the debate on the kingdom of God and the church, it may not be plausible to insist on sharp discontinuity or continuity. Rather, it is more reasonable to see them as complementary; both are found in the scriptures and each needs to be understood in the light of the other. The problem of the kingdom of God and the church in mission is not just confined to Indian Christianity in the 1930s; it is a recurring discussion for those engaged in Christian mission in many other contexts. This is particularly noticeable as we examine the tension between the "global processes and local identities" of contemporary Christianity. The struggle of Indian Christians is a part of this ongoing problem, and the debate may shed some light on our search to interpret contemporary Christianity.

---

70. See Chenchiah, "Church and the Indian Christian," p. 99.

PART III

Domestication, Tooling, and Reinvention: Ministerial Formation

CHAPTER 7

New Evangelical Universities:
Cogs in a World System or Players in a New Game?

JOEL CARPENTER

There is no other event in the world quite like a university convocation. Esteemed members of the faculty, board, and administration — dressed in colorful regalia, bearing mace and medallion — salute, admonish, and encourage the students, whose uniform apparel can scarcely diminish their smiling faces and brimming hearts. Given the worldwide reach of higher education, few celebrations have such global universality today. These academic ceremonies are as likely to be celebrated in Bombay or Banjul as in Boston. Indeed, higher education is one of the most striking contemporary forms of globalization. Universities, one might argue, form a system of interdependent links involving both sovereign states and economic institutions in the exchange of students, professors, ideas, technology, and money. Emanating historically from a still-influential North Atlantic core, this great "knowledge industry" reaches around the globe in complex networks of institutional interaction.[1]

Comparative studies of global higher education abound, but there are some new participants in this vast and complicated enterprise who may surprise even some of its more careful observers. From Seoul, San Salvador, and even the shores of the Baltic, some new universities are arising, and they are coming from an unexpected source, the varied expressions of revivalist Christianity. "Evangelical University" may look like an oxymoron to the aver-

---

1. Lawrence J. Saha, "Universities and National Development: Issues and Problems in Developing Countries," in Zaghloul Morsy and Philip G. Altbach, eds., *Higher Education in an International Perspective: Critical Issues,* International Bureau of Education Studies on Education, vol. 3 (New York and London: Garland Publishing, Inc., 1996), pp. 80-89.

age academic, who knows that the world in which she lives and moves is resolutely secular, and that evangelicals, however defined, operate from a quite different angle of vision.[2] Yet there are new universities arising out of Protestant movements for evangelization and spiritual renewal in many parts of the world. Using the scattered and fugitive materials most readily available for charting these new agencies, I discovered forty-one evangelical Protestant, degree-granting institutions of the arts, sciences, and professions that have been founded outside of North America and Western Europe since 1980. No doubt there are more, because this movement is quite dynamic, and new institutions often escape detection from afar. Yet virtually anywhere in the world that a significant pentecostal, charismatic, or other evangelical movement has taken root, it is now engaged in higher education beyond the training of church workers.[3]

Any attempt to investigate the relationship between the spread of evangelical forms of Christianity in the non-Western world and the forces of global-

2. Even in the United States, where evangelical Christian movements have been around for a long time and church-related colleges and universities are common, the idea of an evangelical presence in academic life seems incongruous and newsworthy in intellectual circles. See Alan Wolfe, "The Opening of the Evangelical Mind," *Atlantic Monthly* (Oct. 2000): 55-76.

3. My hastily improvised research method was to search in the correspondence files of the Council for Christian Colleges and Universities (CCCU) in Washington, DC, and on the websites of the Overseas Council for Theological Education and Missions, the United Board for Christian Higher Education in Asia, and the International Association for the Promotion of Christian Higher Education. Then I posted a query to the e-mail distribution network of the 100 CCCU institutions' academic officers. It yielded more leads, as did further informal personal networking and scores of hours on the Internet, both running down leads with search engines and searching through international listings of universities.

My list of forty-one evangelical universities includes new institutions founded by older Protestant traditions, such as the Methodists, Mennonites, or Anglicans, based on the impression that the new universities reflected the impact of revival movements within those traditions. It excludes new Catholic and Orthodox universities.

It also excludes, perhaps with less justification, the Seventh Day Adventists. This tradition has a substantial record of founding colleges and universities all over the world. Since the 1890s, Adventist missionaries and local SDA church leaders have founded forty degree-granting colleges outside of the North Atlantic region, and a dozen of these were founded since 1980. My source of information is a directory of Adventist educational institutions and personnel, kindly provided by John N. McDowell, vice-president for academic administration at Canadian University College, College Heights, Alberta.

Many of the citations following will be from websites on the Internet. Since these sites are updated periodically and materials appear and disappear, I have printed copies of each source cited and will make items available upon request.

ization would do well to consider these educational movements. They are responding to global economic and political conditions, and they are addressing local dynamics as well. Evangelical universities raise questions, furthermore, about globalization of the more religious sort. Are these new universities the latest occasion for non-Western churches to experience dependency and domination from churches in the West, or do they mark the imminent end of neo-colonial Christianity? Given the pervasively secular character of higher education worldwide and the tensions between Christian values and global economic imperatives, what are the prospects for these new institutions to sustain their religious view of reality and promote a Christian mission in the world?[4] This chapter will offer some preliminary responses to these questions, even as it pursues its more basic task of providing an initial reconnaissance of a little-known movement.

1. New Universities in the Making: A Global Tour

The new evangelical universities are not evenly distributed around the world. I found eleven in Latin America and the Caribbean, ten in sub-Saharan Africa, four in Eastern Europe and the former Soviet Union, one in India, one in Thailand, four in Indonesia, one in Taiwan, one in Japan, and eight in South Korea. A worldwide survey of these universities and their varied contexts would take us beyond the constraints of this chapter, which will concentrate on the three most active contemporary venues: Latin America and the Caribbean, sub-Saharan Africa, and South Korea.

Latin America

Each region of the globe presents a different context for the development of Christian higher education, but Latin America and the Caribbean are definitely "hot spots." The rapid growth of pentecostal and other evangelical movements over the past three decades seems to have provided Latin America with the critical mass of prospective students, faculty, and leaders to make universities possible. Several of the new institutions were formed from earlier educational efforts of missionaries and local Christian leaders. The Universidad Evangelica de las Americas (UNELA), in San José, Costa Rica,

4. I must thank my conference respondent, David Zac Niringiye, for sharpening these questions.

came about in 1999 as a merger of a thirty-year-old study center that was a partnership of local and expatriate mission theologians, and a collegiate venture that the Church of the Nazarene started in 1992 from a pre-existing theological school, but then abandoned. The Universidad Evangelica Boliviana (UEB), chartered in 1982, likewise is the creation of seven national evangelical organizations and five North American missions to "prepare young people for service as responsible citizens, intellectuals, and Christians." The Universidad Cristiana Latinoamerica, however, founded by Methodists in Quito, Ecuador, in 1992, is wholly home-grown and independent of expatriate missionary organizations.[5]

The university incubation process in Latin America seems to have produced its share of failures. There were several attempts in the Dominican Republic between 1960 and 1980 to form an evangelical university. Each succumbed to various pressures, including a government suppression of evangelicals and a mail fraud case. Yet it looks as though a core of viable institutions is being formed across the region, among them the Universidad Nacional Evangelica (UNEV) in the Dominican Republic, founded in 1986 by the survivors of the earlier attempts. UNEV has 1,300 students on three campuses and seems firmly established.[6] The Universidad Evangelica de El Salvador (UEES), in San Salvador, founded in 1981, is also well established, with degree programs in medicine, dentistry, agriculture, education, and a variety of arts and sciences.[7]

In recent years there have been efforts to develop a network of mutual support and accountability among the region's evangelical universities. In July 1997, Latin American educators from seventeen nations came to Bolivia at the invitation of Universidad Evangelica Boliviana to initiate such conversations. They agreed to do some networking and investigation to find like institutions. Two years later they reconvened at Santa Cruz de la Sierra in Bolivia to form the Consortium of Evangelical Universities in Latin America (CONDUCE). This organization included the universities in Bolivia, the Dominican Republic, and El Salvador as charter members, plus three other evangelical universities, including ones from Paraguay and Nicaragua, and a

5. Clifton L. Holland, "Evangelical University of the Americas (UNELA) Financial Development Plan," found at www.prolades.com; "Reseña Historica de la UEB," found at www.ueb.bo/historia/; interview by the author with Dr. Patricio Proano, rector of the Universidad Cristiana de Latinoamerica, in Orlando, Florida, 9 February 2001.

6. John William Medendorp to Joel Carpenter, 8 June 2001.

7. "Facultades" and "Descripción de la Universidad," found at www.ees.edu.sv; "The Evangelical University of El Salvador: A Project Made a Reality," document from the CCCU files, Universidad Evangelica de El Salvador folder.

second institution in Bolivia.[8] CONDUCE is a fragile entity, and it remains to be seen whether it can function effectively across so many nations and miles. The ongoing existence of Latin American evangelical universities, however, is not in doubt. Some of the older ones are major regional fixtures by now. La Universidad de Mariano Galvez (founded in 1966) in Guatemala City now has about 15,000 students, while the Methodist University of Piracicaba, Brazil (founded in 1975), now enrolls some 12,000 students on four campuses.[9]

Africa

The environment for creating evangelical universities is ripe to bursting point in parts of sub-Saharan Africa. I found ten colleges and universities formed over the past two decades by evangelicals from a variety of traditions and movements.[10] Daystar University, a nondenominational evangelical institution, was the pioneer and the prototype of this movement. Daystar began in Southern Rhodesia (Zimbabwe) in the late 1960s as an institute offering studies in communications. It added master's degree courses in the late 1970s (via Wheaton College in Illinois), and an undergraduate degree program in 1984 (via Messiah College in Pennsylvania). Daystar received its university charter from the Kenyan government in 1994, and now enrolls 1,900 students from twenty-eight countries in eight undergraduate majors and four master's programs. Business administration and communications are leading programs.[11] Daystar continues to receive millions of dollars from abroad in support of its ambitious growth, but support from the region is considerable as well.

It is no accident that Daystar eventually relocated to a site near Nairobi. The Kenyan capital is also Africa's ecumenical, missionary, and parachurch

8. "Christian Higher Education in Latin America," *CCCU News*, September 1997, online edition www.cccu.org/news; *"Miembro Enviado,"* 29 July 1999, found at www.forocristiano.com.

9. Universidad Mariano Galvez de Guatemala *(Informacion General y Procedimientos),* 1-3, and David R. Sanford to Robert C. Andringa, 16 September 1997; both in CCCU files, Universidad Mariano Galvez de Guatemala folder; "Reflecting the Past and Projecting the Future," "Affirming Our Identity," and "Four Campuses," all found at www.unimep.br/english.

10. At the conference where this paper was presented, several participants told me of other efforts of which they were aware, but I have not been able to document them.

11. *Operations Report: All the Important Facts About Daystar University: Situation as of March 31, 1997,* a document co-prepared by Daystar University and the SF Foundation, CCCU files, Daystar University folder; "Daystar University," "Our History," "Our Programs," found at www.daystarus.org.

ministries capital, and home to hundreds of highly educated African Christian leaders, both from the region and the continent as a whole. Bible schools and seminaries abound in the Nairobi area, and additional universities are springing up, such as Africa Nazarene University (founded in 1993), which now enrolls 490 students from fourteen nations; and Hope Africa University (founded in 2000), a fledgling Free Methodist school that started in an abandoned dance hall with twenty-seven students.[12] Nairobi is also home to the Catholic secretariat for Africa. In addition to a variety of theological schools, the Catholics operate Strathmore College, a business college created from a merger of older schools and placed on a new campus in 1992; and the Catholic University of East Africa, organized in Karen in 1984.[13]

Elsewhere in East Africa, a number of evangelical universities have appeared recently, notably the Kenya Methodist University in Meru, near Mount Kenya; and Meserete Kristos College in Addis Ababa, Ethiopia, founded in 1997 by the Meserete Kristos Church, an Ethiopian Mennonite fellowship. Much closer to Nairobi is St. Paul's University in Limuru, Kenya. This endeavor was launched in 1999 to build an undergraduate arts and professions program onto an old and distinguished Protestant ecumenical seminary (founded in 1903). Leading the expansion of St. Paul's is Godfrey Nguru, the resourceful former deputy vice-chancellor (Academic) of Daystar.[14]

Time will tell whether old theological seminaries make good bases for building evangelical universities, but St. Paul's is the second seminary in the region to try it. The first was Uganda Christian University, launched in 1997 with the Archbishop of Canterbury, George Carey, laying its cornerstone at the campus of the old Bishop Tucker Theological College (founded in 1923) in Mukono, not far from Kampala. Like African University in Zimbabwe and Daystar University, Uganda Christian University (UCU) has a support foundation in the United States. UCU has grown rapidly to 975 students, and now

12. "Africa Region Institutions," found at www.nazarene.org/iboe/africaninstitutions/africauniversity.htm; Mark R. Moore to Karen Longman, 4 June 1999, and memorandum from Rich Gathro to Jennifer Jukanovich and Ron Mahurin, 7 December 2000, both in CCCU files, African Nazarene University folder; "A Brief History of HAU," "About HAU," "Giving to HAU," "Chancellor's Report," and Bishop Emeritus Gerald E. Bates, "Report on Visit to HAU," all found at www.greenville.edu/hau.

13. "Directory of Catholic Institutions of Higher Education in Africa," found at www.rc.net/africa/catholicafrica/education.htm.

14. "Distinction Between Two Universities in Africa Confusing to Some United Methodists," United Methodist News Service, 15 September 1997, found at www.unms.umc.org/news97; Neal Lettinga to Joel Carpenter, 5 January 2001 (re: Meserete Kristos); Godfrey Nguru to Robert C. Andringa, 18 November 1998, CCCU files, St. Paul's United Theological College folder.

offers majors in education, social work, business, law, and communications as well as divinity. The college's growth came in spite of trying conditions on campus, notably a non-potable water supply and frequent power outages.[15] UCU leaders are well aware, as are those at other evangelical institutions in East Africa, of the religiously plural environment in which their schools compete. New Catholic institutions such as the Uganda Martyrs University, which opened auspiciously in 1994 with the blessing of Uganda's President Museveni, form part of this context. There are several new Islamic universities in the region as well. UCU's vice-chancellor, Stephen Noll, is encouraged that his institution's rapid growth has kept it "nose-to-nose," he says, with the new Islamic university in Mbale.[16]

Southern Africa shows a strikingly different picture. It has both a sturdy network of theological seminaries and Bible colleges, and a powerful array of secular universities and technical institutes. Creating universities out of Bible colleges or seminaries has been more daunting in this region than in tropical Africa, but several such moves are underway. The Africa Bible College in Lilongwe, Malawi, is just starting the process, but the Christian College of Southern Africa, in Harare, Zimbabwe, is quite far along. The latter now enrolls 3,000 with courses in computing, administration, accounting, and communications. The much smaller Cape Evangelical Bible College, located near Cape Town, South Africa, recently renamed itself Cornerstone Christian College and developed programs in management and counseling.[17]

None of these initiatives, however, can match the curricular depth or ability to attract support of their new regional neighbor, Africa University (AU), an upstart Methodist institution in eastern Zimbabwe. The university began in 1992 with forty students and degree programs in theology, agriculture, and natural resources management. In the academic year 1999-2000, AU enrolled 871 students from eighteen African countries. New degree programs now include education, humanities and social sciences, and management and administration.[18] AU is the fulfillment of a dream expressed by the African

---

15. "An Anglican University for Africa," "Uganda Christian University," "Uganda Partners Newsletter," found at www.ugandapartners.org.

16. "History and Mission Statement of Uganda Martyrs University," found at www.fiuc.org/umu; Noll quoted in "Uganda Partners Newsletter," cited above.

17. Stanton Jones to Joel Carpenter, 4 January 2001 (Africa Bible College); "Christian College of Southern Africa: Fact Sheet on CCOSA," appendix to letter from Bill Warner to Robert Andringa, 24 October 2000, CCCU files, Christian College of Southern Africa folder; "Cornerstone Christian College: 2001 Profile," found at www.octeam.org.

18. Andra Stevens, "2000 Graduating Class Largest in Africa University History," United Methodist News Service, 5 July 2000. Found at www.umns.umc.org.

Bishops Conference of the Methodist Church back in the 1980s, and it has become a favorite cause of Methodists in the United States. Millions of dollars have been invested already in the campus at Mutare, 175 miles northeast of Harare. Various American Methodist groups, the American government's USAID program, and private foundations have provided buildings, scholarships, laboratories, and six endowed chairs.[19]

West Africa is a seedbed of rapidly growing pentecostal churches and ministries, with signs, wonders, and Bible schools following. The Central University College (CUC) in Accra, Ghana, arose in 1997 out of a pre-existing Bible college. It is the educational work of the International Central Gospel Church, one of the most prominent of the new independent pentecostal churches in Africa. Its pastor and the university chancellor is the Rev. Dr. Mensa Otabil, an ardent advocate of African self-reliance and an Afrocentric understanding of the Bible and the Church's mission.[20] In marked contrast to African University, the Central University College is for the most part locally funded. Its 1,350 fee-paying students study for bachelor's degrees in business administration, accounting, finance, agribusiness, or theology and missions in a "worker-friendly" environment that offers courses in two shifts, morning and evening, plus a weekend college.[21]

There probably are other institutions like Central University College in Accra that are making the leap from Bible school to university curricula, but my lines of communication have not reached them. There must be more like the Canaan Christian University, a Bible training institution in Lagos, Nigeria, located "behind the Shobor Alluminium [sic] Co., Ltd.," or the True Love Christian College in Ikot Ekpene, Nigeria, that are aspiring to "teach the nations" and "advance the kingdom of God on earth" beyond their current capacities.[22]

---

19. "A brief history," found at www.umc.org/benevol/AfricaUniversity/history.htm; "USAID Grants $2.98 Million to Build Library at Africa University," United Methodist News Service, 24 September 1997; "Pastor Sees Africa University as Hope Against Further Polarization," United Methodist News Service, 14 September 1999; both found at www.umns.umc.org.

20. Christian van Gorder, "Beyond the Rivers of Ethiopia: The Afrocentric Pentecostalism of Mensa Otabil," paper presented at the conference, "Christianity as a World Religion," Calvin College, Grand Rapids, Michigan, 26-28 April 2001.

21. "A Brief History of CUC," and E. K. Larbi, "The Challenges of Leadership," speech delivered by the vice-chancellor on the third matriculation ceremony of Central University College, 13 January 2001, both found at www.centraluniversity.org.

22. Nse E. Ukpong, Essiet E. Akpan, and Monday E. Ukpong to Myron Augsberger, 7 September 1993, CCCU files, True Love Christian College folder; Mike Adeniran to Robert Andringa, 25 November 1996, CCCU files, Canaan Christian University folder.

Africa is not an easy environment in which to launch such endeavors, however. A hopeful letter sent to colleagues in the United States in the spring of 1993 announced the intentions of the Evangelical Friends, Methodists, and pentecostals in Rwanda to open the Protestant University of Central Africa in September of 1994. I am guessing that these efforts expired during the genocidal ethnic violence that erupted earlier that year. Even in a more stable environment, great aspirations can be forestalled. The Hatfield Christian Church, an independent megachurch in Pretoria, announced in July of 1993 that it would be building out its Training Centre into The King's University, with dreams of eventually serving 5,000 students. Something may be happening on that front today, but I could find no evidence of it.[23] Even so, with the movement to charter private universities catching on across the continent, additional evangelical universities surely will be founded.

South Korea

We end our survey of emerging evangelical universities in South Korea, where every kind of church-related college and university exists and the situation is quite dynamic. Like many Asian nations, South Korea has sustained a long and intense buildup of higher education, beginning with mission-sponsored institutions in the late nineteenth century. As in the other nations, the government has become a prominent force in higher education, but the South Korean Christian communities continue to found new universities, and some of them have developed very rapidly. Christian-founded universities in South Korea cover the entire spectrum of academic prowess and Christian commitment. Yonsei University, at one end of the spectrum, is a century old, academically distinguished, and largely secular. Hansei University, at the other end, was founded as a Bible school by the Assemblies of God in 1953, is now affiliated with the world-famous Yoido Full Gospel Church in Seoul, and attained university status only recently, in 1997.[24] I found eight evangelical universities of recent vintage: Hansei University, Handong University (founded in 1995), Kangnam University (accredited university status, 1992), Chongshin University (accredited university status, 1995), Chonan University (founded in 1994), Korea Nazarene University (accredited university status, 1999), SungKyul

23. Willard C. Ferguson to Myron Augsberger, 29 April 1993, CCCU files, Protestant University of Central Africa folder; K. B. Murray to Karen Longman, 8 July 1993, and *The King's University: A Significant and Challenging Project Gains Momentum,* undated brochure, CCCU files, King's University folder.

24. "Mission Statement," found at www.yonsei.ac.kr/eng-www/sub/welcome.

Christian University (accredited university status, 1991), and Hoseo University (accredited university status, 1988). These new evangelical institutions run the range from Kangnam, which is only recently expanding out from a base in theology and social work; to Chonan, a comprehensive university with some 15,000 students in thirty-four undergraduate and nine graduate programs; and Hoseo, billed as a "Christian Polytechnic University," with 520 faculty members and over 10,000 students.[25]

One of the most dramatic stories of academic development is that of Handong University, which opened in 1995 with 400 students, and now has a student body of 2,300. Handong's curriculum now includes about twenty undergraduate majors in two divisions — Engineering and Humanities and the Social Sciences — and five graduate programs in similar fields. Handong has a very strong emphasis on technology, shaped no doubt by its president, Kim Young-gil, an award-winning nuclear engineer in both the United States and Korea. Blessed with distinguished and visionary leaders and attracting a very strong student body, Handong won national awards for excellence three years running, which paved the way for government grants and continued growth.[26]

Handong's board chairman and the former national prime minister, Lee Young-duk, asserted that Handong must not only produce professionals, but "people whose lives are free of shame." The university's website masthead proclaimed that Handong seeks to combine "academic training geared for today's global and information market with moral training to develop personal dignity." Spiritual formation, the integration of faith and learning, and character education are to be the hallmarks of a Handong education.[27]

What a sad irony, then, that the spring of 2001 brought great distress to the campus. On Teacher's Day, a traditional Korean celebration each May for students to honor their mentors, thirty buses filed out from the Handong campus and deposited 1,500 students, 200 parents, and scores of professors

25. "Introduction," found at www.han.ac.kr/english/introduction; "Message from the President of the Board," "General Introduction," found at http://sheep.kangnam.ac.kr/eng/a; "General Information," "Academic Information," "Introduction of the Department: University," found at www.chongshin.ac.kr/eng; Chonan University, 2000-2001 (Chungnam, Korea: Chonan University, 2000); David Strawn to Joel Carpenter, 4 January 2001; "Asia Pacific Region Institutions: Korea Nazarene University," found at www.nazarene.org/iboe/asiapacificinstit/koreanazuniv.htm; "Message from the President," "University Information," found at www.syungkyul.ac.kr/english/information; "A Glimpse of Hoseo: The Past and the Present," "Hoseo's Millennium Vision," found at www.hoseo.ac.kr/eng.

26. "History and Important Facts," and "Admission Requirements," both found at www.han.ac.kr/english.

27. "Chairman and President," found at same Handong website.

outside Kyongju prison. President Kim and Vice-President Oh were incarcerated there, after being convicted of embezzling university funds. The crowd sang and wept, pledged their love and support, and left carnations, signifying their gratitude. Korean newspaper editorials suggested that the officials' alleged mishandling of restricted funds involved no personal thievery, but was rather the result of two earnest and dedicated teachers trying to make ends meet in a school growing faster than its resources. That they were in jail said more about their local political enemies than about their character.[28] Indeed, these cases were summarily overturned by an appellate court in the fall of 2001. Nevertheless, the resistance among local leaders in Handong's home province shows that there are powerful interests working against intentionally Christian universities in South Korea.[29]

South Korea is an education-revering society, in which universities are endlessly ranked and categorized, and where one's university credentials mark one for life. Its best universities are among the finest in the world, and new institutions are driven to improve their academic quality and to prove their worthiness. Seoul National University, the state-founded flagship, sets the standard, and Christian professors there and elsewhere are prone to question the wisdom of establishing new evangelical universities.[30] Nevertheless, new ones appear regularly. Most of them evolve from Bible colleges and theological seminaries, with their emergence marking the aspirations of their host religious movements and denominations. Korea's church history has been marked by steady growth and frequent fragmentation, and each new group seeks via higher education to serve its constituents, reach out to non-Christians, and make its contribution to national development. In spite of daunting competition and even outright opposition, new South Korean evangelical universities are rising, some dramatically indeed.

28. Editorial, "Mismanaging School Funds," Chosun.com 21:1, 18 May 2001, found at http://english.chosun.com/w21/html/news; Chung Yeun-hee, "Teacher's Day Tears That Told Volumes," *JoongAng Ilbo*, 24 May 2001, found at http://english.joins.com/EnglishJoongAngIlbo.

29. Archer Torrey, "In the Love of Jesus Christ," suggests that there has been opposition to Handong for some time. Torrey (Dae Ch'on-dok) dwells at the nearby Jesus Abbey and is a long-time resident of Korea. His essay was found at www.han.ac.kr/english. President Kim gave me word of the successful court appeals in a conversation on 16 April 2002.

30. See, for example, Bong-Ho Son, "Christian Higher Education Where Christians Are a Minority — in Respect to Its Curriculum," in *Rainbow in a Fallen World: Diversity and Unity in Christian Higher Education Today*, proceedings of a conference sponsored by the International Council for the Promotion of Christian Higher Education, Lusaka, Zambia, 29 July–5 August 1987 (Sioux Center, IA: Dordt College Press, 1990), pp. 157-63.

This brief and no doubt incomplete world reconnaissance provides some hints about contextual factors, both religious and secular. It raises important questions, moreover, for assessing the nature of evangelical Christianity's presence and practice in the world today.

3. Evangelical Movements and Higher Education

The emergence of new evangelical universities outside of the North Atlantic world suggests that these movements and traditions are following a historic pattern of development. Puritan, Methodist, and pentecostal movements alike have evolved from peace-disturbing, establishment-upsetting religious upstarts into settled denominations and fellowships. With the revival fires no longer flaring and in need of some tending, institutions or "fireplaces" are built. Converts are gathered and instructed, and excitement about signs and wonders gives ground before an interest in sustaining the movement. People have been saved, sanctified, and filled with the Holy Ghost; battles have been fought to revive sleeping traditions or to break free and start new ones. But Jesus has not come back yet, so there is a new generation to nurture, and a surrounding society in which to sustain a witness. Changing times seem to mandate equipping the saints for the longer term.[31]

Some scholars would interpret this morphology as the process by which evangelical movements begin to make their compromises with the world and move toward decline. A movement like European pietism or American pentecostalism starts as a protest against the comfortable and the compromising, but then begins to join them, undergoing what the Wesleyan theologian Donald Dayton calls "embourgoisment."[32] And what could be more middle-class than developing a university? Other observers, however, see the move from the revival tent to the university as a classic evangelical maneuver rather than a betrayal of a spirit-filled movement's essential character. Evan-

31. One of the most helpful expositions of this process is in R. Stephen Warner, *New Wine in Old Wineskins: Evangelicals and Liberals in a Small-Town Church* (Berkeley: University of California Press, 1987), pp. 284-95, which speaks of the need to distinguish between "nascent" and "institutional" religious orientations as well as the more commonly opposed liberal and evangelical parties in American Protestantism.

32. For Dayton's argument, see his essay, "Yet Another Layer of the Onion; or Opening the Ecumenical Door to Let the Riffraff In," *Ecumenical Review* 40 (Jan. 1988): 87-110. See also Dayton, "'The Search for the Historical Evangelicalism': George Marsden's History of Fuller Seminary as a Case Study," *Christian Scholar's Review* 23 (Sept. 1993): 12-33; and Dayton's "Rejoinder to Historiography Discussion" in the same journal issue: 62-71.

gelicalism, especially in its present-day pentecostal varieties, is a faith of the "aspiring poor," argues sociologist David Martin. If God is good, pentecostals frequently reason, then the Almighty will deliver us from our hopelessness, both our spiritual emptiness and our material poverty. Rather than passively waiting for God to do it, believers live and work as if this promise is true. Pentecostals' faith-driven ambitions and enterprise may be the latest expressions of an abiding material principle in popular evangelicalism, adding a new chapter to the Weber thesis.[33] For the aspiring poor, a university education and a good job are by no means unworthy aspirations, and around the world, evangelical movements and traditions, freshly entering a post-revival stage, are building institutions to open up such opportunities.

When stating the purposes for their institutions, leaders of the new evangelical universities frequently mention two. They want to help students fulfill their aspirations, and they aim to serve the common good of their home societies. "A new generation is seeking reality in their faith in the context of a revived and developing society," states Stephen Noll, the vice-chancellor of Uganda Christian University. "Discipleship for them includes a tremendous hunger for education," he continues, and in equipping them for service, the new university is poised to "become the seedbed for the development of a stable, godly nation."[34] National development has not been a natural first impulse for evangelical movements. The great biblical drama of creation, sin, salvation, and restoration plays out in intensely personal terms early on in revival settings. Fleshing out the idea that a spiritual revival might also bring "healing to the nations" is not high on such movements' initial agendas. Yet for a second generation of contemporary pentecostals, charismatics, and other evangelicals outside of the North Atlantic, such ideas of a broader discipleship and mission are emerging.

The pentecostal leaders of the Central University College in Accra, Ghana, refer to this broader vision as "the great commission of our Lord Jesus Christ in its multifaceted dimensions." They see their task as "sharing in God's concern for reconciliation and justice throughout human society and for the lib-

---

33. David Martin, *Tongues of Fire: The Explosion of Protestantism in Latin America* (Oxford: Basil Blackwell, 1990), esp. ch. 11, "Protestantism and Economic Culture: Evidence Reviewed," pp. 205-32; also his "Evangelical Expansion in Global Society," in Donald M. Lewis, ed., *Christianity Reborn: The Global Expansion of Evangelicalism in the Twentieth Century* (Grand Rapids and Cambridge, U.K.: Eerdmans, 2004), pp. 273-94. For an American version of the story, see Grant Wacker, *Heaven Below: Early Pentecostals and American Culture* (Cambridge, MA: Harvard University Press, 2001).

34. Stephen F. Noll, "An Anglican University for Africa," found at www.ugandapartners.org.

eration of man; evangelism and social action, without fear or favour, denouncing evil and injustice wherever they exist; being part of Christian duty and necessary expressions of Christian doctrines of God and man's love for one's neighbour and obedience to Jesus Christ; to exhibit His Kingdom ethics and to spread its justice and righteousness in the world."[35]

More specifically, according to Vice-Chancellor E. Kingsley Larbi, Central University College aims to help solve "the crisis of leadership [that] is the greatest threat to an African renaissance."[36] Likewise in Latin America, a Christian university spokesman from the Dominican Republic declares, "Pentecostalism is coming of age as a second and third generation begins to ask, 'Now what?' Saving souls has become routine in many cases and there is a desire to make a more significant contribution to the surrounding context." Small groups of Latin American evangelical visionaries who see Christian universities as vehicles for addressing the Great Commission's cultural dimensions are developing educational models and partnerships with which to mount such efforts.[37] The rise of evangelical universities thus marks the emergence of an important second chapter in the story of revivalist Christianity's growth in the non-Western world.

4. Universities and the New Currents in World Christianity

This institution-building "second chapter" in the saga of revivalist and charismatic Christianity's worldwide growth comes at a time when non-Western Christianity more generally is driving a new dispensation in the world history of the faith. As historian Mark Noll recently pointed out, when the delegates at the great missionary conference in Edinburgh in 1910 surveyed the world scene and tried to envisage God's mission in the new century, 80 percent of the world's Christians lived in Europe and North America. Who among them would have thought, Noll asks, that in less than a century, 60 percent of the world's Christians would live outside of that region?[38] In religious demography alone, the world's Christian heartlands have shifted from the North Atlantic region to the South and the East, and we are already seeing harbingers

35. Central University College, *Undergraduate Catalogue, 2000-2002* (Accra: Central University College, 2000), p. 6.

36. E. K. Larbi, "The Challenges of Leadership," cited above, found at www .centraluniversity.org.

37. John William Medendorp to Joel Carpenter, 8 June 2001.

38. Mark A. Noll, "Who Would Have Thought?" *Books & Culture* 7 (Nov./Dec. 2001): 21.

of a corresponding shift in ecclesiastical power and agenda-setting for theology and ministry.[39] Three major trends are riding this wave of change, and they provide a radically different context for institution-building than that of the Western missionary era now passing.

First, the global church is gaining new leaders. The twentieth century was an ecumenical age, in which North Atlantic Christian leaders in missions and theology initiated and led great global fellowships. The vision was worldwide, but the orientation and agenda were European. By the 1990s, however, ecumenical leadership and agendas were changing. In 1994, the Vatican sponsored a historic African Catholic Bishops' Conference, which put the spotlight on one of the fastest-growing regions of the church. It featured such speakers as Francis Cardinal Arinze, the gospel-preaching prelate from Nigeria, who was rumored for some time to be a potential candidate for the papacy in succession to John Paul II. At the Lambeth Conference of the worldwide communion of Anglican Churches in 1998, African and Asian bishops took over the theological and pastoral agenda. They set aside overtures for ordaining practicing homosexuals and emphasized instead the church's calling to evangelize, combat poverty, and overcome political oppression. In 1999, the World Alliance of Reformed Churches, whose secretariat in Geneva had been dominated by Europeans, named Dr. Setri Nyomi, a Presbyterian theologian from Ghana, as its executive head. Conservative evangelical Protestants have experienced similar trends in recent years. The theological commission of the World Evangelical Fellowship (WEF) has been led by Asian, Latin American, and African theologians for nearly two decades, and Jun Vencer, a lawyer and lay ministry leader from the Philippines, has been the WEF's general secretary since the mid-1990s.

The second major trend is the changing agenda for Christian theology. The most pressing issues are shifting from what Mark Noll calls "the jaded discontents of advanced Western civilization" to matters of poverty and social injustice, political corruption and the meltdown of law and order, and Christianity's witness in a situation of religious pluralism. World Christian thought leaders in this new century are thus becoming, as the Anglican evangelical leader John Stott once put it, both more conservative and more radical. They are more conservative in affirming the apostolic doctrines, and especially the immanent presence and power of God. They are more radical in insisting that

39. One of the best summaries of the changed scene at the start of the twenty-first century, which informs the ensuing paragraphs, is Dana Robert, "Shifting Southward: Global Christianity Since 1945," *International Bulletin of Missionary Research (IBMR)* 24, no. 2 (April 2000): 50-58.

Christians offer a prophetic, biblically charged witness against unjust social orders and a vision for a more rightly ordered society and government.[40]

The third major trend has to do with the church's world mission. There are now 400,000 expatriate or cross-cultural missionaries in the world, and those from outside the North Atlantic quadrant outnumber the European and North American missionaries. Koreans, for example, are witnessing in Siberia, Kenya, and Brazil. Nigerians are going to Niger and to "darkest" London; Ghanaians plant new churches in Burkina Faso and in Rotterdam. Ivoireans are preaching in Bordeaux, and Liberians are bringing the gospel to Grand Rapids.

Traditional mission societies and missiologists are scrambling to find their way in the midst of this revolution in world missions. Old-line, ecumenical Protestant agencies are devising schemes for sharing resources with Third World churches and apologizing for historic patterns of patronization and dependency, while younger evangelical agencies are now repeating the "partnership in mission" pattern with their Third World sister churches that the mainline Protestants have been using since at least the 1960s.[41] Third World church leaders point out the inherent problems in such partnerships, notably their tendency to promote North-South or East-West bilateral relationships rather than local interdenominational ones, the persistence of patronizing attitudes on the part of the white partners, the great disparity of financial resources between the partners and the many attendant problems it causes, and the enduring penchant for unilateral decision-making from a distance by the mission boards in the North Atlantic region.[42] And all the while, non-

---

40. Kwame Bediako's recent essays, notably "Facing the Challenge: Africa in World Christianity in the 21st Century — A Vision of the African Christian Future," *Journal of African Christian Thought (JACT)* 1 (June 1998): 52-57; and "A Half Century of African Christian Thought: Pointers to Theology and Theological Education in the Next Half Century," *JACT* 3 (June 2000): 5-11, are indicative of these emerging themes.

41. Bernard Thorogood, "Sharing Resources in Mission," *International Review of Mission (IRM)* 76, no. 304 (Oct. 1987): 441-51; Nicole Fischer, "Towards Reconciled Communities in Mission," *IRM* 79, no. 316 (Oct. 1990): 479-86; Travis Collins, "Missions and Churches in Partnership for Evangelism: A Study of the Declaration of Ibadan," *Missiology* 23, no. 3 (July 1995): 331-39; Joyce M. Bowers, "Partnership and Missionary Personnel," *IRM* 86, no. 342 (July 1997): 248-60; Dwight P. Smith, "Slaying the Dragons of Self-Interest: Making International Partnership Work," *Evangelical Missions Quarterly (EMQ)* 28 (Jan. 1992): 18-23; William D. Taylor, "Lessons in Partnership," *EMQ* 31 (Oct. 1995): 406-15; and Daniel Rickett, "Developmental Partnering," *EMQ* 34 (Oct. 1998): 438-45.

42. Vinay Samuel and Chris Sugden, "Mission Agencies as Multinationals," *IBMR* 7 (Oct. 1983): 152-55; "An Indonesian Leader Speaks to the West, an Interview with Chris Marantika by Sharon Mumper," *EMQ* 22 (Jan. 1986): 6-11; Vinoth Ramachandra, "The Honor of Listening: Indispensable for Mission," *EMQ* 30 (Oct. 1994): 404-9; Tinyiko Sam

Western mission initiatives shoot off in all directions, more of them without partners from Europe and North America than with them.

So what does all this have to do with the rise of new evangelical universities outside of the North Atlantic region? Put succinctly, these institutions are creations of the new spirit of mission agency and agenda-setting that is animating non-Western Christianity. They are being led by Christian professionals and intellectuals who are highly educated, cosmopolitan, more likely laypersons than clerics, frequently experienced in leadership through parachurch ministries, well networked in the North and often in other regions as well, and adept at finance and fund-raising.

The initiative and leadership for the new evangelical universities are not coming from traditional foreign missions. "Partnership" is very much on the minds of North American evangelical mission strategists as a way to sustain missionary work in the new global Christian situation, where in most nations, churches have become well established. Yet these partnerships rarely involve higher education outside of theological seminaries.[43] Indeed, among the variety of tensions that arise from mission-church partnerships, one of the classic conflicts has been over the relative priority of institutions. The missionaries from the North very often are impatient to plant new churches in the less-evangelized regions, while the national churches are eager to consolidate and strengthen their institutional ministries.[44] This is not a new debate; over the past century and a half such disagreements have arisen repeatedly, and education often has been the central issue. In late-nineteenth-century China, for example, it took the threat of a deep rift between local Christian leaders and expatriate missionaries to prompt the founding of a Methodist college in Fuzhou in the 1880s. In central Africa eighty years later, a similar deep split seemed in the offing in the Congo just weeks after national independence. The Congolese members at a meeting of the Congo Protestant Council grew impatient with their missionary colleagues' reluctance to help them develop a college. The national church leaders got up, moved to one end

---

Maluleke, "North-South Partnerships — The Evangelical Presbyterian Church in South Africa and the Département Missionnaire in Lausanne," *IRM* 83, no. 328 (Jan. 1994): 93-100; Martin Repp, "For a Moratorium on the Word 'Partnership,'" *The Japan Christian Review* 64 (1998): 28-34.

43. One prominent exception, as we have seen, is Africa University in Zimbabwe, which has direct links to the missions board of the United Methodist Church (United States).

44. For a paradigmatic expression of such impatience, see C. Peter Wagner, "Mission and Church in Four Worlds," in *Church/Mission Tensions Today,* ed. C. Peter Wagner (Chicago: Moody Press, 1972), pp. 215-32.

of the room, and informed the missionaries that they would "create a Protestant university, whether you help us or not."[45] Universities are costly ventures, and they are not principally involved in saving souls, planting new churches, or even training full-time church workers. Local Christians may want them, but mission leaders generally do not.

Perhaps even more than in the past, today's evangelical mission boards tend to see their mandates in narrow and instrumental terms when it comes to education. Frequently they support ministry education programs, which they see as providing the trained workers for evangelistic endeavors; but universities, by comparison, seem like a diversion. The Church of the Nazarene, for example, which supports eight small universities in the United States and forty Bible colleges and seminaries outside of North America, sponsors only two non-Western universities. The Assemblies of God (United States), which has 1,800 foreign missionaries and supports more than 1,700 overseas Bible schools and extension training programs, sponsors no universities outside of the United States. So while expatriates from the North Atlantic region frequently get involved in the new universities, their presence is no indication of mission support. Whatever the admixture of global or local dynamics and funding behind the founding of these universities, they are not simply an extension of the old missionary enterprise.[46]

The more typical pattern for founding these institutions is an entrepreneurial one, whether the universities have standing with a denomination or not. Local university professors who are evangelicals, pastor-founders of megachurch congregations, evangelical business executives, and leaders of parachurch ministries are the common partners in new evangelical universities. They typically mount an "end run" around denominational and missionary decision-making, priority-setting, and allocation of resources. Who are these educational pioneers and impresarios? Mounting a systematic study

45. Dana Robert, "The Methodist Struggle over Higher Education in Fuzhou, China, 1877-1883," *Methodist History* 34 (April 1996): 173-89; Ben C. Hobgood, "History of Protestant Higher Education in the Democratic Republic of the Congo," *Lexington Theological Quarterly* 33 (Spring 1998): 23-38.

46. "Africa Region Institutions," "South America Region Institutions," "Asia-Pacific Region Institutions," "Eurasia Region Institutions," "Caribbean Region Institutions," "Mexico and Central America Region Institutions," found at www.nazarene.org/iboe; "Statistics on the Assemblies of God (USA)," found at http://www.ag.org/top/about/statistics.cfm. On expatriates' involvement: Samuel Dunn to Joel Carpenter (re: Mariano Galvez University in Guatemala City), 5 Jan. 2001; and *"Descripcion de la Universidad"* (Evangelical University of El Salvador), found at www.uees.edu.sv; Holland, "Evangelical University of the Americas (UNELA) Financial Development Plan," found at www.prolades.com, cited above.

of the emerging evangelical academic leadership is beyond the scope of this chapter, but here are some preliminary impressions. The key agents in this story are a new breed of evangelical leader, very much the products of the new global realities in evangelical Christianity. Three examples will suggest the type.

Dr. Kim Young-gil, president of Handong University in Korea, is an engineer with postgraduate degrees from the University of Missouri and Rensselaer Polytechnic Institute, and several years of research experience in the United States. He was a professor of the distinguished Korean Advanced Institute of Science and Technology for fifteen years, and the winner of American (NASA) and Korean awards for his achievements in technology. He was also the founder of a national network for the integration of faith and science. Since being named president of Handong in 1995, Dr. Kim has built a network of thousands of supporters, both in Korea itself and in the communities of the worldwide Korean diaspora, especially the United States.[47]

Dr. Stephen Talitwala, the longtime vice-chancellor of Daystar University, is from Uganda. He is also an engineer, with a Ph.D. in mechanical engineering from the University of Leeds. He was a lecturer in engineering at Nairobi University and at Makerere University in Uganda, the editor of a regional engineering journal, and the board chair of Youth for Christ in Kenya. Since joining Daystar in 1979, Talitwala has been a frequent speaker at international Christian conferences in Europe, Asia, and North America as well as in Africa. Talitwala has cultivated relationships with many Christian ministry leaders and philanthropists worldwide, and he spends much time traveling every year to sustain those relationships and raise funds for Daystar.[48]

Dr. David Zac Niringiye is not the president of a new evangelical university, but he has been a board member of two of them, Daystar University in Kenya and Uganda Christian University. While currently the director of the Africa work of the (Anglican) Church Mission Society in London, Niringiye has twenty years of parachurch ministry experience in Uganda. He was the founder of FOCUS Uganda, a university student Christian ministry, in the early 1980s. Then he studied at Wheaton College in Illinois for a master's degree. Eventually the International Fellowship of International Students named Niringiye its secretary for all of Anglophone and Lusophone Africa.

---

47. "Introduction: Chairman & President," found at www.han.ac.kr/english/introduction; "Michael Yang and David Friedman Visit Handong," found at www.han.ac.kr/english/news; author's conversations with Kim Young-gil on 16 April 2002.

48. *Operations Report: All the Important Facts About Daystar University*, p. 14.

Yet he found the time to help start a theological seminary and a gospel-and-culture study center in Kampala, and to earn a doctorate at the University of Edinburgh. Niringiye has built relationships with North American and European congregations and Christian philanthropists, and has graced many international student and missions conferences with his Bible teaching. Working both with his own Anglican communion and with a variety of parachurch agencies, Niringiye has encouraged much support in the global North for education and scholarship that is conceived, initiated, and governed in Africa.[49]

Given this kind of leadership and the transnational networks of fellowship and support these new universities enjoy, we can now answer one of the key questions concerning them. The new schools are not merely the latest occasion for non-Western churches to experience dependency and domination from churches in the West, or for the resurgence of missionary-driven religious colonialism. They mark the rise of new players and new patterns in global Christian endeavor, and a new iteration of the "fortunate subversion of the church" as Andrew Walls put it, by the rise of voluntary societies for doing Christian ministry.[50] The parachurch agency revolution, which has transformed North American Christianity, is now making a major impact in the non-Western world, and the growth of new evangelical universities is one of the results.

The first wave of these agencies arriving in the non-Western world — groups such as World Vision, Youth for Christ, Full Gospel Businessmen, Women Aglow, Campus Crusade for Christ, Scripture Union, and the International Fellowship of Evangelical Students — looked like a new missionary invasion, and perhaps, some feared, a new form of religious colonization. In the early 1980s, Vinay Samuel, an evangelical leader from Bangalore, India, complained that these multinational Christian agencies were "evangelical pirates" that siphoned off leaders and initiated projects with no accountability to national churches.[51] By the early 1990s, however, Samuel was the executive secretary of a multinational parachurch agency he had helped to start, the International Fellowship of Evangelical Mission Theologians (INFEMIT). INFEMIT has developed a postgraduate study center in Oxford; a well-

49. Niringiye, via many conversations with the author.

50. Andrew Walls, *The Missionary Movement in Christian History: Studies in the Transmission of Faith* (Maryknoll, NY: Orbis Books, 1996), pp. 247-53.

51. Samuel and Sugden, "Mission Agencies as Multinationals," pp. 152-55. See also Steve Brouwer, Paul Gifford, and Susan D. Rose, *Exporting the American Gospel: Global Christian Fundamentalism* (New York: Routledge, 1996), for a conspiratorial, world-systems view of the worldwide connections of American-style parachurch agencies.

regarded periodical, *Transformation;* a publishing series called Regnum Books; and a well-networked fellowship of evangelical intellectuals and study centers around the world.

The rise of INFEMIT is but one example of a new development: the parachurch pattern, first pioneered by the mission societies themselves, is being taken up and adapted by non-Western evangelical leaders. These new evangelical leaders are highly educated, well connected, and widely traveled. They do not need to rely on the standard channels of support and relationships, but they have learned how to access Western evangelical networks — churchly, missional, financial, and intellectual — for themselves. They have effectively "cut out the middleman" — the Western missionary, ecumenical official, or expatriate parachurch leader — and have taken their causes directly to the North Atlantic evangelical networks and to potential supporters in their own regions. These are the people and the organizations that are bringing their creative and promotional gifts to bear on the launching of new evangelical universities. They are both the beneficiaries of and contributors to the current wave of religious globalization. Instead of bringing forth a new form of Western Christian imperialism, these currents in world Christianity are abetting the great global shift of Christianity's presence, influence, and preoccupations toward the South and the East.

While the new evangelical universities seem to signify the shifting balance of influence and initiative in world Christianity, it would be premature to suggest that they are centers for Christian thought. Integrally Christian cultural and scientific scholarship is in its infancy, at best, outside of the North Atlantic, and is hardly audible as a voice in non-Western Christian discourse. Theology per se is still the dominant Christian intellectual preoccupation. There are trends in the development of the new evangelical universities, moreover, that cast doubt on the prospects of their ever becoming centers for Christian thought and cultural witness. It is here, in the actual structure and work of the new universities, where questions about the impact of globalization are the most pressing.

5. Globalization and Universities

Globalization has become one of the great buzzwords of public affairs discourse. This term was born of the growing recognition among social scientists that there has been a major increase in the volume and rapidity of cross-border exchanges of goods, services, money, people, information, ideas, and artistry in the contemporary world. Globalization means a variety of things to those who use the term, but a fairly standard definition might be the one offered by sociologist Mauro F. Guillén, which combines the concepts offered by pioneering theorists Roland Robertson and Martin Albrow. Guillén defines globalization as "the process leading to greater interdependence and mutual awareness (reflexivity) among economic, political, and social units in the world, and among actors in general."[52] Most of the literature on globalization focuses on its economic and political implications, but there is a significant body of thought about its cultural role as well. The deliberations and debates in both disciplinary camps are very much germane to the rise and development of new universities in the global South and East, including the university ventures mounted by evangelicals.

Higher education rarely has been linked directly to globalization theory, but it can be seen as one of the most striking forms of globalization in one of that term's classic meanings, found in Immanuel Wallerstein's theory of world systems, which sees globalization basically as a worldwide imposition of Western, modernizing values and political and economic hegemony.[53] Higher education does form a global network of interdependent links involving both sovereign states and economic institutions. Global higher education, one might argue further, emanates from a North Atlantic core and reinforces Western values.

In the non-Western world, some scholars have argued, universities are modernizing forces that erode traditional values, bringing individualism, for example, over against traditional communalism. English is rapidly becoming the universal language of high-level scientific and technological study, thus diminishing the use and influence of indigenous languages. The universities teach topics devised in the West, and thus mismatch social and economic needs at home. Their graduates are better suited, some argue, to serve Western economies, and they often do, thus contributing to a depletion of intellectual talent at home. In sum, non-Western universities have been seen as part

52. Mauro F. Guillén, "Is Globalization Civilizing, Destructive or Feeble? A Critique of Five Key Debates in the Social Science Literature," *Annual Review of Sociology* 27 (2001): 236. For recent summative works of the theoreticians to which Guillén refers, see Martin Albrow, *The Global Age* (Palo Alto, CA: Stanford University Press, 1997); and Roland Robertson, *Globalization: Social Theory and Global Culture* (London: Sage Publishing, 1992). See also Donald M. Lewis's very helpful essay, "Globalization: The Problem of Definition and Future Areas of Historical Inquiry," in Mark Hutchinson and Ogbu Kalu, eds., *A Global Faith: Essays on Evangelicalism and Globalization* (Sydney: Centre for the Study of Australian Christianity, 1998), pp. 26-46.

53. Immanuel Wallerstein, *The Modern World-System* (New York: Academic Press, 1974).

of a Western-oriented world system, with professional inhabitants who are globally linked, mobile, and of mixed loyalties.[54]

6. Globalization: A Sober Second Opinion

Not only in higher education but in all other realms, notably economic, political, and cultural, globalization has been seen as one of the great monolithic forces of our time, and assessments of its character have invited extremes. To some, it is the great demon of global capitalist imperialism, sweeping all before it into one world economic and cultural system, everywhere emasculating national governments, depressing wages, destroying the environment, centralizing economic control in multinational corporations, and creating social and economic upheaval in the fragile nations of the global South. Others add to this scenario the alleged impact of cultural globalization, such as the homogenization of culture worldwide, the destruction of indigenous local traits and gifts, the triumph of consumerist values, and the commodification of the values and outlook of daily life.[55]

For others, globalization is a force for salvation, bringing new competition to complacent and inefficient industries, new funding for business growth worldwide, new responsibility to corrupt and inefficient governments, better employment opportunities to the world's poor, unprecedented opportunities for cultural exchange, a "global village" of shared values, and the growth of democracy-producing civil society. These progressive cultural and political trends are being brought on, some argue, by the new world consciousness made possible by global communication.[56]

54. See, for example, the essays in Zaghloul Morsy and Philip G. Altbach, eds., *Higher Education in an International Perspective: Critical Issues,* International Bureau of Education Studies on Education 3 (New York and London: Garland Publishing, 1996).

55. See, e.g., William Greider, *One World, Ready or Not: The Manic Logic of Global Capitalism* (New York: Simon and Schuster, 1997); James H. Mittelman, ed., *Globalization: Critical Reflections* (Boulder, CO: Lynne Rienner, 1996); and Benjamin R. Barber, *Jihad vs. McWorld: How Globalism and Tribalism Are Reshaping the World* (New York: Ballantine, 1996). Unfortunately, quite a few Christian theologians seem to accept this demonizing view uncritically. See, e.g., M. D. Litonjua, "Global Capitalism: The New Context of Christian Social Ethics," *Theology Today* 56 (July 1999): 210-28; Vinay Samuel, "Keynote Address: Evangelical Response to Globalization: An Asian Perspective," *Transformation* 16 (Jan. 1999): 4-7; K. C. Abraham, "Globalization: A Gospel and Culture Perspective," *IRM* 85, no. 336 (Jan. 1996): 85-92; and Oswald Firth, O.M.J., "Globalization: A Christian Perspective on Economics," *Dialogue* (Colombo) 24 (1997): 101-24.

56. Kenichi Ohmae, *The Borderless World* (New York: Harper Business, 1990); Lester

More sober assessments have come to the fore in recent years, so that virtually every claim made by globalization's critics and its proponents has been contested. What has emerged is a set of moderating views among students of international political economy and sociology. Economists find that the international integration of trade and finance has advanced markedly, so there are some truly global markets. One of the main drivers of this integration has been the revolution in communications and information technology. There are very few truly global multinational corporations, but multinationals have become more mobile than ever before. Globalization does not automatically imply the depressing of wages, or the emasculation of governmental regulation, but it does have an impact on both wages and regulation. Globalization is encouraging diversification and resilience in economies. It is true that the income gap between rich and poor nations is growing, but it is not true that a globalizing economy widens income gaps within nations. According to most experts in comparative politics, modern nation states are alive and well, but they have more rivals now as power bases, notably world-class cities. Economic regulation and the welfare state are still eminently viable, but there are plenty of new regulatory issues to consider. Globalization is not the same thing as modernization, say sociologists; it is not homogenizing worldviews and cultural values. It produces more cultural fragmentation and diversification than submission and conformity. Even the global spread of English has resulted in the rise of new, "creolized" versions of it. People do not respond in uniform ways to global communications; rather, mass media provoke widely varying responses, including irony, selective borrowing, re-spinning, and resistance. There is widespread cultural hybridization today; and it is producing a constant and kaleidoscopic re-creation of new and reflexive cultural forms, including new forms of traditionalism. The renowned anthropologist Clifford Geertz aptly sums up the current state of affairs when he reflects that the world is "growing more global and more divided, more thoroughly interconnected and more intricately partitioned at the same time."[57]

Thurow, *The Future of Capitalism: How Today's Economic Forces Shape Tomorrow's World* (New York: Penguin Books, 1996); R. D. Lipschutz, with J. Mayer, *Global Civil Society and Global Environmental Governance* (Albany, NY: State University of New York Press, 1996); and J. Brecher, J. B. Childs, and J. Cutler, eds., *Global Visions: Beyond the New World Order* (Boston: South End Press, 1993).

57. Clifford Geertz, "The World in Pieces: Culture and Politics at the End of the Century," *Focaal: Tijdschrift Antropologie* 32 (1998): 107, quoted in Guillén, "Is Globalization Civilizing, Destructive or Feeble?" p. 253. For helpful summaries of the debates and the emerging moderating opinions about globalization, see Guillén's article; Grahame Thompson, "Introduction: Situating Globalization," *International Social Science Journal*

7. Evangelical Universities and the Privatization of Higher Education

In higher education, one of the most important facets of this global pattern of interconnection and partitioning is "privatization," or the devolution of state control. Difficult governmental decisions about spending priorities, new interest in classic capitalistic themes of competition and private initiative, current democratic theories about the importance of a large and healthy non-profit and non-governmental civil society, and above all, a never-ending demand for more access to higher education, especially to meet the challenges of the new global economy, have led a growing number of nations to decide that their governments will no longer monopolize the organization and financing of higher education. Writing in the March 2001 issue of the *Chronicle of Higher Education,* David Cohen observed that "as the world's hunger for higher education has outstripped the ability of many governments to pay for it, a type of institution has come to the rescue that is well-established in the United States, but a stranger in many other countries: private colleges."[58]

The latest trend for privatization is in sub-Saharan Africa, where economic decline and government fiscal crises have eroded the quality of higher education for several decades, and prompted a continual diaspora of professors and students. At the same time, the governments, eager to keep alive the popular belief in educational opportunity, increased enrollments far beyond universities' capacities.[59] Even so, there is no way that the governments can meet the demand. In Uganda, for example, 35,000 secondary school graduates qualify each year for university admission, but the two public universities can take only 12,000 of them. Over the past decade, however, one nation after another has liberalized its rules for registering universities. When Kenya established new rules for chartering private universities in 1989, sixteen universities lined up for accreditation. More recently, up to two dozen applications

---

(ISSJ) 160 (June 1999): 139-52; Jonathan Perraton, "Review Article: The Global Economy — Myths and Realities," *Cambridge Journal of Economics* 25 (2001): 669-84; Edward Comor, "The Role of Communication in Global Civil Society: Forces, Processes, Prospects," *International Studies Quarterly* (2001): 389-408; and Arjun Appadurai, "Globalization and the Research Imagination," *ISSJ* 160 (June 1999): 229-38. My summary above is drawn from them.

58. David Cohen, "The Worldwide Rise of Private Colleges," *CHE,* 9 March 2001, p. A47.

59. Mary Antoinette Brown Sherman, "The University in Modern Africa: Toward the Twenty-First Century," *Journal of Higher Education* 61 (July/August 1990): 363-85; "African Universities: The Staff Dilemma," *West Africa,* 29 May–4 June 1995, pp. 843-44; Eugene H. Amonoo-Neizer, "Universities in Africa — The Need for Adaptation, Transformation, Reformation and Revitalization," *Higher Education Policy* 11, no. 4 (1998): 301-9.

have appeared in a year. As in other regions, African private universities are focusing on courses that have popular demand, and the universities have been slow to pick up, most notably, in communications, management, computing, tourism, and agriculture.[60]

In East Asia, where private education has had a much longer history and has won a prominent place in the university landscape, the private universities continue to grow in number and capacity. In Japan, the private sector provides nearly 75 percent of all enrollments in tertiary education. Korea, Taiwan, and the Philippines have similar private enrollment rates. The private universities exist in much more highly regulated situations than in Africa or Latin America, and some of the older private institutions rank among the best in the region. Issues of overall quality remain, however, with the institutions often achieving cost efficiency at the expense of high student-teacher ratios and large numbers of part-time instructors. Nevertheless, the East Asian institutions make their contribution by offering high-demand courses in computing, business, and communications, and helping their nations rank high in the world for the access they offer to tertiary education.[61]

In Latin America, where higher education is deeply contested political turf, the private universities are part of politics. Catholic universities came into existence in the mid-twentieth century to protect traditional values and to resist the secular, leftist milieu of the state institutions. Elitist secular private colleges soon followed, and for three decades now, non-elitist privates, focusing on business courses, have opened doors to fee-paying lower-middle-class students. Pressure from international financial agencies such as the World Bank for governments to curb higher educational costs and allow for more privatization has deepened the animosity in the educational sector, but students continue to throng to private institutions. In Brazil, for example, nearly 60 percent of the enrollments are now in private universities.[62]

When private colleges and universities began appearing in larger numbers

---

60. Andrea Useem, "In East Africa, New Private Colleges Fill a Growing Gap Between Supply and Demand," *CHE*, 10 September 1999, p. A65.

61. William K. Cummings, "Private Education in East Asia," in *The Challenge of Eastern Asian Education*, ed. William K. Cummings (Albany, NY: SUNY Press, 1997), pp. 135-52; Cohen, "Worldwide Rise of Private Colleges."

62. Cohen, "Worldwide Rise of Private Colleges"; Daniel C. Levy, "Latin America's Private Universities: How Successful Are They?" *Comparative Education Review* 29 (Nov. 1985): 440-59; Harry Anthony Patrinos, "The Privatization of Higher Education in Colombia: Effects on Quality and Equity," *Higher Education* 20, no. 2 (1990): 161-73; Robert Austin, "Armed Forces, Market Forces: Intellectuals and Higher Education in Chile, 1973-1993," *Latin American Perspectives* 24 (Sept. 1997): 26-58; Cohen, "Worldwide Rise of Private Colleges."

in Latin America and in Asia ten to fifteen years ago, the response from the established educational community was almost wholly negative. Daniel C. Levy, a leading U.S. scholar of Latin American higher education, led the critics. He argued that the region's growing private university sector was achieving its own educational goals and satisfying its own constituencies, but it succeeded because it left the tougher goals to the public sector. These institutions, Levy alleged, siphoned off students, consumed governmental subsidies, priced out the poorer students, and specialized in only the least expensive and most popular courses. They often provided shoddy quality, and added to the number of unemployed graduates. It might even be argued, Levy suggested, that the private universities did not improve higher education overall, and that they flourished "parasitically — off the public sector." An Indian educational planner had a similar verdict: "The goals and strategies of the private sector are on the whole highly injurious to the public interest."[63]

While issues of quality and quality control remain, the perspective over the past decade or so seems more favorable. It is clearer now, for example, that public universities and the governments that fund them simply cannot keep up with public demand. Private institutions fill the gap and provide broader social and economic opportunity. Although the experts predicted otherwise, privates have seriously upgraded their facilities and quality of instruction, added socially responsible (and not just market-demanded) programs of study, and increased student financial aid. In many countries, the privates are still largely unregulated. Shoddy and even fraudulent practices still exist, but overall, the experts seem to be saying today, privatization is a beneficial trend.[64]

It is obvious, strikingly so, that the new evangelical universities are riding this wave of privatization. The evangelical universities are showing up with greatest number and vigor in countries that are liberalizing educational structures. In their course offerings, the evangelicals tend to follow the privatizing trends toward providing the skills students want and will most likely need to get entry-level jobs in the new global workforce. Nevertheless, recently founded evangelical colleges do not follow the curricular pattern of the new privates exclusively. Many of them have found ways to respond to local needs that go beyond training for careers as operatives in the global economy. African institutions are attending to agriculture as well as to accounting.

63. Levy, "Latin America's Private Universities: How Successful Are They?" p. 457; Jandhyala B. G. Tilak, "The Privatization of Higher Education," *Prospects* 21, no. 3 (1991): 227-39, quotation at p. 236.

64. Cohen, "Worldwide Rise of Private Colleges."

Some of the Korean evangelical universities are pushing into the higher-tech and higher-cost fields of engineering and biotechnology. Latin American evangelicals are likely to have programs in health care in their new universities, and to reach out to the poorer rural and small-town districts with extension campuses. For all of their common curricular trends with the new secular private universities, the new evangelical universities are responding to local needs as well. Even so, it is critical for evangelical colleges to consider what they will do in the years ahead to distinguish themselves from the common run of entrepreneurial institutions and to articulate what is in fact Christian and Christ-serving about the curricular patterns they are following.

8. Knowledge Workers for the Global Economy?

Universities have always lived with the tension between the disinterested pursuit of truth and the need to put knowledge to practical use, but in a new era of privatization and globalization, it is quite clear that "usefulness" is winning out. The world is experiencing cultural and economic change of enormous velocity, and the realm of higher education is scrambling to equip people to work effectively within the emerging world market. The result, as we have seen, is that the new privates, evangelical universities included, are not trying to replicate either the liberal arts college, with broad general education requirements, or the comprehensive university, with scores of different concentrations to offer. They are often what one commentator called "boutique" colleges, which offer only a few programs targeted to respond to growing areas in market demand. Daystar University, which asserts a liberal arts approach, listed 1,213 students in bachelor's degree programs in 1997. Yet 1,094 of its students were enrolled in one of three programs: commerce, communication, and community development.[65]

Another important globalizing feature of the new evangelical universities is their ready adoption of computer-based communications technology. Even the poorest African institutions have e-mail, and several of those, which do not have the infrastructure yet to mount web-based communications, have their stories out before the global public via websites constructed by their supporters in the global North. Researching and writing this paper in such a short space of time would have been impossible had I not been able to make electronic contact with so many of these new institutions via the World Wide Web.

65. *Operations Report: All the Important Facts About Daystar University*, pp. 7-8.

Notice too how many of the institutions have English versions of their web pages available. Internet English has become a global phenomenon, and few self-respecting East Asian universities, for example, neglect to connect with English speakers. Beyond the Internet per se, English has become this age's lingua franca in both the academy and the business world. This practice has not brought on the destruction of local languages or diminished their role as the most profound conveyors of cultural meaning, any more than did the international use of Latin in late-medieval Europe or of Swahili over vast stretches of contemporary East Africa. Yet it clearly has been extended and abetted by the global revolution in communications technology.[66]

The new evangelical universities' leaders recognize some of the global economic and technological challenges, and are earnestly promising that their institutions will equip students to meet them. "Our society has impatiently demanded . . . professional workers," says Dr. Sung Kee Ho, president of SungKyul University in Korea. "We are recognizing today's problem and making the well-fitted and capable people prepared for tomorrow in our global community. It is the mission of our University to educate and train the faithful, competent, professional and creative leaders."[67] Likewise, insists Central University College's vice-chancellor, Kingsley Larbi, church-related universities "must relate their programmes to the needs of tomorrow's labour market. The stakeholders of these emergent private institutions must be willing to adapt faster to changing technologies, else they will soon become irrelevant in the realisation of the African dream."[68] These institutions are in fact providing an education for "knowledge workers," or operatives with the technological skills to plug in to the lower-level professional jobs of globalizing economies. But is that enough?

One Indian Christian critic of globalization, who lives in Bangalore, sees little good coming from such trends. Bangalore, he laments, was once called the "Garden City," with verdant parks, clean air, and a lower cost of living than other large Indian cities. Today it is the rapidly growing home of computer software and related companies, 135 of which are foreign-owned. Bangalore's skies are obscured by high-rise buildings and a haze of air pollution, its streets are clogged with traffic, basic utilities strain and break down,

---

66. Joshua A. Fishman, "Globalization at Work: The New Linguistic Order," *Foreign Policy* 113 (1998): 26-41; "The Triumph of English," *The Economist*, 22 December 2001, pp. 65-67; Burton Bollag, "The New Latin: English Dominates in Academe," *CHE*, 8 September 2000, p. A73; Robert Phillipson, "English for Globalization or for the World's People?" *International Review of Education* 47 (July 2001): 185-200.

67. "Message from the President," www.sungkyul.ac.kr/english/information.

68. Larbi, "The Challenges of Leadership," cited above, note 21.

and the job-seeking poor raise new shanty towns on all sides.[69] This is not exactly the new global community for which leaders of the new evangelical universities would want their students to be "well fitted."

Yet one should not dismiss the new evangelical universities' emphasis on professional and technical education. If, as theologian Max Stackhouse suggests, economic globalization is a dominant and enduring force of our time, approximating the "Mammon" of New Testament admonition, then Christians should assert Christ's authority over such powers, and seek to discipline and transform them to serve God's purposes.[70] Contemporary Catholic social teaching may provide a strategic understanding of that task. According to Catholic ethicist Dennis McCann, the recent papal encyclicals on such matters, *Laborem Exercens* (1981) and *Centesimus Annus* (1991), reassert the priority of labor over capital. They argue that the new technological advances emphasize the role of organized intelligence, and they have the potential to help make work more humane in a number of respects. In the emerging global economy, the encyclicals argue, access to technology and skills is a form of ownership, no less important than land or money. The problem of world poverty, they assert, is more a matter of marginalization, of people's lack of access to skills and technologies, than of overt exploitation. People need the means to make their work more knowledge-laden, and thus more valuable. A new assault on poverty thus cannot be simply the redistribution of wealth or the fencing out of foreign capitalists. It has to involve the sharing of skills, so that needy people and nations have the opportunity to add more value to their work.[71] If social justice is tied in fundamental ways to providing more opportunity to acquire skills to participate in the modern, technologically driven economy, then the new evangelical universities are acting as agents of social justice, whether they recognize it or not.

9. The Future of the New Evangelical Universities

It is better, of course, to recognize such strategic agency, and better still to lead students to a fully orbed Christian perspective on globalization and other current realities. Given the new evangelical universities' aims and professed values, one might expect to see signs that they are developing ways and means

69. Abraham, "Globalization: A Gospel and Culture Perspective," p. 85.

70. Max L. Stackhouse, "Globalization, Faith and Theological Education," *Theological Education* 35 (Spring 1999): 67-77.

71. Dennis P. McCann, "Catholic Social Teaching in an Era of Economic Globalization: A Resource for Business Ethics," *Business Ethics Quarterly* 7 (March 1997): 57-70.

to sustain such an outlook. Integrating a sturdy and lasting Christian approach into the new evangelical universities will be important for their ability to sustain a Christian identity and mission into the future. Yet it is difficult to see how faculty and students can cultivate a fully orbed Christian perspective within the narrowly focused curricular tracks that most of these universities have developed. Unless students take courses that address social, economic, theological, cultural, and ethical issues that form the world in which their professions operate, they will have few resources for understanding and applying the Bible's call to work for justice and to love mercy.

There are a few of the new evangelical universities that are providing this sort of educational breadth. Africa University in Zimbabwe emphasizes its "compulsory foundation courses in ethics and Christian values and African history and culture" in fulfilling its aim to produce "well-rounded, socially aware and active professionals." Likewise, Daystar University in Kenya has developed what it calls "a culturally appropriate Christian liberal arts method" with core courses that "provide a basic understanding of Africa's traditional societies, religions and art" as well as "a Christian approach to socioeconomic and political development."[72] Much more common, however, is what one might call a hyper-focused approach, with Christianity appearing as a "value added" around the curricular and co-curricular edges of a narrowly specialized professional or technical education. Hoseo University in Korea, to cite one example, emphasizes professional and technical specialization, and locates its Christian approach in "bimonthly attendance at chapel" for freshmen and sophomores, and a required course, "Introduction to Christianity," for all students. It relies mostly on the co-curricular to make its higher education Christian, with a Pastoral Care Center for counseling, "instructive sermons from the President and pastors," student Christian organizations, a "Gospel Song Contest," and "many missionary programs" for evangelization and service in the region.[73] Such work can sustain a Christian presence and support personal piety, but it has little to offer by way of Christian intellectual depth and breadth. It is difficult to see how the new evangelical universities can sustain a Christian outlook without offering a curriculum that pushes students out into the broad realms of nature and culture that the Bible claims for the Lordship of Jesus Christ, and that equip stu-

72. "Africa University: A Mission to Educate, Empower and Transform," found at http://users.harare.iafrica.com/~auinfo/au.html; Stevens, "2000 Graduating Class Largest in Africa University History," Methodist News Service, cited in note 18 above; *Operations Report: All the Important Facts About Daystar University*, p. 7.

73. "Hoseo University, Light and Salt in the World," found at www.hoseo.ac.kr/english/christian3.html.

dents to bring a "big-picture" Christian perspective to bear on the principalities and powers of this age.

The key to sustaining an integrally Christian identity and mission lies as much with the faculty as with the curriculum. In North America, many a church-related liberal arts college or university with a broad and well-balanced curriculum has become secularized when its faculty no longer cared about making its education distinctively Christian. What are the prospects in the new evangelical universities in this regard? In many of these institutions, Christian professors are not encouraged to integrate their faith into their academic subjects. One veteran Christian educator in Korea recalls a conversation at a conference of Korean Christian professors from church-related universities, where he asked one of the professors how he related his theology to his classroom work. The distinguished gentleman said, "Young man, when I go into the classroom, I leave my religion in the hall."[74] As the newer evangelical universities grow and mature, they face these same pressures. In East Asia especially, where there are now several generations of Christian-founded colleges and universities, there are also several generational stages of secularization as well.[75]

In addition to the tensions inherent to sustaining a Christian purpose and character within a faculty and student body, there are great pressures to secularize from within the academy, because secularity is its dominant ethos. Post-Enlightenment science and the scientific method mandated an approach to scholarly inquiry that excluded all but empirical evidence and shaped a campus ethos, now common worldwide, that is skeptical of received wisdom and claims of divine revelation. Even so, much of the secularization of higher education has come not from a head-on assault against supernaturalism, but from the idea that empirical study is theologically neutral and universally beneficial. Both the natural sciences and the technical and managerial professions have pragmatic, instrumental norms. For them, a Christian morality or view of reality seems not so much at odds with their outlook as irrelevant. What does the Book of Revelation have to do with the price/cost curve? Does a Methodist do chemistry differently than a Buddhist? Perhaps, at best, the secular academy could allow Christianity to be one of the tradi-

74. Dae Ch'on-dok (Archer Torrey), "In the Love of Jesus Christ," www.han.ac.kr.english/news.

75. T. Valentino Sitory, "Rainbow in a Fallen World: Diversity and Unity in Christian Higher Education in Asia Today," pp. 137-52; and Bong-Ho Son, "Christian Higher Education Where Christians Are a Minority — in Respect to Its Curriculum," pp. 157-63, both in *Rainbow in a Fallen World: Diversity and Unity in Christian Higher Education Today* (1987), cited above in note 30.

tions that feed into an auxiliary add-on to professional or scientific studies, such as ethics. Such is the dominant ethos in higher education, and for Christians not to address their views of God, the creation, morality, nature, and human nature within the disciplines they study is to concede higher learning to secularism.[76] Over time, especially as evangelical fervor cools a bit, the add-on strategies of including a Bible and theology department, or fostering religious activities out in student life, will seem less and less relevant to the real business of the university.

In many non-Western settings, the great student demand for university admission and the tiny relative size of the Christian community put pressure on Christian universities to admit large numbers of non-Christian students. Burgeoning enrollments then pressure these universities to hire non-Christian professors to cover all the teaching. Before too long, non-Christian students and professors come to resent the universities' reserving a privileged role for the Christian faith. As early as the 1920s, Chinese Christian colleges encountered student resistance and governmental discouragement concerning their older missionary aims of evangelization and Christian formation.[77] The new Christian universities of Taiwan and Hong Kong in the 1950s were careful, therefore, to state their purposes in the broadest liberal Protestant and humanitarian terms, stressing education for "the whole person, . . . character and personality development, and . . . service to humanity," as Tunghai University's 1953 founding statement of principles put it. Tunghai aimed to convene a dialogue, its founders stated, between "the Christian faith, Chinese traditions, and new ways of thought and life."[78] These universities today are fairly large, well-established, and mostly secular institutions, where Christianity shows up in student circles and has some vestiges in the curriculum, but is not a driving force in the institution. So as new evangelical universities arise in Korea and elsewhere in Asia, one cannot help but wonder how they might resist the secularizing trends of the past.

76. Two definitive studies of the role that the growing influence of scientific naturalism played in the secularization of the American academy are Douglas Sloan, *Faith and Knowledge: Mainline Protestantism and American Higher Education* (Louisville: Westminster John Knox Press, 1994); Jon H. Roberts and James Turner, *The Sacred and the Secular University* (Princeton, NJ: Princeton University Press, 2000).

77. Edgar A. Knight, "Christian Education," in *Laymen's Foreign Missions Inquiry, Fact Finder's Reports: China*, vol. 5, Supplementary Series, Part Two, ed. Orville A. Petty (New York: Harper & Brothers, 1933), pp. 354-408; see also Wen-Hsin Yeh, *The Alienated Academy: Culture and Politics in Republican China, 1919-1937* (Cambridge, MA: Council on East Asian Studies/Harvard University, 1990), pp. 9-88.

78. *Tunghai University: A University with a Pioneering Spirit* (n.p., c. 1996), p. 6; CCCU files, Tunghai University folder.

Might there be some way to break the pattern of progressive secularization? Reformed, Anabaptist, Catholic, Lutheran theologians, and philosophers and historians of ideas in the global North have been coming up with responses lately, and they are well worth pondering. Despite their differences, they agree, as one American Catholic intellectual recently put it, that "the gospel and its Church are gifted, that together they offer a privileged insight" on the realms of thought and research, of scientific and cultural development.[79] A Lutheran theologian puts it this way: "The Christian faith provides an account of all of life, not just of 'private' or 'spiritual' life." Christian teaching and scholarship, he believes, should be "relating Christianity to those many 'non-religious' facets of human life — economic, political, social and cultural."[80] Whether one's university is a place where all faculty members are Christians and are pledged to work according to Christian norms, or whether it is by necessity or principle a more diverse place, there must be a critical mass of leaders who profess this Christian approach. Developing a Christian approach within the "secular" disciplines and professions does not come easily, for it flies in the face of the dominant academic culture. Organizations of Christian professors, such as the Korean Christian Scholarship Institute, founded in 1980, or the Disciples with an Evangelical Worldview, founded in Korea in 1981, are sorely needed to help sustain and develop thinking along these lines, but they simply do not exist in many places outside of North America.[81]

Evangelical universities and their professors would be helped mightily if theologians would take up these themes and lead the way, since in most settings in the non-Western world, theologians are virtually the only integrally Christian scholars. The International Fellowship of Evangelical Mission Theologians (INFEMIT) has launched some pioneering efforts in this direction, attempting to move evangelical theology out of its self-referential ghetto and into the contemporary world's great public debates. What Christian scientists and humanists need is cultural theology, public theology, theology of mission. They need theological reflection on how the gospel can be brought to bear on society and on the ideas and techniques that drive the current world. Theologians, of course, cannot develop such perspectives out of their own disciplinary realms alone; they need to engage Christian thinkers in

79. James Tunstead Burtchaell, *The Dying of the Light: The Disengagement of Colleges and Universities from Their Christian Churches* (Grand Rapids: Eerdmans, 1999), p. 851.

80. Robert Benne, *Quality with Soul: How Six Premier Colleges and Universities Keep Faith with Their Religious Traditions* (Grand Rapids: Eerdmans, 2001), p. viii.

81. Youn-Sik Han, "Status of Korean Christian Scholarship," document in the author's possession (n.d., circa Feb. 2002).

other disciplines: philosophers, literary scholars, historians, social scientists, and natural scientists. Out of such discourse may come the insights, convictions, and commitments that will strengthen and enrich the new evangelical universities. The conversation needs to be planted and to grow within these new institutions, and it needs to mold them in ways that reflect a more holistic understanding of their mandate.[82]

10. Conclusion

The new evangelical universities have arrived at a time when the world is exceedingly protean and kinetic. Ideas, ideologies, people, goods, images, money, and technologies are sailing about with great speed, and they are being exchanged, borrowed, reacted to, and transmuted more rapidly than ever before. The evangelical and pentecostal movements that are creating these new universities are themselves a global phenomenon; they are at once a product of this speedup of cultural transmission, but everywhere transmuting into unique local forms and expressions.[83] The new evangelical universities are at once the responses of local change agents to urgently felt local needs, and reactions to global economic and cultural trends. These young and fragile institutions rise on the hopes and dreams of the born-again and spirit-filled of their regions to provide a better life for the eager and aspiring students who enter their portals, to further the welfare of their homelands, and to respond, out of a Christian imagination, to the dynamic forces they see at play in the larger world.

As part of a new wave of non-Western Christian institutions beyond the churches themselves, the new evangelical universities have the potential to play a seminal role in the formation of Christian thought and action in the

82. One pioneering effort in mounting and sustaining these lines of thought and discourse is the International Association for the Promotion of Christian Higher Education (IAPCHE). This international network was founded a quarter-century ago by Reformed educators, at first mostly of Dutch heritage, who eventually welcomed other evangelical Christian educators and some Russian Orthodox professors as well. IAPCHE has held a number of regional conferences in Asia, Latin America, Africa, and Eastern Europe for Christian university professors and officials to share ideas regarding the integrality of faith and learning and to plan further organizational moves. In August 2000 IAPCHE met at Dordt College in northwest Iowa, and attracted Christian educational leaders from thirty nations. Out of that meeting have come new initiatives to organize and operate on a regional basis.

83. Peter L. Berger, "Four Faces of Global Culture," *National Interest* 49 (Fall 1997): 23-29.

decades to come. Christianity, Andrew Walls keeps telling us, enters the twenty-first century as a mainly non-Western religion. While the demographic center of the faith has shifted southward, its ways of thinking and engaging culture have not yet caught up with that shift. Thus "the quality of twenty-first-century Christianity as a whole," Walls concludes, will depend on the quality of its interaction with the cultures of Africa, Asia, and Latin America. "If the quality is good, we may see . . . a great creative development of Christian theology; new discoveries about Christ that Christians everywhere can share; mature, discriminating standards of Christian living; . . . [and] a long-term Christ-shaped imprint on the thinking" of these emerging heartlands of the faith. "If the quality is poor," Walls warns, "we shall see distortion, confusion, uncertainty and, almost certainly, hypocrisy on a large scale." There is much riding on the quality of Christian scholarship arising from these regions, so there is much at stake in the intellectual maturation of the new evangelical universities. At present, original Christian scholarship is far down these institutions' lists of urgent priorities. Given their structures and orientations, the new universities run a great risk of missing this deeper calling. Yet there are resources available nearby, especially in the quickening movement of evangelical "mission theology," to help these uncommon schools become agents for "thinking Christ into the entire cultural framework" of their lands.[84]

84. Andrew F. Walls, "Christian Scholarship in Africa in the Twenty-First Century," *JACT* 4 (Dec. 2001): 44-52, quotations at pp. 46 and 48.

CHAPTER 8

The North China Theological Seminary: Evangelical Theological Education in China in the Early 1900s

KEVIN XIYI YAO

From the very beginning, theological education has been an important part of Protestant missions in China. Before the 1860s theological education in China was started and carried out in the form of training classes for native evangelists and preachers. From the mid-1860s to the Boxer Rebellion of 1900, theological seminaries began to emerge. They were all denominational institutions staffed by foreign preacher-teachers, and their curricula were "Biblical, practical and conservative."[1] During the early twentieth century numerous denominational theological schools merged into larger union seminaries staffed by an increasing number of specially trained theological teachers. The most prominent were the Nanjing Theological Seminary and School of Religion of the Yenching University. The seminaries' academic standards were raised, and their curricula were broadened to include a number of aspects of social and religious studies. Furthermore, Protestant seminaries were increasingly dominated by liberal theological teachings.

Among the largest and the best-known Protestant seminaries in China of the first half of the twentieth century, the North China Theological Seminary (NCTS) was a unique institution. For the most part during the 1920s and 1930s, the NCTS remained the most influential conservative seminary in

---

1. C. Stanley Smith, *The Development of Protestant Theological Education in China in the Light of the History of the Education of the Clergy in Europe and America,* part 2 (Shanghai: Kelly and Walsh, Ltd., 1941), p. 87.

China and had the largest enrollment of students of any theological school in China. However, the NCTS has been intentionally or unintentionally neglected by the liberal-dominated theological educational establishment in China and China mission scholarship.[2]

In fact, the NCTS was an excellent example of evangelical theological education in China before 1949. A study of the NCTS can help us understand the conservative model of theological education, the conservative mission approach, and the link between the Chinese evangelical churches and the international fundamentalist movement in the 1920s and 1930s. This chapter will trace the history of the NCTS; analyze the major aspects of its approach to theological education; highlight its contributions to the emerging Chinese evangelical churches; and explore its influence in the international evangelical movement.

1. A Brief History of the NCTS

The NCTS was born out of a doctrinal and administrative controversy within Shandong Christian University. The predecessor of the Shandong Christian University was Tengchow [Dengzhou] College opened in 1864 by the conservative Shandong Mission of the [American] Northern Presbyterian Church. In 1902 the Northern Presbyterian mission and the English Baptist mission united their schools in Shandong Province to form the Shandong Christian University. As the university grew, more missionary societies joined the enterprise.

Throughout the 1910s, however, internal tensions built up within this union enterprise. The tensions were largely administrative, personal as well as doctrinal. In particular the differences between the Northern Presbyterians and British Baptists, the two major segments of the university's constituency, played a crucial role in the developing controversy. The issues at stake included the school administration's control of student life, the final authority of faculty administration, and the style of the president's leadership. The conflict culminated in the summer of 1919 when J. Percy Bruce, an English Baptist and the university president, was forced to resign by the majority of the

---

2. For instance, in Cressy's survey of Christian higher education in China for the year 1925-1926, the NCTS was not even mentioned. See Earl Herbert Cressy, *Christian Higher Education in China, A Study for the Year 1925-26* (Shanghai: China Christian Educational Association, 1928). In Smith's study of Protestant theological education in China, only some statistics of the NCTS were given in the appendix. See Smith, *Protestant Theological Education*, part 2.

Presbyterian faculty. The controversy also led to the resignations of two prominent Presbyterian faculty members, L. J. Davies (1892-1935), the dean of the Arts College, and Watson Hayes (1882-1941), the acting dean of the Theological College.

The controversy within the Theological College was especially intense. Although some issues involved within the theological school were similar to those debated in other schools, the controversy at Shandong had its own unique features. One was that it was the Chinese Presbyterian churches, rather than the missionaries, who took the initiatives in opposing some of the current policies. As the Chinese Presbyterian churches in Shandong had become quite strong, independent, and theologically conservative in the early twentieth century, they became increasingly dissatisfied with the seminary. First, they were frustrated by the fact that the British Baptists often attempted to strengthen foreign control and weaken the power of the Chinese churches at the seminary. Secondly, the Chinese churches complained that erroneous teachings were permitted at the seminary, and "certain traditional doctrines were publicly challenged by a few liberal-minded faculty members."[3]

For years the Chinese churches had trusted Watson Hayes as the champion of their rights and opinions. Not surprisingly the forced resignation of Hayes from the theological school upset the Chinese Presbyterian students and the churches backing them. As a result, eighteen Presbyterian students left the theological school of Shandong Christian University and followed Hayes to Weihsien [Weixian], where he continued to tutor them.[4] Determined to establish a new seminary according to their own vision, the Chinese Presbyterian churches threw their support behind these students and one by one officially withdrew their support of the seminary.

In December of 1919 eight Chinese church leaders and foreign missionar-

3. According to Hayes, some of the teachings "can only be described, even from a mildly conservative standpoint as 'erroneous'; the teaching in regard to the O.T. especially cannot be regarded with approval.... [A faculty member] openly scoffed at O.T. teachings, and held up prayer for rain as a superstition of a bygone age" (M. Hayes to the Secretaries of the Presbyterian Board of Foreign Missions, 1 May 1920, Presbyterian Church in the U.S.A. Board of Foreign Missions, Secretaries' Files [PCUSABS], RG82, 20-5, Presbyterian Historical Society [PHS], Philadelphia). Another missionary wrote: "The virgin birth is scoffed at, the bodily resurrection of Jesus Christ is explained away, and even the Deity of Christ is questioned by some of the foreigners on the faculty" (Extract of Letter, Attachment to the Letter from E. C. Lobenstine to J. Walter Lowrie, 12 August 1921, PCUSABS, RG82, 20-13, PHS, Philadelphia).

4. Charles Hodge Corbett, *Shantung Christian University* [*Cheeloo*] (New York: United Board for Christian Colleges in China, 1955), p. 143.

ies formed a provisional board of directors for the new seminary named NCTS. The board drafted the constitution and raised funds, and Hayes was asked to assume the presidency of the seminary.[5] In 1922 the NCTS moved to its permanent campus in Tenghsien [Tengxian], Shandong Province. A Women's Bible Seminary was opened in connection with the men's in the fall of the same year.[6] Later the conservative North Jiangsu Mission of the Southern Presbyterian Church joined the new seminary and assigned a few missionaries to teach there.

When the NCTS was founded in 1919, it only had eighteen students, but it quickly experienced dramatic growth. For the school term of 1923-1924, the student body already included seventy-five men and nine women from nine different provinces and even from Korea, and the number of faculty reached six.[7] The peak of the seminary's enrollment, 135 men and fifty-one women, was reached just before the spring of 1927.[8] By the mid-1920s, the NCTS had surpassed the Nanjing Theological Seminary and become the largest seminary in China, especially in terms of student enrollment,[9] but the size of the NCTS faculty was small in comparison with other seminaries.[10] During the late 1920s, mainly because of escalation in fighting between the warlords and the Northern Expedition of the Nationalist forces, the work

5. Minutes of a Meeting of the Provisional Board of Directors of the Shantung Theological Seminary, held at Weihsien, Shantung China, 4 December 1919, PCUSABS, RG82, 20-8, PHS, Philadelphia.

6. The Women's Bible Seminary was under different administration. The women students attended classes with the men, even though their curriculum was different, and they did not take all the courses the men took.

7. Report of the North China Theological Seminary, August 1923–January 1924, PCUSABS, RG82, 26-7, PHS, Philadelphia. The Northern Presbyterian missionaries were W. M. Hayes and A. B. Dodd, and the Southern Presbyterians were B. C. Patterson and G. P. Stevens. After 1927, M. A. Hopkins of the PCUS and A. L. MacLeod of the PCUSA also joined the faculty. Chinese faculty members changed considerably throughout the years.

8. The North China Theological Seminary, Printed Materials, China Mission Papers, PHS, Montreat, NC, p. 7.

9. In the fall of 1926 the Nanjing Theological Seminary had 100 students, and the theological school of Shandong Christian University had forty-three. Cressy, *Christian Higher Education,* p. 121.

10. For the school term of 1925-1926, the NCTS had seven faculty members, some of whom split their time between the NCTS and the Mateer Memorial Institute. (Report of the NCTS, August 1925–January 1926, PCUSABS, RG82, 26-7, PHS, Philadelphia). In 1926, Nanjing and Yenching had respectively twenty-seven and thirteen teachers on faculty, and at least five other seminaries had more than seven faculty members (Cressy, *Christian Higher Education,* p. 125).

of the NCTS was interrupted from time to time, and its growth slowed considerably. The NCTS quickly regained its strength in the early 1930s, however, and the number of students reached 102 men and thirty-one women for the 1933-1934 term.[11]

After the Sino-Japanese War erupted in 1937, Tengxian soon became a major battlefield. The life of the NCTS community was seriously affected by the consequences of the war: an increasing number of refugees, damage to property, and a decline in the enrollment of students. When the Pacific War broke out in 1941, all students were forcefully dismissed and American faculty members were sent to a concentration camp by the Japanese troops.

During the brief period of peace following the Second World War, the faculty and board members of the NCTS made tremendous efforts to re-open the seminary. The board of directors held a couple of important meetings in 1946, the seminary property was registered according to the new laws in China, an American council was formed by the NCTS's conservative constituencies in the United States, and a Restoration Fund was set up for the rehabilitation and reconstruction of the seminary.

The NCTS officially re-opened in early 1946. As an all-out war broke out between the Nationalists and Communists, however, Tengxian found itself in the battle zone again. The school had to be temporarily located in the city of Hsuchowfu [Xuzhou] in the North Jiangsu region. As the battle lines moved southward, the NCTS was forced to move to Wuxian [Wusih] near Shanghai in 1948. Furthermore, the civil war made the return of foreign missionaries to China extremely difficult, and the NCTS was thus handicapped by the shortage of teaching staff.

As the Communists were winning the war in the late 1940s, the NCTS rapidly declined. In the fall semester of 1950, the NCTS had eighty-one students.[12] By the spring semester of 1952, there were only thirteen.[13] The last foreign missionary was forced to leave China in early 1951 and the financial support from overseas also stopped. Under Chinese leadership, the NCTS managed to carry on for a couple of years before it finally closed.

From the time of its founding to the Second World War, Watson M. Hayes was the dominant figure in the NCTS. The growth of the seminary and the formation of its character owed much to his leadership. Hayes arrived in

11. North China Theological Seminary President's Report for 1933-1934, PCUSABS, RG 82, 26-7, PHS, Philadelphia.

12. Martin A. Hopkins to Lloyd S. Ruland, 12 November 1950, PCUSABS, RG82, 67-14, PHS, Philadelphia.

13. Martin A. Hopkins to the American Council of the NCTS, 29 February 1952, PCUSABS, RG82, 68-14, PHS, Philadelphia.

Shandong Province in November of 1882 under the auspices of the [U.S.] Northern Presbyterian Mission Board. The next year he started teaching at Dengzhou College and was elected its president in 1889. During this period Hayes established himself as one of the most outstanding educational missionaries in China. Theologically very conservative, Hayes gained a reputation as "a rock of orthodoxy."[14] It was said that "Dr. Hayes is by far the ablest exponent of the fundamentalist theology in China. Of the dogmatic school of President Patton and Dr. Machen of Princeton, he is doing for conservative Christianity in China what these scholars have done in America."[15] After the Pacific War began, he spent his last years in the Japanese concentration camp in Weixian and died there in August of 1944.

2. NCTS and Fundamentalism

The NCTS was unique among the seminaries in China not only because of its dramatic rise and the size of its student body but also because of its distinctive teachings and administrative policies, which most explicitly embodied the conservatives' vision and understanding of theological education and mission. For years the NCTS firmly maintained its own identity as an institution championing the conservative cause.

The NCTS was founded at a turbulent time in China's mission history. In the early twentieth century, the spread of higher criticism, modern theology, and social gospel caused growing oppositions from conservative missionaries. The founding of the Bible Union of China in 1920 marked the beginning of an organized fundamentalist offensive against modernists among China missionaries. In the 1920s and 1930s the missionary community in China was deeply divided by the modernist-fundamentalist conflict.

The NCTS made its own conservative theological position very clear from its beginning. In March 1920, the provisional board of directors of the NCTS defined the purpose of this new institution as follows: "First, To teach the fundamental doctrines of the Christian church as found in the Word of God. Second, To emphasize the Bible as the only sufficient rule of faith and practice. Third, To preserve conservative teaching with regard to Theology, Bibli-

14. Extracts of Letter, attached to the letter from E. C. Lobenstine to J. Walter Lowrie, 12 August 1921.

15. Stanley Ross Fisher and H. Paul Douglass, "The Church and Its Leadership," in Orville A. Petty, ed., *Laymen's Foreign Missions Inquiry Fact-Finders' Report, China*, vol. 5, Supp. Series, Part 2 (New York: Harper and Brothers Publishers, 1933), pp. 237-301, quotation at p. 281.

cal criticism and Exegesis."[16] Obviously the authority of the Bible took a central place in the vision of this seminary.

As the fundamentalist missionaries launched offensives against the modernists in the early 1920s, the NCTS did not hesitate to express its sympathy with the fundamentalist cause and started to stress its own conservative agenda and its differences from theological liberalism. The Creedal Statement of the NCTS declared: "We unreservedly believe what orthodox Christians of every denomination accept as the Bible; namely, the sixty-six books of the Old and New Testaments. We believe the entire record to have been made under the guidance (inspiration) of the Holy Spirit. We believe what it records as history to be genuine history, its miracles to be actual facts, its prophecies to be truly prophecy, and its teachings to be the unique and supreme rule for faith and life."[17] Christ's deity, propitiatory sacrifice, resurrection, and the second coming were all firmly asserted by the statement. All faculty and board directors were required to subscribe to the statement annually.[18] To be a "Bible honoring" school and defend the "old gospel" against modernism became the essential spirit of the NCTS.

Throughout his years at the NCTS, Watson Hayes envisioned the NCTS as a counter-attack against the modernist tide and as an institution deeply rooted in the principle of the infallible authority of the Bible. He believed that it was the NCTS's responsibility to "never graduate Christ-belittling, Gospel-doubting men who imagine that their ideas are as good, if not superior to those of St. Paul."[19] As a result of this conservative vision of theological education, the curriculum of the NCTS was dominated by Old and New Testament courses. For instance, the NCTS President's Report for 1933-1934 stated:

> While new courses have been gradually introduced into the curriculum, the main stress is, as before, laid on the plain teachings of the Scriptures and on what "by good and necessary inference" is deduced from the same. There is no substitution of mere human surmises for the Divine Word, nor any attempt made to correct inspired language. The empha-

16. Minutes of a Meeting of the Provisional Board of Directors of the Shantung Theological Seminary, held at Weihsien, 12 March 1920, PCUSABS, RG82, 20-5, PHS, Philadelphia.

17. North China Theological Seminary, Printed Materials, 4.

18. Report of the North China Theological Seminary, August 1923–January 1924, PCUSABS, RG82, 26-7, PHS, Philadelphia.

19. W. M. Hayes to Swarthmore Church, 4 January 1930, PCUSABS, RG82, 41-20, PHS, Philadelphia.

sis laid on God's own teaching we see as the main reason for students coming long distances to take their theological course with us.[20]

Again the following year's Report stressed that the NCTS's curriculum emphasized "particularly direct Bible study."[21] It would be a mistake, however, to treat the NCTS merely as a Bible-training school. Even in the early 1920s, in addition to biblical studies, its curriculum included considerable training in systematic theology, church history, homiletics, and such general studies as the biblical languages, English, music, and even comparative religion.

As time went by, the NCTS curriculum was also enlarged by courses in Old and New Testament theology, Christian sociology, Old Testament archeology, geology, and biology. Even the broader curriculum, however, reflected the NCTS's anti-modernist stand. For instance, the courses on archeology, geology, and biology were geared to testify to "the historical accuracy of the Bible, and to the creation of the world by Divine fiat, and not by methods of evolution."[22] In summary, the NCTS's curriculum was designed to equip the Chinese Christians with orthodox doctrines and biblical literalism, and the relatively small number of courses on science and other secular knowledge were also offered to serve this ultimate goal.

In Christian schools in China of the 1920s and 1930s, as Peter Tze Ming Ng has pointed out, religious teachings moved "beyond the mere teaching of the Christian Bible, to give more attention to its relevance to the Chinese cultural environments and social issues."[23] He called this development "secularization or modernization." This trend was common not only on college campuses but also within certain theological educational institutions. Such well-known seminaries as the School of Religion at Yenching University were eager to change their aim from "training men for the Christian ministry" to "laying the foundation of Christian thought for China and . . . building up Christian life in China." Consequently, Yenching began to significantly broaden its curriculum and offer courses in the fields of Psychology of Religion, Philosophy of Religion, History of Religion, Religious Literature, and Religious Arts.[24] The NCTS's Bible- and doctrine-centered approach and curriculum stood in

20. North China Theological Seminary President's Report for 1933-1934, PCUSABS, RG82, 26-7, PHS, Philadelphia.

21. Report of North China Theological Seminary, 1934-1935, PCUSABS, RG82, 26-7, PHS, Philadelphia.

22. Fisher and Douglass, "Church and Its Leadership," p. 280.

23. Peter Tze Ming Ng, "Secularization or Modernization: Teaching Christianity in China Since the 1920s," *Studies in World Christianity* 5, no. 1 (1999): 1-17, quotation at p. 5.

24. See Ng, "Secularization or Modernization," pp. 7-9.

sharp contrast to this secularizing trend, and the school never had any intention of broadening its curriculum in the way Yenching did.

3. The NCTS and Evangelism

One of the important characteristics of the NCTS was its emphasis on evangelism. To strengthen the evangelizing forces of the emerging Chinese churches was a crucial mission of the NCTS.

While the social gospel advocated the importance of social reform and service as an inseparable part of the Christian missions and many missionaries were busy building universities and hospitals in the 1920s and 1930s, the NCTS persistently held on to its single-minded evangelistic goal. This was viewed not only as the best way of spreading the gospel in China but also as a protest against the modernists' re-interpretation of mission goals and emphasis. Hayes was a staunch believer in the evangelicals' classical stress on "direct evangelistic work" as the primary task of the Christian missions and the prerequisite for social services. He insisted that "the main business of the missionary is not to teach modern methods of farming, political science, philosophy, or modern languages, . . . but to lead men to know God and Jesus Christ."[25] He believed that the Christian missions in China were in great danger of overemphasizing social reform at the cost of evangelism.[26]

Hayes was very critical of "the grand mistake that had been made in pouring money by the thousands of dollars into the large purely educational institutions."[27] Consequently the financial resources and personnel were drained from direct evangelistic work. In his opinion these "extensive and expensive enterprises" were definitely not "proper objects of missionary work."[28] Sometimes he made a sharp contrast between the missionary "elite" busy with the institutional work in the cities and these "pastor-evangelists" winning souls for Christ under harsh environments. He claimed that "it is not the men who receive big salaries, dress well, and are prominent (not in actual work) but in

25. W. M. Hayes to Swarthmore Church, 16 February 1928, Blackstone Papers, Billy Graham Center (BGC), Wheaton College. His words earned him a reputation of opposing "education." See C. H. Fenn to W. M. Hayes, 28 June 1930, PCUSABS, RG82, 41-20, PHS, Philadelphia.

26. See W. M. Hayes to Swarthmore Church, 18 January 1927, Blackstone Papers, BGC, Wheaton College.

27. W. M. Hayes to Swarthmore Friends, 19 November 1927, Blackstone Papers, BGC, Wheaton College.

28. W. M. Hayes to Swarthmore Church, 10 May 1927, Blackstone Papers, BGC, Wheaton College.

the so-called Councils 'telling others how to do it' who are really advancing the Kingdom, but men like Paul, willing to endure hardship."[29] Hayes also constantly advocated the recalling of personnel not directly involved in evangelistic work and cutting the expense in the central offices instead of the field work.[30]

Hayes's negative view of the growing missionary social programs and his stress on evangelism was shared by the faculty, the board of directors, and student bodies of the NCTS. Therefore, the curriculum and school activities of the NCTS were designed to give the students not only knowledge of the Bible and theology but also the opportunity to be involved in evangelistic work during the school year. Each school year lasted usually from August of one year to January of the next, so the students were free for more than six months between school years. This unique arrangement was intended to "give its students ample time for evangelistic work and thus test their ability to serve the churches, so that on graduation they will not be inexperienced novices but men qualified by educational culture and practical experience to build up the church."[31]

To sharpen their evangelistic skills, the seminary encouraged its faculty members and students to engage in the evangelization of the neighboring areas. The majority of the NCTS faculty took an active part in leading revival meetings, Bible study conferences, and other evangelistic events. In 1934 Shankiang Presbytery of Shandong Province designated an area with fifty-eight villages to be the seminary parish. A number of student gospel teams composed of five to six members were sent out to the villages, preaching at the hall, the jail, the railway station, and the leper asylum on Sundays. In the first year of operation, more than fifty people were converted by these gospel bands.[32] For the school year of 1936-1937, the total number of the gospel teams reached twenty-eight, and 125 people were admitted into local churches by baptism.[33] The students' evangelistic teams gradually gained a good reputation in the surrounding areas and were often in high demand.

---

29. Hayes to Swarthmore Church, 19 November 1927. Hayes repeatedly expressed similar views in some of his correspondence with Robert E. Speer. See W. M. Hayes to Robert E. Speer, 27 June 1933, PCUSABS, RG82 47-17, PHS, Philadelphia. See also W. M. Hayes to Robert E. Speer, 16 February 1933, PCUSABS, RG82, 47-17, PHS, Philadelphia.

30. W. M. Hayes to Robert E. Speer, 12 September 1933, PCUSABS, RG82, 47-17, PHS, Philadelphia.

31. North China Theological Seminary, PCUSABS, RG82, 26-7, PHS, Philadelphia, 2.

32. Report of North China Theological Seminary, 1934-1935.

33. Report of the North China Theological Seminary, 1936-1937, in Minutes of the Shantung Missions of PCUSA, 1937, China Mission Papers, PHS, Montreat, NC, 92.

Watson Hayes and the NCTS's standing for evangelism reflected evangelicals' understanding of mission and their response to the social gospel and institution-building trend in the 1920s and 1930s. The old balance between evangelism and social services became a casualty of the fundamentalist-modernist division. The so-called "Great Reversal" or the weakening of evangelicals' social interests took place among the conservative missionary circles in China of the 1920s and 1930s.

4. The NCTS and the Chinese Churches

Another very significant feature of the NCTS was its persistent policy of maintaining Chinese control of the seminary and strengthening the role of self-support of the Chinese churches. From the moment of its founding, one of the indispensable aspects of the self-identity of the NCTS was that it was a Chinese theological school governed by the Chinese Presbyterian churches, especially in Shandong and North Jiangsu. There is no doubt that, for the period of 1920 to 1937, Watson Hayes was the dominant figure in the life of the NCTS. He taught theology, raised funds, and almost single-handedly ran the school administration. Nevertheless, the board of directors was elected by the Chinese churches, and the majority of the board members were Chinese Christians. Even foreign members of the board were chosen by the Chinese Presbyterian churches.[34]

Chinese Christians also assumed significant roles in teaching at the NCTS. For most of the years, at least half of an average of seven to eight full-time faculty members were Chinese. Among all the Chinese faculty members, Ting Li Mei [Ding Li-mei] and Kia Yu Ming [Jia Yu-ming] were most prominent. Ding (1871-1936) was one of the earliest Chinese evangelists with a "nation-wide reputation."[35] Jia (1880-1964) was one of the top conservative Chinese systematic theologians, exegetes, and educators. He was appointed to the vice-presidency of the NCTS in the early 1920s. In 1937 W. M. Hayes started to transfer the NCTS leadership to Chinese Christians, and a Chinese faculty member, H. K. Chang [Zhang Xue-gong], was appointed co-president with Hayes.

Chinese Christians even took on significant responsibilities in financial support of the seminary. When the seminary was founded, Chinese Chris-

---

34. Report of the North China Theological Seminary, August 1923–January 1924.

35. Daniel H. Bays, "The Growth of Independent Christianity in China, 1900-1937," in Daniel H. Bays, ed., *Christianity in China: From the Eighteenth Century to the Present* (Stanford, CA: Stanford University Press, 1996), pp. 307-16, quotation at p. 313.

tians made considerable financial contributions. Hayes always stood firmly for the self-support of the Chinese church. He was keenly aware that the NCTS aimed to train the future leaders for the Chinese churches especially in rural areas. In his view, the students' capacity for enduring hardship and self-support was just as crucial as the orthodoxy of their beliefs for the future of the churches in China. Hayes summarized his view and the NCTS's position as follows:

> We would like to see the student body practically entirely self-supporting, believing that the student who earns his education will value it all the more. . . . All will probably realize the importance of men on graduation being willing to accept the small salaries which the churches, with few exceptions are able to pay: otherwise the problem of the rural church, constituting the bulk of the Christian constituency in China, presents a serious problem. The culture of the students during their seminary course has a very direct relation to this problem.[36]

Under his leadership these visions and principles were applied to the financial matters and student life at the NCTS. For years the NCTS pursued two related policies: keeping the expenses of the seminary low and encouraging financial commitment on the part of the Chinese churches.[37] As the seminary with the largest enrollment, the NCTS had considerably lower expenses and a higher percentage of Chinese contributions to its budget than a number of other seminaries. For the school year of 1933-1934, the total expenditure of the NCTS was approximately M $5000[38] and [NCTS] ranked number seven among the top eleven seminaries in China.[39] In addition, the NCTS was one of only two schools that did not receive any significant income from the mission boards but received contributions from the Chinese churches,[40] even

36. Report of the North China Theological Seminary, August 1925–January 1926, PCUSABS, RG82, 26-7, PHS, Philadelphia.

37. Of course the adoption of these policies had to do with the lack of financial backup from the mission board of the Northern Presbyterian Church and poor economic conditions of the rural areas from which the NCTS drew most of its students. However, they also significantly reflected Hayes's inclination toward anti-institutionalization and his vision of theological education and its relation to the emerging Chinese churches.

38. North China Theological Seminary President's Report for 1933-1934. "M" stands for the Mexican dollar, the currency in China in the 1930s.

39. Smith, *Protestant Theological Education*, Appendix B, "Statistical Chart of Theological Seminaries and Bible Schools, 1933-34."

40. Since the NCTS was a project initiated by the Chinese Presbyterian churches and a few Northern Presbyterian missionaries like Hayes outside the Northern Presbyterian

though the contributions from the Chinese sources never accounted for more than half of the school's expenses. During the same school year Yenching School of Religion and Nanjing Theological Seminary had the largest expenditures and relied heavily on endowments from the foreign sources.[41] The relatively small budget enabled the NCTS to endure the impact of the Great Depression rather easily.

The low expenditure made the costs of living and studying in the NCTS relatively cheap and thus enabled many students with very modest economic means to accept theological training there. Throughout the years the NCTS charged neither tuition nor housing for all students and maintained low costs of board, heat, baths, and electric light. Furthermore, the NCTS persisted in steps to reduce financial assistance to the students.

When the seminary was established in 1919 Chinese churches and students paid no part of their board, travel, books, or other expenses, and presbyteries also subsidized the students for the support of their families. Six years later this subsidy for families was completely dropped. By 1925 the majority of the student body also paid for the actual cost of board, clothes, travel, and books.[42] In the meantime the NCTS helped create the opportunities for students to obtain the means for self-support. In fact one major purpose of having a single five-and-a-half-month semester per year was to free the students so that they could make a living and provide for their families.[43]

Strengthening the Chinese self-government and self-support was just a part of the NCTS's efforts to build an indigenous church in China. While other seminaries like Yenching and Nanjing sought to raise the academic standard of theological studies by offering higher-grade theological courses in English to college graduates,[44] the NCTS continued to shun any attempts at Westernizing the teaching or students' lives. All classes in the NCTS were conducted in Mandarin, and English was simply taught as an elective course. In guiding the students' life, "the school also aims by its Chinese dormitory

---

Mission Board's plan, the board never took on the responsibility for any expenses of the new seminary, besides a couple of missionaries' salaries and a very small amount of annual allowance. Throughout the whole history of the NCTS, the seminary's relationship with the board was ambiguous and controversial.

41. Smith, *Protestant Theological Education,* Appendix B, "Statistical Chart." According to Smith's survey, from 1933-1934, Nanjing had eleven full-time faculty and fifty-eight students, and Yenching had five full-time faculty and thirty students. The NCTS had only ten faculty but 133 students.

42. Report of the North China Theological Seminary, 1925-1926.

43. See North China Theological Seminary, PCUSABS, 2.49, Extracts of Letter, Attached to the letter from Lobenstine to J. Walter Lowrie, 12 August 1921.

44. See Smith, *Protestant Theological Education,* p. 122.

system and mode of life to avoid training its men to a semi-foreign style of living beyond the ability of the Chinese churches to sustain."[45] The NCTS always carefully avoided detaching its students from their own indigenous cultural and living settings.

To establish Three-Self churches had been the goal of many Protestant missionaries in China since the early years of the nineteenth century.[46] By the mid-twentieth century, however, the accomplishment of their efforts was minimal. Daniel Bays observed that this was especially the case with the so-called "Sino-Foreign Protestant establishment" dominated by modernists and moderates.[47] The rapid development of expensive educational and medical institutions made the goal of the Three-Selves even more difficult to achieve. On the other hand, the emerging indigenous conservative Christian groups were Three-Self from the very beginning. The case of the NCTS showed that conservative missions were in general more consistent in their efforts to make the churches indigenous and also achieved more than their liberal counterparts. In contrast to several rather academic and urban-based seminaries in China, the NCTS created and maintained a culture serving grass-roots Christian communities and providing them with an opportunity of theological training in their own cultural and economic environments.

Controlled and staffed by the Presbyterian churches, the NCTS aimed to train church leaders for all Chinese churches regardless of denomination. Minimizing the particular Presbyterian teachings on the curriculum, it was able to gather an inter-denominational student body on the basis of common conservative beliefs. Over the years a large number of Chinese Christians across the country came to get their theological education there. From 1919 to 1933, 204 students graduated from the NCTS,[48] and served the churches throughout the country. The NCTS did not produce prominent Chinese Christian thinkers and scholars but educated generations of pastors and evangelists for a great number of rural and urban churches. Through these graduates, the NCTS exerted an important and long-lasting influence on the character of the Chinese churches and contributed to the formation of the evangelical and conservative tradition of the Protestant churches in China.

The 1920s and 1930s witnessed the dramatic rise of independent Chinese

45. North China Theological Seminary, PCUSABS, 2.

46. For a survey of the Three-Self movement in China, see Wilbert R. Shenk, "The Origins and Evolution of the Three-Selfs in Relation to China," *International Bulletin of Missionary Research* 14 (Jan. 1990): 28-35.

47. See Bays, "Independent Christianity," pp. 308-9.

48. Hayes to the Supporters of the North China Theological Seminary, 16 October 1933, PCUSABS, RG82, 26-4, PHS, Philadelphia.

evangelists and evangelical revival movements. The Chinese evangelists and revivalists' message of repentance and rebirth and their conservative theological views were largely compatible with the positions of the NCTS. Not surprisingly, several Chinese faculty members of the NCTS were among the prominent figures of these revivals. The Presbyterian missionaries associated with the NCTS also reacted positively to most of the revivals and their leaders, but the NCTS reacted negatively to one strain of the revival movement, namely the "Spiritual Grace Movement." This was a pentecostal type of revival movement rising in Shandong Province in the early 1930s. Watson Hayes and most of the NCTS faculty were deeply troubled by the movement's emphasis on the experience of being filled by the Holy Spirit, speaking in tongues, visions, miracles, and its crude exegesis, and they took official actions to resist the movement's invasion of the NCTS community. The NCTS's conflict with the pentecostal revival in Shandong highlighted the tension between the conservative Reformed tradition and holiness teachings. With its strong Calvinistic background, the NCTS had a lot in common with the Bible-centered and Reformed-oriented mainstream of the revival movements within the Chinese churches.

5. The NCTS's International Influence

In the 1920s and 1930s the North China Theological Seminary attracted much attention from the fundamentalists in both China and North America. The split within the Theological College of the Shandong Christian University was often cited as evidence of the widespread modernism in the mission field.[49] In the case of the NCTS, the fundamentalists clearly saw a useful weapon for agitation against and attack on the modernists and the mission boards. It was no wonder that, among the fundamentalist groups, the NCTS quickly gained the reputation as "a protest against the rationalistic teaching of our missionaries,"[50] "a shining example of true testimony,"[51] and "the only theological school in China of seminary grade which is conservative."[52] The NCTS partic-

49. Extracts of Letter, Attached to the letter from Lobenstine to J. Walter Lowrie, 12 August 1921.

50. Quoted in the Board of Foreign Missions of PCUSA to China Council and Missions in China, 8 December 1925, PCUSABS, RG82, 27-17, PHS, Philadelphia.

51. Charles G. Trumbull, "Foreign Missionary Betrayals of the Faith, a Crisis Confronting the Whole Church," *The Sunday School Times* (March 23, 1935), p. 195.

52. W. M. Hayes to George T. Scott, 22 November 1923, PCUSABS, RG 82, 26-4, PHS, Philadelphia.

ularly featured prominently within the fundamentalist network of evangelist and missionary training institutions in North America. It became a symbol of anti-modernist battle in the mission field. In 1926 John Innis of the Bible Institute of Los Angeles declared that "it is very encouraging to see how the numbers at the North China Seminary are increasing. It is another unquestionable evidence we have that, in spite of all the fuss and noise made by Modernists, the heart of the church in China is beating true, and I believe that the great rank and file of the missionaries and Chinese Christians are absolutely loyal to the Gospel of Jesus Christ."[53] During the 1930s the NCTS was constantly compared with the newly founded Westminster Seminary in Philadelphia, sometimes simply referred to as "the Westminster Seminary of China,"[54] because both were viewed as strongholds of conservative theological education. In the eyes of the fundamentalists in China as well as abroad, the NCTS was one of the theological educational institutions they could still trust. They spoke highly of both the spiritual life and academic standard of the seminary, and the NCTS was claimed to be "by far the largest Theological Seminary in all China as well as second to none in educational standard."[55]

Soon after the NCTS was established, it began to raise funds from over-

53. John Innis to W. E. Blackstone, 14 October 1926, Blackstone Papers, BGC, Wheaton College.

54. "News from the Front," *Independent Board Bulletin* 1 (Jan. 1935): 12. See also J. Edward Blair: An Open Letter to Dr. Robert E. Speer, 8 April 1935, J. Gresham Machen Papers, Westminster Theological Seminary, Philadelphia.

55. See Albert B. Dodd, "The General Assembly of the Presbyterian Church of Christ in China," *China Fundamentalist* (Jan.-March 1930), p. 15. An article in the *Sunday School Times* praised the NCTS and the affiliated Women's Bible Seminary in these words, "These two schools combined are not only the largest theological center in China, of high grade teaching and real scholarship in the Chinese and foreign professors, . . . but they also constitute a bulwark of evangelical religion for the nascent Church of China" (Charles Ernest Scott, "A Great Missionary's Fifty Years in China, Watson M. Hayes, DD., Evangelist, Teacher, Author, and Scholar," *Sunday School Times* (10 June 1933), p. 388. But many educational missionaries questioned the academic standard of the NCTS. A common view among many missionaries was that the academic standard at the NCTS was lower than such seminaries as Nanjing and Yenching. According to the NCTS statement of 1924, the qualification for entrance into the seminary was college and middle school graduates who were required to take some extra junior college courses. (See North China Theological Seminary, PCUSABS, 3.) According to the *Laymen's Inquiry Report*, which was considered to be unexpectedly objective and generous toward the NCTS, the actual entrance requirement for the NCTS was junior middle school, and lower than Yenching, Nanjing, and some other schools. Most of the students at the NCTS belonged to the category of junior middle school, and "with the exception of three teachers, the scholastic equipment of the faculty is not of a high degree" (*Laymen's Inquiry Fact-Finders' Report*, p. 281).

seas. Conservative organizations in North America, such as the Milton Stewart Fund[56] and individuals such as William B. Riley of Minneapolis, had secured funds toward the founding of the NCTS.[57] For the most part of the 1920s, the Milton Stewart Fund continued to provide the NCTS with financial support. As the largest conservative seminary in China, the NCTS was indeed a big attraction for many potential conservative donors who began to lose confidence in the mission boards of their churches. Certain NCTS faculty members appealed directly to the conservative home constituency for funds. Even W. M. Hayes wrote numerous letters to his home churches and constantly stressed the conservative status of the NCTS and its differences from liberal seminaries.

Throughout the years the NCTS built extensive constituencies in North America. In the post–Second World War era, NCTS's supporters in North America were determined to "perpetuate N.C.T.S. as it had prospered in Dr. Hayes' days."[58] In other words, they insisted that "N.C.T.S. should be maintained as a distinctly Presbyterian Seminary, genuinely conservative, committed to an inspired Bible as our only infallible rule."[59] Conservative churches and individual Christians began to pour considerable financial resources into the rehabilitation of the NCTS. An American council of the NCTS was set up to muster the support for the seminary. This council worked hard to resist any attempt to change its conservative foundation and identity.

The history of the NCTS shows that sympathy and support from the conservative forces overseas contributed to its growth. As a joint venture of American missionaries and Chinese Presbyterian churches, the NCTS served as a link between the fundamentalists in North America and evangelicals in China. In their efforts to fight liberalism, the two sides reinforced each other. The case of the NCTS shows that the emerging evangelical movement in China was a part of the international phenomenon.

56. The Milton Stewart Evangelistic Fund was set up by Milton Stewart, the brother of Lyman Stewart, in 1917. Theologically conservative, the fund aimed to strengthen evangelistic forces in mission fields. The fund heavily invested in China and supported numerous conservative missionary enterprises. See J. H. Blackstone, "The Milton Stewart Evangelistic Fund," in E. C. Lobenstine, A. L. Warnshuis, and others, eds., *China Mission Year Book 1918* (Shanghai: Kwang Hsueh Publishing House, 1918), p. 359; "The Milton Stewart Evangelistic Fund," in *China Mission Year Book* (1917), p. 367.

57. See B. C. Patterson, Memoir of Brown Craig Patterson, Brown Craig Patterson Papers, PHS, Montreat, NC, 53-54.

58. Horace G. Hill, Jr., to C. E. Macartney and others, 14 April 1949, PCUSABS, RG82, 67-3, PHS, Philadelphia.

59. Horace G. Hill, Jr., to D. Kirkland West, 3 June 1949, PCUSABS, RG 82, 67-3, PHS, Philadelphia.

The North China Theological Seminary deserves a special place in the history of Protestant theological education in China. It was the best embodiment of the evangelical vision of theological education. The mission of the NCTS was always to equip the Chinese churches with well-trained ministers and evangelists who held orthodox beliefs, committed themselves to the evangelization of the masses in the urban and rural areas, were willing to work independently under harsh conditions, and were capable of building indigenous churches. This vision of theological education was certainly different from the social-service oriented, rather academic, and mostly urban liberal seminaries in China. For more than three decades this vision made the NCTS the foremost theological training institution for evangelical Protestantism in China and thus produced a significant impact upon Protestant churches in China in the twentieth century.

PART IV

Local Agency:
Charismatic and Pentecostal Transformations

CHAPTER 9

Consuming Fire: Pandita Ramabai and the Global Pentecostal Impulse

EDITH L. BLUMHOFER

Readers of the *Chicago Daily News* on Tuesday, 14 January 1908, stumbled on a startling tale. A few pages in, among advertisements for house furnishings, Clark's thread, and cotton pillowcases, was an article by the noted journalist William T. Ellis detailing a recent visit to Mukti, a Christian community forty miles south of Poona, India.[1] Drawn by the reputation of the community's founder, Pandita Ramabai, and by accounts of unusual religious stirrings at Mukti, Ellis — who had gone abroad to explore the missionary enterprise at his own expense — had detoured from his planned itinerary. What he found made the detour worth his while, and became the subject of the article Chicagoans read with their morning coffee. "Have Gift of Tongues," the title announced: "Girl Widows of Christian Church in India Develop Wonderful Phenomena."

A seasoned Christian author and editor, Ellis earned his living in 1908 by writing editorials for the *Philadelphia Evening Bulletin*,[2] but his Christian sympathies sensitized him to religious news as well. Wherever he traveled, Ellis had found people talking about a new wave of revival. When he learned of the revival in Mukti, he chose to go, for, like countless thousands, he had long known of Mukti's legendary founder, Pandita Ramabai. If the perplexing revival phenomena occurred under her purview, Ellis knew he could sell his story, for Protestants around the world revered and supported Ramabai.

---

1. Poona is now known as Pune.

2. For a brief biographical sketch, see "Ellis, William Thomas," *The Encyclopedia Americana* (New York: Americana Corp., 1953), p. 257.

Ellis found at Mukti "an extraordinary religious manifestation, as remarkable as anything in connection with the great revival in Wales." Unwilling to pass judgment, he chose simply to "narrate, soberly and consecutively, what I have seen and heard concerning this 'baptism with fire' and pouring out of 'the gift of tongues,' whereby ignorant Hindoo girls speak in Sanskrit, Hebrew, Greek, English, and other languages as yet unidentified." Ellis puzzled over a small, noisy prayer meeting with thirty girls, some praying aloud, others crying "at the top of their lungs." Some sat on the floor, with heads touching it; others stood and swayed; a few knelt and rocked; still others twitched and jerked as if convulsed. The girls seemed unconscious of one another, and amid the clamor, their intense concentration surprised Ellis. He thought he heard one speaking English. Oddly, he learned that occasionally one or another could not speak at all. These believed God "smote them dumb" and obliged them to write messages rather than to speak them. "Sometimes," Ellis reported, "the girls will go about their tasks for days, unable to utter a word though they understand perfectly all that is said to them and are able to pray in other tongues. And when they specially pray for the power to do so, they are able to speak in religious meetings."

When Ellis confronted Ramabai for an explanation, she told him that she did not "make a special point of the gift of tongues." She never "exhibited" the tongues speakers, and she admitted an ongoing problem of "weeding out the false from the true." "There are other spirits than the Holy Spirit," she reminded him, "and when a girl begins to try to speak in another tongue, apparently imitating her sisters without mentioning the name or blood of Jesus, I go up to her and speak to her or touch her on the shoulder, and she stops at once. On the other hand, if a girl is praying in the Spirit I cannot stop her, no matter how sharply I speak to her or shake her."

Ellis had stumbled on one piece of the larger story of the emerging global pentecostal movement. In several ways, Ramabai stood at the center of the beginning of that story in India, and her community offers an opportunity to track the movement's unfolding. Her reputation at home and abroad seemed to Western pentecostals to lend a certain credibility to the movement. Her networks in India briefly helped nurture a certain credibility for the movement and to extend it in its critical early years. Under her auspices, people found space to explore the essentials and meaning of revival in relationship to pentecostalism. In the end, however, Ramabai held herself aloof from pentecostalism as a movement that attempted to promote the revival that had ebbed and flowed among Indian Christians for at least two years. One could argue that Western pentecostalism played a primary role in ending the Indian revival. A brief look at Ramabai's past suggests why events surrounding this "most famous Hindoo woman" matter to the larger story of global pentecostalism.

1. "Pandita" Ramabai Dongre

Though she became the protégé of such prominent late-nineteenth-century activists as the American scientist and educator Rachel Bodley, Oxford professor F. Max Müller, the American reformer Frances Willard, and the English educator Dorothea Beale, Ramabai's life began obscurely in a mountainous and remote corner of Bombay Presidency on 23 April 1858. Born to a Brahman family living outside India's urban centers of influence, Ramabai owed her later prominence to two daring decisions her father (Anant Shastri Dongre) made. He infringed caste strictures by teaching her to read and then master Sanskrit and Hindu sacred literature, and defied caste customs by refusing to contract a marriage for her. He thus opened to her a vastly different future from that available to most Indian women.

Ramabai's teenage years were spent on the move. She was taken in a wicker basket at the age of six months and never knew anything other than the road for the next twenty years. Walking with her family the length and breadth of India, they stopped at sacred places, performed the customary rituals, fasted, presented offerings, and bathed in sacred rivers. Her father's learning made him much in demand, and he eked out a meager living reciting scriptures, teaching, and accepting gifts from the faithful. The tremendous hardships that accompanied this nomadic lifestyle took their toll.

Desperate poverty and hunger afflicted the family, and in the summer of 1874, Ramabai's parents succumbed during a severe famine. Ramabai and her brother trudged on, covering an estimated 2,000 miles in the next six years. What they saw everywhere "made us think much of how it was possible to improve the condition of women and raise them out of their degradation."[3] Ramabai's fluency in seven languages and her general learning in Hindu sacred literature astonished her male cohorts. When Ramabai and her brother arrived in Calcutta, she came to the attention of the university community. In 1878 she became "the news of the hour," one admiring missionary contemporary later enthused. "Papers all over published her with doubtings, trumpetings and amazement. She was unimaginable — a woman of purest

---

3. Pandita Ramabai, "An Autobiographical Account" (1883), in Meera Kosambi, ed., *Pandita Ramabai Through Her Own Words* (New Delhi: Oxford University Press, 2000), p. 117.

Brahman birth, twenty-five years old and unmarried, beautiful and impossibly learned. She dazzled India."[4] In an unprecedented move, a panel of Sanskrit scholars or *pandits* associated with the University of Calcutta bestowed on her the title of "Saraswati" ("Goddess of Learning"), and from that point on she was given the further honorific title of "Pandita." In Calcutta she delved deeper into Hindu texts and Hindu law and was appalled by their views of women.[5]

Even as she gained acclaim, personal tragedy continued. Her brother died in 1881. Ramabai broke caste to marry Bipin Behari Medhavi, a lawyer and member of the theistic reformist sect, the Brahmo Samaj. Influenced by Western (especially American Unitarian views), the Brahmo Samaj endorsed a forward-looking social program that Ramabai found appealing. Her marriage was happy and remarkably egalitarian, but cholera claimed her husband less than two years later, leaving her with an infant daughter, Manoramabai. Ramabai decided to return to the Bombay Presidency and to the study of English. She and her husband had talked of visiting England; now she would pursue that goal on her own.

Ramabai arrived at the Government Female Training School in Poona in March 1882. She also became the private pupil of an English missionary, a Miss Hurford, with whom she read the Bible in Marathi and pursued her study of English. This was not Ramabai's first encounter with the Bible. With her brother, she had attended a Christian meeting in Calcutta where missionary translators presented her with a Sanskrit Bible. She had found a Bengali Gospel of Luke among her husband's books. A British Baptist missionary from Silchar in Assam had occasionally called, preaching the gospel and explaining the Genesis account of creation.[6] Ramabai professed no interest in conversion, but she found the Bible intriguing and became a willing reader.[7] Through Miss Hurford, Ramabai came to know the Sisters of St. Mary the Virgin, members of an Anglo-Catholic order, that ran a mission in Poona. Ramabai coped tactfully with their manifest interest in her soul and graciously accepted their introduction to a prominent Indian convert, Father Nehemiah Goreh.

4. Mary Lucia Bierce Fuller, *The Triumph of an Indian Widow* (New York: The American Auxiliary of the Ramabai Mukti Mission, 1928), p. 17.

5. Pandita Ramabai, *A Testimony of Our Inexhaustible Treasure* (Kedgaon, India: Mukti Mission Press, 1907), in Kosambi, ed., *Pandita Ramabai Through Her Own Words*, pp. 302-3.

6. Kosambi, ed., *Pandita Ramabai Through Her Own Words*, pp. 305, 326.

7. Pandita Ramabai, "The Word-Seed," in Kosambi, ed., *Pandita Ramabai Through Her Own Words*, pp. 325-27.

In May 1882, shortly after her arrival, Ramabai established in Poona the Arya Mahila Samaj, a society dedicated to promoting female education. A few months later she founded a Bombay branch. In February 1883 she testified before the Indian Education (Hunter) Commission in support of legislation to improve educational opportunities for Indian women. Her prominence in such endeavors led English journalists to introduce her to their readers before her dream of visiting the West materialized. It was reported that Queen Victoria herself had read Ramabai's remarks to the Hunter Commission and that the Government of India had gradually implemented some of her suggestions.[8] Ramabai's name first surfaced in the American religious press in 1883, just after her testimony before the Commission. *The Presbyterian,* like other Protestant papers, dutifully apprised its readers of glimmers of social progress on the world's mission fields. Of Ramabai *The Presbyterian* commented:

> One of the most interesting characters in India just now is Ramabai, a
> gifted and highly educated young Brahmin widow, who has undertaken
> the difficult task of creating a public sentiment against the social cus
> toms which bind down Indian women. She has already achieved a great
> deal. Her lectures in Bombay have created a wide interest, not only from
> the novelty of a woman assuming such a position, but from her schol
> arly and forcible manner of placing her views before the public. She is
> spoken of as on the "border line of Christianity," and her influence in
> certain directions can scarcely be overrated.[9]

On 17 May 1883, Ramabai realized her dream of going to England. She funded her trip with the proceeds from a small Marathi book, *Stri-dharma-niti,* describing the duties of women. Before her departure she had publicly promised that she would not convert to Christianity.[10] The government having purchased rights to her book, Ramabai sailed away to embrace a future that she hoped would focus on the study of medicine. The Indian press followed her plans and kept her before an eager public.

Prominent people welcomed Ramabai to England. She enchanted the venerable F. Max Müller, the foremost Indologist of his day and professor at

8. Frances Willard, *Glimpses of Fifty Years: The Autobiography of an American Woman* (Chicago: H. J. Smith, 1889), p. 9. Willard attributed to Ramabai's efforts the opening to girls of primary and secondary schools in Poona and Bombay.

9. Reprinted in *The Union Signal* 10, no. 2, 10 Jan. 1884, p. 15.

10. Translated by Meera Kosambi, this book is included in Kosambi, ed., *Pandita Ramabai Through Her Own Words,* pp. 35-104.

Oxford University.[11] Müller lent his support to contemporary efforts urging reform of marriage laws in India. He exerted his considerable influence on Ramabai's behalf and enthusiastically promoted her as a "representative of Indian progress." Another supporter was Alfred Dyer, a Quaker journalist and reformer, in the limelight at the time in part because of his support for the British feminist social reformer, Josephine Butler.[12] Dyer, about to become editor of *The Bombay Guardian*, shared Ramabai's horror at state regulation of prostitution and the opium trade. Dyer was a colorful figure who did prison time for his journalistic revelations; he and his wife, Helen, proved stalwart and influential lifelong friends.[13]

Ramabai moved in such socially prominent reform-minded circles despite the vehement objections of her English hosts, the Sisters of St. Mary. These religious preferred to circumscribe her access to English reform politics and to occupy her time in the regulated life of the convent. There they exposed her to the Church of England in its most Catholic expression, and there she "crossed the border line" and embraced Christianity. Although she had much difficulty with the doctrines of the Trinity and atonement, Ramabai found herself drawn to Christ. She later claimed that Hinduism had offered no rest to her soul whereas in Christ she found rest. When asked to name her favorite hymn, she responded immediately: "I heard the voice of Jesus say, 'Come unto Me and rest.'" Correspondence with Father Goreh in India eased some of her theological doubts. Nevertheless, Ramabai's understanding of her conversion did not completely satisfy the Sisters of St. Mary. She regarded herself as a Christian, not an Anglican. She acknowledged membership in no specific earthly communion, nor would she embrace exclusively the rituals and creeds of any one church. With such provisos, on Michaelmas Day, 29 September 1883, she was baptized at Wantage parish church by Canon W. J. Butler, a leading Anglo-Catholic.[14]

11. *The Life and Letters of the Right Honourable Friedrich Max Müller*, 2 vols. (New York, London, Bombay: Longmans, Green & Co., 1902), vol. 2, pp. 148-49; F. Max Müller, *Auld Lang Syne*, 2 vols. (London and Bombay: Longmans, Green & Co., 1898-99), vol. 2, pp. 133-42; F. Max Müller, "Marriage Reform in India," *Our Day* 6 (1890): 258.

12. Nancy Boyd, *Three Victorian Women Who Changed Their World* (New York: Oxford University Press, 1982).

13. For Dyer, see *Dictionary of Quaker Biography* (typescript) (London: Library of the Religious Society of Friends in Britain); *The Friend* (London) 34 (1894): 452; *The Friend* (London) n.s., 66 (1926): 1026. It seems that Ramabai did not meet the Dyers until her return to India. See Helen Dyer, *Pandita Rambai: The Story of Her Life* (London, New York: Fleming H. Revell, c. 1900), pp. 45, 51.

14. For a provocative discussion of religious, nationalist, feminist, and political aspects of Ramabai's conversion, see Gauri Viswanathan, *Outside the Fold: Conversion, Modernity and Belief* (Princeton: Princeton University Press, 1998), pp. 118-52.

Much later, she would reminisce that she had "found the Christian *religion*, which was good enough for me; *but I had not found Christ Who is the Life of the religion,* and 'the Light of every man that cometh into the world.'"[15]

News of Ramabai's baptism provoked turmoil in India. Though she had long since abandoned Hindu practice, her cohorts loudly criticized her failure to resist conversion and predicted dire consequences for her future usefulness in India. Meanwhile, her limited opportunities among the Sisters of St. Mary intensified Ramabai's longing for the wider world.[16] In September 1884 she found it at one of England's premier girls' schools, Cheltenham Ladies' College, presided over by the pioneer of female education, Dorothea Beale.[17] Beale's Broad Church sympathies permitted Ramabai's questions without concern about her soul, and Ramabai, in turn, welcomed Beale's religious instruction. The prime minister, W. E. Gladstone, provided funds for Ramabai from the Queen's Scholarship, easing the burden on her sponsors at Wantage. Ramabai developed a course in Sanskrit. Manoramabai remained at Wantage and, despite Ramabai's instructions for her religious education, imbibed High Church thinking that shaped her lifelong spirituality.

Severely impaired hearing forced Ramabai to exchange her dream of a medical career for a life devoted to education. Education had emancipated her, and she now turned her hopes to high-caste Hindu widows. Educated widows, freed from dependency and subservience, she believed, could actively contribute to an emerging new India as teachers, physicians, and nurses. With this new goal in mind, Ramabai accepted an invitation to the United States. A distant married cousin, Anandibai Joshi, was about to become the first Hindu graduate of the Women's Medical College of Philadelphia, and planned to return to India to preside over a hospital for women.[18] She pressed Ramabai to attend her graduation, and Ramabai agreed, planning a long visit to study American education, especially the newly popular adaptations of Froebel's concept of the kindergarten.

Ramabai arrived in Philadelphia on 6 March 1886.[19] The next week, Ra-

---

15. Kosambi, ed., *Pandita Ramabai Through Her Own Words,* p. 309.

16. For Ramabai's complex relationship with the Sisters of St. Mary see A. B. Shah, ed., *The Letters and Correspondence of Pandita Ramabai,* compiled by Sister Geraldine (Bombay: Maharashtra State Board for Literature and Culture, 1977).

17. A. K. Clarke, *A History of the Cheltenham Ladies' College, 1853-1953* (London: Faber & Faber Ltd., n.d.); Elizabeth Raikes, *Dorothea Beale of Cheltenham* (London: Archibald Constable & Co., Ltd., 1908).

18. Caroline Healey Hall, *The Life of Dr. Anandabai Joshee* (Boston, 1888).

19. "Woman's Day," *Philadelphia Evening Bulletin* (hereafter *PEB*), 12 March 1886, p. 4; "Commencement Day," *PEB,* 11 March 1886, p. 6.

chel Bodley, resident of the Women's Medical College, hosted a tea in Ramabai's honor at which the latter first publicly shared with nearly one hundred Philadelphians the germ of her plan for the education of Indian women.[20] She proposed to open a boarding and day school for high-caste Hindu widows where the women could keep caste. Convinced that success demanded a religiously neutral facility, Ramabai announced she would work with the local board of Hindus and enlist financial support and administrative oversight from an American committee.

Over the next three years, Ramabai took American Protestants by storm. She was the missionary curio table come to life. Whatever she said about India carried enormous weight, and she found herself invited to public forums, feminist events, and religious gatherings. On her part, she later recalled bewilderment "at finding such a Babel of religions in Christian countries, and at finding how very different the teaching of each sect was from that of the others."[21] The sheer force of her personality, her refusal to be sidetracked by sectarian differences, and her winsome ways won her friends wherever she traveled. Frances Willard provides a winsome description of Ramabai, who spent several weeks as a guest in the stately Willard home on Chicago Avenue in Evanston, Illinois:

> She is delightful to have about; content if she has books, pen and ink, and peace. She seems a sort of human-like gazelle; incarnate gentleness, combined with such celerity of apprehension, such swiftness of mental pace, adroitness of logic and equipoise of intention as to make her a delightful mental problem. She is impervious to praise, and can be captured only by affection. . . . The Pundita is a woman-lover, not as the antithesis of a man-hater, for she is too great-natured not to love all humanity with equal mother-heartedness, but because women need special help, her zeal for them is like quenchless fire. . . . I cannot help cherishing the earnest hope that, under Pundita Ramabai's Christian sway, women never yet reached by the usual missionary appliances of the church may be . . . led from their darkness into the marvelous light of the gospel that elevates women, and with her lifts the world toward heaven.[22]

---

20. "Pandita Ramabai in America," *PEB*, 13 March 1886, p. 4.

21. Kosambi, ed., *Pandita Ramabai Through Her Own Words*, p. 308; also cited in R. E. Frykenberg, ed., *Pandita Ramabai's America: Conditions of Life in the United States* (Grand Rapids & Cambridge: Eerdmans, 2003), p. 21.

22. Willard, *Glimpses of Fifty Years*, pp. 557, 561.

Ramabai had come at a critical moment. Reform sentiments of many sorts enjoyed popularity, and the ever-expanding mass print culture kept the claims of Indian women before Americans. Ramabai found staunch friends among the thousands who rallied to Frances Willard and the Women's Christian Temperance Union (WCTU).[23] She charmed audiences in Boston, where in December 1887 in Channing Hall such luminaries as Edward Everett Hale, George A. Gordon, Joseph Cook, and Phillips Brooks helped establish the Ramabai Association.[24] The mix of Unitarian and orthodox on her board did not trouble her; she assumed that Christian theological differences resembled "those existing among the different sects of Brahmanical Hindu religion."[25] The Association pledged ten years' support, at which time Ramabai hoped her school would be self-supporting. Donations came as well from Miss Porter's school in Connecticut, from the newly formed Ramabai Circle at Cornell University, from countless individuals, and from WCTU and women's missionary Ramabai Circles. In 1888 Ramabai published *The High-Caste Hindu Widow* to promote and explain the radical potential of her intentions. With an introduction by Rachel Bodley and the marketing expertise of the WCTU, the book proved a valuable asset to the cause. It was believed to be the first publication in English by an Indian woman.

Plans proceeded apace. With the appointment of "the grand woman," Mary Livermore, as national superintendent for the American Ramabai Circles, success seemed assured. Livermore, a talented promoter, was the wife of a Universalist minister, a feminist, social reformer, editor, and national lecturer with a reputation as "queen of the platform."[26] Ramabai could not have envisioned a more efficient supporter. Frances Willard, going beyond Ramabai's announced intentions, looked ahead to a day when White Ribbon missionaries would assist Ramabai in India. She planned a role for Ramabai in the emerging International Women's Christian Temperance Union.[27] Early in 1888, at its inaugural meeting in Washington, DC, Ramabai graced the plat-

23. For example, Frances Willard, "President's Address," *Minutes of the NWCTU,* 1887, pp. 83-84; Frances Willard, "The High Caste Hindu Woman," *Union Signal,* 4 Aug. 1887, p. 12.

24. See "The Ramabai Association," *Boston Journal (BJ),* 14 December 1887; "Fast Day Services," *BJ,* 6 April 1888; "Pandita Ramabai's Plans," *Union Signal,* 13 October 1887, p. 5.

25. Kosambi, ed., *Pandita Ramabai Through Her Own Words,* p. 309.

26. "Ramabai's Circles," *Union Signal,* 22 December 1887, p. 4; Mary A. Livermore, *The Story of My Life* (Hartford, CT: A. D. Worthington & Co., 1899).

27. Both Ramabai and her later associate, Minnie Abrams, assumed leadership roles in the Indian WCTU. *Woman's Missionary Friend (WMF)* 28 (April 1897): 280; "Woman's World," *The Missionary Review of the World (MRW)* (June 1897): 472.

form of the International Council of Women where she mingled with such luminaries as Clara Barton, Lucy Stone, Antoinette Brown Blackwell, Susan Anthony, and Elizabeth Cady Stanton.[28]

Ramabai sailed for India from San Francisco in the fall of 1888. Thousands of attendees of the National Education Association's annual meeting in that city had given her their enthusiastic blessing.[29] The *Indian Witness* commented on her return to Bombay in March 1889: "The Pandita Ramabai has met with a kind reception from all parties in Bombay. As to opposers, she has none."[30] The *Missionary Review of the World* predicted a "fair trial" for Ramabai's scheme and noted that in America she had received "more liberal assistance than . . . had ever before been given to any one person for missionary purposes."[31] On 11 March she opened the long-anticipated home, the *Sharada Sadan* (House of Learning/Wisdom). In 1890, she moved the Sharada Sadan from Bombay to Poona — a healthier and cheaper city with a population of some 150,000 — 140 miles away. By July 1891 the boarding school was well established, and American support enabled the purchase of a commodious residence for the school. Some forty widows had enrolled, and Ramabai had kept her promise of religious neutrality. She had, however, established a chapter of the King's Daughters, an association established for benevolent purposes by the American Episcopalian Margaret Bottome and promoted in India especially by the Methodist Women's Missionary Society.[32] A high-caste Indian Christian teacher and reformer, Soonderbai Powar, worked closely with Ramabai, bringing crucial experience in education.[33] Everything about the home was Indian: food, furnishings, dress, schedule. Ramabai objected strenuously to the missionary tendency to picture Indians and their culture as "vile" (referring to the depiction of the Indian subcontinent in Reginald Heber's hymn, "From Greenland's Icy Mountains," in which "only man is vile"). "My father was a Brahmin," she once told Frances Willard. "I don't like to hear that every man is vile when I know that my father was so true and so good that he had me taught to read, and to read such books."[34] Such evident devotion to India helped deflect criticism that Ramabai had

28. *Union Signal*, 23 February 1888, p. 9.

29. "Visiting Teachers," *San Francisco Chronicle (SFC)*, 14 July 1888, p. 8; "The Pundita Speaks," *SFC*, 16 July 1888; "The Pundita," *SFC*, 21 July 1888.

30. "The Pandita Ramabai," *MRW* (July 1889): 523.

31. "General Missionary Intelligence, India," *MRW* (July 1889): 523.

32. "Uniform Study for May: The King's Daughters in Heathen Lands," *Heathen Woman's Friend*, Supplement no. 4 (April 1892): 1-2.

33. "Miss Soonderbai Powar," *MRW* (March 1892), p. 240.

34. WCTU, *Convention Minutes*, 1892, p. 63.

compromised her national pride to become the tool of wealthy Westerners. While she capitalized on the Western will to address India's social needs, her own heart beat for India. Westerners marveled at what seemed her transparent simplicity. The "Hindu Minerva" surprised them by her adeptness in scholarly disputations as well as in gospel services. In a curious way, Ramabai apparently belonged to all Protestants and to reform-minded Indians of other faiths.[35] Denominational periodicals published updates of her work without claiming her as their own. Indian reformers and British officials watched supportively. She achieved a degree of Western goodwill and support that few Westerners rivaled.

Then came a crisis. A few of Ramabai's child widows converted to Christianity.[36] Families withdrew one-third of the students. Her Hindu board deserted her. Physical violence erupted, and the storm of opposition nearly crushed Ramabai.[37] "Very fiercely has native society turned upon her," reported a missionary of the Free Church of Scotland, "and very severely has she been handled as 'a wolf in sheep's clothing' by the native papers."[38] Max Müller echoed the dismal outlook: "Accounts that reach us from India are very discouraging," he wrote. "The law did not protect her. . . . She had to give up girls on demand of families. A woman in India always belongs to someone else. She cannot exist by herself."[39]

The Sharada Sadan survived and was reorganized as a Christian enterprise. This Christianity had the distinct Indian style of Ramabai's personal piety, and she continued to welcome non-Christians without forcing them to convert. Her own spiritual journey, meanwhile, distanced her from some of her most lavish American supporters. In India she discovered American and British evangelicalism, complete with camp meetings.[40]

She warmed to the books of the Anglican evangelist William Haslam, the revival message of George F. Pentecost, and the summons to a deeper life brought by missioners from the Keswick Convention. She now said she had come to know Christ, and in her dependence on him she found new joy. A fascinating public debate over Ramabai's evolving understanding of personal Christian experience intrigued American readers. George Pentecost proudly

35. One of her admirers was the distinguished Methodist Bishop James Thoburn. See "A Hindu Lady Reformer," *MRW* (Feb. 1890): 130.

36. "Pundita Ramabai and the Sharada Sadana," *Indian Witness (IW)*, 11 January 1896, p. 6.

37. "General Missionary Intelligence," *MRW* (Sept. 1896): 716.

38. "India," *Christian Alliance* 16 (12 June 1896): 572.

39. F. Max Müller, "Child Widows in India," *Our Day* 13 (March-April 1894): 563.

40. "Pandita Ramabai's Camp Meeting," *Earnest Christian*, April 1899, pp. 131-32.

claimed Ramabai as a convert, while she admitted only to having gained a new perspective on personal Christian experience.[41] Evangelicals applauded Ramabai's growing affinity with their views and offered her increased support.[42] By 1896 they replaced some of the Unitarians and Universalists who had been her staunchest allies. Some of her Unitarian friends had had misgivings and sent a representative to investigate Ramabai's work; when child widows began to convert to Christianity they resigned *en masse* from her American board.

After 1895, two severe episodes of famine accompanied by plague greatly expanded Ramabai's responsibilities.[43] When Louis Klopsch, editor of the *Christian Herald,* toured India to assess famine work in 1900, he visited Ramabai whose work he praised as "the most remarkable missionary enterprise of the age, so well known all over Europe, India and America."[44] At Mukti he found hundreds of child widows whom Ramabai had rescued at her own initiative, many from appalling conditions in government-run relief camps. The new arrivals overcrowded the Sharada Sadan and did not necessarily fit its mission. Ramabai responded by designing a Christian community at Kedgaon, forty miles south of Poona, where she eventually took full responsibility for some 2,000 people. The Sharada Sadan retained its original purpose and remained in Poona. She named her new center Mukti, meaning "Liberty."

As her work expanded, so did Ramabai's communications skills. She carefully cultivated her many supporters. A wide variety of American publications carried letters and reports from Ramabai as well as from the considerable array of visitors who flocked to Mukti. Readers of the *Bombay Guardian* or the *Indian Witness* were well informed about her as well as about the worldwide church. Such papers dutifully reported famine in China, revival in Korea, or pre-millennialism in England, along with lists of recent publications and secular news. Births, deaths, publications, heresies, financial woes, or scandals found space in popular religious publications in India. Denominational periodicals enabled Christians in India to keep abreast of religious

41. "Questions to Specialists," *Our Day* 11 (1893): 68-75 details the various exchanges among Pentecost, Ramabai, and her American friends. See also H. B. Hartzler, "Dr. Pentecost at Northfield," *Record of Christian Work* (January 1893): 26, 28.

42. For example, *MRW* (March 1899): 234; Arthur T. Pierson, "Ramabai and the Women of India," *MRW* (July 1899): 481-88.

43. Delavan L. Pierson, "Famine and Plague in India," *MRW* (April 1897): 296-98; Grace Wilder, "Pandita Ramabai and Her Work," *MRW* (Sept. 1897): 669-74; Pandita Ramabai, "Famine Experiences" (1897), in Kosambi, ed., *Pandita Ramabai Through Her Own Words,* pp. 247-60.

44. Louis Klopsch, "Famine in India," *Topeka Daily Capital,* 24 June 1900, p. 10.

issues abroad. And so in 1904, when revival burst out in Wales, Indian Christians joined those who eagerly followed its course and yearned for its stirrings in their own hearts.

Ramabai shared the keen hunger for revival. As early as 1898, her circular letters urged prayer "for the outpouring of the Holy Spirit upon our mission" and solicited suggestions from Western friends.[45] The same year she stood on the Keswick Convention platform in England to plead for 1,000 "Holy Ghost missionaries" for India's 140 million women, some 8.5 million of whom were child wives under 14.[46] She extended the same call to Americans through the pages of D. L. Moody's *Northfield Echoes*. Hundreds of famine widows had swelled the population of Mukti, and few manifested interest in Christian faith. Also in 1898 Ramabai accompanied her daughter and three widows from Mukti to Rochester, New York, where Augustus Strong, president of Rochester Theological Seminary, introduced her to an admiring audience as "one of the greatest, if not the greatest, heroine of the century."[47] She enrolled the girls in the A. M. Chesbrough Seminary (later Roberts Wesleyan College).[48] Situated in North Chili, New York, the small school was a hotbed of holiness fervor. On completing her studies, Manoramabai represented her mother at the impressive Ecumenical Missions Conference in New York in 1900 and then sailed for India, stopping briefly in England en route to speak at the Keswick Convention.

Meanwhile, Ramabai's new American colleague, Minnie Abrams, manifested her own revival longings. Abrams had arrived unannounced at Mukti in 1898 to assist Ramabai.[49] Her prolific pen made her the most prominent of the changing list of American, English, Scandinavian, and Australian women who spent long periods heading Mukti's various enterprises. A seasoned India missionary, Abrams had first arrived in India in 1888, the first missionary graduate of Lucy Rider Meyer's Chicago Training Institute.[50] For the next eleven years, she worked with the Woman's Board of Foreign Missions. Then she severed her ties with the board to go to Mukti as a faith missionary.[51]

---

45. Pandita Ramabai, "Teach Us to Pray," *WMF* 30 (Aug. 1898): 44.

46. *The Keswick Week*, 1898, p. 188.

47. Emma Sellew Roberts, "Pandita Ramabai and Her Work," *Missionary Tidings* (June 1898): 5.

48. See *The Annual Catalogue of the A. M. Chesbrough Seminary*, 1897-1898 (North Chili, NY: A. M. Chesbrough Seminary), pp. 6-7.

49. "Personal Mention," *WMF* 29 (March 1898): 267. The *WMF* chronicled Abrams's earlier work in India, e.g., "Our Post-Office Box," *WMF* 28 (March 1897): 256.

50. "Minnie Abrams," Alumni Card File, Chicago Training Institute, Archives, Garrett Theological Seminary, Evanston, IL.

51. Minnie Abrams, "A Bible Training School," *WMF* (Feb. 1901): 56 gives a sense of Abrams's pre-revival responsibilities at Mukti.

Almost all that can be learned of Abrams comes from her own pen. She represented herself as especially sensitive to revival inklings and wrote that news of revival in Australia prodded Ramabai in 1903 to commission Abrams to travel with Manoramabai to Australia "to see how they got" revival. During a visit of several months, the two also succeeded in establishing lucrative support for Ramabai among Australian Christians (probably the primary objective of the trip). Abrams concluded that Australia, where R. A. Torrey and Charles Alexander had recently concluded a remarkable evangelistic tour, saw revival because of a handful of people who "poured their lives out" in prayer. Upon returning to India, she told Ramabai they must begin to pray for revival.[52]

When revival came to parts of India from 1905 to 1907 Ramabai was possibly the best-known Indian Christian. Certainly American Protestants promoted her as such. She also had perhaps the most ambitious single Christian enterprise, one that intrigued Indians and Westerners alike. Indian scholars still debate her choices and explore her importance for emerging Indian nationalism. Ramabai would have declared that national interests stood at the core of her being: she saw no conflict in being fully Indian and thoroughly Christian.

2. Revival

The Welsh revival that so energized similar movements elsewhere first erupted in 1904. There, to use the words of G. Campbell Morgan, one of a host of prominent British evangelicals who visited the scene, "apparent disorderliness was characterized from first to last by the orderliness of the Spirit of God."[53] Expressive, physically engaged prayer, confession of sin, protracted meetings, testimony, and irrepressible song rather than preaching characterized the Welsh revival. Welsh missionaries in India's Khasi Hills reported similar outbreaks in 1905. Unusual emotional outbursts, trembling, trances, public confessions of sin, and renewed commitment to faith became commonplace at Welsh Presbyterian mission stations in the hill country. Such phenomena were not new to India: strikingly similar "physical symptoms" had been noted in the South Indian revival of 1873: "flinging the arms

---

52. Minnie F. Abrams, "How the Recent Revival Was Brought About in India," *The Latter Rain Evangel*, July 1909, p. 8.

53. G. Campbell Morgan, "The Lesson of the Revival," in Arthur Goodrich et al., *The Story of the Welsh Revival Told by Eyewitnesses* (New York: Fleming H. Revell, 1905), p. 55.

into the air, shaking in every limb, violent contortions, falling on the ground and rolling about."[54] The 1873 revival had even been followed by speaking in tongues among adherents of the radical revival-inspired "Six Years' Movement."[55]

In 1905 the Reverend Pengwern Jones offered voluminous accounts of the revival stirrings and analyzed their waxing and waning in the widely circulating *Indian Witness*. One wonders what course these events might have taken had Jones not been their indefatigable chronicler. His enthusiastic publicity made what had happened in the Khasi Hills a standard for other Indian revivals. When revival occurred in other parts of Bengal, for example, reports tied its manifestations to what their authors had read of the Khasi Hills.[56] Jones found encouragement and a soul mate in an American Presbyterian missionary, John Hyde. Considered "odd" by cohorts (who dubbed him "Praying Hyde"), Hyde as a result achieved a sort of sainthood among Americans who associated prayer with revival. Popular renderings of his exploits in prayer gave the Indian revival publicity in American Sunday School libraries.[57] This dawning revival had no warmer supporter than Bishop Thoburn's successor in the Methodist episcopate, Frank Warne.[58]

By her own account, at least, Minnie Abrams was to revival at Mukti what Pengwern Jones was to the Khasi Hills: tireless, determined, focused. In January 1905, Ramabai invited her girls to join the workers in prayer for revival. Seventy girls promptly formed a "praying band." They met daily for Bible study and prayer, and before long numbers surpassed five hundred.[59] Reports from the Khasi Hills prompted Ramabai to enlist volunteers to go out to the villages to preach. Beset by illness, meanwhile, Abrams left for six months of rest at a hill station determined to be not too far away when revival came. There, she later claimed, she made her consecration: "Oh God, in this coming revival I am a candidate for service."[60]

Abrams believed that God sent her back to Mukti before she fully re-

---

54. "Revival Begins in 1873," *The Missions Conference: South India and Ceylon, 1874* (Madras: Addison & Co., 1880), vol. 2, p. 165.

55. "Revival Begins," pp. 166-67.

56. "The Revival in Bengal," *IW,* 21 March 1907, pp. 187-88.

57. *Reminiscences of the Late Rev. J. N. Hyde — Known as Praying Hyde of India* (Madras: SPCK Depository, 1923).

58. Frederick DeLand Leete, *Methodist Bishops: Personal Notes and Bibliography* (Nashville: The Parthenon Press, 1948), p. 188. See also E. G. Carré, *Praying Hyde: A Challenge to Prayer, or A Present Day* (London: Pickering and Inglis, n.d.).

59. Helen S. Dyer, *Revival in India: A Report of the 1905-1906 Revival* (New York: Gospel Publishing House, 1907), p. 32.

60. Abrams, "Recent Revival," p. 9.

gained her health. She immediately rallied Ramabai's village girls to seek the "enduement of power," a subject she had pondered during her enforced idleness. One June morning at 3:30, Abrams awakened to pounding on her door. She found an excited student who summoned her to a dormitory. There Abrams found a woman who the night before had agonized in prayer for the baptism with the Holy Spirit. Abrams put it as follows:

> At three o'clock in the morning the Lord awoke her with the fire coming down upon her. It was a wonderful time. She cried out in fright. She had never heard of such a thing, and the young women sleeping on either side of her sprang up and saw the fire. One of them ran across the room, picked up a pail of water and brought it to dash upon this young woman when she discovered she wasn't on fire. It was a case of the "burning bush" over again. All the young women got up; I got there at a quarter of four, and the young women in that compound were kneeling about, weeping, and confessing their sins to God.[61]

So began the long-anticipated revival at Mukti. The next day, 30 June 1905, Abrams was summoned with the news that "the Holy Ghost has come into the church." She found "all in the room weeping and praying, some kneeling, some sitting, some standing, many with hands outstretched to God. . . . Words of help were of no avail. God was dealing with them and they could listen to no one else."[62] In fact, the confusion had interrupted Ramabai's typically calm exposition of John 8, making it impossible for her to continue. For several months following, noisy boisterous waves of confession and repentance swept Mukti. The two daily meetings of the prayer band became "great assemblies, morning and evening, and the Bible school was turned into an inquiry room. Girls stricken down under the power of conviction of sin while in school, in the industrial school, or at their work were brought there. Regular Bible lessons were suspended, and the Holy Spirit, Himself, gave to the leaders such messages as were needed by the seeking ones."[63] All the while, evangelistic bands traversed the countryside. "Secular studies" gave way to concentrated Bible reading.

If fervor impressed Abrams, Manoramabai, like her mother, found "peace entering souls" most striking. While she thrilled to the prospect of "a great

---

61. Abrams, "Recent Revival," p. 10.

62. Minnie F. Abrams, *The Baptism of the Holy Ghost and Fire* (Kedgaon: Mukti Mission Press, 1906), p. 6.

63. Abrams, *Baptism*, p. 7.

work in our midst" and noticed that the Holy Spirit chose "one of our quiet-est and most insignificant girls" to arouse spiritual concern among the rest, Manoramabai's reports are far less effusive than Abrams's descriptions.[64]

Occasionally during 1905 and 1906, what Abrams called "testing times" interrupted the emotional fervor. She later intimated that these "tests" were financial, though both Ramabai and Abrams refrained from identifying specific needs. Amid hunger and poverty, workers spent hours agonizing in prayer for basic necessities. In 1907 revival fires burned with renewed intensity, and this time a few of the devout at Mukti spoke in tongues.

The tongues-speaking that occurred from 1907 must be considered in the context of this revival that dated to 1905 and drew its inspiration from Wales, from accounts of the Torrey-Alexander global evangelistic mission, and from awareness of local stirrings in India and Korea, all duly noted in publications like the *Bombay Guardian* and the *Indian Witness*. A clear awareness of inter-connectedness is apparent. Participants in the Indian revival certainly saw tongues, a phenomenon soon associated with emerging pentecostalism, as continuous with the ongoing awakening. For years, evangelicals in various networks in India had been fascinated by teaching on spiritual empower-ment. Now they found conditions ripe for pursuing it.

Before considering Mukti and its relationship to the larger Indian pente-costal story, it will be helpful to look at the community's understanding of the revival. What did Ramabai mean when she urged her girls to seek the baptism with the Holy Spirit? What did Abrams intend when she told them they could not do effective village evangelism without receiving a special "enduement with power"? From 1905 on, the revival in India, as interpreted by Indians and foreign missionaries, had evangelism and Christian fruitfulness at its core. Even as they reveled in revival manifestations, Ramabai's community ex-pressed disappointment that the revival had not stirred hearts outside the Christian community. Evangelism, then, is the backdrop against which what follows must be understood.

Three notable features seemed ubiquitous in this Indian revival: fire (felt and seen), intense joy, and public confession of sin. In 1906, the prolific Minnie Abrams offered the fullest explanation of the teaching that shaped and emerged from the revival at Mukti. Reprinted numerous times until her death in 1912, the booklet established Abrams as the principal interpreter of the revival phenomena in Ramabai's far-flung network.

Abrams presented steps to revival sequentially, beginning with the "new

---

64. "Growth and Revival in Ramabai's Work," *Record of Christian Work* (October 1905): 857.

birth." Holiness understood as "dying daily to self" and "consecration" came next:

> We must take by faith our position on the cross as dead to sin, but alive to righteousness through the power of His resurrection life. . . . When we consent to death on the cross, the Holy Spirit comes in to empower us to die to the flesh and to the world, and through abiding in Christ to maintain the position of death. This means to be given over to Christ, in absolute surrender; desires, will, time, strength, body, mental powers, possessions, friends, all given up to him.[65]

The "fire of the Holy Ghost" followed. This fire — often eerily visible to its subject and to onlookers — "searched out sin" and then compelled its exposure "by means of confessions to individuals and in public." This public confession, Abrams maintained, brought Christians to an essential "realization of [Christ's] humiliation and shame when he bore our sins. These confessions also bring us into a position with Himself of oneness with the vilest sinner, by making us feel the depravity of our nature and being."[66]

Abrams remained adamant on this point, despite objections. Even past sins "already put under the blood" needed to be publicly confessed as part of "the calling to remembrance of the pit from whence we were digged." Abrams insisted that confessions prompted by the Spirit came "under the Spirit's covering," assuring that "only good can come to the hearer."[67] Public confession of individual sins was God's way of "breaking the power of sin" in believers.[68] Old Testament sacrificial law provided a graphic illustration: Christians were to be "cut in pieces and laid on the altar of burnt sacrifice, morning and evening. The fire consumes bleeding lambs. Without holiness no man shall see the Lord. As we keep our position on the altar the Holy Spirit works out that union with Christ which brings new life and power."[69]

Physical as well as visual signs accompanied this experience of fire. Far more subjects testified to the warmth of fire within than saw flames without. Distinct physical discomfort attended the fire's exposure of sin, but the persistent soon learned that repentance and confession replaced physical suffering with "wondrous joy and consciousness of the presence and approval of Jesus." Even momentary withdrawal of this pleasing sense of burning fire was

65. Abrams, *Baptism*, p. 27.
66. Abrams, *Baptism*, pp. 42-43.
67. Abrams, *Baptism*, p. 43.
68. Abrams, *Baptism*, p. 48.
69. Abrams, *Baptism*, p. 48.

cause for concern, and typically resulted in agonized heart-searching and confession.

The process leading to "enduement of power," then, might be summarized as "pardon" and "purity." Power followed, wrought by the Holy Spirit's "revealing Jesus, forming Him within us, imparting to us the life and nature of Christ, and uniting us with Him in the work of saving souls."[70] These steps, Abrams cautioned, were always sequential. Abrams concluded with an impassioned defense of "manifestations." The tokens that accompanied revival in India varied from place to place but generally included trembling, loud crying in prayer, falling on the ground in trances, writhing, clapping, shouting praises, singing, and "losing strength as under an 'exceeding weight of glory.'"[71] At Mukti, Ramabai attempted to maintain order but claimed she "stopped the work of the Holy Spirit by interfering with it." Thus convinced, she "took her hands off the work." "Most of us have been praying for a Revival," she observed. "Are we willing that it should come in God's way and not ours?"[72] But Ramabai and Abrams cautioned against making manifestations an end in themselves. For them what happened — or did not happen — was incidental to "fruit in life and service."

It is important to recognize that all of this was in full swing in India before word of the baptism with the Holy Spirit accompanied by tongues arrived from the West. The language associated with this ongoing revival was suitable for pentecostal use, but it had already been invested with particular prepentecostal meaning. The striking custom of simultaneous loud individual prayer that visitors to the Mukti church invariably noted also predated outbursts of speaking in tongues. Dreading the inevitable publicity, Ramabai only reluctantly permitted the *Bombay Guardian* to publish initial accounts of the revival at Mukti. She escorted a band of girls to Poona, where they began a series of prayer meetings targeting Indian Christians. Europeans came, too, as did non-Christian Indians. Revival followed at the Methodist Boys' School at Poona, at the Zenana Training Home run by Ramabai's erstwhile colleague, Soonderbai Powar, and at the large Boys' Christian Home at nearby Dhond led by Albert and Mary Norton, one-time Methodist missionaries whom Ramabai had recruited in 1898 to return to India.[73] Revival radiated directly to a Famine Orphanage in Allahabad, to a Rescue Home near Bangalore and to the American Methodist Episcopal Mission in Telegaon, east of Bombay. Ramabai an-

---

70. Abrams, *Baptism*, p. 47.
71. Abrams, *Baptism*, p. 78.
72. Pandita Ramabai, "Lessons from the Revival," in Dyer, *Revival*, p. 45.
73. W. K. Norton, "The Rewards of a Life of Faith," *Latter Rain*, April 1917, p. 16.

nounced that her concern for the "lukewarmness" of Indian Christians motivated these forays beyond the tumult at Mukti. "Our work will bear lasting
fruit if we work less and pray more," she urged.[74] As she took her girls beyond
the privacy of their community, she considered that her praying band of more
than 700 had become "fools" for Christ: "The Spirit-filled girls cannot sup-
press their sorrow for sin or their joy in salvation. They burst into loud crying
and laughing, they shake, they tremble, some of them dance with joy, and almost all pray simultaneously in loud voices."[75] This reckless abandon persisted
as the revival moved into its next phase.

In the fall of 1906, reports about a revival emanating from southern California reached India via both post and the press, and advocates soon followed
in person. Participants in the Los Angeles–based event associated speaking in
tongues with the baptism with the Holy Spirit. Their worship and agonized
prayer resembled that of the ongoing revival in India, but their practice of
speaking in tongues in association with the baptism with the Holy Spirit set
them apart, as did their clear evocation of restored apostolic experience. These
early pentecostals frequently linked tongues speech and missionary service
and manifested eager willingness to circle the globe with their message:

> I'm so glad the promised Pentecost has come
> And the Latter Rain is falling now on some.
> Pour it out in floods, Lord, on the parched ground
> 'Til it reaches all the earth around.[76]

Already primed for revival, many foreign missionaries in India manifested
curiosity if not outright interest. Among the movement's emissaries from the
United States were some of the peripatetic stalwarts of early pentecostalism.
India beckoned A. G. Garr, while China seemed to summon his wife, so that
early in 1907 they stopped in Calcutta on the way to Hong Kong.[77] Garr believed he had spoken "the Hindustani language" at the moment of his Spirit
baptism, confirming a call to India, and his brief visit stirred up controversy

---

74. Ramabai, "Lessons," p. 44.

75. Ramabai, "Lessons," p. 44.

76. D. W. G., "The Latter Rain," in *Psalms, Hymns and Songs Spiritual,* ed. Charles A.
Squire et al. (St. Louis: Squire & Kinne, 1910), no. 62, cited in Gary B. McGee, "'Latter Rain'
Falling in the East: Early-Twentieth-Century Pentecostalism in India and the Debate over
Speaking in Tongues," *Church History* 68, no. 3 (Sept. 1999), p. 648.

77. Mary Johnson, "In Calcutta, India," *Apostolic Faith* (Los Angeles), February-March
1907; Mary Johnson, "Ye Are My Witnesses," *Apostolic Faith* (Los Angeles), May 1907; A. G.
Garr, "Divine Wisdom Given the Faithful Missionary," *Latter Rain,* July 1914, p. 18.

that persisted after his departure, fed in part by new arrivals. The irrepressible Frank Bartleman and his colleague, Daniel Awrey, passed through, as did Thomas Ball Barratt, a Norwegian pentecostal leader, and Joseph King from Georgia. These generally targeted foreign missionaries as the surest way to get their message to Indians. They mingled at missionary retreats, distributed pentecostal literature, and spent time with any seeker they encountered. Max Wood Moorhead from Colombo, Sri Lanka, gained access to Lal Bazaar Baptist Church in Calcutta for the Garrs' meetings. Moorhead briefly acquired a commodious Calcutta home, welcomed seekers day and night in its drawing room, and began a short-lived publication, *The Cloud of Witnesses to Pentecost in India*.[78] The long-time missionary Maude Orlebar, proprietress of a Bombay home known as Beulah, promoted the message by opening her residence to seekers.[79] The impressionable Minnie Abrams longed for "God's best" and hoped the Garrs would come through Mukti to explain their point of view, but activities in north India occupied them, and tongues came to Mukti without help from Calcutta.[80]

Tongues came among those already immersed in revival, and they flourished among a few without connections, being drawn by Ramabai or her colleagues to the baptism with the Holy Spirit. Ramabai did not speak in tongues, but she did not hinder those who did. By 1907 she seemed resigned to such manifestations as long as transformed lives followed. It was reported that some of her girls (generally fluent only in Marathi and Hindustani) uttered Sanskrit or English prayers or miraculously spoke other languages unknown to them.[81] Her neighbor, Albert Norton, marveled at the apparent miraculous ability of a handful of untutored famine widows to pray in "idiomatic, distinct and fluent English."[82]

Abrams noted: "Only a small proportion of the girls and boys have received the pentecostal baptism, but the other Christians have been quickened and are living better lives than before."[83] Neither Ramabai nor her colleagues

---

78. B. F. Lawrence, "Apostolic Faith Restored," *Weekly Evangel*, 1 April 1916, p. 4; "Items from the Apostolic Light," *Word and Work*, October 1908, p. 314.

79. Maude Orlebar, "India Stretching Out Her Hands to God," *Latter Rain*, October 1910, p. 16.

80. For the debate that followed, see McGee, "'Latter Rain' Falling in the East," pp. 659-62.

81. Albert Norton, "Tongues in India," *Word and Work*, June 1907, pp. 174-75.

82. Albert Norton, "Natives in India Speak in Tongues," *Apostolic Faith* (Los Angeles), April 1907.

83. Minnie Abrams, "A New Outpouring of the Holy Spirit at Mukti, Accompanied by the Gift of Tongues," *Faith Work in India*, 10 July 1907, p. 3.

believed the girls should anticipate tongues as evidence of Spirit baptism. Significantly, they noticed that in the revival of 1907 (that included tongues speech), physical manifestations were less remarkable than at the beginning of the revival in 1905.[84]

Accounts of tongues at Mukti vary widely, colored by their source and context. The impressionable Max Moorhead (whose inclinations toward extremes later kept him on the fringes of the American pentecostal movement) enthused about Mukti in his *Cloud of Witnesses,* relishing "the glad scene of a continuous Pentecost as day after day seekers come into fullness of blessing."[85] He boldly asserted what both Ramabai and Abrams denied. "Both," he opined, "were deeply impressed by the truth contained in the reports which came from Los Angeles concerning Pentecost" and believed God would send "like pentecostal blessings to Mukti . . . after the manner described in Acts 2." He claimed that Ramabai had set her converts to seeking Spirit baptism marked by tongues.[86] That this pentecostal lens distorted both her teaching and events as they unfolded was irrelevant. Moorhead's rendering, popularized by the *Apostolic Faith,* became a standard early pentecostal text.

When she raised support among pentecostals in the United States, Abrams sometimes gushed similar hyperbole. "God poured out upon us a mighty wave of speaking in other tongues," Minnie Abrams reminisced before an American audience in 1909, "and a mighty wave of interpretation; He used the Spirit of prophecy in witnessing to the heathen, and He sent us out on several occasions a hundred at a time . . . to preach the everlasting gospel."[87] Abrams's hearers might easily have imagined that most Mukti residents spoke in tongues, rather than that few manifested the ability. Nevertheless, accounts agree that outreach from Kedgaon multiplied, and Ramabai began writing to her supporters requesting missionaries to help in this newly energized phase of her work.

In the September 1907 issue of her monthly journal, the *Mukti Prayer Bell,* Ramabai defended the manifestations at Mukti. "Love, perfect divine love, is the only and most necessary sign of the baptism of the Holy Spirit," she insisted. "But other gifts, such as the power to heal, to speak with tongues, to prophesy, are not to be discarded. Indeed, we should seek from God such gifts as will enable us to preach the gospel of Jesus Christ with power and draw

84. Abrams, "New Outpouring," p. 4.
85. Max Moorhead, "Pentecost in Mukti, India," reprinted in the *Apostolic Faith* (Los Angeles), September 1907.
86. Moorhead, "Pentecost in Mukti."
87. Abrams, "Revival," p. 11.

men unto Him."[88] One admiring Mukti visitor from the Church Missionary Society, Canon L. B. Butcher, remarked that Ramabai's Mukti did not "suffer through the manifestation of tongues" because of Ramabai's steadying hand.[89] He applauded Ramabai for "fostering" revival in a way that enabled hundreds to come to faith while avoiding "spiritual disorder."[90]

Like Ramabai, Abrams claimed little personal experience of tongues. Twice during revival services at the Nortons' Home for Boys in Dhond, she said she sang brief choruses in tongues. God, she concluded, had bestowed other gifts on her, and she was content.[91] But visitors insisted that the two must take a clear "stand" on tongues. Missionaries who had spoken in tongues flocked to Mukti from Calcutta, Coonoor, Bulsai, and Colombo. Abrams sensed trouble ahead and proposed that they agree to differ. She attempted to shift the focus to the long view of the Mukti revival experience during which Spirit baptism (without tongues) had, she claimed, "so united the workers in the love of the Spirit that we are able to work in love and harmony, as one man, for the salvation of souls."[92] While she agreed that all might (perhaps even should) speak in tongues, she denied "that no one is Spirit-baptized who has not received this Sign."[93] The Methodist-controlled *Indian Witness* ventured that a link between tongues and Spirit baptism appealed where the revival had not occurred, but where Christians yearned for its fervor.[94] Certainly it was strikingly absent in both the Khasi Hills and Mukti.

By 1908 distinct boundaries were thus evident. Western voices helped make sense of an emerging party spirit. The experience in 1908 of Thomas Barratt, pioneer of pentecostalism in Norway, is a case in point. Barratt arrived in India at the invitation of a planter, an A. N. Groves, who had read Barratt's dramatic religious testimony, *When the Fire Fell.* Groves lived near Coonoor, a favorite retreat for foreign missionaries during the hot season, and he circulated an invitation to special meetings in March. Barratt began in Bombay where he encountered the same opposition he had faced in Europe. Readers of the English press now had at their disposal recent warnings from the prolific pen of the Welsh Jesse Penn-Lewis, who worried that tongues en-

---

88. *Mukti Prayer Bell*, September 1907, p. 11.

89. Quoted in N. MacNicol, *The Story of Pandita Ramabai: A Builder of Modern India* (Calcutta: Association Press, 1926), pp. 172-73.

90. MacNicol, *Ramabai*, p. 174.

91. Abrams, "New Outpouring," p. 4.

92. Minnie Abrams, "A Message from Mukti," *Confidence*, September 1908, p. 14.

93. Abrams, "Message," p. 14.

94. "Shall We Go On?" *IW*, 5 March 1908, p. 1.

thusiasts failed to discern spirits and magnify the cross,[95] as well as harsh judgments about tongues from prominent German evangelicals.[96] The American missionary statesman, Arthur T. Pierson, chimed in with the growing chorus of reservations, urging caution. The *Indian Witness* had gone on record in 1907 with the observation that the revival was most marked among those who were nominally and quite loyally Christian, especially among young people in schools and orphanages and Christian workers. "God is revealing Himself to many in India," its editor agreed, but "it did not follow that absurd and ridiculous things are being done by Him."[97] Letters to the editor regularly mixed uncritical revival enthusiasm with considerable hesitation. One caution appeared frequently: "There is too great a tendency to give the result of some experience that we have had in connection with revival and to long to see that experience reproduced in others, rather than quietly and zealously to give the teachings of God's Word."[98] By August 1907, the *Witness* (an enthusiastic pro-revival organ since 1905) had concluded:

> Certain men have come among us claiming that the gift of tongues is the one and only true sign of the gift of the Holy Spirit, and they have alleged that certain phenomena exhibited by them . . . are evidence of the gift of tongues like that experienced by the apostles at Pentecost. The first statement Dr. Pierson and others have been shown to be absurd. It involves the discount of all the great work of revival . . . that has gone on over the world for centuries. . . . On closer examination there is found no evidence that the mutterings and gabblings these people have are the Bible gift of tongues. One feels perfectly safe, so far as the truth is concerned, to declare against both this doctrine and this alleged gift of tongues.[99]

Barratt felt the force of mounting concern in Coonoor, but reported nonetheless that "not a few missionaries received a full Pentecost."[100] Barratt's accounts are couched in a language of attack and conflict. In the name of Pentecost, he waged war and won a few skirmishes. People took sides, and

95. "Mrs. Penn-Lewis on the True and False in the Revival," *IW*, 28 March 1907, pp. 22-23.

96. "The 'Tongues' Movement in Germany," *IW*, 27 Feb. 1908, p. 133.

97. "The True and the False in the Revival Movement," *IW*, 28 February 1907, p. 133.

98. "The Revival in India," *IW*, 4 April 1907, p. 3.

99. Edward G. Saunderson, "The 'Witness' and Speaking with Tongues," *IW*, 15 Aug. 1907, p. 522.

100. Thomas Ball Barratt, *When the Fire Fell, and an Outline of My Life* (Oslo: Alfons Hansen and Sonner, 1927).

disagreements over initial evidence soon threatened the revival over which Pengwern Jones and Minnie Abrams had valiantly labored since 1905. Abrams moved easily from one scene of revival manifestations to another, but when doctrine intruded, her sympathies stood with Ramabai. For her part, in this as in other controversies, Ramabai felt no need to take sides.

The late spring of 1909 brought Daniel Awrey, a much-traveled evangelist who made a whirlwind tour of the handful of sites in India where people had spoken in tongues. Like most of the others, he did not take the time to comprehend the meaning of revival in the local context. Rather, he arrived from China, stopped at such obligatory Indian destinations as Mukti, then hurried off to Egypt. The pace of his travels leaves the reader breathless. He wasted few words on comments except to say that Mukti was "surely a great work of God."[101]

Minnie Abrams spent much of 1909 in the United States where — despite her reluctance about initial evidence — she found a welcome among pentecostals. Her association with the venerated Ramabai assured her acceptance. She apparently opened opportunities for Rachel Nalder, the North American spokesperson for the Ramabai Association, to speak and publish in pentecostal venues.[102] While home, Abrams recruited eight single women to return to India with her.[103] On their arrival in 1910, Abrams and several of the new recruits left Mukti to cultivate two new evangelistic outreaches farther north.[104] While she remained identified with Mukti mission — where she spent Christmas and other holidays — her labors now focused directly where her heart had been all along, in pioneer village evangelism. Ramabai supplied literature, money, and co-workers.[105] In 1912 Abrams finally succumbed to the ill health that she had suffered for years.

Between 1910 and 1912, Ramabai welcomed a changing array of would-be pentecostal faith missionaries from Britain and the United States.[106] Those recruited by Abrams tended to head to Mukti until they found openings else-

101. Daniel Awrey, "On Missionary Wings," *Missionary World,* July 1909, p. 7.

102. See, for example, Rachel Nalder, "God's Wonderful Work Through Pundita Ramabai," *Latter Rain (LR),* November 1908, pp. 7-12; Rachel Nalder, "The Child-Widows of India," *LR,* January 1909, pp. 13-17; *LR,* December 1908, p. 14; "Evangel Tracts," *LR,* May 1909, p. 12; *LR,* June 1912, pp. 4, 10.

103. Minnie L. Houck, "On Board S.S. Arabic," *The Pentecost* 2, no. 11-12 (Nov.-Dec. 1910): 14.

104. Their progress is amply documented in various correspondence in Pentecostal periodicals. See, for example, *Confidence,* March 1912, p. 71; "India," *Confidence,* May 1912, pp. 118-19.

105. See, for example, Minnie Houck, "At a Mela in North India," *LR,* September 1911, p. 12; "India," *LR,* March 1912, p. 4.

106. Edith Baugh, "Some Missionary Jottings," *LR,* February 1911, pp. 7-8.

where.[107] Some acknowledged that Ramabai had long ago aroused their interest in India.[108] Some identified with fledgling pentecostal efforts in India; others did not.

With Abrams's death, Ramabai's principal fund-raiser among American pentecostals passed from the scene. Abrams had, however, put pentecostals on Ramabai's mailing list, and for the rest of Ramabai's life, circular letters from Mukti regularly appeared in American pentecostal periodicals. These raised significant support for missions, and Ramabai's name was often near the top of recipients' lists. In the second half of 1910, for example, *The Latter Rain Evangel* forwarded over $1,000 to Ramabai.[109] Editors and chroniclers of the spread of pentecostalism liked to quote Ramabai or to reprint her words on the revival years. In 1916 *The Weekly Evangel*, organ of the Assemblies of God, introduced her reflections on the 1907 revival in India as follows: "Pandita Ramabai's words on this matter are very worthy of consideration, coming as they do from one respected for her piety, work, and learning by Christians the world over."[110] The same column listed her among the well-known Christians who were "in the present movement."

But was she? Given what Americans meant in 1916 by "the present 'Movement,'" she certainly would have said "no." Western Christians failed to comprehend her disinterest in their turf wars. She valued their goodwill, depended on their money, but rejected their boundaries. As she saw it, no aspect of the revival at Mukti mandated doctrinal changes, nor did she find in the revival a conclusive restoration of apostolic faith. Ramabai coveted the peculiar, intense manifestations of revival far less than she valued inner rest and effective outreach. In her mind, "Holy Ghost revival" might not always include tongues, but it would consistently translate into "fruit." "The Lord is doing a deeper work in the hearts and lives of many of the children who were blessed in the revival," she wrote thankfully in 1909.[111] *The Indian Patriot* (billed by its American citers as a "Hindoo" nationalist publication) commented: "In India, the [Welsh] revival seems to have manifested itself notably in the Kassai [*sic*] Hills, in Pandita Ramabai's home, and other places. Whatever the Revival may have been, there is no doubt there was a great spiritual awakening among Christians all over the globe."[112] The *Patriot* writer sug-

---

107. See, for example, "Word from Our Recent Outgoing Missionaries," *LR*, January 1911, p. 12.

108. Minnie Houck, "One Year in India," *LR*, March 1912, p. 19.

109. *LR*, December 1910, p. 3.

110. Bennett Lawrence, "The Works of God," *Weekly Evangel*, 10 June 1916, p. 5.

111. Lawrence, "Works of God," p. 5.

112. "From Ramabai," *The Pentecost* 1, no. 7 (June 1909): 9.

gested that tongues had erupted in the ongoing revival like "a bolt from the blue." They were part of a larger whole and signified nothing more. By 1911 pentecostals reluctantly agreed that, though Ramabai "never obstructed the working of the Holy Ghost," she did not "see things in the same light" as they.[113]

Ramabai undeniably energized early pentecostalism in India and heartened pentecostals around the world. The timing of tongues speech at Mukti seemed to pentecostals providential. In the excitement of the moment, they believed Ramabai and her well-known "work" had become one with them. They waxed eloquent citing reports from Mukti in their publications, with a special focus on 1907. They thrilled to stories of visible fire and the strange behavior often seen in their own gatherings elsewhere. The Khasi Hills and Mukti found an enduring place in pentecostal lore.

What happened in India seemed to pentecostals to prove that the apostolic faith was, indeed, the global end-times "latter rain" that Western pentecostals thought had begun. As late as the 1940s, *The Pentecostal Evangel* occasionally offered entire articles taken from Ramabai's revival writings.[114] But it is noteworthy that during the period from 1908 to Ramabai's death when they reprinted her writings on the Mukti revival, American pentecostals were evoking the past, not celebrating the present. While they hallowed memories of revival at Mukti and wove Ramabai into their mythology, they learned — as had others before them — that Ramabai defied Western classification.

In November 1910 two of the most widely traveled and most ardent American pentecostal evangelists, Frank Bartleman and Daniel Awrey, came through Mukti. Each — unknown to the other — was circumnavigating the globe by faith. They met (providentially, they were sure) at the rail station in Poona and hurried with Albert Norton to Mukti where for two days they preached and prayed. Bartleman's comments on Mukti are instructive:

> There seemed to be very little demonstration as far as one could see, but I was conscious of a steady, moving faith that brought reality and results. . . . I felt very unworthy. The humility of these great leaders (Ramabai and Manoramabai) was very touching. I left Mukti feeling I had been very near to heaven.[115]

---

113. *Indian Patriot,* cited in *Confidence,* Sept. 1910, p. 223.

114. "The Place of Tongues in the Pentecostal Movement," cited in *Confidence,* August 1911, p. 176.

115. Frank Bartleman, *Around the World by Faith* (Los Angeles, privately published), pp. 68-69.

Other contemporary accounts concur. One wonders if most non-pentecostals took special notice of tongues speech at Mukti. Everyone remarked on the concerts of prayer, but visitors other than Bartleman, though they found much to impress in the way of fervor, also neglected to notice tongues.[116]

3. Ramabai and Global Pentecostalism

Without ever becoming a pentecostal, Ramabai played a significant role in the spread of pentecostalism. The pentecostal press spread the news of revival among her young child widows. Her established reputation and the interest with which the missionary world had long regarded her spiritual pilgrimage made her a central figure in reports of Indian revival. India had long fascinated the West, and the revival at Mukti was reported widely in Protestant periodicals because it swept mission communities, too. It heartened those who had toiled long and coveted results. Reports generally emphasized the evangelism that flowed from the revival and the prayer that nurtured it. Pentecostals, on the other hand, seemed to revel in the manifestations that accompanied it.

While pentecostals seized especially on the Mukti revival because it belonged to no one else (as did the revived stations in the Khasi Hills) and because Ramabai had always had an "open door policy," the revival at Mukti contrasted in several ways with the scenes that animated Western pentecostalism. At Mukti, revival emerged in the context of an awakening that had already been in progress for two years. It objected to tongues speech as the inevitable sign of Spirit baptism. Speech uttered "in tongues" was typically in languages Ramabai recognized — English, Sanskrit, Greek, Hebrew — rather than in the "missionary tongues" as many American pentecostals claimed. Unlike pentecostals in the United States, those of Ramabai's widows who spoke in tongues did not feel called to the ends of the earth. For them, the Great Commission was what it always had been: a command to village evangelism at home. The small percentage of Ramabai's girls who spoke in tongues, then, did not use miraculous speech to identify new venues for Christian service. In fact, tongues speech was generally confined to the prolonged and intense periods of simultaneous vocal intercessory prayer. When the visiting journalist William Ellis asked Ramabai "why tongues that served no useful purpose being incomprehensible [to the speaker] should be given,"

116. Emma Dean Anderson, "A Visit to Ramabai's Home at Mukti," *MRW* (April 1909): 289-91.

Ramabai responded: "I, too, wondered about that. But it has been shown to me that it is to rebuke unbelief in the gift of tongues that [the girl in question] has been given the gift."[117] Ramabai remained untroubled when "manifestations" did not occur and unfazed when they did. What mattered to her was the outflow in effective prayer and vigorous evangelism that seemed to follow the revived, whether or not they spoke in tongues.

Nonetheless, she helped ignite the global pentecostal flame. She had a well-established place in Western Protestant lore, and pentecostals were gratified when tongues speech among some of her girls apparently linked her with them, just as George F. Pentecost had boasted, a decade before, of her ties to him. Entirely apart from tongues, tales of the intensity of the Mukti revival heartened countless people to expect spiritual renewal and suggested what a revival might look like. Ramabai's devotion to the evangelism of her people encouraged hundreds of struggling pentecostal missions around the world.

Though pentecostals rushed to count Ramabai in their ranks, the revival at Mukti is better described in relationship to Ramabai's unfolding personal spiritual journey. Her aloofness to pentecostalism forced pentecostals to content themselves with recounting the "glory days" when tongues speech had briefly intruded at Mukti. Pentecostalism progressed in India independently of Mukti. Already in July 1908 George Berg (fresh from Azusa Street) boasted that a total of fifty overseas missionaries had "received Pentecost" and that at least twenty mission stations "were just flooded with pentecostal power and light."[118] But that was less than what readers of the *Apostolic Faith* in 1907 might have anticipated. Under the title "The Work in India," the paper had boasted that "some of the choicest spirits of India have been baptized with the Holy Ghost," and that "five or six hundred witnesses in India today earnestly contend for the faith once delivered to the saints."[119]

The convergence between Mukti and pentecostalism was a matter of timing. Tongues were tongues, and pentecostals were heartened by tongues wherever they found them. They deemed the timing providential, and they never openly relinquished their claim to Ramabai. When she died on 5 April 1922, *The Pentecostal Evangel* carried a long obituary, reprinting familiar excerpts from Minnie Abrams's ramblings on the revival of the 1905-1907 years. A more poignant personal tribute from Ramabai's long-time col-

---

117. William T. Ellis, "Christians in India Are Given 'Gift of Tongues,'" *The Weekly Evangel,* 24 June 1916, pp. 5-6. This is taken from the *Erie (PA) Daily Times* and is a fuller rendering of Ellis's observations than Chicago papers carried.

118. George E. Berg, "Latter Rain Mission in India," *Word and Work,* September 1908, p. 282.

119. "Work in India," *Apostolic Faith* (Los Angeles), June-September, 1907.

league, Albert Norton, now a devout pentecostal, followed a month later. With no references to the revival, Norton praised Ramabai, not because a handful of people had once manifested spiritual gifts at Mukti, but for the consecration that had marked her life.[120] Indian compatriots, too, caught glimmers of the meaning of her life lived for India and sensed she had earned greater international esteem for her homeland. Sarojini Naidu, a leading Indian nationalist and poet, paid her tribute as "the first Christian to be enrolled in the calendar of Hindu saints."[121] A contemporary biographer suggested that she brought into Christianity "the glory and honor of the Hindu spiritual heritage — a heritage marked by the devotion and passion of its long search for God."[122]

In the course of Ramabai's busy life, then, the emerging pentecostal movement converged briefly with a revival already in progress. She refused to oppose its distinctive practice, but she resisted deriving doctrine from practice. In Mukti as in the Khasi Hills, the more vivid "manifestations" that accompanied the Indian revival floundered on the shoals of pentecostalism. Pentecostals deflected the revival's momentum. Though Ramabai facilitated pentecostalism's early Indian stirrings, she resisted the tidal wave that followed. And so while the Mukti revival helped convince Western pentecostals that their movement was "of God," pentecostalism in fact followed its own trajectory while the revival that dated from 1905 followed another. The two converged superficially, and Ramabai's international acclaim lent momentary legitimacy, but just as quickly, the streams diverged.

Set apart from her willing supporters abroad by her Hindu upbringing and from her compatriots by her education, her international acclaim, her devotion to India and its women, and her lifelong pursuit of the holy, Ramabai in the end stood aloof from Western attempts to classify or to claim her. The handful of Westerners who glimpsed her significance for India were often experienced "India hands" such as F. Max Müller or James and Isabella Thoburn. Some extolled her for her determination to give Christ place as "the architect" of India's future. Indian contemporaries recognized her unstinting devotion to the search for God. One proposed that in her dependence on the Christian God she discovered the Hindu's ultimate goal of perfect rest. Contemporary feminists regret that she professed to find that rest in dependence. Few found a more enduring place in pentecostal memory. Few helped (un-

120. Albert Norton, "A Warm Tribute to Ramabai," *The Pentecostal Evangel*, 27 May 1922, p. 9.

121. Padmini Sengupta, *Pandita Ramabai Saraswati: Her Life and Work* (London: Asia Publishing House, 1970), p. 325.

122. MacNicol, *Ramabai*, p. 195.

wittingly, to be sure) more to spark the pentecostal flame around the globe. Yet Ramabai's disinterest in the historical and doctrinal views that molded Western pentecostalism made it impossible for her to identify pentecostalism with the baptism of the Holy Spirit and Fire that beckoned her ever onward.

CHAPTER 10

Pentecostalism and Christian Utopia in China: Jing Dianying and the Jesus Family Movement, 1921-1952

FEIYA TAO

1. Introduction

A great change took place in the Christian movement in China in the first half of the twentieth century. One of the most conspicuous results of the pressure of Chinese nationalism was the development of the Chinese indigenous church and the emergence of a group of Chinese Christian leaders.

The Jesus Family, founded by Jing Dianying (1890-1957) in 1927 in Mazhuang, Taian, Shandong Province, was one of the most important rural indigenous churches. Established in the 1920s, it underwent a very interesting and strange experience in the early 1950s. At first, it was regarded as thoroughly indigenous, a burgeoning "proletarian church" that allegedly had something in common with communist theory. As a result the Jesus Family was extremely popular in the arena of Chinese religions from 1950 to 1951, and Jing Dianying was elected as the one of the leaders of the Three-Self Patriotic Movement. However, the Family was soon attacked as "a hell on earth" (in 1952) and broken up in the church reform movement. Its history has remained obscure since then.

A few academic articles published since the 1980s have touched on the story of the Jesus Family and revealed its many special features. Among scholars, Daniel H. Bays described its social structure as "remarkably egalitarian and communitarian."[1] Zha Shijie also mentioned its strange communal way

---

1. Daniel Bays, "Christianity in China: A Case Study of Indigenous Christianity: The Jesus Family, 1927-1952," in *Religion* (journal of the Kansas School of Religion) 26, no. 1 (Oct. 1988): 3.

of life.[2] Even Bishop Ding Guangxun, the former chairman of the Chinese Christian Association, pointed out that the Jesus Family was "communism with a feudal flavor."[3]

Obviously, people recognized that a certain relationship existed between "communism" and the Jesus Family though they viewed it from different perspectives. This is the first issue that this chapter will explore. How should the so-called "communism" of the Family be characterized and identified? Bryan Wilson has distinguished three types of sects that are more likely to lead to alternative communities than others.[4] One category is "utopian," which in all cases resort to their own community, not as an end in itself, but as a way of fulfilling a perfect manifestation of God's will that can then be spread to the rest of society.[5] G. and P. Gutek discussed some cases in the United States and found that among others "in American history, 'Utopia' needs to be expanded to include the concept of Communitarianism, a societal arrangement in which property is owned jointly by a group rather than by individuals."[6] In a certain sense, the Jesus Family could be categorized as a Christian utopia in China according to Wilson's theory, and it did have many similarities with various so-called American Christian utopias.

If this is so, there arises the second question: Why and how did the Family evolve into a Christian utopia over nearly thirty years? Bays has proved its close connection with the American Assemblies of God church in Taian city, and suggested that the example of the Home of Onesiphorus (a philanthropic institute run by the Assemblies of God in Taian) "fed directly into Jing's formation of the Jesus Family in 1927."[7] R. J. Burden, however, said he would "resist claiming that they are merely a Chinese version of U.S. pentecostalism," and thought the Jesus Family was something of a "traditionary invention."[8] Bays thus attributed its uniqueness to the mode of the American pentecostal

2. Shijie Zha, "Shandong 'Yesu Jiating' de Jingji Xingtai Chutan, 1927-1942" [the economic activities of the 'Jesus Family' in Shandong, 1927-1942], *Guoli Taiwan daxue lishi xuexi xuebao* 15 (1990): 218.

3. Winfried Glüer, *T. C. Chao's Thought* (Hong Kong: Christianity Literature Press, 1998), p. vii.

4. Bryan Wilson, *Religious Sects: A Sociological Study* (London: Weidenfeld & Nicolson, 1970), pp. 43-44, 46-47.

5. Dennis Hardy, *Alternative Communities in Nineteenth-Century England* (London and New York: Longman, 1979), p. 121.

6. Gerald and Patricia Gutek, *Visiting Utopia Communities* (Columbia: University of South Carolina Press, 1998), p. 1.

7. Bays, "Christianity in China," p. 3.

8. R. J. Burden, "Cleaving Traditions: The Yesu Jiating, Chinese Pentecostal Sectarians," unpublished paper, p. 6.

church in Taian while Burden tried to explain it in terms of Chinese religious tradition, though an invented tradition. A close analysis of the Jesus Family shows that on the one hand it was indeed influenced by both the Assemblies of God and Chinese traditions. On the other hand, it differed in many ways from the Assemblies of God, and many elements of the Family cannot be found in Chinese tradition either. For example, the Assemblies of God did not advocate the "communitarian" way of life, and whereas the advocacy of "communism" was virtually unknown in Chinese tradition, the Family advocated "public ownership." It would seem that something besides American pentecostalism and indigenous Chinese traditions contributed to the development of the Jesus Family movement.

This chapter will discuss how various social and religious forces contributed to the formation and growth of the Jesus Family, and in particular, how and under what circumstances Jing Dianying combined new social thought and the pentecostal movement to create the Chinese Christian utopia. It will also consider how he and his followers reassessed the pentecostalism and the utopian system in the 1950s. In addition, the place of the Jesus Family in the historical process, based mostly on the record of the Family itself, will be considered.

2. From Taoist to Methodist to Pentecostal

Jing Dianying, the founder of the Jesus Family movement, was born into the family of an impoverished landlord in Mazhuang, Taian, Shandong, in 1890 when the Qing dynasty was approaching its end. His father taught in several old-style private schools and sometimes practiced Chinese medicine to earn extra money to support his family. Neither of Jing's parents had religious beliefs except that his father was obviously influenced by Confucianism. Young Jing was attracted to religion for various reasons: his parents both died when he was a teenager (he was thirteen when his mother died and fifteen when his father died); his family's economic situation declined continuously, and the alleged disloyalty of his wife hurt him very badly. The Qing government's abolition of the imperial examination system in 1905 blocked his chance of upward mobility through entering the bureaucracy. Jing was very disappointed and turned to religion, which could help him to escape from "reality." First he converted to Taoism, which was very popular in the area around Tai Mountain, the site of many temples and performances of the folk operas based on Taoist stories. The young man followed the teaching of Taoism literally and adopted its ascetic lifestyle.

Something is known of Jing's initial religious development. First, as a lay Taoist, he hoped he could become an immortal or a very healthy man through practicing Taoism. Second, he believed that a human being could associate with the deity by a certain combination of body movement and devout prayer. Both Jing's religious purpose and practice revealed his connection with and experience of the popular religions in the area. Jing had to find a job. After the overthrow of Qing in 1911, he went to the American Methodist Middle School in Taian city in 1912 and became a student at the age of twenty-two. He did not become a Christian, however, until he was hired as a teacher of Mandarin by Nora Dellinbeck, a single female Methodist missionary. It was alleged that Jing became a Christian in 1914 because of his attraction towards this missionary. Whatever the actual reason, he later affirmed his belief that he had not been spiritually "reborn" simply because he had become a Christian.[9] He believed that he had not received the "gift of the Spirit" or entered into personal communication with the Holy Spirit.

Jing was hired as a preacher by the hospital attached to Shandong Christian University in Jinan in 1918 and worked there for almost five years. He participated in Sage Taoism [Shengxian Dao], one of the newly formed popular religions in Shandong. Jing explained that he did so because he wanted to understand Sage Taoism in order to dissuade his nephew from severing connection with it and converting to Christianity. This may suggest that Jing's faith in Christianity was not yet that firm and that his disposition was one of pragmatism in religion. According to Jing's own account, however, he finally experienced a personal encounter with the divine when preaching in the hospital hall. He was sick at the time but while preaching he suddenly felt the force of the Holy Spirit.[10] This mystical experience convinced him that he had finally found the true religion.

Jing's stay in the provincial capital exposed him to new experiences in the turbulent years when the May 4th Movement swept across Shandong Province. New ideas were disseminated, leading to the establishment of different organizations, one of which was the communist group in Jinan in the 1920s. Jing, however, was more concerned with the rural problems of Mazhuang, where flood, drought, and a plague of insects, in addition to the corrupt warlord government, had caused the farmers' situation to worsen.

In 1919 Jing had the idea of organizing a Christian cooperative economy, the Christian Trust and Saving Society, which was finally established in 1921.

9. "An Autobiography of Jing Dianying," Tai Mountain District Archive, Taian, Shandong [hereafter Tai Archive] 1-16-9, f. 147.

10. "Autobiography of Jing Dianying," f. 142.

He explained that China was poor because people did not trust each other, and the only way to solve this problem was to organize the Christians, whom he considered had virtue and could be trusted, to do business together. What was more, he criticized "the evil world" and hoped to build a new society under the guidance of Christian principles as he outlined in his opening speech to the society.[11] It is important to note that Jing had the idea of uniting poor rural Christians for secular and religious purposes even *before* he made contact with the pentecostal church in Taian. On the other hand, both "trust" and "saving" were new words that could not be found in Chinese tradition. Hence this venture demonstrated Jing's pragmatism and willingness to adopt and incorporate new thoughts into his own creation from the beginning. More importantly, Jing believed his invention was of universal significance and that was one of the characteristics of utopianism.

Jing grew dissatisfied with his hospital job, which he used as a base to establish his small organization, but he still worked in the provincial city and made his new organization his nephew's responsibility. His problem was that he did not have a degree, or even a middle school diploma, and saw no future for himself as the lowest-level preacher in the hierarchy of the institutional church. On one occasion he condemned the church leaders for only paying attention to people with high qualifications, and in particular, with foreign degrees.[12] He resigned his position several times and was later invited to be a Bible teacher in his alma mater. In 1923 he returned to Taian to teach in the middle school, where he became associated with the Assemblies of God, a connection that was to change his life.

As Bays suggests, it is possible that Jing found illumination from a particular Assemblies of God missionary called Anglin, who established the "Home of Onesiphorus." He was gradually attracted by both its pentecostal religious teaching and its combination of the sacred and secular life. In 1924 it was in the meeting hall of the Assemblies of God that Jing experienced the "strong shock" that convinced him he had been baptized by the Holy Spirit, for at last he could now speak in tongues. It seems that Jing highly appreciated "the strange and beautiful feeling" derived from this experience and found happiness from this encounter with the divine.[13] The Rev. Perry Hanson, the principal of the Methodist Middle School in Taian, warned that what Jing believed in was "heresy." Jing was ousted from both the school and the

11. "A Survey of the Jesus Family in China," Tai Archive, 1-16-7, f. 69.

12. "An Account in Jing Dianying's own words," Tai Archive, 1-16-7, f. 47.

13. Letter from Jing Dianying to Cao Shuseng, 30 March 1942, Taian Municipal Archives, 18-13-17, ff. 37-38.

Methodist church because he refused to retreat from pentecostalism. After that he worked in the Home of Onesiphorus in 1925. This pentecostal institute was very prosperous at the time and enjoyed a high reputation in the locality. Its success would have left a deep impression on Jing, and the name he chose for his establishment, "the Jesus Home," was strongly influenced by the "Home of Onesiphorus."[14]

Jing's Christian Trust and Saving Society was unsuccessful, and by 1924 he began to transfer his economic activity from business to agriculture. He hoped that silkworm-breeding and silk-reeling would support the Christian group, which was renamed the "Jesus Home" or the "Jesus Family" in 1927. Strangely, Jing's autobiography never mentions either his work in the Assemblies of God or the Jesus Family's connection with that church. Hanson had warned Jing that pentecostalism was a heresy, but this type of religious experience was familiar to the Shandong farmers. The pentecostal messages would be interpreted in the local idiom by Jing and led to his formation of a Chinese Christian utopia.

3. Pentecostalism and the Christian Utopia

The Jesus Family developed gradually after 1927. In addition to the family in Mazhuang, which was called the "old family," Jing began to build "small families" along the lines of the old family from that year. The pattern of the development of the small families was uneven. Jing and his followers established only eleven small families between 1927 and 1937, but they founded sixty-three during the Sino-Japanese War (1937-45) and thirty-nine new ones during the civil war of 1946-1949. It is clear that the suffering of the two wars helped in the development of the Family.[15] The total number of families reached 127 in 1952, spread over northwest, east, and south China. At first most of the families were in rural areas, but small families began in cities from the mid-1940s, and even in some large cities such as Nanjing, Wuhan, and Shanghai. The total population of all the families grew from only around a dozen Christians in the Mazhuang family to about ten thousand members in 1948.[16] This number probably included two types of people; those who

14. The title "Jesus Home" was printed on the songbook of the Family in 1940.

15. During the Sino-Japanese war, 900,000 Shandong people lost their lives. See Liu Dake, Ma Fuzhen, and Shen Guomin, *The History of Japanese Invasion of Shandong* (Jinan: Shandong People's Press, 1990), pp. 276-83.

16. Ma Honggang, ed., "An Introduction of a Burgeoning Chinese Christian Sect: The Jesus Family," *Xiejin* 7, no. 5 (16 Oct. 1948): 7.

lived in the family communities, and others who supported the family but did not live in it. Fewer than 3,000 Christians lived in the Jesus families country-wide according to governmental statistics in 1952.[17]

Compared with the surrounding society, the social life of the Family ex-hibited many distinctive utopian characteristics. First, it adopted the commu-nitarian principle and denied private ownership. The Family initially copied the idea from the Home of Onesiphorus, and even its first three looms were bought from that institution. Jing, however, encountered many problems as soon as he convened his followers to live together as the Home of Onesi-phorus did. The most important thing was that he had no funds to support his small community and often lacked enough food and appropriate shelter for his people. He could not pay them anything for their labor, as Anglin did. In this way, Jing's group adopted utopianism at the beginning of its history. Like all Christian utopians, he advocated that the true Christian should fol-low what Jesus asked the young man to do in Matthew 19:16, and he called on members to follow the mode of life of the primitive Christian community in the first century (Acts 2:43). This meant no private property, the sharing of all goods, and not paying much attention to one's family ties or material con-cerns. The Family was, Jing said, the best life a Christian should practice. The communitarian system naturally led to an egalitarian way of life. Adult mem-bers of the Family shared the same standards in food and dress and all lived in the same rooms except for babies and older people who received some special treatment.

Second, the Jesus Family established socially isolated but economically self-sufficient communities governed by specific rules based on scriptural patterns. It was believed that such separation, a most important requirement of communitarian life, would not only protect community members from persecution but also from enticements to deviate from the founder's pre-scriptions for the true way of life. Most of the Jesus families were located in the countryside or in the suburbs of cities with no close neighbors. Based on economic functionalism, all the Jesus families relied on industry and farming, which made them self-sufficient. Production was efficient as a result of a planned division of labor. The foundation was agriculture, and upon this were built various enterprises and departments, which in the Mazhuang fam-ily were carpentry, boot-making, baking, operation of a smithy, a machine shop and electrical department, stone masonry, schools and a kindergarten, an outside relations department, a finance department, printing, and book-

17. Xu Jiashu, "The Thirty-One Years' History of the Jesus Family," Shandong Provin-cial Archive, f. 21.

binding.[18] The Family characteristically maintained a profitable economic connection with the larger society. The original family sent people to Shanghai to sell green bean noodles and apples, and most of the small families made and sold bean curd for profit. They also deliberately created communal agencies that would efficiently perform necessary services, for example, communal child-care centers, kitchens, dining rooms, and laundries were used to free women to perform other economic functions in the community. As community-builders, they endeavored to develop profitable agricultural and secondary products that would contribute to the maintenance of the Family's very modest standard of living in the chaotic years.

Third, the Family was a total social and economic communal milieu. Life in it was a totally formative experience that involved the mutually reinforcing elements of prayer, work, and learning. Usually, the members prayed five hours a day on weekdays, eight hours on Sunday, and nine hours when they held two large retreats every winter and summer. Their working and prayer hours were almost the same in the slack season. Courses provided in the Family school were strongly religious in content. The importance of work both to economic production and religious indoctrination was a key element of community life. Religious communities were to create a spiritual "we-feeling" among the church membership and build into their psyches a willing conformity to the religious practices and lifestyle prescribed by Jing. Living in these communities involved a high degree of social, economic, and religious integration but also profound social control that erased individuality. Their lifestyle, social and economic organization, and educational practices were heavily influenced by the theology of Jing Dianying, who was known as Jiazhang (Family Head) and later as the only Laoren (Old Man), which confirmed his unique authority over all the families.

Fourth, like all Christian utopias in the West, Jing and the members of the Jesus Family considered themselves to be a separate and consecrated people who were to live apart from a sinful world. As a chosen people, they thought Jesus lived among them and they awaited the Second Coming of Jesus Christ, which would usher in the thousand-year reign of harmony, peace, and holiness. Jing described his ideal society in the long poem "The Jesus Family." The Family, he said, was filled with love, and all the people could spend their lives there. He stressed that the Family was better than the Great Harmony of Confucius and of communism. Members hoped to reform the whole of China,

---

18. D. Vaughan Rees, *The 'Jesus Family' in Communist China* (London: Paternoster Press, 1976), pp. 26-27.

even the whole world, and they dreamed of spreading the Family to Western countries.[19]

Richard C. S. Trahair has noted that "the realization of human potential through collective ownership, reduction in aggression, and commitment to communal residence and to work for the community are at the core of utopian ventures."[20] The Jesus Family seems perfectly to fit these categories of "utopian ventures." Actually, as early as 1933, Paul Abbott, an American missionary in Shandong, pointed out that the Jesus Family practiced "Christian communism."[21] Our question here is that if such a communitarian utopia was something brand new at that time in China, what caused Jing and his people to establish and live in such an organization?

There is no doubt that the Jesus Family had close connections with the Assemblies of God church in Taian. The pentecostal ritual and religious experience were identical with the ones that the Shandong peoples were familiar with in the performance of shamanism. In such religious practice the adherents believed that they were able to listen and talk with the Holy Spirit by praying with loud crying and shouting, and proved their communication with the Spirit by certain bodily actions and speaking in tongues. Jing's pentecostalism, however, contained something different and new. Early pentecostals often claimed that speaking in tongues was speaking a foreign language, but the Family members voiced only two monosyllabic words (ba and da), and the vocalization of such sounds meant the Holy Spirit had fallen on the speaker. This obviously made speaking in tongues easier to replicate than speaking an identifiable foreign language: the way was open for anyone to prove their relation with the Holy Spirit. Jing merged various elements of Chinese popular religion with experiences drawn from the Assemblies of God, such as trance, dancing in the Spirit, seeing visions, special dreams, and other forms of possession by the Spirit, and in this way gave more freedom to his disciples to prove their relation with the Holy Spirit. Pentecostalism is a highly enthusiastic form of Christianity that gave Jing and his followers the confidence to regard themselves as a special category of Christians whom Jing described as the "vanguard of the kingdom of God."[22] Such enthusiasm helped the members of the Family to retreat from normal secular life and to accept the Family's radically new way of life. Although Jing stressed the effi-

19. Rees, 'Jesus Family,' p. 24.

20. Richard C. S. Trahair, *Utopias and Utopians: A Historical Dictionary* (London and Chicago: Fitzroy Dearborn Publishers, 1999), p. x.

21. Paul R. Abbott, "Revival Movements," *China Christian Year Book, 1932-1933* (Shanghai: Christian Literature Society, 1933), p. 188.

22. Ma Honggang, ed., "Burgeoning Chinese Christian Sect," p. 6.

cacy of prayer, he did not overemphasize the healing function of pente-costalism, and he built up a clinic staffed by well-trained doctors with university degrees. This also helped to safeguard people's faith in pentecostalism in the long term.

Theologically, pentecostalism advocated the pre-millennial advent of Christ, a doctrine that stressed the evils of the world and predicted natural disasters and wars as signs of the end of the age. This explanation was extremely pertinent to the miserable situation of Shandong in most of the first half of the twentieth century and was accepted by Jing and the Family members. Jing explained that the signs of the end of the age were evident in the many natural disasters and wars that afflicted Shandong during the years when the Family was relatively prosperous. Jing explained the phenomenon literally according to the Bible and told people that the Family was "Noah's ark."[23] Given that the world would end soon, why should Christians care too much about their family and property? In this sense, although pentecostalism did not advocate utopianism, it did endow the Jesus Family with a meaning and reasonable explanation for it.

Jing's Jesus Family was not merely the result of American pentecostal influence, but neither was it an "invented tradition." In fact, it was a unique mixture of elements drawn from pentecostalism, Taoism, Confucianism, and socialism. For instance, Jing interpreted pre-millennial teaching to his followers in light of the nihilism of Chinese Taoism. He was able to convince them that the communal way of life was the best one for them while waiting for the Second Coming of Jesus, because Taoism holds that secular life is transient and teaches that people should get rid of their family and property to reach true eternal life. Similarly, his ethics for his Family were based both on the Christian teaching of love and on Confucius's ideal of commonwealth [*Datong*], in which people should help each other and live in harmony.

As for the economy, Jing advocated the typical small farmer's ideal society where man tills and woman spins and weaves. Here too, Jing imbibed new ideas characteristic of his time and combined them with Chinese tradition. The social gospel ideas of E. Stanley Jones were very popular in the 1920s and 1930s in China, where his advocacy of social reform and attacks on "economic injustice" received a ready hearing. Jones's books were translated into Chinese. Jing collected and read many of them, such as *Abundant Living*, and *Christ at the Round Table*. According to his followers, Jing was very attracted to Jones's ideas and often said that he followed Jones's writings.[24]

23. *Preaching Song of the Jesus Family*, p. 95, Tai Archive.
24. Xu Jiashu, "Thirty-One Years," f. 13.

Communist propaganda appeared in Jing's poems. As early as 1931, Jing's long poem "The Jesus Family" cited "communism" as a way of highlighting the advantage of his Family. "From each according to his ability, to each according to his needs" was the popular and standardized Chinese Communist slogan. This exact same sentence was cited in a long poem by Jing written in 1941.[25] This tendency became more and more evident. During the Sino-Japanese War, Jing told his people that the system of the Jesus Family was a kind of communism.[26] In early 1951, in a letter he wrote: "I often said that every Christian should be a true Communist though they are without membership; as for communism, it is needless to say that Jesus, and his disciples Peter, James, John and Paul and so on fully deserved to be called communists."[27] It was not strange that Jing was familiar with Communist ideas, because the Communists had established base areas behind the Japanese lines that had been adjacent to the Family since 1938. What Jing absorbed from Communism, however, was only these few sentences, cited just as he cited a few words from the Confucian classics. It is certain that what appealed most to Jing was the egalitarianism and communitarianism.

We have shown that pentecostalism, Confucianism, social-gospel teaching, and Jing's own brand of communism together formed the ideological basis of the Jesus Family. Among them pentecostalism was the most important. In his three hundred poems he reiterated pre-millennial eschatological themes many times but only casually mentioned Confucianism and communism. In fact, neither the Confucian attachment to one's family and clan nor the socially revolutionary nature of communism could easily be applied to the Jesus Family movement. A distinctively pentecostal ethos supported the Family's life. War and famine became identified as the characteristics of the pre-millennial era in the Shandong area. All this supported Jing's teaching and served to strengthen the Family system. Jing's theology heavily relied on the practical situation, however, and it would meet challenges as soon as the war ended.

4. From a Pentecostal to a Transient Figure in the Church Reform Movement: The Disintegration of the Chinese Christian Utopia

The civil war ended in Shandong in 1948 and the Communists established a new government and introduced new policies to reconstruct the country. For

25. Xu Jiashu, "Thirty-One Years," f. 13.
26. Xu Jiashu, "Thirty-One Years," f. 12.
27. Xu Jiashu, "Thirty-One Years," f. 21.

all the churches, it was a totally different new society. To the Jesus Family the new era brought distinctive challenges, though Jing Dianying was still optimistic in the early 1950s when he married Dr. Chen, who had graduated from the medical school of Hong Kong University in the 1930s. Economically, because of the land reform movement, the Family in Shandong was compelled to return many lands to the poor farmers who had sold them to the Family in famine years. The Family therefore faced a serious land shortage. In addition, Christians who supported the Family but did not live in it gradually stopped donating to the Family, though the members who lived in the Family continued to increase, particularly because of children of the old members. As a result, the Family began to disperse its inhabitants to the small families in the northeast and northwest of China.

The early 1950s in Chinese history were eventful years. Soon after the Korean War broke out the government mobilized the people to support the war, and officials often went to the Family and borrowed their churches for political meetings. In early 1951 the government recruited the youth of China for the army, and Jing proposed that the Jesus Family would organize a medical team and go to the battlefront to help the Chinese soldiers. This idea was highly praised and accepted by the local officials. In June 1951, Jing himself led the medical team to Beijing and delivered many public speeches in Taian, Jinan, and Tianjin on their way to Beijing. His action became news in governmental newspapers and church publications, and he became almost a hero in church circles. The reform movement of Chinese Christianity was launched by a group of Christian leaders almost at the beginning of the Korean War, and Jing was very active in the campaign. He condemned American imperialism and the churches supported by foreign missionaries. He claimed that his Jesus Family was an indigenous church that had no connection with foreign missions. To show their support to the Three-Self and Patriotic Movement of the Chinese Church, all the members of the Jesus Family signed a statement published in the *People's Daily,* and the Jesus Family became a so-called "new church." Jing was elected as a member of the presidium of the Chinese Christian Three-Self and Patriotic and Anti-Imperialism Organizing Committee, the only member of the Chinese pentecostal churches on that committee. Jing became more politically radical soon after he was elected as a committee member, asserting that the members of the Jesus Family were actual party members without needing formal membership, and that he himself would no longer live for the Jesus Family alone but for all the Chinese churches.[28]

28. Song Minzhu's speech, 25 May 1952, Tai Archive, 1-16-9, p. 66.

Along with the change of his political attitudes, Jing began to re-evaluate the pattern of his church and his theology. In fact, as was the case with most of the communal churches at this time, the internal problems of the Jesus Family became more and more serious. Religious enthusiasm aroused by pentecostalism was on the wane as the new regime stabilized society and promoted economic development. The younger generation that had grown up within the Family did not treat the pentecostal experience as seriously as the old members. Filling with the Holy Spirit and speaking in tongues became routine business for some of them. On the other hand, the living standard of the farmers around the Family improved, since they now owned land and the government encouraged them to build up family fortunes. In relative terms the people who lived in the Family found that they were still as poor as before. For almost thirty years when the country was at war, Jing Dianying had preached the Second Coming and predicted the approach of the last days, but now he had to stop repeating his predictions of the end of the world. Jing found it very difficult to control the Family members after the liberation from the Japanese and the civil war. Though he at first wanted to maintain the Family, he gradually changed his mind and decided to seek the cooperation of the government to solve the job problem of his disciples. It is very significant that Jing himself did not hold the beliefs about the Second Advent and the end of the world as firmly as before.[29]

At the end of 1951, Jing went to Shanghai for a political study meeting where he wrote many reminiscences and discussed pentecostalism. He thought the pentecostal religious experiences were good and that they helped converts to reach a condition of physiological happiness, but the people in the Family abused them. He pointed out that some of the Family members had become conceited and looked down on Christians from other denominations, claiming that they could receive the Holy Spirit but others could not. He admitted that the Jesus Family had been a life raft in the old society, but was now an ugly wart that should be removed from the new China, and he and the members of the Family should live in their own families. Jing expressed the view that for the Christian, "grace" would come from God but material life should be left to the government and was not the business of the church. He admitted that the structure of the Family was not as good as those of the common churches and should be reformed.[30]

It is evident that by the early 1950s Jing's theological stance had undergone substantial change. What caused this transformation? Probably it was the re-

29. Collection of *Poems of Jing Dianying*, ed. Yang Jiemin, mimeographed, 1985, p. 29.
30. An account in Jing Dianying's own words, Tai Archive, 1-16-9, p. 59.

sult of external political pressures and internal problems, but his pragmatism, in particular, played an important part. The change in Jing's theological stand is not beyond comprehension, because he always wanted to adapt his religion to his time and social environment.

The end of the Jesus Family did not come in the way that Jing had expected. In the new political climate, the mainstream of the Chinese church did not appreciate pentecostalism. In the journal of the Chinese Christian Association many articles attacked the spiritual churches because they overstressed the mystery of religious experience, paid too much attention to religious activities, and ignored the responsibility to increase production that the people dearly needed.[31] In a word, the Jesus Family was deemed incompatible with the new system of the socialist country. Finally, the Family was "reformed" and disbanded in the middle of 1952 with the help of a work team organized by the members from the local government and the Three-Self Patriotic Movement Organizing Committee. The Jesus Family, the only Chinese Christian utopia, thus disappeared from the religious arena.

5. Conclusion

It is clear that Jing Dianying's conversion to pentecostalism led to the establishment of the Jesus Family, because the Assemblies of God had given Jing an example of how he could get Christians to live and practice their religion together. The Chinese Christians were hardly passive recipients of Western culture and religion, however, and they read their own significance into pentecostalism. Owing to the practical conditions, Jing's pentecostalism was adapted to the social context and helped to form a Chinese Christian utopia. Chinese tradition, the social gospel, and a smattering of knowledge of communism all made their contributions to his utopian enterprise. The enthusiasm aroused by the millennial teaching of pentecostalism and the actual acute daily social distress were always the cornerstones of the Christian utopia. As soon as the local situation improved, and the cornerstone was shaken, the utopian system was deeply challenged and brought to the brink of collapse. Jing's pragmatic attitudes towards synthesizing elements of Taoism, Methodism, pentecostalism, and communism illustrate the complexity of interaction between the faith and social life of Chinese Christians in this period. It was this interaction that enabled Jing to combine ideas from

31. *The Newsletter of the Rural Church* 18 (1 Sept. 1950) (Shanghai: The Rural Church Press of the Chinese Christian Association).

pentecostalism, Chinese tradition, and newly introduced communism to create a unique Chinese Christian utopia. The Jesus Family remains a vivid example of how pentecostal forms of Christianity have been contextualized and localized in Chinese society.

CHAPTER 11

Local Portraits of Christ in Africa Today: Jesus as Chief/King in Ghanaian Christianity

DIANE STINTON

Jesus! You are the one
who has gone out to save the nations.
You wear a chief's crown.
The flag of a conqueror leads you in battle.[1]

Mmp'wmmeahene and Gyaasehene:
Chief of many small villages
and steward of God's household,
Jesus, who walks on gold dust,
with great strides he reaches this place,
while gold-nugget stars lead the way.

Chief among chiefs, when you stretch forth your hand,
widows are covered with festive beads
while orphans wear kente!
'hemmer'fo: humble King,
your words are precious jewels.
We don't buy them, we don't beg for them;
you give them to us freely![2]

1. Afua Kuma, *Jesus of the Deep Forest: Prayers and Praises of Afua*, trans. Jon Kirby (Accra: Asempa Publishers, 1981), p. 6.
   2. Kuma, *Jesus of the Deep Forest*, p. 11. The following definitions are provided in the

Local portraits of Christ in Africa are exemplified in the vernacular prayers and praises of Afua Kuma, a non-literate farmer and midwife in Ghana. The recent recording, translation, and publication of these prayers illustrate an important observation concerning world Christianity today: namely, that despite the homogenizing tendencies of contemporary globalization, local expressions of Christianity offer distinctive christologies as Jesus "tabernacles" among various cultures. That is to say, contemporary African christologies reveal conscious appropriations of Jesus not only in light of biblical revelation and Christian tradition, but also in terms of African realities both past and present. In so doing, these christologies represent an important landmark in the development of modern African theology. Given Africa's prominent place in Christian history at the turn of the third millennium, emergent African christologies warrant careful consideration for their significance to global Christianity.

Of the many creative christologies currently flourishing across the continent of Africa, this chapter concentrates on only one image in a particular context: Jesus as chief/king in Ghanaian Christianity.[3] Attention is focused on the contemporary church in its Protestant and Catholic expressions arising out of the modern missionary movement. In view of the vitality of Christian experience in sub-Saharan Africa today, informal expressions of christology warrant serious consideration. Research findings are therefore based on oral as well as textual sources, the former gained through qualitative field research in Ghana. Voices of urban, educated Christians are captured through interviews conducted with selected theologians, church leaders, and laity.[4] Further

---

glossary: "Mmp'wmmeahene — chief over many villages," p. 48; "Gyaasehene — official in charge of the chief's kitchen and household," p. 47; "kente — costly hand-woven cloth of intricate pattern," p. 47; "'hemmer'fo — chief who has time for ordinary people," p. 48.

3. The material here is derived from wider research presented in my *Jesus of Africa: Voices of Contemporary African Christology* (Maryknoll, NY: Orbis Books, 2004).

4. Among the African theologians selected for consideration in the wider research project are two Ghanaians: Mercy Amba Oduyoye and John S. Pobee. Their christological reflections are gained through an examination of relevant publications and through individual interviews conducted in person. Additionally, thirty-five individual interviews and six with focus groups were undertaken in Ghana according to the following categories: (1) Catholic clergy, (2) Catholic laity, (3) Protestant clergy, (4) Protestant laity, (5) The Circle of Concerned African Women Theologians, and (6) Pan-African Christian Women's Alliance. Individual interviews were also extended to include (7) Christian traditional leaders. All interviews were conducted, fully transcribed, and analyzed by the researcher, with a computer software program (QSR NUD*IST 4) enhancing the comprehensiveness of analysis. All respondents were fluent in English (employed in the interviews), although I purposely elicited vernacular expressions of christology and ob-

indications of current christologies are gleaned through participant observation in a variety of Christian settings and through photographing visual expressions of Christ-devotion.[5] In the following discussion, the portrait of Jesus as chief/king is presented in terms of its sources, its prevalence in the Ghanaian context, and its meaning according to the selected Christians. Finally, conclusions are drawn regarding the significance of the christological image, first for Ghanaian Christianity and then for world Christianity.

1. The Chief/King in Traditional Ghana[6]

Various African communities naturally have different ideas and practices of authority. John Pobee, a well-known Ghanaian theologian, notes that "[w]hatever the leadership concept and practice, they can be a very powerful avenue for articulating the answer to the [fundamental christological] question 'Whom do you Africans say that I am?'"[7] In view of the divergent leadership patterns, contextual grounding for the present discussion is located in one ethnic group: the Akan of Ghana. Given the commonalities in concepts of leadership among many African peoples, however, the relevance of the African heritage to contemporary christologies in this respect extends beyond this particular people group.

Spokespersons regarding traditional Akan leadership include the Anglican theologian John Pobee, Methodist leader Robert Aboagye-Mensah, and Catholic bishop Peter Sarpong. Pobee explains that "the institution of chief-

---

tained translations from the respondents themselves or from Ghanaian research assistants.

5. The term "Christ-devotion" is taken from New Testament scholar Larry Hurtado. In his research on the origins of Christian devotion, he employs the term to encompass "Christology" as "the beliefs about Jesus held by earliest Christians and the factors that shaped them," and also "the wider matters of the role of Jesus in the beliefs and religious life of ancient Christians." Larry W. Hurtado, *One God, One Lord: Early Christian Devotion and Ancient Jewish Monotheism*, 2nd ed. (Edinburgh: T. & T. Clark, 1998), p. viii.

6. The use of the term "traditional" in relation to aspects of African culture is not intended to be derogatory in any way, as it might be considered in other contexts. The aim is to discern those beliefs, customs, and values, derived from African realities prior to the coming of Europeans and Christianity, which exert enduring influence upon African worldviews. Furthermore, it must be acknowledged that in reality, the traditional and the modern intermingle in contemporary Africa and cannot be separated. However, they are distinguished in this paper for purposes of analysis.

7. John S. Pobee, "In Search of Christology in Africa," in Pobee, ed., *Exploring Afro-Christology* (Frankfurt: Peter Lang, 1992), p. 17.

taincy is the focal point of culture and a model for leadership patterns in society."[8] Aboagye-Mensah adds that the "lineage system is vital to the understanding of kingship/chiefship,"[9] with descent and privileges being traced through the mother since Akan society is matrilineal. Each lineage comprises a political unit with its own headman acting as representative on higher councils, from the household head through successive levels of chiefs administering larger political units. At each level the leader is responsible for maintaining defense, law and order, harmonious relationships within the group, and communication between God or the gods, the living, and the departed. In descending order of importance, the main leaders include the chief/king *(Ohene)*, the queen mother,[10] and other subchiefs.

Pobee, Aboagye-Mensah, and Sarpong all emphasize the pervasive influence of religion in the socio-political structures of the Akan. Pobee cites the sociologist K. A. Busia regarding the institution of chieftaincy among the Asante,[11] one of the linguistic and cultural groups within the Akan, as follows:

The most important aspect of Ashanti chieftaincy was undoubtedly the religious one. An Ashanti chief filled a sacral role. His stool, the symbol of his office, was a sacred emblem. It represented the community, their solidarity, their permanence, their continuity. The chief was the link between the living and the dead, and his highest role was when he officiated in the public religious rites which gave expression to the community values. He then acted as the representative of the community whose members are believed to include those who are alive, and those who are

8. John S. Pobee, *Christ Would Be an African Too,* Gospel and Cultures Pamphlet 9, *West Africa* (Geneva: WCC Publications, 1996), p. 24.

9. Robert Kwasi Aboagye-Mensah, "Socio-Political Thinking of Karl Barth: Trinitarian and Incarnational Christology as the Ground for His Social Action and Its Implications for Us Today" (unpublished Ph.D. thesis, University of Aberdeen, 1984), p. 425. The English terms "king/kingship" and "chief/chieftaincy" are used interchangeably in the literature, although certain oral interviews reveal a slight difference in connotations which will be noted in the later discussion on Jesus as king/chief.

10. Aboagye-Mensah explains that among the Akan, the queen mother is actually the sister of the chief/king but is described as the "mother" because of the matrilineal bond. Her roles include participating in the selection of a new chief, in consultation with the elders who represent the populace, and advising the chief on his conduct. In the latter regard she has greater freedom to scold and reprove than the other councilors. See his "Socio-Political Thinking of Karl Barth," p. 461, n. 32.

11. *Asante* is the indigenous term which was used in the nineteenth century and which has recently regained currency over the Anglicized form *Ashanti*. Therefore *Asante* is employed in the discussion while quotations retain their original usage.

either dead or are still unborn. The sacral aspect of the chief's role was a powerful sanction of his authority.[12]

Aboagye-Mensah explains further that since the Akan king combines religious, social, and political leadership in occupying the stool, "he is described as the Priest-chief/king."[13] Thus the office of kingship is clearly composite.

2. Jesus as King/Chief

It is not surprising that many African theologians have called for serious consideration to be given to traditional concepts of kingship/chiefship in formulating African christologies. For example, Pobee is said to speak for many Africans, particularly Akan Christians, when he asserts that "the court of the royal house in Akan society can serve the cause of Christology in Akan African theology."[14] Likewise, Aboagye-Mensah asserts that:

Akan Christians have no hesitation in transferring to Jesus Christ descriptions and titles which were used for our traditional kings. More strikingly, in this form of transposition they also portray Jesus Christ as one greater and superior to them. They are mere chiefs/kings in comparison to Jesus Christ. Jesus is their leader and is sovereign among them.[15]

Closer examination of Jesus as king/chief[16] entails analysis of the field research data and the substance of the image before conclusions are reached.

12. K. A. Busia, *Africa in Search of Democracy* (London: Routledge & Kegan Paul, 1967), p. 26; quoted in John S. Pobee, *Toward an African Theology* (Nashville: Abingdon, 1979), pp. 94-95.

13. Aboagye-Mensah, "Socio-Political Thinking of Karl Barth," p. 431. In a corresponding summary of chiefly functions, Sarpong stresses that "[t]his religious role is so important that if a chief fails to play it, he can easily be dismissed or destooled." See Peter K. Sarpong, "Asante Christology," *Studia Missionalia* 45 (1996): 193.

14. Pobee, *African Theology*, p. 94.

15. Aboagye-Mensah, "Socio-Political Thinking of Karl Barth," pp. 437-38. Aboagye-Mensah supports his statement with quotations from Afua Kuma, including the citation included at the outset of this chapter.

16. The combined expressions "king/chief" and "kingship/chieftaincy" appear in the literature, indicating dual terms for the singular office of traditional leadership. However, in the interpretive discussion I use them in conjunction but separately (i.e., "king/chief";

3. Field Research Data

Contextual evidence from Ghana points to the kingship of Jesus being a prevalent theme in local expressions of Christianity. Participant observation in a wide variety of churches exposes numerous references to Jesus as king in songs, prayers, liturgy, and preaching. Undoubtedly, royal imagery for Christ is at least partially spawned by the biblical and the Western missionary inheritance, as many hymn books, for example, attest. *Asímpa Hymns,* published in Accra (1982), contains classic British hymns expressing the theme of Jesus as king, such as Isaac Watts's "Jesus Shall Reign Where'er the Sun," and Charles Wesley's "Rejoice, the Lord Is King."[17] It also offers English choruses adapted from various vernaculars, like the following one adapted from Ga:

> You are the king of kings,
> Other gods are lifeless things.
> Lord Jesus, who can be compared with you?
> You are the king of kings.[18]

In addition to biblical and Christian traditions, there is clear indication that traditional leadership symbolism further informs christological images of kingship/chieftaincy. The Catholic bishop Charles Palmer-Buckle confirms that "[a] lot of the Akan songs present Jesus Christ as king, as king of kings, you hear it very, very often, *'Ahenfo mu Ohene.'"*[19] The Protestant clergyman Dan Antwi adds, on a more personal note, that "the vernacular compositions, . . . the local choruses, have been very, very powerful. . . . [A]nytime I hear such a piece like *Momanoso Yesu na Oye Ohene,'* you know, Lift him up. Jesus is the king!' *Ahenfo mu hene,* he's the king of kings. *Ey'-se obiara kotow no,* everybody must bow unto him, . . . it's such a powerful piece that I love very much."[20]

Furthermore, Aboagye-Mensah notes that "Jesus as chief or Jesus as king is also another common terminology people use in prayer."[21] While the

---

"kingship/chieftaincy") to acknowledge some degree of nuance as expressed by respondents concerning the English terms in relation to Jesus. That is to say, presumably no African Christian would disavow Jesus as "king," yet not all agree with the ascription of "chief" to Jesus.

17. *Asímpa Hymns* (Accra: Asempa Publishers, 1982), song numbers 62, 64.
18. *Asímpa Hymns,* song number 7.
19. Charles Palmer-Buckle, oral interview, Koforidua: 1 September 1998.
20. Dan Antwi, oral interview, Legon, Accra, 24 July 1998.
21. Robert Aboagye-Mensah, oral interview, Accra, 20 September 1998.

meanings of the vernacular terms await further explication below, Sarpong concurs that "[i]n the spontaneous prayers of ordinary people, one hears their kings and chief. They would address Jesus as *Osagyefo, Kantamanto, Kurotwiamansa, Oduyefoo, Paapa, Ahummobro.*"[22]

Besides songs and prayers, several Catholic respondents speak of liturgical celebrations employing local terminology and customs related to kingship, especially in Easter dramatizations and the annual Feast of Christ the King on 22 November. Describing the latter, Catholic priest Joseph Aggrey relates how the Corpus Christi is carried in a palanquin: "[W]e carry Jesus Christ amidst dancing and drumming, and praises, some of which I will say are very traditional. Yes, very traditional."[23] In the focus group of Catholic clergy, Anthony Kornu adds the further detail that Christians including traditional chiefs even go and kneel down on their bare knees and go through the whole village. "You see it in Cape Coast — all the regalia of chieftaincy! He's [i.e., Jesus, symbolized in the Eucharist] even sometimes brought from the king's palace to the church adorned with all the paraphernalia for the procession with the blessed sacrament. . . . [T]hose who are Christian chiefs are there, and they are kneeling down doing obeisance. . . . [W]e associate with him *all* that goes with kingship and *more!* So he is chief, king of kings."[24]

One last clue to the importance of Jesus' depiction as king lies in the visual indicators apparent in the Ghanaian context. A signboard in Kasoa, Ghana, advertises "King Christ Medical Laboratory." On the outskirts of Accra, another one displays "Jesus Is King Metal Works." In Akuapem Region, a roadside refreshment stand boasts "King of Kings Chop Bar." These few examples are representative of many similar signboards in Ghana. Also, among the ubiquitous slogans on vehicles are indicators of Jesus' perceived kingship/chiefship. One *trotro* (local transport vehicle) publicizes "Osahene Yesu," a Twi military metaphor used of conquering war heroes applied here to Jesus.[25] So simply being in the context of Ghanaian Christianity allows ample opportunity to witness the widespread conviction that Jesus is king/chief as expressed in churches and in wider society.

Further corroboration comes to light in the oral interviews. Effort was made to elicit the respondents' own perceptions of Jesus as far as possible, be-

22. Sarpong, "Asante Christology," p. 202.

23. Joseph Aggrey, oral interview, Mampong-Akuapem, 31 August 1998.

24. Anthony Kornu, focus group, Accra, 4 September 1998.

25. As part of the observational research in Ghana, I recorded a list of those slogans referring to Jesus that were personally witnessed on vehicles. Other slogans suggestive of Jesus' kingship, though unconfirmed, include "He Reigns" and "Yesu Tumi Nyinaa Wura," Twi for "All power belongs to Jesus," with "wura" denoting either "owner" or "source."

fore the interviewer raised specific images for their consideration. Out of thirty-five individuals interviewed, eight respondents (23 percent) offer the image of Jesus as "king," and four (11 percent) initiate perceptions of Jesus as "chief." Therefore, combining the two terms, eleven of the thirty-five respondents[26] (31 percent) volunteer the king/chief image of Jesus as a christological category meaningful to them personally. Later in the interview, questions were posed to the interviewees concerning Jesus as "chief" and as *Nana* (a Twi term associated with "king/chief" and "ancestor," to be further discussed below). Due to the overlapping of terminology including "king" and "chief," plus other vernacular titles such as *Nana*, precise statistics isolating any single term are inadvisable.[27] However, the overall pattern of evidence from the individual interviews is decidedly favorable towards the cluster of "king/chief/*Nana*" images by an approximate ratio of two positive to one negative response.[28] Thus the data from participant observation in the context of Ghanaian Christianity and from the oral interviews leave little doubt as to the widespread conviction of Jesus' kingship/chieftaincy.

4. Rationale for the Image of Jesus as King/Chief

Among the early proponents of Jesus as chief, Pobee provides a clear rationale for depicting Jesus in this way. He explains that the Supreme Being in Akan religion is conceived of as a paramount chief so great that he must be approached through subchiefs and his official spokesperson, the *'kyeame*. The *'kyeame* is as the chief in public affairs and exercises royal authority, although such authority is subordinated to the paramount chief. Moving from the Akan heritage to the Bible, Pobee notes similarities between the two sources regarding the kingship of God. He cites biblical teaching regarding God as

26. One interviewee suggests both images of "king" and "chief"; hence the total of eleven respondents. Dan Antwi, oral interview, Legon, Accra, 24 July 1998.

27. Respondents repeatedly explain the approximate equivalence between two or sometimes three of the terms "king," "chief," and "*Nana*." For example, Protestant clergyman Theophilus Dankwa responds to the specific question of Jesus as "chief," explaining, "Well, 'chief,' *Nana*, 'king,' all go together, if one is thinking in terms of his kingship, his rule and authority. . . ." Theophilus Dankwa, oral interview, Accra, 16 August 1998. In addition, respondents sometimes answer the question of Jesus as "chief" using vernacular terms such as the Twi *ohene*. With such difficulty in isolating particular terms, it is advisable to treat this leadership image in terms of a cluster of descriptions carrying slightly different nuances, and seek to discern the overall pattern of response for the composite image.

28. Focus group materials from Ghana reflect similar findings.

king[29] and Jesus as king,[30] yet notes that "Jesus shares in the kingship of God and holds his kingship under God."[31] In order to convey this teaching to local Christians, he suggests, "In our Akan Christology we propose to think of Jesus as the *'kyeame,* or linguist, who in all public matters was as the Chief, God, and is the first officer of the state, in this case, the world. This captures something of the Johannine portrait of Jesus as the Logos, being at one and the same time divine and yet subordinate to God."[32]

Further parallels are drawn between the Akan chief and Jesus, with Jesus' role superseding that of the human leader in each case: (1) in their sacral role, although Jesus is distinguished as both priest and sacrificial victim in accomplishing salvation; (2) in their role as head of a community, in Jesus' case, the church; and (3) in their authoritative role as leader, judge, and the one to whom allegiance is due. A new element with Jesus as chief is that his community cuts across political and ethnic boundaries to embrace all humanity.[33]

On the basis of this functional analogy, various honorifics used of chiefs in traditional society are said to capture aspects of New Testament christology. Of the many examples, only two are highlighted at present. Pobee proposes the christological title *Nana* as a term traditionally attributed to God, to the ancestors, to chiefs, and to family heads.[34] He also recommends the title *Osagyefo,* meaning "one who saves in battle; therefore, a deliverer." The basic idea of this term is comparable to the Old Testament judges who saved their people from the tyranny of oppressors. While this appellation is applicable to Jesus as deliverer, according to Pobee, one key difference is that Jesus' deliverance is not through a "literal battle" but rather a figurative rescue from "the inimical forces of legalism, self-sufficiency, and the cosmic forces."[35] After delineating the traditional concept of chieftaincy and these praise names attrib-

29. Pobee, *African Theology,* p. 95; citing Psalm 10:16; 44:4; 47:7; Matthew 5:35; 1 Timothy 1:17; 6:15.

30. Pobee, *African Theology,* p. 95; Matthew 25:32; cf. the charges against him claiming to be king in the trial scene, and Revelation 17:14; 19:16.

31. Pobee, *African Theology,* p. 95; cf. 1 Corinthians 15:24, 25, 28.

32. Pobee, *African Theology,* explains further: "There are two types of *'kyeame:* (a) Ahenkyeame, who is also a chief, and that is hereditary; (b) a common linguist who is appointed by the Chief because he was judged to be responsible and reliable and was generally capable of fulfilling the roles of a *'kyeame."* See p. 167 n. 21.

33. Pobee, *African Theology,* pp. 95-96.

34. Pobee, *African Theology,* p. 94, recounts how reflecting on Jesus as *Nana* prompted his further reflections on Jesus as chief. His observation underlines how this cluster of images, including "chief," *Nana,* and other vernacular titles, overlap with one another and also with that of Jesus as ancestor.

35. Pobee, *African Theology,* pp. 96-97.

uted to the chief, Pobee concludes with their relevance to contemporary Christianity: namely, that "among the African tribe of the Akan of Ghana a royal priestly Christology aptly speaks to their situation."[36]

Within this brief summary of Pobee's rationale for portraying Jesus as chief, three elements come to light: theological grounds for the analogy in the kingship of God being extended to Jesus, similarities in chiefly functions, and titles of respect associated with the chief that carry christological meaning and significance. These three elements find corroboration among other Ghanaian Christians selected in this study.[37]

Theological grounds for conferring God's kingship/chieftaincy upon Jesus are confirmed with respect to *Nana* as a christological title. For example, Lawrence Darmani, a Protestant layman, explains that *Nana* is a title for "Supreme," and confirms that he conceptualizes God as *Nana Nyankop'n*. Since he associates the title *Nana* with God, he needs a "bridge" to associate Jesus with *Nana*. That bridge he finds in the Bible, and he explains the significance for him personally as follows: "[B]ecause of what I understand from the scriptures, I'm very much privileged to be able to connect Jesus to God, and therefore to be able to use *Nana* for Jesus. Because immediately, I see him not just like the man walking by the shore of Galilee, or . . . being led to the cross to be crucified. But as the God now, who came in the form of man. Then I can see Jesus as *Nana*."[38]

Thus the ascription of *Nana* to Jesus clearly carries potential for conveying to Akan Christians the universal rule of Christ and his incarnation. It is worth noting, however, that when probed as to whether the image of Jesus as *Nana* is operative in his own life and specifically in his ministry as editor of *Step* magazine in Ghana, Darmani replies:

36. Pobee, *African Theology,* p. 97.

37. While the present discussion focuses on the Ghanaian context, further support is found elsewhere in sub-Saharan Africa. For example, when asked about images of Jesus meaningful to Africans, the first one offered by Ugandan Catholic religious sister Mary Cleophas is that of king. From her background within the Baganda, she explains, "[W]e have great respect for kings. And . . . I see Jesus as king, for example. So tracing back how Baganda treat their kings, I place Jesus also there. Yes, I have that image of him too." She then describes traditional customs of honoring the king, like the subjects' joyful willingness to lie down on the path for him to walk on, and how this background enhances her image of Jesus as king, especially in relation to Palm Sunday. Mary Cleophas, oral interview, Jinja, 6 May 1998. See also Douglas W. Waruta, "Who Is Jesus Christ for Africans Today? Prophet, Priest, Potentate," in J. N. K. Mugambi and Laurenti Magesa, eds., *Jesus in African Christianity: Experimentation and Diversity in African Christology* (Nairobi: Initiatives, 1989); François Kabasélé, "Christ as Chief," in Robert J. Schreiter, ed., *Faces of Jesus in Africa* (Maryknoll, NY: Orbis Books, 1991), pp. 103-15.

38. Lawrence Darmani, oral interview, Accra, 30 July 1998.

We have not used that word, or that title, "*Nana* Jesus," but we have presented him as king. . . . He came in a humble way but in my mind, . . . I see him as . . . a great one who is actually sitting as a chief, as a king! And therefore in my own devotion, prayer, thought, I'm able to see him as the king with powers! Powers to liberate me. Powers to guide me and to lead me. In that sense, we have presented him in our publication. So I'm able to say "King Jesus," that's almost like saying "*Nana* Jesus," just that I've not used the word *Nana*. But otherwise, in my mind, yes, he is *Nana*.[39]

Therefore, even when the vernacular title "*Nana* Jesus" is not expressed publicly, it evidently functions conceptually within many Ghanaian believers as part of the cluster of king/chief images.

The functional analogy Pobee develops between the traditional Akan chief and Jesus as chief is also witnessed among other Ghanaian Christians. The most obvious parallel, remarked upon by many respondents, is the rule and power exercised by the chief over the subjects. For instance, when asked about the image of Jesus as chief, Protestant laywoman Grace Nartey replies: "Chief, as ruler, as judge, as someone who has authority, yes, one can think of Jesus as chief. The family head or the chief is somebody that one should be able to look up to, somebody that you respect and somebody who provides support and protection. And Jesus does all this and more. . . ."[40]

A Protestant clergyman, Thomas Oduro, brings out another aspect of the subject's allegiance to the chief in the sense of personal identity gained through association, for the chief is "somebody you can be proud of, to re-

39. Darmani interview, 30 July 1998.

40. Grace Nartey, oral interview, Accra, 2 September 1998. It is noteworthy that Protestant clergyman Samuel Aboa responds negatively to the image of Jesus as chief, first outlining the functions of a chief and then stating he does not see Christ in this way, for reasons to be set forth below. Yet in discussion, as he reflects upon the analogy, he concedes as follows:

Except that, I think of his [Christ's] power over the world, then of course I would say, a chief in his own small way, he has power over his subjects and all that the reign is. Because he is also the custodian of even the land for the people. So in a way, he commands all, as God or Christ is the creator of the world and has power over everything that is in the world and of the world. It is only in this respect that I would somehow equate God with the chiefs.

So even when a respondent disagrees with the chiefly image for Jesus, he nonetheless acknowledges certain aspects of the analogy. Samuel Aboa, oral interview, Mampong, Akuapem, 17 August 1998.

late yourself to."[41] In addition, a Protestant layman, Kingsfold Amoah, affirms the fundamental concept of lordship inherent in the image of Jesus as chief. He explains that "when you talk of a 'lord,' a 'king,' then the word 'chief' has the same connotations. . . . [I]f I was trying to explain his supremacy and . . . what is meant by 'Lord of all lords,' then I could say that he's the greatest chief."[42] Once again, however, a respondent admits that the image of Jesus as "chief" is not verbalized in his own experience or ministry. Yet Amoah states unequivocally that it is meaningful conceptually and that it holds potential for ministry, in that a lot of Ghanaians know a chief as the depository of authority and control and power and that sort of thing. So one could use that same thing that they know and transfer it to describe the lordship of Christ upon their lives. So, just as a chief makes laws and a chief is supposed to be obeyed, and a chief is to be honored, one could use that to present the lordship of Christ.[43]

So whether or not such terms as "chief" and *Nana* are actually voiced in relation to Jesus, they are acknowledged by many respondents as mentally operative and potentially constructive for ministry purposes in Ghana.

The most common reason expressed for affirming Jesus as king/chief/*Nana,* on par with Pobee's third rationale, is the respect or reverence accorded through ascribing these titles. Protestant clergyman Dan Antwi's explanation is telling, for when asked specifically if the term *Nana* comes naturally to him in relation to Jesus, he replies: "You have the imagery of a chief, — a king, — lord of lords and king of kings, then in that respect you wouldn't address him in any other way but as you would address a chief — *Nana* would be quite a convenient way. Because, in any case, if Jesus is the heir to the throne of God, . . . then he deserves the title *Nana!*"[44]

Striking evidence also comes from Nana Addo Birikorang, himself the chief linguist to the regional king. When asked about Jesus as *Nana,* Birikorang responds enthusiastically, with slight laughter, "Jesus is super-*Nana!* Yes! He is super-*Nana!* Because if I go before God, I feel that Jesus is the only means by which I can go unto God."[45] He likewise affirms Jesus as "super-chief," thus validating Aboagye-Mensah's assertion cited above that Akan Christians transpose titles for traditional kings to Jesus while maintaining his clear superiority over them.

Finally, Pobee's exposition of traditional Akan accolades capable of ex-

41. Thomas Oduro, oral interview, Akropong-Akuapem, 14 August 1998.
42. Kingsfold Amoah, oral interview, Accra, 18 August 1998.
43. Amoah, oral interview, 18 August 1998.
44. Dan Antwi, oral interview, Legon, Accra, 24 July 1998.
45. Nana Addo Birikorang, oral interview, Akropong-Akuapem, 27 August 1998.

pressing facets of New Testament christology is echoed by other Ghanaians. The title most commonly voiced is *Osagyefo,* the king/chief who delivers his people in battle.[46] Described as a "brave warrior, conquering king,"[47] *Osagyefo* is said to "very aptly describe who Christ is to a believer."[48] Especially instructive here is the conflict that arose between church and state when the title *Osagyefo* was applied to Kwame Nkrumah, Ghana's first president who led the people of Ghana from colonialism to independence. Certain church leaders vehemently opposed it as "a blasphemous equation of Nkrumah with Jesus the savior."[49] Yet Pobee explores the use of the term in Asante tradition and in the lyrics of the Fanti Methodist Church, where *Osagyefo* was commonly applied to God, and notes how African and church traditions overlapped so that the same term was used with different connotations. Full explanation of this controversy, involving *Osagyefo* and other chiefly titles, lies beyond the scope of this chapter. However, the point emphasized here is the extent to which Ghanaian Christians have adopted vernacular appellations for traditional leaders and ascribed them to Jesus. Aboagye-Mensah follows Pobee in criticizing the church's attitude of monopolizing the title for Christ without adequate awareness of the term's usage in its tradi-

---

46. This title is introduced by nine out of the thirty-five individual Ghanaian respondents (26 percent): two in publications, including Aboagye-Mensah and Sarpong, and an additional seven in conversation. However, one respondent, Catholic layman Samuel Asubonteng, takes issue with the aspect of "strife and wars" conveyed by the *osa* in *osagyefo.* Instead, he favors simply *gyefo* or "savior," since "there has not been the need for him [Jesus] to go to war." Samuel Asubonteng, oral interview, Accra, 1 September 1998.

47. S. S. Quarcoopome, oral interview, Legon, Accra, 4 August 1998.

48. Amoah, oral interview, 18 August 1998.

49. John S. Pobee, *Kwame Nkrumah and the Church in Ghana 1949-1966* (Accra: Asempa Publishers, 1988), p. 143. The incident is also referred to by Protestant laywoman Grace Nartey, which suggests that the controversy and its significance regarding christological titles are common knowledge among Ghanaian believers. Nartey summarizes as follows:

> [T]here are specific words that may be used for chiefs and elderly, respectable people, but which in actual fact are restricted to, . . . [or] most of the times . . . used in terms of Jesus. I can think of the Twi word *Osagyefo,* . . . which was used for our first President, Kwame Nkrumah. And when first he took that title, in fact a lot of people were affronted. They felt that he was . . . projecting himself as divine. . . . And there are words like that, . . . I think originally in the traditional society, these were given to the chiefs. But when Christianity came, Christianity adopted those words and now they've become almost restricted to [Jesus], so that now if you want to apply them to the chiefs, they sound like you are being sacrilegious.

Grace Nartey, oral interview, Accra, 2 September 1998.

tional context. He then draws an important conclusion, worth citing in full for its explication of the meaning and significance of *Osagyefo* as a christological title:

> [I]n the traditional usage, the title referred to socio-political liberation. The Church in Ghana gave it a religious or divine interpretation. Arguably, the Church understood the term in the spiritual sense. In applying the title to Jesus, we must include both interpretations, traditional and church. Thus Jesus Christ will be understood as the One who delivered and continues to deliver us from socio-political domination and oppression. At the same time He is the One who sets us free from spiritual bondage. In this sense when the title is applied to Him we are stressing the fact that He is concerned about the liberation of our entire life, from the social, political and religious realities that ensnare us. Jesus Christ has come and continues to come to liberate us from all structural and private sins which hold us captive. He is indeed the *Osaagyefoo* and all the other leaders and kings are His subordinate *asaagyefoo*.[50]

The importance of this particular portrait of Jesus warrants further consideration in relation to contemporary liberation christologies.

These examples of vernacular titles suffice to illustrate how traditional Akan praise names are applied to Jesus in order to convey his kingship/chieftaincy. Besides this rationale for the image of Jesus as king/chief, grounds for casting Jesus this way have been identified in respondents reasoning theologically from the kingship/chieftaincy of God to that of Jesus, and developing analogies between the functions of Akan chiefs and Jesus as chief. Despite the amassing of such evidence, however, not all Ghanaian believers support the christological image of chief, as indicated by the data outlined above. The reasons for their reluctance must therefore be considered.

5. Problems with the Image of Jesus as King/Chief

From the outset of his proposal regarding Jesus as chief, Pobee acknowledges that the image is necessarily limited. He pinpoints the key danger as the chief analogy being "a *theologia gloriae*, lacking a *theologia crucis*."[51] That is to say, it denotes chiefly power and authority attained through means other than

---

50. Aboagye-Mensah, "Socio-Political Thinking of Karl Barth," pp. 449-50.
51. Pobee, *African Theology*, p. 97.

suffering. In contrast, biblical tradition discloses Jesus entering his kingly glory only through humility, suffering, and martyrdom as symbolized in the cross. Despite the slight modification Pobee makes to his proposal, drawing upon certain chiefs who gain their position through some act of devotion to society, a fundamental tension remains between concepts of power and authority as demonstrated by Jesus and as associated with African chiefs.

Negative connotations surrounding African chieftaincy account for the greatest number of objections raised by the selected Christians in Ghana to the image of Jesus as chief. Catholic priest Matthew Edusei explains: "The image of Jesus as the king of the kings is powerful, and very biblical. He rules over all. Unfortunately, *'Nana'* has all kinds of connotations — imposing on people, taking the first place. And then the area of service — death on the cross for salvation. Most *Nanna* wouldn't do that, they wouldn't dirty their hands. So we need to be careful how we see Jesus as *Nana*."[52]

Contrary to traditional kings who shared their resources with the people, reservation is expressed about portraying Jesus as chief because of contemporary chiefs "who rather grab and don't share."[53] Moreover, Catholic layman George Hagan summarizes problematic associations regarding the chiefly lifestyle as follows: "But the Jesus that people see cannot easily be projected as *Nana*, you see, because we associate in our minds a certain gorgeous way of life with *Nana*. A certain opulence with *Nana*. Jesus as *Nana* will mean Jesus who married so many wives, Jesus who has so much wealth. So the image doesn't quite fit."[54]

Further problems with the christological image stem from traditional chiefs having lost some degree of status, authority, and credibility through the changes brought by colonialism and independence. The Protestant clergyman S. S. Quarcoopome explains that the word "chief" has gained derogatory connotations in Ghana due to the British custom of calling African rulers "chiefs" instead of "kings" so as to avoid equating them with the king of England.[55] The Protestant clergyman Kwesi Dickson adds that the British tended to use the chiefs to implement their own colonial policies, thereby influencing people's perceptions of the traditional leaders. He also voices the present problem of "absentee chiefs" who live and work in distant cities, returning home for festival occasions, in contrast to traditional chiefs who lived among their people, were known by them, and served them regularly. Hence

---

52. Matthew Edusei, oral interview, Accra, 1 September 1998.
53. Palmer-Buckle, oral interview, 10 September 1998.
54. George Hagan, oral interview, Legon, Accra, 28 July; 6 August 1998.
55. Quarcoopome, oral interview, 4 August 1998.

Dickson concludes that "the chief concept has gone through various vicissitudes, and I don't think it's such a vital concept now, christologically."[56]

In light of these and other reservations regarding African chieftaincy, several respondents stress the distinction between the biblical imagery of Jesus as the "king of kings" and "lord of lords" and the traditional chief. The pivotal point in these arguments is the conviction of Jesus' divinity. For instance, African chiefs are said to be subject to human weakness and failure and are consequently dethroned, while Jesus' reign is eternal. Earthly kingdoms are necessarily limited to particular territories and peoples, while Jesus' rule is deemed universal. Aboagye-Mensah grants that the Akan king is described as "sacred" as long as he sits on the stool, yet stresses that "he is never considered divine. Even when he dies and becomes an ancestor, he still remains man, for the ancestors are not thought of as deities." Hence he sums up the contrast as follows: "[A]n Akan king is no more than a mere man, but for Jesus Christ we are talking of one who indeed was man like all men and yet more than man. He is the Word-become-man."[57]

This fundamental affirmation regarding the supremacy of Jesus over earthly rulers receives forceful expression by the Pan-African Christian Women's Alliance (PACWA) representative Florence Y. B. Yeboah. In response to the question of Jesus as *Nana*, she exclaims, "He is higher than *Nana*. He's the creator of all *Nanas!* He made all presidents and prime ministers, and all *Nanas*." She continues, when asked about Jesus as chief, "He is *greater* than every *chief!* Chief, . . . *Nana*, they are human beings! And like the *radiance* that fills the heavens, a little atom of his dignity he gives to the *Nana*. . . . And we have *no words*, we have no mentality to picture his greatness, the *awesomeness* of his power, and the *radiance* of his glory. . . . So *if we* compare him to *Nana*, we are belittling him. We dare not!"[58]

Related to these theological objections are those that stem from perceived discontinuities between the African heritage and the Christian faith. Protestant clergyman Samuel Aboa argues that "the chief in our thought is the epitome of our traditional culture, including our religion," and therefore insists he cannot "connect Christ with our religion" in this way.[59] Similarly, the PACWA leader Felicia Opare-Saforo counters any suggestion of Jesus as chief or *Nana*, declaring that "he's the king of kings, and lord of lords. And I want to take it that way, [rather] than bringing it to our cultural way of calling our

56. Kwesi Dickson, oral interview, Legon, Accra, 2 September 1998.
57. Aboagye-Mensah, "Socio-Political Thinking of Karl Barth," p. 442.
58. Florence Y. B. Yeboah, oral interview, Accra, 30 July 1998.
59. Aboa, oral interview, Mampong-Akuapem, 17 August 1998.

leaders."[60] Hence these two typify some respondents who favor biblical terminology over indigenous expressions for Jesus.

A few additional problems are noteworthy. First, feminist theologians have criticized ruler images for Jesus on the basis that human experience of hierarchies, which are usually patriarchal, does not commend itself to those being alienated and oppressed. For example, Elizabeth Amoah and Mercy Oduyoye stress that "patriarchal/hierarchical structures have little room for the participation and inclusiveness that those whose humanity is being trampled upon yearn for."[61] Second, a few Protestant clergymen remark that their common use of English inhibits their use of vernacular titles for Jesus. For instance, while Theophilus Dankwa agrees that *Nana* is fitting for Jesus, he admits, "[F]or me personally, I don't think I often refer to Jesus as *Nana*. But maybe that's my problem, that I pray more in English than in Twi!"[62] One final limitation is that the image is naturally context-specific. Those Ghanaian respondents not from traditional chieftaincies are less inclined to identify with the image of Jesus as chief — for example, Peter Kodjo, chairman of the Ga Presbytery, who admits he is highly critical of chieftaincy.[63]

A variety of factors thus hinder more widespread acceptance of the christological portrait derived from Akan kingship/chieftaincy and its associated titles. Historical and contemporary realities have given rise to certain negative connotations of African chiefs, which in turn fuel attempts to emphasize the theological distinctions between these human rulers and Jesus as divine ruler. Convictions regarding discontinuities between the traditional African heritage and the Christian faith make some respondents reluctant to consider Jesus in indigenous categories of thought. Further obstacles to employing the

60. Felicia Opare-Saforo, oral interview, Akropong-Akuapem, 3 August 1998.

61. Elizabeth Amoah and Mercy Oduyoye, "The Christ for African Women," in Virginia Fabella and Mercy Oduyoye, eds., *With Passion and Compassion: Third World Women Doing Theology* (Maryknoll, NY: Orbis Books, 1988), p. 41. They also criticize Pobee's portrayal of Jesus as *okyeame* or chief linguist, stating that for Pobee "the okyeame can be nothing else but male. Whereas in the Akan system of rule the okyeame can be either a man or a woman" (p. 43). However helpful their clarification is in this regard, there is no evidence of gender restriction in Pobee's *African Theology*, pp. 94ff.

62. Theophilus Dankwa, oral interview, Accra, 16 August 1998.

63. Peter Kodjo, oral interview, Accra, 3 September 1998. As a Ga, Kodjo explains that the chieftaincy tradition "is very new, in my context. We have a dominant traditional priest, and priesthood in the African context from where I come is very acceptable. . . . Jesus is not the showy leader who has power and who . . . can order everybody about, to work for him and all that. Jesus for me is not a chief." The same point is underlined by Protestant laywoman Irene Odotei, who is also a Ga. Irene Odotei, oral interview, Legon, Accra, 4 August 1998.

image are voiced by women concerned about perpetuating authoritarian male images, by those communicating primarily in English, and by those from non-chieftaincy traditions. These factors must therefore be borne in mind when considering the overall effectiveness of the christological image.

6. Conclusion

Analysis of the research data suggests that the majority of selected Ghanaian Christians favor the images clustering around Jesus as king/chief/*Nana* and other vernacular titles for socio-political leaders. Reasons that prompt the composite image have been set forth, as well as those that constrain its usage. While the core concept of Jesus' kingship is virtually undisputed,[64] controversy surrounds the depiction of Jesus according to categories derived from traditional Akan/African leadership. Cognitive associations are crucial; as Protestant clergyman Abraham Akrong emphasizes, "because once you use a model, you have to look at the ready meaning that it evokes, whether it's going to hamper or enhance what you intend to do."[65] If the intention is to communicate the identity and significance of Jesus Christ to contemporary Ghanaians, then certainly some respondents believe the African kingship/chieftaincy image hampers that goal. In contrast, the majority are evidently convinced that it enhances their understanding of Jesus, and would presumably identify personally with Catholic bishop Peter Sarong's verdict as follows: "Now the Asante Catholics consider these [leadership] roles as applicable to, and indeed perfectly fulfilled by the Lord Jesus. They see Jesus as a chief, a king, over them. With the qualities Jesus exhibits — qualities of humility, goodness — the Asante see in him a person who is their leader in a superhuman way."[66]

Indications of the image's relevance for Christian individuals and communities have emerged throughout the discussion, confirming Pobee's assertion that a royal priestly christology speaks aptly to the Akan context. Parish priest Joseph Aggrey affirms, simply, "[W]e can refer to God, or Jesus Christ, as *Nana*. . . . [I]t makes sense to me, and to my people. . . . They will understand that."[67] The Protestant clergyman Thomas Oduro assigns even weight-

---

64. That is, one Ghanaian respondent consents that Jesus is king of kings, but cautions that he is a "spiritual king" whose "kingdom is not of this earth." George Hagan, oral interview, Legon, Accra, 28 July; 6 August. Similar comments were made by one Kenyan respondent. J. B. Masinde, oral interview, Nairobi, 11 June 1998.

65. Abraham Akrong, oral interview, Legon, Accra, 27 July 1998.

66. Sarpong, "Asante Christology," p. 194.

67. Joseph Aggrey, oral interview, Mampong-Akuapem, 31 August 1998.

ier significance to the image of Jesus as chief in suggesting that it communicates more effectively the meaning of the original Greek word translated "lord." In his words: "[T]he word 'lord' in the Greek and its interpretation, to me, does not have a connotation in the Twi version. For instance, [in] Twi, when you say somebody is 'my lord,' it means nothing. . . . But if you take the image of somebody as my chief, . . . you don't even need an interpretation. The person already knows what you mean."[68]

Theological relevance is also attributed to the chiefly portrait by Protestant clergyman Abraham Akrong. In particular, he spells out the concept of chief as potentially valuable in explicating the incarnation according to Akan thought: "[W]hen it comes to an attempt to explain the relationship between God and Christ, the chieftaincy pattern is very, very important. . . . [W]e understand that technically, the chief is the incarnation of the ancestors. And that is why we give them reverence. . . . I'm not saying that the chieftaincy model will exhaust the mystery of the incarnation, but at least it helps people. So if you tell them that 'if you see Jesus, you've seen God'; . . . 'if you have seen the chief, you've known the ancestors!' . . . It resonates. It's a similar logic."[69]

The portrait of Jesus as African king/chief not only enhances respondents' understanding of Christ, but it may also influence their manner of worship. In the context of discussing Jesus as chief, Protestant layman Lawrence Darmani relates: "Because I see him as king, I've seen him also as chief, . . . [a] great chief . . . with a lot of subjects, meaning people who are worshipping him daily. The reason I can *lie* down prostrate, *really* lie down prostrate, before Jesus, is because I'm able to see him as chief."[70] By way of background, he narrates childhood memories from his home area of people removing their sandals, crawling and lying prostrate before a certain chief. He also points out further postures, such as crossed legs or wearing a hat, on which he comments, "*[D]efinitely,* I wouldn't be able to do that [in prayer]. Because in my mind, I've just gone before the chief or the king."

Nana Dokua bears similar witness, which is all the more striking in light of her own position as a traditional leader. In response to the question of Jesus as chief, she states: "He is king of kings. Chief is *Ohene,* and king is *Ohene.* In our language we say '*Ahane mu hene,*' 'king of all kings.' . . . So whenever I mention his name, I bow, because I am a chief, a queen mother. So he is my superior. . . . Yes, when worshipping him, . . . I cannot stand straight like that. I bow!"[71]

68. Thomas Oduro, oral interview, Akropong-Akuapem, 14 August 1998.
69. Abraham Akrong, oral interview, Legon, Accra, 27 July 1998.
70. Darmani, oral interview, Accra, 30 July 1998.
71. Nana Dokua I, oral interview, Akropong-Akuapem, 18 September 1998.

These personal accounts from layman and a queen mother alike thus amplify previous evidence of the christological image in context, such as the liturgical celebrations honoring Christ the King. Contemporary Ghanaian Christianity, as one particular test case, therefore provides strong indication of the prevalence, meaning, and significance of Jesus as king/chief.

Finally, what relevance do these findings have for world Christianity? Two main conclusions suffice for the purpose of this paper. First, and most fundamentally, the image of Jesus as chief/king in Ghanaian Christianity clearly illustrates the universality of the gospel. As Ghanaian Christians appropriate Jesus in light of biblical revelation and the African heritage, they demonstrate that Christianity can truly find a home in every cultural context. Even the voices of reservation regarding the image generally serve to underline key aspects of contemporary African christologies evidenced in the present research: (1) the uncompromising commitment to upholding the humanity and divinity of Jesus as "the two non-negotiables of any authentic christology";[72] (2) the awareness that particular images like Jesus as chief/king are necessarily context-specific; and (3) the acknowledgment that no single christological image can ever encompass the mystery of Jesus' identity and significance. Nonetheless, by proffering Jesus as chief/king in the Ghanaian context, these African Christians contribute to the multiplicity of christological images that enhance our corporate understanding of Christ in the worldwide church.

Second, these research findings corroborate Andrew Walls's important observation, that for the first time in history, Christianity is becoming a truly universal faith not only in principle but also in practice.[73] With the fundamental shifts in world Christianity in recent times, new local forms of Christian faith are developing in accordance with the conceptual categories and the contextual realities of the new heartlands of the gospel. Given the prominence of African Christianity at the present time, manifestations and priorities of the Christian faith from this continent will likely have a decisive impact upon the shaping of Christian thought and practice in the future.[74]

72. Pobee, *African Theology*, p. 83.

73. Andrew Walls, "The Christian Tradition in Today's World," in Frank Whaling, ed., *Religion in Today's World: The Religious Situation of the World from 1945 to the Present Day* (Edinburgh: T. & T. Clark, 1987), p. 76.

74. See A. F. Walls, "Towards Understanding Africa's Place in Christian History," in J. S. Pobee, ed., *Religion in a Pluralistic Society* (Leiden: E. J. Brill, 1976), p. 183; "Africa in Christian History: Retrospect and Prospect," *Journal of African Christian Thought* 1, no. 1 (June 1998): 2; Kwame Bediako, "The Significance of Modern African Christianity — A Manifesto," *Studies in World Christianity* 1, no. 1 (1995): 51-67.

Without denying or downplaying the impact of current globalization upon the church worldwide, the evidence from this research suggests that creative christologies expressed in local idiom serve to stem the tide of homogenizing forces within globalization.[75] In so doing, contemporary African christologies, like Jesus as chief/king, afford a glimpse of the heavenly scene in Revelation 7, when a great multitude from every nation, people, and language will offer their distinctive praise to the Lamb of God upon the throne.

75. See Kwame Bediako, "Africa and Christianity on the Threshold of the Third Millennium: The Religious Dimension," *African Affairs* 99, no. 395 (April 2000): 313-14.

CHAPTER 12

Gendered Appropriation of Mass Media in Kenyan Christianities: A Comparison of Two Women-Led African Instituted Churches in Kenya

PHILOMENA NJERI MWAURA

The dynamic growth of Kenyan Christianity has become a prominent feature of Kenyan society. Christianity here takes a variety of forms. Apart from the considerable number of former mission churches established at the beginning of the twentieth century,[1] there exists a large, enduring, and expanding body of African Instituted Churches (AICs).[2] These churches are an illustration of the diverse and profound response of Africans to Christianity. Ever since the encounter of Western Christianity and culture with African religion and culture in the nineteenth century, there has developed a variety of responses to the gospel that has created different Christianities. The late nineteenth century and the beginning of the twentieth century saw the development of Ethiopian Christianity,[3] which was a religious and cultural protest

1. Examples of former mission churches in Kenya are: the Anglican Church of Kenya, Presbyterian Church of East Africa, Roman Catholic Church, Methodist Church of Kenya, and Pentecostal Assemblies of God.

2. These churches are also known in the literature as African Independent; Initiated; and Indigenous Churches.

3. Ethiopian-type churches are known in Kenya as Nationalist churches. In Nigeria they are referred to as African churches. See John Padwick, "Towards a Change in Spirituality? Working in Development with Kenyan Spirit Churches," in D. Shenk, ed., *Working in Partnership with African Churches* (Elkhart, IN: n.p., 1991); Harold W. Turner, *The Life and Faith of the Church of the Lord Aladura*, 2 vols. (London: Oxford University Press, 1967); Bengt G. M. Sundkler, *Bantu Prophets in South Africa* (London: Oxford University Press,

against white hegemony in culture and church. In various places in Africa indigenous prophetic figures inspired a charismatic response to the gospel, and through their commitment and innovations, Christianity grew.

By the mid-1920s, Ethiopianism yielded to further new churches. These are known in Kenya as Spirit churches, in Southern Africa as Zionist, in West Africa as Aladura (Praying Churches), and in Ghana as Sunsum Sore.[4] They grew from prophet-founded religious movements that were increasingly creative in their pneumatic emphasis, in the use of the Bible, innovative gender ideology, and African religion and culture.[5] These churches changed the face of Christianity in Africa by their enlarging of religious space for women and their reclaiming of the pneumatic and charismatic experience, which had been suppressed by mainline Christianity but resonated well with African spirituality. They emphasized healing, and the use of African symbolism, music, musical instruments, and leadership patterns.

By the 1970s, charismatic revivals from within the mainline churches soon fed into pentecostal forms as young puritans emerged from the mainline churches and formed charismatic ministries and churches. Scholars have viewed the pneumatic factor as the link between the spiritual churches and the charismatics. According to Ogbu Kalu, "Both lie on the same side of the typology of Christian forms. Both draw from the same issues raised in primal religion."[6] They operate from the same map of the universe but color it differently. These churches have certain distinguishing characteristics, for example, prominent roles for women and youth; the appropriation of the American prosperity gospel in the 1980s; and "riveting" to holiness and intercessory traditions in the 1990s.[7] They are also noted for their aggressive use of mass me-

---

1961), pp. 53-59; J. D. Y. Peel, *Aladura: A Religious Movement among the Yoruba* (London: Oxford University Press, 1968).

4. See John T. Padwick, "Change in Spirituality?"; Sundkler, *Bantu Prophets;* Turner, *Life and Faith;* Kwabena Asamoah-Gyadu, "Renewal Within Christianity: A Historical and Theological Study of Some Current Developments Within Ghanaian Pentecostalism" (unpublished Ph.D. thesis, University of Birmingham, 2000), p. 35.

5. Ogbu U. Kalu, *Power, Poverty and Prayer: The Challenges of Poverty and Pluralism in African Christianity, 1960-1996* (Frankfurt: Peter Lang, 2000), p. 105.

6. Kalu, *Power, Poverty and Prayer,* p. 105.

7. These churches are known as African pentecostal churches or neo-pentecostal churches in Kenya, charismatic churches in Ghana, pentecostal churches or "born-again" churches in Nigeria. See Maurice Onyango, "Churches of the Poor: African Independent Churches," *Wajibu* 2 (1997): 6-8; Ruth Marshall-Fratani, "Mediating the Global and the Local in Nigerian Pentecostalism," *Journal of Religion in Africa* 28, no. 3 (1998): 278-315; Kwabena Asamoah-Gyadu, "'Fireballs in Our Midst': West Africa's Burgeoning Charismatic Churches and the Pastoral Role of Women," *Mission Studies* 15-16, no. 29 (1998): 18-19.

dia and new media technologies. These churches have also been influenced by North American neo-evangelical and pentecostal Christianity. They adopt a faith-gospel focused on a *this-worldly* blessing and deliverance theology, which, though built on "African traditional conceptions is expressed strongly in terms of modern western charismatic thinking."[8]

These churches have shown tremendous growth all over Africa, and they are said to have replaced the spiritual churches "as the growing edges of independent indigenous Pentecostal churches."[9] Scholars have noted that the charismatic churches demonize spiritual AICs, which they view as compromised by traditional African culture and therefore anti-Christian. They perceive them as potential mission grounds.[10] As a result of this, spiritual AICs are either losing members to the charismatic churches or have been forced to "charismatize" and reinvent themselves.[11]

The growth of the charismatic/neo-pentecostal churches has been viewed by scholars of religion as linked to the current globalizing trends in other spheres of life. Most noteworthy is the inherent tendency of pentecostalism to align itself with modernity. In their quest for modernity, they have tended to adopt Western technology. This increases the force of externality in African Christianity. Indeed, Adrian Hastings postulated that pentecostals are an extension of the American electronic church. This does not mean, however, that African Pentecostal Christianity is totally foreign. There have been local initiatives, and as Gifford rightly observes, "Africa's Christianity is both localized and part of the world religion."[12] He further observes, "The growth of Christianity in Africa was never unrelated to its relations with the wider world; externality has always been a factor in African Christianity."[13] Being a Christian for individuals and communities meant being part of the global community with its philosophies, values, and economic, political, and social systems. It also meant the construction of local identities. Globalization, described by Robertson as "the compression of the world and the intensification of con-

8. Paul Gifford, *African Christianity: Its Public Role* (Bloomington: Indiana University Press, 1998), p. 306. See also Klaus Hock, "'Jesus Power — Super Power': On the Interaction Between Christian Fundamentalism and New Religious Movements in Africa," *Mission Studies* 13, no. 1 (1995): 56.

9. Gifford, *African Christianity*, p. 306. See also Hock, "Jesus Power," p. 56.

10. Asamoah-Gyadu, "Renewal Within Christianity," p. 144. Cf. Ruth Marshall, "God Is Not a Democrat: Pentecostalism and Democratization in Nigeria," in Paul Gifford, ed., *The Christian Churches and the Democratisation of Africa* (Leiden: E. J. Brill, 1995).

11. Ogbu U. Kalu, "Estranged Bedfellows: The Demonization of the Aladura in African Pentecostal Rhetoric," *Missionalia* 28, no. 2/3 (2000): 121.

12. Gifford, *African Christianity*, p. 47.

13. Gifford, *African Christianity*, p. 318.

sciousness of the whole world,"[14] is a process evident not only in the economic but also in political, technological, and cultural spheres. Giddens too argues that traditions connected with religion have undergone major transformations. Hence aspects of religion such as fundamentalism "originate from a world of crumbling traditions."[15]

In no other area has the impact of globalization been so pervasive as that of communication. Instantaneous electronic communication is possible from one side of the world to another. This is not "just a way in which news or information is conveyed more quickly. Its existence alters the very texture of our lives, rich and poor alike."[16] One area in which AICs reveal their connection to global mechanisms, tools, and values is in their use of mass media in evangelization and witness.

The use of media technology in Christianity, particularly among AICs, has not only transformed methods of evangelization, but it has also impacted on personal values and how spirituality is viewed as part of a global faith. All over Africa, "Visual representations of the communities of the saved and their leaders — whether on television, on book covers or magazines — now abound."[17] A casual observation of patterns of worship, types of ministries, and evangelistic methods in these churches shows similar approaches. This is evidence of the globalizing effect that mass media has wrought on the new emerging Christian expressions in Africa.

This chapter explores the access to, and appropriation of, mass media communication by women evangelists in two African Instituted Churches in Kenya. One is a spiritual AIC, the Jerusalem Church of Christ, founded in 1985 and led by prophetess Mary Akatsa. The other is the Jesus Is Alive Ministries (JIAM), a charismatic/neo-pentecostal church founded in 1993 and led by Bishop Margaret Wanjiru. The chapter compares two approaches to evangelization in the city of Nairobi, one drawing heavily on indigenous media (verbal: use of language, proverbs, anecdotes, gestures, songs, dance, drama, and role-play) as well as modern media technologies (use of a public address systems, audio-visuals, photographs), while the other relies heavily on print and electronic media to reach its audience. The chapter also analyzes the styles of preaching, some of the dominant beliefs and the rhetorical sig-

---

14. Roland Robertson, *Globalization: Social Theory and Global Culture* (London: Sage Publications, 1996), p. 8.

15. Anthony Giddens, *Runaway World: How Globalization Is Reshaping Our Lives* (New York: Routledge, 2000), p. 22.

16. Giddens, *Runaway World*, p. 29.

17. Rosalind I. J. Hackett, "Charismatic/Pentecostal Appropriation of Media Technologies in Nigeria," *Journal of Religion in Africa* 28, no. 3 (1998): 263.

nificance of these beliefs, and the impact of the relative growth pattern of each church in its influence in Kenyan Christianity, particularly in Nairobi and its environs. It is assumed and argued that the patterns of appropriations of global cultural forces at the local level provide a helpful way to interpret globalism. They show how global forces are gestated at the local level, creating different identities and Christianities. It is also argued that pneumatic-driven environments such as those evident in spiritual AICs and charismatic churches are more gender-friendly. Hence the preponderance of females in these churches where they are given space and recognized as change agents.[18]

1. Women in AICs

The preponderance of women in AICs has been noted by several scholars.[19] Not only are women there as participants, they have also assumed significant roles as pastors and hence mediators of God's grace and Spirit. This is a marked departure from the Western mission-founded churches' practice in which women were only participants. Despite the fact that some mainline churches ordain women and have opened more avenues for their participation in church life, leadership still remains a male domain. Classical AICs, particularly spiritual ones, draw from traditional African religious structures and hence women are evident as founders, healers, prophetesses, prayer-leaders, and evangelists.

Hastings[20] and Jules-Rosette[21] argue that spiritual AICs have provided women a chance to recover some of their traditional status and positions that

18. Research was conducted on the Jerusalem Church of Christ and Jesus Is Alive Ministries between October 2000 and May 2001 in Nairobi and surrounding districts. Methods of data collection included participant observation of worship services and informal interviews with church leaders and members. Content analysis of sermons and audio- and videotapes on church functions and sermons was also done. A total of fifty people were interviewed and over thirty worship meetings and services were observed.

19. See Marie France P. Jassy, "Women in the Independent Churches," *Risk* 7, no. 3 (1971): 46-49; Benetta Jules-Rosette, "Cultural Ambivalence and Ceremonial Leadership: The Role of Women in Africa's New Religious Movements," in John C. B. and Ellen Low Webster, eds., *The Church and Women in the Third World* (Philadelphia: Westminster Press, 1985); Rosalind I. J. Hackett, "Women and New Religious Movements in Africa," in Ursula King, ed., *Religion and Gender* (Oxford: Blackwell, 1995); Asamoah-Gyadu, "'Fireballs in Our Midst.'"

20. Adrian Hastings, *A History of Christianity in Africa 1950-1975* (Cambridge: Cambridge University Press, 1979).

21. Jules-Rosette, "Cultural Ambivalence."

had been undermined by the teachings of the mission churches. Nevertheless, the functions of women leaders and even ordinary participants are circumscribed by traditional taboos surrounding menstruation, which thus exclude them from certain sacramental roles. Traditional taboos and beliefs about women are reinforced by the Levitical code and by Pauline and Petrine teachings on household codes in the New Testament.[22] Mary Akatsa of the Jerusalem Church of Christ is thus limited in her functions as founder and prophetess-healer. Hers is only the charismatic ministry of healing and prophecy. The sacramental functions of baptizing, joining in matrimony, and ordination are performed by male clergy sometimes "loaned" from other spiritual AICs.

Nevertheless, neo-pentecostal churches (NPCs) have initiated a departure from this paradigm. In these churches, just like the spiritual AICs, women may be vehicles of the Spirit and receive spiritual gifts in the same way as men. However, unlike the spiritual AICs, they are not bound by any traditional or ecclesiastical restrictions. As Asamoah-Gyadu observes: "The charismatic ministries do not impose any Levitical or traditional taboos on women. They regard these as being inconsistent with New Testament teaching, particularly with the missionary experiences that followed the outpouring of the Holy Spirit in Acts."[23]

These new churches have even set up Bible schools where among those being trained to be pastors and leaders are women converts. According to Bishop Margaret of the Jesus Is Alive Ministries, God's call to women is not passive but a compelling call to participate fully in Christian missions at all levels. God's power, through the Holy Spirit and Christ's death and resurrection, has dismantled the hold of negative cultural traditions. Thus women are free to participate in ministry. They have also been able to apply a liberating hermeneutic in their readings of scripture in this respect and hence Pauline prohibitions directed to women are critiqued within their cultural and historical context. However, as Hackett observes with regard to Nigerian NPCs, there still exist ambivalent attitudes towards women. At one level they may enjoy greater participation and leadership opportunities in God's army, but at another level they are frequently stigmatized and demonized (notably those of the unmarried and "liberated" variety).[24]

Asked how they view Bishop Margaret as an unmarried, single mother, members reiterated that they hold her in high esteem as one with God's

---

22. Leviticus 12; Ephesians 5:21-33; 1 Peter 3:1-7.
23. Asamoah-Gyadu, "'Fireballs in Our Midst,'" p. 21.
24. Hackett, "Charismatic/Pentecostal Appropriation," p. 261.

anointing, hence her gender and status are irrelevant because she has been renewed in Christ. Though she confesses that she has been subjected to insults because of her personal status, Margaret sees herself as God's servant. Being a woman has endeared her to her followers, particularly single mothers. Her deliverance ministry is particularly appealing to those who perceive themselves as victims of witchcraft, misfortune, and afflictions of life attributed to the devil and his cohorts. She presents a comprehensive theology of salvation encompassing new life and victory over all evil. Members argue that since she was delivered from the forces of evil, she understands affliction, poverty, prostitution, hunger, and all wants. It is safe to say that there is here a gender dimension in ministry. Nevertheless, a fuller inclusion of men and women, if nurtured, would make mission a cooperative venture between men and women whom God has called. We shall now turn to the origin of Jerusalem Church of Christ (JCC) and Jesus Is Alive Ministries (JIAM).

2. The Origins of the Jerusalem Church of Christ

The Jerusalem Church of Christ was founded by the female prophet Mary Sinaida Dorcas Akatsa in 1985. She was born in 1964 into a polygamous household in a small village in western Kenya.[25] The stories of her birth are marked with mysteries and are reminiscent of those of Jesus' birth and other prominent founders of new religious movements. It seems that she was born in Kima mission hospital (in western Kenya) through a caesarian section five hours after her mother was pronounced dead. Her childhood was marked with neglect as her father and his wives did not want her. She was therefore raised by her maternal grandmother in poverty. She had only three years of schooling because of poverty but also because of the tug-of-war throughout her childhood between her grandmother and father over her custody. Ultimately this was to lead to her running away from home to get married at the age of thirteen to Francis Akatsa in 1981. Before that, she attended the local pentecostal Assemblies of God (PAG) church where she was an active member of the church choir. She traces her calling to prophetic religious ministry to a prophetic call when she was nine years old and received power to expose evil forces.

In 1982, Mary fell sick and allegedly "died." In her state of death, she experienced Jesus calling her to go back to earth and call people to repentance. After

---

25. Interview, Mary Akatsa, Nairobi, 6 October 2000; interview, Enoch Lumits, 10 December 2000; cf. Jack M. O. Nandi, "The Jerusalem Church of Christ: A Historical and Theological Analysis" (unpublished M.A. thesis, University of Nairobi, 1993).

this experience, her spiritual powers increased and on top of her other activities, she was able to heal the sick. Her continued exposure of evils elicited hostility from her victims and, fearing death, she and her husband left for Nairobi on God's command. In Nairobi, she worked as a house-help and continued in her healing ministry. When this became overwhelming she quit the job to devote her time to the healing ministry. Then she was known as Dada Mary (Sister Mary in Kiswahili). She joined the Church of Bethlehem East Africa, a spiritual AIC from western Kenya, where her healing ministry also led to disagreement with the church authorities. Her followers convinced her to start a church. Thus the Jerusalem Church of Christ began in a small plot donated to her by her landlord in the sprawling Kawangware slums in the western part of Nairobi. Her healing services held on Wednesdays, Saturdays, and Sundays attracted huge crowds of people from all walks of life, and several people reported being "healed" of various types of diseases and others having their businesses, marriages, and broken relationships restored. Akatsa has been able to captivate crowds by her dramatic preaching methods and her genuine concern for people's problems, particularly those related to witchcraft.

This church has created a community with new personal collective values. It regards itself as a family, and members experience spiritual and social support in the light of the alienation that they may experience in a strange, harsh urban context characterized by crime, violence, and little regard for human life and dignity. There is pneumatic spirituality in this church due to the emphasis on health; spiritual protection from evil; fertility; moral and physical well-being; and the recognition of the mystical causation of illness and misfortune. The church regards its mission as mediating healing in a holistic manner. It has shown a capacity to transcend ethnic, racial, and national boundaries. Nevertheless, it still bears a strong cultural stamp from the founder's background and hence it is viewed as a Luhya church despite its attempt to appear a national church.

3. The Origins of Jesus Is Alive Ministries

The Rev. Margaret Wanjiru founded the Jesus Is Alive Ministries in September 1993. She was born into a very poor family in 1961, to the late Samuel Kariuki and Mrs. Louise Wanjiru Kariuki. Her childhood was characterized by poverty and its attendant hardships. According to her, her mother worked very hard to make ends meet and to put her and her siblings through school, for her father was irresponsible. She claims that she was unwittingly initiated into witchcraft at the age of ten when, in a time of desperation, a wizard convinced her mother to subject her and her elder sister to witchcraft rituals that would guarantee their protection from harm by evil spirits. From then on they were, as she says, "covenanted with the powers of darkness." She sees this experience as sowing the seed for her deeper initiation into evil. It had an ambivalent impact on her, and she oscillated between success and failure. At sixteen she entered into a dysfunctional relationship that resulted in two children and was then dissolved. She returned to her mother's home and went back to finish high school while her mother took care of her children. All this time she was a member of the Anglican Church of Kenya in Westlands, Nairobi, and she even conducted Sunday School classes.

Eventually Margaret finished school and got a job as a toilet cleaner with a meager salary, but she says: "I was very ambitious to see my life change for good than the life of poverty that we had gone through while we were young."[26] Margaret is a very courageous and bold person. This is evident in her determination to change her circumstances. She enrolled in a sales and marketing management course and was able to rise through the ranks and become a sales girl and later a sales executive in a leading private company. However, the dark forces still stalked her. Whatever she was earning in employment and extra work in advertising was not enough, and she engaged in trade within Kenya and abroad. This brought her wealth, but she became involved in witchcraft in order to outdo her competitors. In her own words: "I went deep into witchcraft and passed to a very high degree called Red witchcraft. Finally Satan gave me a short time to decide if I wanted to sell my soul to him."[27] She had an uncanny flirtation with the satanic world, and that is why any "success" she encountered was eventually characterized by failure.

While she was indecisive as to whether to give her soul to the devil, she attended a crusade by a Nigerian evangelist, Emmanuel Eni, in March 1990.[28] "He was preaching against Satanism and witchcraft. Every issue he raised in his sermons was just too familiar. It was as if he had been sent to talk to me about the kinds of iniquities I was involved in."[29] Days after the crusade, she "gave her life to Jesus Christ." She recalls, "While in my small office I prayed a prayer of repentance and asked the Lord to forgive a sinner like me who had

---

26. Interview, Margaret Wanjiru, Nairobi, May 2001.

27. Interview, Wanjiru; see also *Sunday Nation*, 17 June 2001.

28. Emmanuel Eni is a self-confessed convert from witchcraft and Satanism. He has written *Delivered from the Powers of Darkness* (Ibadan, Nigeria: Scripture Union, 1987). His ministry and literature are popular in Kenya owing to their emphasis on deliverance theology.

29. *Sunday Nation*, 17 June 2001.

done worse things in life and from that moment after repenting I purposed in my heart to live for Jesus and for Jesus alone and preach the gospel."[30]

She strove to live a righteous life and not to be "separated from the presence and love of God." In the meantime she continued in her business that was now on the verge of collapse, and she was also engaged part-time in Christian ministry. God spoke to her, asking that she give up all the things she had acquired while in the "devil's kingdom." She destroyed all of them and overnight she was penniless. She had to move from Westlands, an upper-middle-class neighborhood, to the Eastlands part of Nairobi, a low-income, densely populated neighborhood. Losing her worldly possessions did not "shake me, my thirst was to please the Lord and to do his will." She says of these hardships, "One thing I have made up my mind is that I do not live in my mistakes but I learn from them. Mistakes do not keep me from marching to my destiny."[31]

Margaret later became actively involved in missions and evangelism through World Intercessory, a Christian ministry started by Pastor Mutimba. This entailed traveling all over the country evangelizing. She encountered hostility from both male and female evangelists, particularly those who knew her past.[32] She remarks that even though she was "born again," and prayed and fasted, the devil still "held her captive." Over the years, Margaret learned the word of God and was delivered. This explains why deliverance is so crucial to her ministry. She started preaching in the streets of Nairobi and many people were "born again." Through God's command, she started Jesus Is Alive Ministries in September 1993 in order to nurture the faith of the new converts. She experienced discouragement and persecution from fellow evangelists, both male and female, particularly because of her past lifestyle. In 1996, she abandoned the church and started preaching in Britain, America, Uganda, and South Africa.

Once, while in South Africa, God spoke to her through a preacher while she was attending a ministerial conference and asked her to concentrate on her fledgling church. In the course of that week, God revealed to her his vision and plans for the evangelization of Africa and her role in it.[33] The vision

---

30. Interview, Wanjiru.

31. Interview, Wanjiru.

32. According to Pastor Karuri and Rev. Ruth Ndaka, some people did not believe that Margaret had changed. They were also discouraged from following a woman with apparently unbecoming conduct and particularly someone who was a single mother. Interview, Karuri and Ndaka, Nairobi, May 2001.

33. Interview, Wanjiru; *Miracle Magazine*, 2001, p. 3; *Let's Talk About You.* This is a television program held weekly on Family Media Television. It features prominent personalities, particularly those in Christian ministry. Margaret was featured in May 2001, and the recording has been repeated several times since.

occurred as Margaret was lying down on a couch, and it lasted for nine hours. In the vision, God took her through the Gospel of Luke and the story of Mary the mother of Jesus and said, "I chose Mary because she was God fearing and humble. Because you are obedient and humble, I will send you to restore my church."[34] God then took her through the book of Nehemiah and said, "You will bring souls and rebuild the church like Nehemiah." After this, she was shown a black book with writings inside but no title. God touched it with a finger and drew the map of Africa and wrote "Revival for Africa." This was subsequently rubbed out and replaced with "Africa shall be saved."

Margaret considers this as her inaugural vision. While before this she was full of doubts and almost succumbed to discouragement and despair, the vision confirmed to her that her mission was part of the divine scheme for the salvation of humankind. She felt compelled like Mary and Nehemiah to fulfill God's calling to preach the gospel of salvation to the nations of the world. She also believes she has a burden to restore churches that are ailing; hence she goes out of her way to mediate reconciliation and even give financial support not only to churches but also to fledging ministries.[35]

On 28 June 1997, Margaret was ordained by Bishop Arthur Kitonga of the Redeemed Gospel Church, in Kenya.[36] Since then her church has experienced tremendous growth, and "is one of the biggest gospel crusades and outreach programmes in Africa."[37] She launched a media ministry in 1998 after the Nairobi bomb blast. According to her, "The Lord spoke to me to launch a media ministry that would reach many people who were hurting and so I started a television programme on the national broadcasting service entitled 'Healing the Nation' which was later changed to 'The Glory Is Here.'"[38]

Between 1993 and 2002 Margaret published several spiritual works, including *The Wiles of the Devil, The Work of the Holy Spirit Sanctification,* and *The Joy of God's Sanctification.* She is in the process of completing another one titled "Revealing the Spirit of Free Masonry" in which she chronicles her flirtation with the Masons before becoming "born again."[39] She also started

34. *Let's Talk About You,* May 2001.

35. Interview, Wanjiru; *Miracle Magazine,* 2001, p. 6; *Let's Talk About You,* May 2001.

36. On 5 October 2002, Bishop Kitonga consecrated her a bishop.

37. *Sunday Nation,* 17 June 2001.

38. On 7 August 1998, the U.S. Embassy building was bombed by Arab terrorists. Over two hundred people died and several buildings in the vicinity were destroyed. The church is located near the bomb blast site, which was also the area of her street evangelism. The bomb blast had a serious impact on her church, for some of the dead and injured were members (interview, Wanjiru).

39. Interview, Wanjiru.

a magazine, *Faith Digest,* and she contributes extensively to other neo-pentecostal magazines such as *Victory, Revival Springs,* and *Miracle.* According to Margaret, she has been able to reach thousands of people who attribute their conversion to her evangelization through the media. Today the church has a seating capacity of 3,500.[40] It conducts twenty-two services in a week, three of them on Sundays. Other services include a miracle service on Tuesdays and Wednesdays; and morning, lunchtime, and evening services. The whole month is also marked by various evangelistic activities including Bible study; choir practice; youth, women, men, and business fellowship; as well as monthly conferences. The church has established several departments and ministries, for example, Home Cells, Youth Aflame, Good Samaritan Project, Prison and Hospital Ministries, Evangelism, Intercessory, Counseling, Sunday School, and Television Ministries.

What has led to the growth of JIAM and JCC and what role have the personalities and methods of Mary Akatsa and Margaret Wanjiru contributed to that growth? What has been the impact on Christianity in Nairobi? These issues will be explored below, but first one has to consider what religious communication implies.

4. Defining Communication

Communication can be defined as a process by which human beings share information, ideas, and attitudes.[41] Sharing implies that the sender and the receiver of the message are actually involved and working together for common understanding. Implicit in evangelization is the belief that communication for evangelization is regarded as proclamation, witnessing, and persuading people to respond to Christ's message of salvation. In Christian communication the message is not created by human beings, for it is already "given"; it is Jesus Christ incarnate. Christian communication, according to Essayas, "is not just the dissemination of information. It is not the sharing of ideas or the exchange of news. It is not moral edification. It is not the instructing of ignorance. Primarily and basically, it is the *commemoration* of

40. The church (Worship Center) is called the Nairobi Miracle Center. In March 2002 the church purchased a large building.

41. Stan Le Roy Wilson, *Mass Media, Mass Culture: An Introduction* (New York: McGraw-Hill, 1993), p. 6; Menkir Essayas, "Content and Context of Christian Communication," in Robert N. Kizito, ed., *Communication and Human Rights in Africa: Implications for Development* (World Association for Christian Communication — Africa Region Publication, 1992), p. 84.

an event."[42] He continues by saying that Christian communication is explicit and implicit witness to God, who is deeply concerned about social justice and human rights. It is encountering the God incarnate within human experience. While accepting his definition we argue that sharing ideas, moral edification, and elimination of ignorance are all part of Christian communication, particularly when they are geared towards conversion and transformation. Crabble identifies the importance of the media in Christian communication, viewing it as a "multiplying factor of the church's ministry in society."[43] Options open to the church for evangelization include traditional and new technology.

5. Communication for Evangelization in JCC and JIAM

How do JCC and JIAM use communication in their evangelism? What do they see themselves communicating? In order to understand the dynamics of communication in the two churches, we use the ritual model of communication developed by James Carey.[44] This is regarded as the expressive model.[45] Here communication is seen as a means through which shared culture is engendered, altered, and then transformed. A ritual view of communication is not so much concerned with the extension of messages in time; not with mechanisms of dispensing information but rather with more complex interactions involved in creating, representing, and celebrating shared attitudes and beliefs.[46] This model can apply to religious activities in JIAM and JCC, whether through broadcasts, church services, or other aspects of evangelization. Those who view or listen to broadcasts or participate in live religious activities share and celebrate common symbols, values, and a moral culture.

Evangelization Methods in JCC

In the JCC, Mary Akatsa uses traditional media in the main. As Dyer observes, "Africans have indigenous, functioning, powerful, accurate, valuable,

42. Essayas, "Content and Context," p. 84.

43. Richard Crabble, "The Role of Christian Media in Church and Society," *Christian Media* 2, no. 1 (1991): 3.

44. James Carey, "A Cultural Approach in Communication," *Communication* 2 (1975): 1-22.

45. Denis McQuail, *Mass Communication Theory: An Introduction*, 3rd ed. (London: Sage Publications, 1994), p. 51.

46. Stewart M. Hoover, *Mass Media Religion: The Social Sources of the Electronic Church* (London: Sage Publications, 1988).

low-cost non-dependent creative systems of communication."[47] Considering that she appeals mostly to the poor in Nairobi who form 40 percent of the city's population, and who are most likely to be illiterate or semi-literate, her use of spontaneous and traditional media is very effective. Spontaneous media includes word of mouth, music, poetry, proverbs, riddles, song, dance, drama, prayer, gesture, and narratives. Traditional or indigenous media in Africa includes the talking drum, the town crier, the gong, fire and music rituals, folktales, and speeches.[48] Although not all of these are used in JCC, prominent among the traditional media used are speeches/sermons, songs, stories, drums, gestures, anecdotes, riddles, and feedback techniques that lead to conversation between Mary and the audience. In traditional African society, folktales and songs are significant in perpetuating the people's cultural values. Apart from reflecting the indigenous abilities of the composers, they bear ethical teaching. The Old Testament also depicts the importance of music, song, and poetry, not only as means of worshiping God but also for prophecy.

In the JCC through stories and songs enacted by the prophetess, the history of the church is recounted, and in every service the members are acquainted with it. Stories also edify the community through the recounting of healing testimonies. This has had the effect of drawing more members to the church. Akatsa is also a comedian; she cracks jokes, admonishes, disciplines, and at the same time restores people's confidence through her singing. Although modern musical instruments such as guitars, drums, percussion, and keyboard are used in JCC, the traditional drum is very significant. Its use draws instantaneous response from the older members and the migrant youth from the rural areas to whom this form of religious communication and entertainment is still very valid. This is evidence of the church's Abaluhya cultural background.

Traditionally, certain drum rhythms symbolize certain words or messages — for example, joy, celebrations, or death. Like all African people the Abaluhya community, to which Akatsa belongs, are a song-loving people. Evangelizing through song is one way of reaching the people with the gospel message. Worship services are joyous and entertaining occasions that involve everyone. Akatsa also uses ritual words such as *Riswa!* (Kiswahili for "Depart!") to exorcise evil spirits. The word has come to acquire a significant religious meaning and is used almost magically. The practice of ritual words that

47. Paul D. Dyer, "The Use of Oral Communication Methods in Health Education, Evangelism and Christian Maturation" (unpublished D.Min. thesis, Bethel Theological Seminary, 1994), p. 9.

48. Dyer, "Oral Communication Methods," p. 9. See also Nabban J. Corbit, "Music as Prophecy in the African Church," *Christian Media* 7 (1993).

acquire magical value is also evident in Aladura churches in Nigeria.[49] While this word *Riswa* is meaningful in JCC it would be meaningless in JIAM, which operates within a different worldview.

The *lingua franca* in JCC is Kiswahili, which Mary employs to great advantage. She uses metaphors and euphemisms, particularly when addressing adults in front of children. She also has a tendency to use vulgar language that may be embarrassing to the young. It has a shocking impact on the adults, whose attention is drawn to the gravity of the immoral and sinful situation to which Akatsa may be alluding. In using culturally relevant communication procedures, however, her message of hope, deliverance, and healing become more effective. Her use of technological media is limited to the public address system, video and audio recording of services, and photographing of events and subjects of her healing. There is no evidence that these recordings are circulated to members. A number of members, however, record the proceedings of services on audiotapes and possibly replay them for their own edification. The rhetorical features and significance of Akatsa's evangelism and how they contribute to her appeal are explored below.

Evangelization Techniques in JIAM

JIAM employs some of the oral methods of communication used in JCC but not the traditional media. It can best be described as a modern church, for it aggressively uses mass communication in the form of books, pamphlets, tracts, magazines, posters, direct-mail circulars, electronic mail, websites, video, audiotapes, telephone, radio, and television. Scholars of mass communication have underscored its power to persuade, change attitudes, elicit opinions, and even lead to conversion.

Like the pentecostal and neo-evangelical churches in the United States, JIAM is keenly aware of the power of the media. In 1998 it started a half-hour broadcast on Kenya Broadcasting Corporation (KBC) Television. By the year 2003, it was broadcasting its messages five times a week, both in English and Kiswahili, on KBC and Family Television, a new religious broadcasting service sourced from Trinity Broadcasting Network of the United States. Margaret Wanjiru says that the impact of the television broadcast — with its different message on deliverance, success, healing, spirituality, prayer, and Bible study — was so great that she had to increase the number of programs in response to public demand. JIAM now owns a studio, which records and edits

49. Turner, *Life and Faith*.

her messages whether they are church sermons, talk shows, or Bible study programs specially prepared for broadcasting.

Because of the heavy cost of producing and broadcasting the programs[50] and the limitations imposed by the government on access to the airwaves, the number of local owners of private stations is negligible. Other churches, mainline or NPC, do not use the TV media as aggressively as Margaret. She appears to apply her business skills to this ministry. She has also recently started to broadcast on Family Radio. In addition, JIAM spreads its messages through video- and audiocassettes that are sold and distributed or loaned from the church library.

The church recently started two websites, and uses e-mail, telephone, and fax to reach its audience.[51] Its publications include a quarterly magazine. The TV ministry has spread to other parts of the world. In Margaret's words, "Currently we are on television in Uganda (Lighthouse Television), Europe (Inspirational Channel) and we are also trusting God for airtime in America and South Africa."[52] The impact has been such that "We receive testimonies either by phone, fax, letters, e-mail and hear of how God has changed and transformed them. Businesses have been restored, finances restored, and marriages restored, not forgetting the many souls that have gotten saved and many healing of diseases."

How pervasive is this impact given the current viewing and listening public in Kenya? According to Steadman Media Researchers, the KBC covers 40 percent of Kenya's landmass and is concentrated in urban areas of the country. There are about 1,740,000 households with television sets and an adult audience of 29 percent in the country as a whole and 50 percent in Nairobi.[53] Family TV, which started broadcasting in July 1999, has a reach of only a 100-km radius from Nairobi and broadcasts mainly in English. According to the director, its television broadcasts have approximately 27 percent of viewers

---

50. JIAM spends 1 million Kenya shillings (12,500 U.S. dollars) a month. This money is sourced from church members and non-members who view the program throughout the country, as well as foreign mission, prayer, and TV partners.

51. The websites are www.jiam.org and www.jiam.com. They are both operated from London. They target audiences and viewers outside Kenya, for the majority of their members in Kenya do not have access to the Internet or are totally unaware of its existence. The church sees its mission as reaching the whole world. The websites provide information on the church, its vision, mission, and ministries; disseminate healing through prayer requests; and provide information on salvation, the Holy Spirit, healing, and how to prosper.

52. Interview, Wanjiru; *Faith Digest*, 1999.

53. Roger H. Steadman et al., eds., *The Advertisers Guide 2002* (Nairobi: Steadman Associates, 2000), pp. 48-51.

and radio 47 percent of listeners.[54] KBC Radio has a national reach; however, since JIAM does not use KBC Radio yet, it cannot claim to reach the whole country. The fact that JIAM does not own a station that can carry broadcasts that run for twenty-four hours a day limits its impact on potential viewers.

Unlike American televangelists like Pat Robertson, who own television networks and compete with commercial television for audience and adhere to the same production values,[55] JIAM only disseminates selected sermons recorded in the church or produces teaching programs on various themes in a simple manner. It has, however, installed other mechanisms that ensure that the church is in touch with the viewers. Telephone numbers, e-mail, and website addresses are thus superimposed on the screen during entire programs for prayer and money pledges. Viewers are urged to call in for prayer, counseling, and healing. The impact of the programs is measured in terms of feedback from telephone counselors, and by anecdotal evidence obtained from unsolicited letters, phone calls, e-mails, and faxes.[56]

The church does not solicit members on television, but the fact that it advertises its services and video library is a subtle way of doing the same thing. A number of members interviewed claimed to have known about the church through television, and pastors attribute 75 percent of its growth and membership to the impact of the TV broadcasts.[57]

Hackett rightly observes that television and radio are very powerful tools of evangelization, and used effectively they have led to church growth. She points out that "Younger people in particular are attracted to the evangelists who have developed modern media images of themselves and their churches."[58] Through simulated conversation, media evangelists like Margaret are able to create a re-

---

54. Interview, Leo Slingerland, Nairobi, May 2001. Slingerland is the founder and managing director of Family Media TV.

55. Hoover, *Mass Media Religion*, p. 177.

56. The TV department records all these responses. The records show that depending on the nature of the broadcast message, about fifteen to forty people call from all over the country during the program. Some people claim to have received healing, deliverance, and salvation while others request to be given directions to the church. Some have joined the church this way, and others continue to finance the TV ministry. They need not be church members.

57. Pastor Karuri informed the author that before the TV broadcasts, there was only one Sunday service comprising fewer than one hundred people. There are clearly other factors contributing to the growth — among them a combination of various evangelistic methods through the Home Cells, personal evangelism, crusades, and door-to-door evangelism. Visitors to the church are given cards to complete; so too are those who are converted and join the church. The church also has a roster for permanent members.

58. Hackett, "Charismatic/Pentecostal Appropriation," p. 266.

lationship with their audiences. Discussing the relationship between religious media personalities and their audiences, Goethals notes: "Television is especially compatible with those religious traditions that have emphasized the charismatic qualities of leadership and played down the office of priesthood and saving role of the sacraments. Sacramental power becomes concentrated in the person who has been divinely called to teach, preach and heal; television offers an unprecedented opportunity to focus on the personality and forcefulness of religious leadership."[59]

These observations are true of JIAM, which, unlike JCC, uses television broadcasts. The medium of television is not only used to evangelize but also to mediate healing and dispel evil powers. During JIAM broadcasts, the television is viewed ritually as imbued with power. Several people interviewed claimed to have been healed or saved during Margaret's broadcasts. Although she does not encourage viewers to touch television screens, recipients of healing have claimed that they did. Hence the television is a ritual object. Hackett observes the ritual use that pentecostals in Nigeria make of their radio and television. She says, "It is not uncommon for an evangelist to encourage his listeners to place their hands on the radio to receive healing and spiritual power."[60]

Audio- and videotapes of sermons are sold and loaned to thousands of people all over Kenya, which means that the same messages are not only consumed by thousands but are recycled and marketed. They are "shared between friends and family members and virtually critiqued in terms of performance, presentations, results, etc., so this type of praxis is arguably reshaping the religious landscape, dissolving boundaries and [creating a] standardized form of communication."[61] Since several other factors contribute to the growth and impact of JCC and JIAM, we shall now examine the content, significance, and impact of Akatsa's and Wanjiru's rhetoric.

6. Rhetorical Exigencies: Hope for the Hopeless

Although Akatsa and Wanjiru have a different audience and style of evangelism, their rhetorical situations do not differ radically. As faith healers they

59. G. T. Goethals, *The Electronic Golden Calf: Images, Religion, and the Making of Meaning* (Cambridge, MA: Cowley, 1990), p. 17, cited in L. B. Nadler et al., "Why Do People Give Money to Televangelists? A Pentecostal Development Explanation," *Journal of Communication and Religion* 19, no. 2 (1996): 49.
60. Hackett, "Charismatic/Pentecostal Appropriation," p. 267.
61. Hackett, "Charismatic/Pentecostal Appropriation," p. 267.

seem to be responding to the maladies of the day.[62] Lewis points out that in general, charismatic religious leaders "emerge in times of deprivation and disenfranchisement." Followers converge toward a religious figure "because they have been unable to resolve feelings of estrangement and fatality in other normal contexts." In other words, charismatic figures provide their followers with hope for a better future or the means to regain losses.[63]

A survey of the characteristics of people who attend crusades in Nairobi revealed that the poor dominate, followed by the middle class and then the rich.[64] Their problems include unemployment, poverty, sickness, stress, sin, housing, food, family issues, and even non-performance of business enterprises or financial ruin.[65] The same people frequent AICs like JCC and JIAM, although in the latter, the middle class is dominant. Both Akatsa and Wanjiru view God as the "greater physician." Margaret usually exclaims, "It is time for our salvation to shine and our glory to break forth."[66] She mediates healing by calling people "to receive your healing! Receive the Holy Ghost! Receive your breakthrough."[67] All problems are attributed to the devil, witchcraft, and its attendant evils. Both Akatsa and Wanjiru are in agreement in locating evil in the area of witchcraft and other malevolent forces. While Wanjiru teaches and discusses the problems from an informed position of biblical exegesis, however, Akatsa relies on the Holy Spirit. Both continually emphasize that if God rescued them from poverty, sin, and despair, he can do the same to anyone who has faith, no matter the circumstances.

Rhetoric of Humility and Sincerity

Both Akatsa and Wanjiru claim to have no power of their own to heal. Akatsa calls herself Jesus' "watchman" and Wanjiru asserts that "I have no power to heal. I am God's servant." She claims, however, to have God's anointing to enable her to perform the ministry of deliverance and healing. One of the at-

---

62. JIAM conducts healing services, but Wanjiru sees herself more as a teacher of the word. However, she has a powerful deliverance ministry.

63. V. L. Todd Lewis, "Charisma and Media Evangelists: An Explanation and Model of Communication Influence," *The Southern Communication Journal* 54 (1988): 97.

64. However, JIAM and most NPCs attract mostly the middle class, since they are predominantly urban churches.

65. Zachariah W. Samita, *Christian Crusades in Nairobi: An Analysis of Social-Religious Factors Underlying Their Upsurge* (Addis Ababa: OSSREA, 1998), p. 40.

66. *Faith Digest*, 1999, p. 4.

67. *Faith Digest*, 1999, p. 4.

tractive features of Akatsa and Wanjiru to their followers is their humility, which, ironically, they constantly advertise. They have maintained their humble stance before their followers by reminding them of their own less-than-ideal beginnings. Wanjiru for instance asserts: "I became very poor when I got saved, I lost everything. I got it all from witchcraft."[68] Akatsa recounts her misery as a child; however, both also advertise their current status of blessings seen in material wealth and social status.

Dynamic Personalities

The rhetoric of these charismatic leaders features the appeal of their dynamic personalities. This, coupled with their beauty, is certainly one of the greatest attractions. Not only are they physically compelling, they are also entertaining to watch. Margaret usually dresses in long African dresses of various striking colors. She engages her audience in the sermon with rhetorical questions, for example, "Hello! Am I talking to somebody?" She leads songs and dances on stage. Her followers describe her as "beautiful," "energetic," and one who "displays a wide range of dramatic moods and voices." In her television broadcasts she has been able to harness the power of the media technologies to build an "interpersonal relationship" with her audience. As Nadler observes in relation to U.S. televangelists, people connect to media evangelists because they appear vividly real.[69] They relate to them as if they are intimately involved with them.

The feedback JIAM gets of its media broadcasts attests to this fact. Wanjiru has acquired celebrity status and effectively applies oral communication to convey the illusion of intimacy. This is a strategy that can effectively be used to elicit conversion and raise funds. The content of the broadcast is important too, for it has relevance to daily life and meets the spiritual and psychological needs of the viewers. Those interviewed for this research confirmed that religious television broadcasts play this role in their lives.

Akatsa too is a spectacle to behold, and leads the singing and dancing in traditional Luhya movements and tunes. Lewis points out that the "superior ability to communicate verbally and non-verbally may result to attribution of charisma to a leader/communicator," thereby causing an audience to be attracted to him or her.[70]

---

68. *Faith Digest,* 1999, p. 11.

69. L. B. Nadler et al., "Why Do People Give Money to Televangelists?" p. 50.

70. Lewis, "Charisma and Media Evangelists." See also Samita, *Christian Crusades in Nairobi,* p. 41.

Another rhetorical strategy is that of ultimate legitimizer. Overcoming the vicissitudes of life helps to legitimize one's existence. Hence Akatsa and Wanjiru validate their beliefs and practices to their audience by describing the terrible shape their lives were in before God wrought miracles on them. This rhetorical strategy can be a powerful force in persuading others to accept their positions. Since the mission of both is to win souls to Christ, they consistently remind their listeners of their own positive conversion experience in the hope that they too might be compelled to accept Christ. In addition to testimonies, they constantly attempt to legitimize their teaching and miracles through personal experiences.

7. Conclusion

We have argued that Christianity in Africa has experienced phenomenal growth since the beginning of the twentieth century as a result of the rise of African Instituted Churches. Neo-pentecostal churches have been a major force in the last thirty years. Their chief characteristics are a theology of health, wealth, deliverance, and healing. They are also known for their use of mass media in evangelism, and women play key roles as founders, leaders, and participants. There is a gender dynamic in the AICs that is evident in preaching and ministry. The fact that women predominate in leadership in churches with pneumatic orientations suggests that charismatic/spiritual churches are more "gender-friendly" than others. Women are able to use their special resources for the growth of the church. Their healing roles, which are interpreted holistically, are an extension of their gendered roles in society. One can rightly argue that women-led churches are gaining appeal in Africa because of women's ability to engage in ministry from a material perspective.

The use of a variety of media, both traditional and technologically new, has contributed to the growth of JCC and JIAM. Some scholars argue that mass media content alone is not sufficient to change human behavior.[71] Others like Klapper and McQuail, however, argue for the media's potential to influence opinion, lead to conversion, and to control and inform.[72] It is true, nevertheless, that interpersonal communication remains more effective. In JCC, the evangelism styles of Akatsa encourage interpersonal interaction

---

71. Louise Bourgault, "The Jim Bakker Show: The Programme, Its Viewers and Their Churches," *Journal of Communication and Religion* 11 (1988): 32.

72. Joseph T. Klapper, *The Effects of Mass Communication* (New York: Free Press, 1960); McQuail, *Mass Communication Theory.*

through the use of folk media, while in the JIAM ministry, television, radio, cassettes, and video ministries are reinforced by other interactive and intensive evangelism procedures. This has contributed to the transformational impact of their form of Christianity. A ritual view of media shows how a shared culture is engendered, altered, and transformed. The use of culturally relevant media in JCC and modern media that appeals to a middle-class group in JIAM, coupled by the various rhetorical dimensions of their preaching, provide inspiration, entertainment, and an opportunity to express and share common values in the two churches. The use of mass media has also enabled the building of links with global Christianity.

The potential of modern media technology has its limitations in a country like Kenya, where literacy levels are low and only 40 percent among the educated can access print or electronic media. Hence Akatsa's approach is more appropriate for a rural-oriented or -based audience, but Wanjiru's methods are also suited to a middle-class urban environment. Responses to JIAM's media ministry is evidence, however, that the use of mass media should be encouraged, not discouraged. Electronic media has been criticized for being impersonal and superficial and for promoting cultural imperialism. These are problems inherent in any media, whether print, electronic, or folk.

CHAPTER 13

Globalization and African New Religious Movements in Europe

AFE ADOGAME

The African continent, more than ever before, has come to represent one of the major global "theaters" for the dramatization of religion. Christianity, Islam, and the indigenous religions continue to engage and negotiate enduring processes of renewal, revitalization, and contextualization. The vigor and vitality demonstrated by these religious initiatives are such that it has launched them and their activities within and beyond local and global space. As Africans migrate to Europe and elsewhere, they are often accompanied by their religion in a way that helps to maintain and reinforce their identity, but also inadvertently results in the charting of new ones. New circumstances and contextual factors in the new host cultural context often goad these migrants to reconstruct, organize, and identify "their religion" both for themselves and for the non-Africans around them. In more recent times, African New Religious Movements (ANRMs) have experienced remarkable proliferation outside of Africa, where they are increasingly engaged in the task of "self-insertion" and "self-assertion" on the global religious scene. African churches have become particularly creative and innovative when they encounter the unfamiliar socio-cultural environments of Europe, insinuating themselves into the local contexts and adapting the traditions of an African church to new geo-cultural boundaries and non-African realities.

This chapter examines African churches' religious geography in Europe, discusses their stakes in the ongoing processes of globalization, and demonstrates how they attempt to assimilate notions of the global while simultaneously averring their local identity. It also looks at the extent to which African Christians in Europe have been able to spread their religious ideologies, taking advantage of new forms of communication technologies in particular, as well as the religious, economic, and socio-political developments in Europe.

1. Globalization as a "Kaleidoscopic" Concept

Globalization has become the buzzword in several academic discourses such as communication, sociology, cultural studies, political science, advertising, and in history of religions. It is a term that has come from "nowhere" to occupy almost "everywhere," thus becoming a household name in public-private domains, especially in the last decade. As globalization is a dynamic process, still unfolding and revealing itself in many domains of social and private life, there can be no final word on the phenomenon of globalization. What does this mean to us? What is the nexus between religion and all the talk about globalization? Can this be understood in the same way as other usages and meanings of the term?

Although the focus on globalization is very diverse,[1] what seems to run through it all is the view that "the world is experienced as a single place, or even a non-place, an abstract sign space, or as subject to time-space compression."[2] But this one world also has its shadow world. There is often talk of a tension between the universal and the particular, the global and the local, and this has led to the coinage of terms such as "glocalization" by Roland Robertson.[3] Globalization has stimulated postmodern interest in fragmentation, not so much in relation to the global, but much more in relation to the local translations of the global. Droogers aptly remarks that the fascination with globalization does not stem from the characteristics of the global, but from the attitude developed locally in order to survive in an era of globalization.[4]

As David Vanter rightly observes, "The application of globalization theo-

---

1. Cf. Christopher Chase-Dunn, "Globalization: A World-System Perspective," *Journal of World-System Research* 5, no. 2 (1999): 165-85. Robert Keohane and Joseph S. Nye, Jr., "Globalization: What's New? What's Not? (And So What?)," *Foreign Policy* (Spring 2000): 104-19.

2. Cf. Roland Robertson, *Globalization: Social Theory and Global Culture* (London: Sage Publications, 1996); Marc Augé, *Non-Places: Introduction to Anthropology of Supermodernity*, trans. from the French by John Howe (London: Verso, 1995).

3. Robertson, *Globalization, Social Theory*, p. 73.

4. André Droogers, "Globalization and Pentecostal Success," in André Corten and Ruth Marshall-Fratani, eds., *Between Babel and Pentecost: Transnational Pentecostalism in Africa and Latin America* (Bloomington and Indianapolis: Indiana University Press, 2001), pp. 41-61.

ries to religious movements is relatively undeveloped."[5] Some notable attempts at linking or seeing the relationship between religion and globalization are evident, however, in the works of Roland Robertson[6] and Peter Beyer.[7] It would appear, however, that most of the scholars who have attempted to see the link between religion and globalization have done so solely with reference to the so-called Christian and Islamic fundamentalist forms, thus giving the impression that this is the only way to view this connection. This chapter demonstrates one of several other ways: the steady spread of African religions and other religious ideologies deriving from African indigenous spiritual ideologies can be viewed as forms of "globalization from below."

In non-Western contexts such as Africa, indigenous Christianity has shown how people can adopt a "global view" and at the same time remain faithful to their local, traditional "identities." Although the popular adage has been "Think globally, act locally," much of the thinking also takes place at the local level.[8] Thus, we could reverse the aphorism by saying, "Think lo-

5. David Vanter, "Globalization and the Cultural Effects of the World-Economy in a Semi-Periphery: The Emergence of African Indigenous Churches in South Africa," *Journal of World-Systems Research* 5 (1999): 105-26.

6. Robertson is undoubtedly the pioneer in this academic endeavor. Since the mid-1980s, he has written extensively on the theory and processes of globalization. He writes of "the crystallisation of the entire world as a single place," "the emergence of the global-human condition," "the consciousness of the globe as such." On religion, he bases his analysis on how state-religion tensions across the globe arise from the politicization of religion, and the religionization of politics — the result of globalization. See Robertson, "The Sacred and the World System," in Philip E. Hammond, ed., *The Sacred in a Secular Age: Toward Revision in the Scientific Study of Religion* (Berkeley: University of California Press, 1985), pp. 347-58; "Church-State Relations and the World-System," in R. Robertson and T. Robbins, eds., *Church-State Relations: Tensions and Transitions* (New Brunswick, NJ: Transaction Books, 1987), pp. 39-52; "Religion and the Global Field," *Social Compass* 41, no. 1 (1994): 121-35; and Robertson, "The Globalization Paradigm: Thinking Globally," in Peter Beyer, ed., *Religion im Prozeß der Globalisierung* (Würzburg: Ergon Verlag, 2001), pp. 3-22.

7. See Peter Beyer, *Religion and Globalization* (London: Sage Publications, 1994); and Peter Beyer, ed., *Religion im Prozeß der Globalisierung*. Beyer attempts a theoretical and applied examination of globalization and its application to religion by combining four world-system theorists to show globalization as resulting in a global economy (Wallerstein), a global culture (Robertson), a global society (Luhmann), and a global polity (Meyer). Beyer identifies Christian and Islamic fundamentalist forms as both flourishing in the new globalizing climate. Prior to the term "globalization" gaining wide currency, the expansion of Christianity was always viewed as a transnational phenomenon with globalizing tendencies. In this sense, the Roman Catholic Church for instance has been depicted as a religious multinational.

8. Droogers, "Globalization and Pentecostal Success," pp. 12ff.

cally, act globally." As Droogers rightly points out, "This then is the somewhat gloomy globalizing world within which Pentecostal expansion occurs. In it, space and non-space intermingle, just as the global and the local — or even the fragmented. . . . Religion is part of the globalizing forces, as well as of the local translations. It is part both of the global impact and the local reaction."[9]

It is within this context of globalization that we can better understand the intricate links between ANRMs and the processes of globalization.

2. Debut and Proliferation on European Soil

African New Religious Movements refer, from a historical-descriptive point of view, to the various religious initiatives that emerged in different parts of Africa, especially from the end of the twentieth century onwards.[10] The movements that fall under this wide categorization may not be entirely new in terms of their doctrines and ideology. They are considered new in the sense that these indigenous religious initiatives and creativities are historically unprecedented in the African religious context. For instance, within Christianity, new religious movements refer to the newer forms of Christianity that succeeded mission or mainline Christianity. These recent waves have reshaped Christianity and ushered it into a conspicuous place in contemporary global religious maps of the universe.[11] This includes the so-called African Instituted Churches (AICs) and African pentecostal/charismatic movements. Many other new movements have emerged from Islam and the traditional religions, but this chapter shall draw examples mainly from Christian NRMs. In Europe, they reveal a complex variety in terms of their historical origins, social composition, geographical distribution, belief content, and ritual traditions. Global and local can be interpreted as two faces of the same movement from one epoch, a process that is dynamic and multi-directional, not static or uni-directional. For the ANRMs, Europe represents both a local and a global space at the same time. The proliferation and expansion of African churches

9. Droogers, "Globalization and Pentecostal Success," p. 13.

10. This definition also embraces African-initiated and African-led religious movements and groups that emerged elsewhere beyond the African shores. For a definition of new religious movements from the African context, see Afe Adogame, "Traversing Local-Global Religious Terrain: African New Religious Movements in Europe," *Zeitschrift für Religionswissenschaft* 10 (2002): 33-49.

11. Cf. Philip Jenkins, *The Next Christendom: The Coming of Global Christianity* (Oxford: Oxford University Press, 2002).

beyond their contexts of origin is a significant manifestation and indication of their local vitality.

AICs and pentecostal/charismatics have come to represent a very significant factor in the contemporary life situation of the African Diaspora in Europe and elsewhere. From the 1920s onwards when they made their debut in Great Britain, ANRMs have increasingly made their footprints more conspicuous on the European religious scene. Emerging from varied socio-ethnic milieus and religious constituencies, these groups operate on new levels of organization in which doctrinal differences and ethnic exigencies do not seem to serve as the most vital reference points. Utmost in the minds of many Africans is a space where similar sentiments can be reciprocated. The groups are as varied and complex as the factors accounting for their rapid spread in Europe, in the many different African Christian communities. The Nigerian and Ghanaian Christian initiatives represent one of the largest and most widespread African religious communities in Europe. Their historical emergence in Europe can be located under different epochs.

One of the earliest Christian initiatives was the African Churches Mission (ACM) established in Liverpool in 1922. Daniel Ekarte, trained by the Scottish Mission in Calabar, Eastern Nigeria, was the prime mover behind the movement, promoted by a group that was financially supported by churches in West Africa. The ACM emerged following a successful attempt at gathering a handful of followers. Within a decade, the mission had grown into a center with considerable socio-religious significance, catering to the multifarious needs of the poor black and white population in one of Liverpool's slums. "In the 1930s and 1940s Pastor Daniel was a popular and respected figure in the Hill Street community, both Black and White. His concerns and hence his work were as rooted in the practical as the spiritual."[12] In 1938, the mission worked among about 1,000 men and women and approximately 3,000 children.[13] Owing to the suspicion, distrust, and the high-handed reprehension of the white establishment, he did not fully realize his long-term vision of providing a permanent abode for abandoned children, or of establishing a well-equipped social center and better educational facilities for black children. Financial constraints also stifled the Mission's

12. Marika Sherwood, *Pastor Daniel Ekarte and the African Churches Mission Liverpool 1931-1964* (London: Savannah Press, 1994), p. 32.

13. National Archives, Ghana: CSO 18/12/51. C. Daniel Ekarte, *The African Churches Mission & Training Home*, p. 5, cited in Frieder Ludwig, "Nigerian Christian Initiatives in Great Britain. The African Churches Mission in Liverpool and the Aladura Churches in London Compared: Six Theses," paper read at conference on "The Significance of the African Religious Diaspora in Europe," University of Leeds, 8-11 September 1997, p. 2.

growth, as it had to depend solely on donations and occasional help and assistance from the locality as well as from Africa. The untimely closure of the Mission building, the forceful ejection of Ekarte, and the relocation of the children by the Home Office were conscious attempts at obliterating Ekarte's works and achievements. However, the enthusiasm and vigor with which he pursued his mission and vision shot him into the religious, social, political, and humanitarian limelight and occasioned legacies that have endured until now.

The predecessors of this pioneering effort and initiative were the AICs. Although Africans headed all the churches, the features that distinguished the ACM and the churches that surfaced subsequently within this new geo-cultural space were their ritual systems, worldviews, and modes of operation. The introduction into Europe of a brand of Christianity largely influenced by African culture can be said to have started only from the 1960s, first in Great Britain and afterwards in continental Europe. As Nigerians represented one of the largest African immigrant groups in the United Kingdom, the most visible indigenous group within these religious initiatives was the Aladura.[14] The Aladura presence has been noticed since the inception in London of the first branch of the Church of the Lord-Aladura (CLA) in 1964, the Cherubim and Seraphim (C&S) in 1965, and the Celestial Church of Christ (CCC) in 1967. Other Aladura churches such as the Christ Apostolic Church (CAC) and the Evangelical Church of Yahweh (ECY) followed. As of today, branches of these churches as well as their splinter formations abound in different parts of Europe.

This emergent phase in the early 1960s was characterized by initiatives and activities of temporary migrants, mainly students (of Nigerian origin), businessmen, and some sectors of the diplomatic community. Their transient status in Europe had a corresponding impact on the nature and scope of their proliferation. The last three decades, however, have witnessed the rapid expansion and stability of these churches, in a way that significantly altered and enhanced their earlier membership structure. The possibilities of family reunion and the rising birth rates (first and second generation) within the migrant communities have led to a major shift towards long-term or permanent

---

14. The Aladura movement (one of the AICs) refers to a group of indigenous Christian movements that emerged mainly from western Nigeria from the 1920s. They are so-called because of their penchant and proclivity for prayer, prophecy, visions, dreams, and other charismatic features. "Aladura" literally translates as "the praying people" or "owners of prayers." Churches in this category are the Christ Apostolic Church, the Cherubim & Seraphim, the Church of the Lord — Aladura, the Celestial Church of Christ, and the Evangelical Church of Yahweh, as well as their various appendages and splinter formations.

migrants or settlers, thus bringing far-reaching implications for the status and growth of these religious communities.

Evidently, Africans still largely dominate these religious communities, but through inter-personal contacts and networks, inter-marriages, and conscious evangelistic strategies targeted at both Africans and non-Africans, they have steadily widened their clientele in a way that makes them inter-ethnic and international in outlook. Thus, some of the nucleus groups that met for fellowship and Bible studies in private homes later metamorphosed into full-fledged churches, many with branches all over Europe.[15] Variants of the Aladura category (as described above) have emerged in Europe, either by severing from an existing church or by emanating from the charismatic quality of a leader. A remarkable example is the Aladura International Church with headquarters in London founded by Olu Abiola.[16] As an ordained minister of the Anglican Church in Nigeria, Abiola encountered frustration and humiliation within the Anglican Church when he came to London. Obvious racism led him to shift his religious allegiance and affiliation.

The scramble by African churches for European public space has become more diversified and competitive with the latest entry of pentecostal-charismatic movements such as the Redeemed Christian Church of God (RCCG), the Deeper Christian Life Ministry (DCLM), and the Church of Pentecost International (CPI), which have opened branches or mission posts in European cities. Added to this repertoire are several African-led pentecostal churches in various parts of Europe. Examples are the Christian Church Outreach Mission International (CCOMI) led by Abraham Bediako (Hamburg), Kingsway International Christian Centre (KICC) led by Matthew Ashimolowo (London), the Born-Again Christ Healing Church International led by Fidelia Onyuku-Opukiri (London), and the True Teachings of Christ's Temple (Holland) to mention a few. There are also inter-denominational prayer/fellowship groups and other parachurch organizations that are characterized by rather loose, flexible, and non-formalized organizational hierarchies and administrative structures. These African-led churches and organizations that have proliferated in several parts of Europe from the 1980s may

15. Branches of these churches have been established in parts of the U.K., and in Germany, Austria, the Netherlands, Italy, France, Belgium, and Spain among other places. Some of these churches already experienced schisms in their histories prior to their inception in Europe. Thus, for a particular group, there may now exist some factions that are represented in the European religious context.

16. See Afe Adogame, "Aladura Churches in 20th Century Europe," in Klaus Koschorke, ed., *Transcontinental Links in the History of Non-Western Christianity* (Wiesbaden: Harrassowitz, 2002), pp. 73-86.

be categorized as those that are indigenously African and self-sustaining, and others that rely on external input and assistance.[17]

Individual initiatives or the initiatives of small groups have resulted in the founding of many African churches or church-related organizations. The last two decades have witnessed a new dimension in which conscious strategies for missionary expansion are discerned among the mother churches in Africa that serve as the international headquarters. Old mission departments of churches have been overhauled and streamlined to cope with current socio-economic and political realities while new ones are established. Pastors and missionaries are now commissioned to head existing branches or parishes in Europe or to establish new ones. Such missionaries in most cases rely on finances and stipends from their international headquarters in Africa. The churches often describe this development as "the re-missionization of the (spiritually) dark continent of Europe." This process of "reverse mission" is of immense historical significance, marking one of the ways in which global religious maps are being redrawn. As a novel feature and development, it marks a major change from the earlier period of their existence in Europe, where a nucleus group emerged and sought official recognition or affiliation with headquarters in Africa.

The multiplicity and proliferation of African migrant churches in Europe is also linked to a high rate of schisms. Individuals and groups often sever from each other as a result of issues such as personality clashes, leadership preferences, and socio-ethnic and economic factors. Schismatic groups seem to emerge much more as a result of the inordinate ambition of a member to lead a group, or as a means of controlling financial and material resources, than as a consequence of doctrinal controversies or disagreement. While some members see this splintering trend as detrimental and unhealthy to the general course of African religious communities, others perceive it as one of the most dramatic ways their geographical expansion can be realized.

The membership structures of African migrant churches reveal varied levels of identity, with members emanating from wide-ranging religious backgrounds and orientations to form new religious identities in Europe. Members have switched religious denominational affiliation, or have consciously maintained dual or multiple religious affiliations. These levels of reli-

17. This categorization here does not portray the distinction to be mutually exclusive. It is not rigid but rather elastic in nature. Another distinction lies in the fact that while some exist as branches and parishes of mother churches with headquarters in Africa, others began and have their headquarters in Europe, though with the intent of establishing branches in Africa and elsewhere. For the latter, they emerged and are operating in the new environment while adhering to a particular African religious tradition or worldview.

gious action are largely occasioned by a multiplicity of prevailing socio-economic, cultural, and political circumstances. Although individual preferences prevail, specific circumstances and contextual exigencies in the host society are major elements dictating the nature of identity — single or multiple — forged and desired by migrants. Examples abound of Africans who became Christians for the first time while residing in Europe. The collective identity "African," hitherto not an issue among Africans within their continental shores, comes to assume immense meaning and relevance, thus coalescing the several, multiple identities (ethnic, religious) into what may seem a complex, whole, African identity.

Religious praxis in African migrant churches has also been transformed by new lifestyle characteristics in Europe. Lifestyle and the differences in the balance of work and leisure have changed religious expression. For a number of pragmatic reasons, worship services are sometimes held in the afternoons or evenings instead of the traditional Sunday morning. Ritual time is often carefully selected and negotiated in view of appropriateness and suitability to a majority of the membership. The encounter of African churches with Germans, for example, has indirectly affected the duration of their church services and programs. A typical African worship service could run into several hours. However, as a strategy to attract the German public, many of whom are not used to such prolonged church events, and coupled with financial problems and paucity of space, most African churches are now cautious about long services and have taken deliberate measures to regulate them. Because of harsh climatic conditions and societal values, church programs such as open-air revival services or open-air night vigil rituals cannot be held in Europe in winter, or in summer due to complaints of breach of peace (loudness) from the respective neighborhood. Incessant harassment by and confrontation with their white neighbors has led to a growing preference for a physical space in the industrial sectors of European cities. This tendency of relocating and acquiring landed properties (abandoned warehouses) in the industrial areas for religious purposes is a new phenomenon in Germany, one that I describe as "warehouse churches." As a member of the Christian Church Outreach Mission (CCOM) in Berlin has remarked:

> The choice of buying a property in this industrial part of the city has several advantages. At least since we moved here, we have said bye-bye to complaints and confrontations from German neighbors who continually harass us for being too loud with our music and worship. Here, we can continue without any inhibition to worship our God the way we are used to and in the way God Himself will appreciate. These entire indus-

trial premises are usually like 'ghost yards' on Sundays, that is why we can feel so free to shout as much as we like.

These migrant churches represent pivots of attraction, particularly to their African membership, owing to the fact that they largely replicate the cultural and religious sensibilities of their home context in a way that creates a "home away from home" or a "comfort zone" for many unstable African migrants. The preponderance of language (English and African languages) and the invigoration of the indigenous worldview in their belief and ritual systems explain why they have successfully attracted and converted Africans. For instance, the official language for communication in both the RCCG and CCOM is still predominantly English, but African languages (i.e., Twi, Yoruba, Igbo, Edo) are commonly used in informal social settings within the churches. The emergence of a second branch of the CCOM in Hamburg, with Ghanaian (Twi) language as the sole medium of communication, was in order to cater for Ghanaians who do not comprehend English or speak German fluently. The use of the local language also serves other primary purposes, such as re-creating a sense of the homeland, thereby creating a sense of comfort and familiarity for newcomers who often feel estranged in their new communities. In other words, it is a concrete way of reinforcing cultural or ethnic identity outside the home context. This can be interpreted as a local action of the Ghanaian migrants within the context of global influences.

The African migrant churches have not only served as avenues where old and new identities are reinforced and negotiated, they often forge ways through which new migrants gradually adapt and integrate into the new society. One of the adaptive strategies is through the conscious inauguration of language instruction courses within their church precincts, where languages of the host societies (German, Dutch, French, Italian) and aspects of the local culture are taught to fresh migrants. Language proficiency is stressed as one of the keys to socio-cultural integration, a practical tool for evangelization and an essential asset in job-seeking. As we have shown above, African languages such as Twi are being preserved in a way that articulates and reinforces cultural identity. On the other hand, other churches such as the RCCG forge strategies both to integrate members into the host society and to draw Europeans into their fold. The founding of a German-speaking RCCG parish in Cologne is a forum envisaged to bring Africans and Germans closer together. Such an initiative is meant to draw in interested Germans, many of whom also complain of language barriers in African churches.

3. Appropriation of Media Technologies

Communication has become an integral issue on the question of globalization because it builds bridges between the universally human, the one global place, and local translations of the global.[18] The dramatic increase in the use of transport and new communication facilities suggests that we live in a somewhat "global village," in which each fellow-human being can be reached at short notice, if not instantly. World society is presented as a system of mutual dependency. People, nations, transnational corporations, and religions are all joined to each other.[19] ANRMs are already using new forms of media technologies in information processing and dissemination in their self-insertion and -assertion on the European religious scene. The phenomenon of intra-religious networking among African communities has been further stimulated and enhanced through their access to and appropriation of these new forms of communication (media) technology. This involves the creation and use of computer websites, fax and electronic mail systems, televangelism, audio- and videotapes (home video), books, tracts, magazines, handbills, and leaflets. While openly embracing all sorts of media technologies, most African churches frown on and prohibit the use of cell phones during services within the church precincts. As they claim, the use of these phones disrupts and interrupts communication with God and the heavenly forces, and becomes a distraction during the ritual services. Bold warning notices on bulletin boards at church entrances — "Switch off your mobile phones! Only God's calls are received here!"; "Make and receive God's calls here but not men's!" — vividly illustrate one of the ways in which African migrant churches negotiate modernity.

Hitherto, media such as print, radio, and television have been used for the translation and transmission of their messages. What is relatively new is their creation and appropriation of space on the Internet and the production of Christian home videos. We argue that the recourse to new, alternative evangelistic strategies is intricately tied to the socio-cultural realities of the host European society. The somewhat individualistic nature of the society has largely rendered some of the known conventional modes inept and far less productive. Thus, the "personal" modes of communication (i.e., door-to-door, street-to-street, marketplace and bus evangelism) have given way to more "impersonal," "neutral" modes (i.e., computer websites, e-mail, fax). The rele-

---

18. Barrie Axford, *The Global System: Economics, Politics and Culture* (New York: St. Martin's Press, 1995), p. 28.

19. Droogers, "Globalization and Pentecostal Success," p. 51.

vance and urgency these alternative modes of communication demand in the host European context suggest why virtually all these websites have been established, developed, and maintained in Europe, the United States, or elsewhere outside Africa.[20] Analytically, however, the new development in mission strategies with the increasing use of the new media for membership recruitment and evangelism has resulted more in a qualitative change in their religiosity rather than a quantitative change in membership.

The CCC[21] seeks to create a global network through the use of Internet websites and e-mail.[22] In a "web release" on 15 December 1997, announcing its (Riverdale, U.S.) presence on the Internet, it stated *inter alia:*

> Halleluyah!!! . . . Celestial Church of Christ now has a dominant presence on the World Wide Web. The main focus of this page is to present a unified and cohesive communication vehicle for Celestial Church as a whole, world-wide. . . . As the web site evolves, we hope to use it as a vehicle to communicate news about Celestial Church of Christ on a global basis, both information geared toward Celestians and non-Celestians alike.

The U.K. site complements this objective through its mission statement, which reads in part: "To introduce CCC to the whole world . . . to bring all the parishes together by obtaining free e-mail addresses for interested parishes and contribute to the free flow of information in the church . . . to use the medium of the Internet as a vehicle to recruit new members. . . ."

The official website of CLA was established in 1999.[23] One of its introduc-

---

20. Closely related to this is the fact that a large percentage of their members in Africa do not have access to the World Wide Web, are totally unaware of the existence of these church web pages, and even what and how the shape of a PC system looks like.

21. For details on the use of media by the CCC, see A. Adogame, *Celestial Church of Christ: The Politics of Cultural Identity in a West African Prophetic-Charismatic Movement* (Frankfurt: Peter Lang, 1999), pp. 82-89.

22. See for instance the website address: http://www.celestialchurch.com (operated by a parish in Riverdale, U.S.). Similar website services operate in the United Kingdom and France.

23. See the official Church of the Lord (Aladura) web page at the address: http://www.aladura.de. It was created and managed by Dr. Rufus Ositelu, who was the founder and leader of the Langen-Frankfurt (Germany) branch and also the General Overseer of the European branches of the church. He is currently the Primate of the Church of the Lord Aladura Worldwide (CLA). The web administrator still remains the incumbent Primate as his e-mail address shows: aladura-rufus.ositelu@t-online.de; rufus-ositelu @beta.linkserve.com; primate-cla@beta.linkserve.com.

tory statements announces that "the Church of the Lord (Aladura) is conscious of her mission to spread the good news of our LORD Jesus Christ to every nook and corner of the world." It describes the four tenets of the church as "Pentecostal in Power, Biblical in Pattern, Evangelical in Ministry, and Ecumenical in Outlook." The Internet could serve as a kind of status booster for the CLA, as it contains a long list of local and international religious and ecumenical organizations to which it belongs or to which it is affiliated. This in our view gives some kind of religious credibility to the group, especially in a society where such a group could be easily "demonized" and waved off as a cult or sect.

In the RCCG Internet Outreach, the introductory statement on the parish directory states *inter alia:*

> Over the years The Redeemed Christian Church of God has experienced an explosive growth with branches being planted all over the world. It has become pertinent to create a directory and online database for all The Redeemed Christian Church of God parishes worldwide — this will enable us do a complete, relational online database that will be useful for the Body of Christ. Furthermore the online database will help us in our evangelism, fellowship and interaction among member parishes. It will also serve to assist travelers in their efforts to find a place of worship wherever they find themselves.[24]

The vision and goals of the members as expressed in the RCCG "Mission Statement" published on their site include the following:

> It is our goal to make heaven. It is our goal to take as many people as possible with us. In order to accomplish our goals, holiness will be our lifestyle. In order to take as many people with us as possible, we will plant churches within five minutes walking distance in every city and town of developing countries; and within five minutes driving distance in every city and town of developed countries. We will pursue these objectives until every nation in the world is reached for JESUS CHRIST OUR LORD.

Though these goals may appear too ambitious, idealistic, and utopian to attain, it is significant that the church has demonstrated optimism and enthusiasm towards the realization of its global vision. The church is not only

24. See the official website of the RCCG at www.rccg.org created and maintained by the RCCG Internet Project, Houston, Texas.

concerned with the local setting but what transpires beyond it, within the so-called "developing" and "developed" countries. The increasing gaze on the global scene is made clearer through the "annual prophecies" vouchsafed to the church by the General Overseer, Pastor E. A. Adeboye. Until 1999, the prophecies had been categorized into three: for individuals, for Nigeria, and for the RCCG. In the RCCG Prophecies for 2000 and 2001, the scope of the prophecies was enlarged to include the international scene. As Adeboye himself has said, the reason for going into this area is that the world has become a global village.[25] Such a remark by the leader reveals its self-understanding within a global framework.

African (Ghanaian) migrants founded the Christian Church Outreach International (CCOMI) in Hamburg, Germany, in 1982. Although the aim of the group was to establish what it called an "international faith organization," yet at the moment, Africans still largely dominate its membership. From Hamburg, the church has spread to other parts of Germany, Europe, and the United States, as well as to Africa.[26] The church is involved in establishing ecumenical and intra-religious networks. The opening statements of the CCOM website lend credence to the extent of their intra-religious affiliation: "We are a member of the International Communion of Charismatic Churches (ICCC) and a member of the Bund Freikirchlicher Pfingstgemeinden (BFP) Germany (Association of German Pentecostal Churches)."[27]

Another way through which the ANRMs have appropriated new technologies is through the production and distribution of what has been called Christian home videos on the one hand, and through their space appropriation in global religious TV networks. Two examples that readily come to mind are the Mount Zion Faith Ministries International (MZFMI) and the Kingsway International Church Centre (KICC). The MZFMI self-identification is as a "full-time evangelical drama and film ministries" whose mission is "to evangelize the world through drama."[28] These films have become very popular in sub-

---

25. Unabridged (unedited) versions of the Annual Prophecies delivered by the General Overseer, Pastor E. A. Adeboye, are published on the RCCG website. The prophecies are usually publicly announced at the Annual Special Holy Ghost Festival.

26. The phenomenon of African New Religious Movements established and with headquarters outside the African continent and now establishing branches in parts of Africa is an interesting feature of globalization. This supports our earlier view that expresses the fluidity and dynamism of globalization processes. See also KICC founded in London (1992) by a Nigerian migrant, Matthew Ashimolowo. The church plans to plant branches back in Africa, starting in Nigeria and Ghana.

27. See CCOMI official website at http://www.ccomi.org.

28. The MZFMI started in Nigeria but now has branches in Europe and America. As of

Saharan Africa (particularly in Nigeria and Ghana) through domestic and public screening, as well as among African Diaspora communities. As Femi Awoniyi aptly notes:

> Video film as an entertainment medium is becoming a bulwark against the much-feared cultural repercussion of globalisation — the home video culture in Nigeria is transcending the whole continent. Apart from having inspired a similar industry in Ghana and the Gambia, films released in these countries find their way to the other English-speaking countries on the continent and to the African Diaspora worldwide.[29]

The religious and social impact of this video genre on the viewers cannot be underestimated.[30] A section of the page is devoted to "testimonies" and "comments" of a wide range of viewers. The fact that such testimony genres emanate from Africa, Europe, America, and other parts of the world explains the local-global nexus these "home videos" have come to assume. The successful commodification of home videos in and outside Africa has also drastically reduced the quality of production as well as the cogency of their storylines or messages. Although piracy and the absence of effective copyright laws in Nigeria have bedeviled the burgeoning industry, it is having tremendous influence in shaping African popular culture.

The KICC is often described as one of the largest pentecostal churches in the U.K. The churches are known for their prodigious appropriation of the new media technology. As the church asserts, "We recognise the effectiveness of using the media to communicate and draw the attention of the world to the good news. We do this by our Winning Ways Programme."[31] The Winning Ways television program claims to transmit across twenty-one European nations and has a potential viewing audience of several million in Europe as well as in Africa. Programs are aired on the following channels:

2000, it had produced at least twenty films, including *Agbara Nla, Perilous Time, Ide Esu,* etc.

29. See Femi Awoniyi, "Video Film Uniting Africa," *African Courier* 6, no. 31 (April/May 2003): 9, 26.

30. See details of testimonies and views expressed on the Testimony section of the MZFMI website at www.mzfm.org/.

31. "The Winning Ways Programme" is broadcast on radio and television both within and outside the U.K. The programs are produced from the various teachings of Pastor Matthew Ashimolowo. The Winning Ways Programme is categorized into TV/Radio, T.O.P. 1000 Club, Video Technical, Audio Technical, and Tape Production. See details at http://www.kicc.org.uk.

Europe (Christian Channel Europe,[32] Premier Radio London, BBC Radio Leicester), Nigeria (NTA 2 Channel 5, NTA Channel 10, OGTV Channel 22, PRTV Channel 21, and Radio 90.5), and Ghana (Ghana TV). The church is involved in intra-religious networks and organizes conferences and crusades that draw worldwide participants. The annual conference tagged "Gathering of Champions" is a forum that attracts an international audience of Christians.

4. Are We Not Also Global and International?

From an analytical standpoint, this chapter makes a basic distinction between the global self-assertion and understanding of African churches on the one hand, and actual global structures or networks on the other. For instance, viewed from the level of systems (insider view), the self-understanding of most African churches in Europe is revealed in the assertion that their churches transcend geographical, racial, color, and social-class distinctions. This is largely exemplified by their self-identification as global, worldwide, and international. Such appellations indicate their religiously inspired transnationalism and their wide variety of international linkages. In this way, Christian religious identity is placed above ethnic (African) identity. While some of these churches are geographically spread across Europe, others are seeking to plant branches too. Thus, there are groups with a single branch that already attach such labels as global, worldwide, or international, so declaring their intent to transcend local boundaries. It was this noticeable global dispersal of these churches that perhaps informed Ter Haar's suggestion to re-christen them "African International Churches," retaining the old initials AIC but assuming a new, contemporary meaning. She hints that "Most churches in fact label themselves as 'international churches,' expressing their aspiration to be part of the international world in which they believe themselves to have a universal task."[33]

Examined from the outside, these churches have yet to gain significant inroads judging by the membership ratio of Europeans and other non-Africans. The dual strategy according to these churches was first to reach the African public in Europe with the end purpose of using them as a bridge to further

---

32. The Christian Channel Europe is now known as "the God Channel"/"God Digital." Matthew Ashimolowo is on the Board of Reference of the Christian Channel Europe, and the KICC program is screened from time to time on "the God Channel."

33. Gerrie Ter Haar, *Halfway to Paradise: African Christians in Europe* (Cardiff: Cardiff Academic Press, 1998), p. 24.

reach out to the wider European public. The relatively small non-African (for example, German) membership is largely through inter-racial couples or friendships, and sometimes as a result of personal/impersonal evangelism. Although the membership structure may be transformed in the future as the churches gain inroads in Europe, it currently appears that African churches in Europe continue to oscillate as the loci of identity, community, and security primarily for African immigrants.

The conspicuous and symbolic display of global operational frameworks through the hoisting of flags or banners at the pulpits and within the church vicinity forms another common characteristic of African churches. Thus, around the pulpit or altar in a typical African church, at least ten to twenty colorful national flags or flags representing some ecumenical organizations may be counted. Each flag represents a country to which the church has branched out or where there is some form of religious affiliation, or a body/group with whom they have already established ecumenical relationship. This is seen somewhat as a feature that adds credibility or boosts the image and strength of the local church.

5. Forging Intra-Religious Networks

The initiative of the African religious communities towards joining and creating new ecumenical links or ties at local, national, continental, and inter- and trans-continental levels is worth mentioning. Examples of such intra-religious networks include the African Christian Council[34] (ACC) Hamburg, the West Yorkshire African Caribbean Council of Churches[35] (WYACC), the Council of African Churches in Germany (CACG), the Council of African and Caribbean Churches (CACC) in the U.K., Churches Together in Britain and Ireland (CTBI), the British Council of Churches (BCC), the Council of African Christian Communities in Europe (CACCE), and the World Council of Churches (WCC). The motives for joining or engaging in intra-religious

---

34. ACC has a membership of twenty-two churches, and German congregations for the purpose of worship services temporarily accommodate most of them. The Council seeks to promote cordial relations with German churches and also to work with other Christian bodies in and outside Germany. See Alex Afram, "African Christian Council, Hamburg," *International Review of Mission (IRM)* 89, no. 354 (July 2000): 434-35.

35. WYACC is a collection of some nineteen congregations from the inner city areas of the country, viz. Leeds, Bradford, Huddersfield, and Halifax, covering some ten different denominations. See Tony Parry, "West Yorkshire African Caribbean Council of Churches, England," *IRM* 89, no. 354 (July 2000): 436-37.

networks are various and complex. Basically, most African Christian communities will locate this phenomenon as a vital strategy for global mission and evangelism, or what they popularly refer to as "mission reversed" or the "re-missionization of heathen Europe."[36] Others express their interest in net-working, and engage in such processes as a way of acquiring status or legitimacy within European societies. The public denigration — including by the host European churches — of these African religious communities as sects, cults, and exotic religions has generated fear of exclusion, ostracism, and further "demonization" within the European spiritual marketplace and society at large.[37] Thus, while some of the relatively "young" religious groups may see their involvement in such networks as a means of status enhancement in Europe, there are some institutionally and financially well-established groups that exercise restraint in such networking endeavors on the grounds that they are already secure and well established.

The significance of local and global networks among African churches in Africa and in Europe cannot be overemphasized. One way of comprehending this process is to see how such networks, in the "home" (African) and the "host" (European) context, are assuming increasing importance for African migrants. The range and nature of ties include new ecumenical affiliations, pastoral exchanges between Europe and Africa, special events and conferences, prayer networks, Internet sites, international ministries, publications, video, and televangelism. This reveals a two-directional "flow," both sending and receiving links. Thus, the relevance of African migrant churches within the framework of globalization is not merely with reference to the unique expression of African Christianity they exhibit, a feature described above as their self-assertion and preservation of religious identity. Rather, their pertinence lies in the fact that they constitute international ministries and groups that have implications on a global scale.[38] The impact and import of their geo-numerical spread, driven by a vision of winning converts, is that it offers a unique opportunity to analyze their impact at a local European level.

The proliferation of social ties and relationships among African migrants, and between migrant churches and their home bases, has implications that need to be understood contextually. African churches in Europe frequently organize programs that are local in nature but have a focus link-

---

36. Communication with Rev. Dr. Rufus Ositelu, Primate of the Church of the Lord — Aladura Worldwide, 15 June 2001. See Rufus Ositelu, "Missio Africana! The Role of an African Instituted Church in the Mission Debate," *IRM* 89, no. 354 (July 2000): 384-86.

37. Roswith Gerloff, "Editorial," *IRM* 89, no. 354 (July 2000): 276-77.

38. See Stephan Hunt, "'A Church for All Nations': The Redeemed Christian Church of God," *Pneuma* 24, no. 2 (2002): 185.

ing the local church with other pentecostals globally. In addition, these churches play a central role in providing a social space where members can meet one another and forge other networks for mutual support and assistance. Such social networks often transcend religious boundaries into social, cultural, and economic spheres in the form of social-cultural associations (i.e., Ghana Social Club, Oduduwa Descendants Union, Igbo Forum). These networks serve as "social capital," especially for the new African migrants into Europe. The sense of mutual obligation (the practical and emotional support given to one another, often among individuals who did not know one another prior to joining the church) is akin to relationships found within families, friendships, and neighborhoods in the home context.

One feature that is becoming popular among the African congregations is what may be called "the switching or exchange of pulpits." As a result of the increasing network processes, different churches now embark on joint worship services and programs. A leader of a particular church could be invited to preach in another, irrespective of doctrinal leanings and emphasis. This development is not restricted to the African communities alone, but also between them and their host European churches,[39] which in most cases have provided accommodation for the African congregations through rent, lease, or mutual agreement. Instances of tensions between Africans and their host German churches may be lucidly illustrated by an incident that occurred during a "Healing-Deliverance Ritual" organized by an African migrant church in Cologne. As a leader of the African church described it:

> Members of the host local German church were in attendance in their numbers. As prayers were enacted during the "altar call," a German woman alongside some Africans fell flat on the nave of the church. Members of the African Pentecostal congregation recognized and interpreted this phenomenon as the action and visible manifestation of the Holy Spirit. However, the visiting Germans, whose pastor swung instantaneously and dashed to his office where he called the attention of the city ambulance service, understood this differently. All attempts to restrain him and to explain the actual situation proved abortive. Although the emergency doctors who rushed the woman to the hospital ended their examination without any negative results, yet this singular event

39. It must be noted that such collaboration is not devoid of restraints on both sides, especially bearing in mind the concern about loyalty and potential loss of members to other groups.

had strained the relationship between the African and German congregations respectively.

Thus, while various attempts have been made through language instruction, joint services, etc., at adapting African members into the new German context, the varied religious worldviews and cultural backgrounds have perpetuated a "stark cultural wall" that defies any wholesome process of integration. Our interpretation is that this "wall" on the one hand symbolizes a reproduction of religio-cultural identity as well as the construction of a new migrant identity, thus creating and reinforcing a kind of locality (as opposed to globality) at the religious level within the German public sphere. The other end of the "wall" encapsulates the strains and tensions experienced by Germans in the task of adjusting to these new processes and worldview, or at least in the juxtaposition of both worldviews.

6. Conclusion

This chapter has demonstrated how and to what extent ANRMs, particularly African migrant churches, are burgeoning in Europe. In spite of its multi-ethnic configuration, the relative membership dominance by Africans suggests that the phenomenon largely represents loci of identity, community, and security. These religious communities also serve as an abode of spiritual solace, especially for many political and economic asylum seekers, refugees in Europe. The religious roles — in addition to the social, economic, and political roles — that African churches have come to assume in Europe help us to understand the meaning and significance of migrant churches for Africans within local and global ambits. The variety of physical manifestations of the African churches in Europe could be referred to as "the localization of African immigrant religious culture." This includes the overwhelming display of traditional African garb during services and other programs, the ebullient rendition of songs and choruses in local languages (Twi, Akan, Yoruba, Igbo, Edo) side-by-side with the English language, and the provision and collective sharing of meals during services and other programs. Through the replication of these distinctive objects and worship styles, the churches formally recognize, support, and thereby reinforce and re-enact ethnic-religious identity and cultural continuity. These attributes and features are evident in such a way that they are sometimes alienating to non-Africans, who readily opt for groups where they will not constitute an apparent "minority of outsiders." Thus, African migrant churches comprised largely of immigrants typically develop a set of structures and practices designed simultaneously to help their members maintain and reproduce their cultural and religious heritage on the one hand, while assisting immigrants in adapting to the new, host European context on the other. In this way, the churches both ensure continuity of worldview and assume adaptive strategies of change. In the new geo-cultural setting of Europe, African churches face a myriad of "roadblocks." These vary from cultural barriers such as language, paucity of religious space, loud services (and hence hostility from neighbors), transience of their membership, finance, weather conditions, the nature of some practices (i.e., prohibition of alcohol and cigarette smoking), and even the long duration of their services. The forging of, and involvement in, intra-religious networks may in the long run make their presence more visible and their impact more deeply felt within the European religious scene. Since the physical presence of many ANRMs on the World Wide Web is relatively recent, it will no doubt take a while before one can ascertain the effectiveness of the impersonal medium as an alternative vehicle for evangelization, and in fact how and whether it has made significant impact on members as well as on the religious landscape of Europe.

PART V

Cultural and Socio-Political Dimensions of Global Processes

CHAPTER 14

Christianity, Ethnicity, and Structural Violence: The Northeast India Case

JOHN PARRATT

1. Introduction

The majority of former colonies may fairly be described as colonial constructs, in that their borders and the ethnic composition of their populations (and thus the resulting stresses of inter-ethnic and inter-religious conflict) were determined by the historical processes of colonial expansion. India, by contrast, could not unreasonably be called a *post-colonial* construct.[1] Negotiations for its independence involved not only partition (ostensibly on religious grounds) but also the beginnings of the incorporation into the newly independent India of the princely states and other (mostly tribal) territories that were only very loosely administered by Britain. This process was still ongoing in 1975 (with the taking over of Sikkim). Around two-fifths of present-day India was never directly part of the British Empire, and only joined the Indian Union by processes of negotiation, backed up in several cases by intimidation and military action.[2] This process (which came to the attention of the international community specially in the cases of Hyderabad, Kashmir, and Goa) also significantly affected the northeastern region of India. Of the seven states in the northeast, only Assam (which then included the present Magalaya) was fully administered by the British. The princely native states of

1. A point acknowledged by Sunil Khilnani, *The Idea of India* (London: Hamish Hamilton, 1997).

2. V. P. Menon's highly partisan and sanitized *The Integration of the Indian States* (Hyderabad: Orient Longman, 1956) is an "official" history that skates over the real issues of conflict. His date for the absorption of Manipur and Tripura is two years too early.

Manipur and Tripura became independent in 1947, and the tribal areas of the Naga Hills (which became the basis of the present Nagaland), Lushai Hills (now Mizoram), and NEFA (now Arunachal Pradesh) were loosely administered but not fully integrated into British India.

The northeastern region in general is sharply different from the remainder of the subcontinent. In contrast to the broadly Aryan-Dravidian peoples of the heartlands of India, the peoples of the northeast are ethnically Mongoloid, and the bulk of its peoples migrated into the region from the east. Its languages furthermore are unrelated to Sanskrit, but belong to the quite different Tibeto-Burman language group. Its cultures, despite influence from the Indian subcontinent, in many ways resemble more those of east Asia. Historically, too, the region was never part of the great empires of the subcontinent, nor was it greatly involved in the Indian Congress struggle for independence. After Indian independence in 1947, ethnic, historical, and cultural differences were reinforced by geographical isolation. With the removal of West Bengal to become East Pakistan (and subsequently Bangladesh) the northeast became tenuously linked to the rest of India only by the fourteen-kilometer-wide Siliguri corridor, so that now less than 1 percent of its borders are with the rest of India. The Congress policy of aggressive integrationism after 1947, paradoxically, reinforced this isolation. Foreign investment is practically nonexistent, internal investment very limited, and all communications go through Delhi or Calcutta. Much of the region has been declared a "restricted area"; foreigners are scarcely permitted access, international media and human rights organizations are excluded, and some areas are off limits even to Indian nationals.

This isolation was reinforced by a form of narrow ethnocentrism which assumed that the Hindi-speaking "Aryan" tradition represented the only valid form of Indianness. The resulting "integrationist" policies, which lasted until comparatively recently, thus pressured a region that is ethnically and linguistically quite different to conform to what has been called the culture of the Hindi cow-belt. While the distinctiveness of the "Dravidian" south had to be recognized, the peculiarities of the Mongoloid cultures of the northeast (which have an equally great cultural history) have never yet been fully acknowledged. As Verghese comments, "The dominant Aryan bent of national thinking has accommodated the Dravidian reality but has yet to appreciate the Mongoloid feature of the Indian ethos."[3]

The claim that India is unified by an underlying Hindu cultural tradition,

3. B. G. Verghese, *India's Northeast Resurgent: Ethnicity, Insurgency, Governance, Development*, 2nd ed. (New Delhi: Konark, 1997).

often used by integrationists, is unconvincing. As far as the northeast is concerned it is only the Brahmaputra valley and the valley of Manipur that were extensively hinduized. Even in the latter, Hinduism is a comparatively recent importation, and Meitei (i.e., plains people as opposed to hill tribals) society now shows many signs of becoming post-Hindu, as political identity has become entangled with religious identity.[4] The hills, which were never hinduized, are today mainly Christian, with Mizoram and Nagaland being around 80 percent Christian, and Meghalaya also having a large Christian population.

Indian integrationism is based on what one might call the fallacy of the concept of the "mainstream." Naorem Sanajaoba quotes a telling comment of Sunanda K. Datta-Ray. Speaking of the ignorance of Indians in general about the "Mongolian" heritage of the northeast, Datta-Ray writes: "Deep in the Indian psyche lies the belief, lately encouraged by obscurantist political groups, that Bharat is really Aryavrata, or the Hindi heartland, and that outlying districts which do not conform to its manners, customs, language and religion are colonial possessions and must be ruled as such until they can be absorbed in a superior code."[5] The Mongoloid peoples of the northeast frequently claim that in the rest of the country they are regarded as foreigners and that an attitude of misplaced racial superiority and disdain has characterized their treatment by "mainstream" Indians. The parochialism of successive Delhi governments and the widespread ignorance about the region, even on the part of educated Indians, has created a "them and us" mentality on both sides that has been one contributory factor to civil unrest and armed conflict. As late as 1988 one of the government's own reports could speak of a "two way deficit of understanding with the rest of the country." It is therefore no surprise that an area as large as the northeast, separated as it is from the bulk of the subcontinent by its geography, history, ethnicity, languages, and for a majority by its religion, and which was only marginally affected by the independence struggle, should regard itself as not part of the so-called "mainstream" as defined by the Delhi-wallah. Unfortunately central governments have deliberately reinforced the marginalization of the region by a policy of isolation.

---

4. As long ago as 1980, V. I. K. Sarin, *India's North East in Flames* (New Delhi: Vikas, 1980), p. 116, could claim that "of late Meiteis are refusing to be recognized as Hindus," and the revival of the pre-Hindu Sanamahi religion continues apace; see S. N. Arambam Parratt and J. Parratt, "Reclaiming the Gods: A Neo-Traditional Protest Movement in Manipur," *Archiv Orientální* 67 (1999): 241-48.

5. "The Genesis of Insurgency in Manipur," in Naorem Sanajaoba, ed., *Manipur Past and Present: The Heritage and Ordeals of a Civilization*, 3 vols. (Delhi: Mittal Publications, 1988-95), vol. 1, p. 262.

It is the only area of India for which special permits are required.[6] From soon after independence large tracts have been classified as "disturbed areas" and subject to oppressive military occupation, without however the formal declaration of an emergency.

B. K. Roy Burman has pointed out that claims of neo-colonialism are justified and that there has been a sharp suppression of talk of self-determination.[7] Resentment at political subjection, and economic and social neglect, have understandably given rise to protest, both civil and insurgent,[8] both peaceful and violent. This has resulted in turn in the attempt by Delhi to impose its will by military force. Some political advance has been made, notably in Mizoram. But half a century of severe military repression has in the main solved nothing, but rather increased the feeling of alienation, even on the part of peace-loving civil populations. Sadly, there seems to be little political will on either side to create a climate of basic human rights that alone would make development a possibility.

6. It is true that these restrictions (like much other oppressive legislation) are built upon colonial regulations, in this case the "inner line." The inner line restrictions were originally meant to preserve tribals from exploitation by Indians from the rest of the subcontinent. Its present operation certainly does not succeed in doing that, and there are justifiable complaints (especially from Manipur) that outsiders dominate the economy out of all proportion to their numbers, and flood the region with unwanted unskilled labor. The modern version of the inner line, "restricted areas," functions simply to prevent outside access to sensitive areas and thus prevent the dissemination in the media of the true conditions in those states.

7. B. K. Roy Burman, "Insurgency: Its Dynamics and Vision for Northeast India," in B. Pakem, ed., *Insurgency in North East India* (New Delhi: Omsons, 1997), p. 26.

8. The term "insurgency" is far from satisfactory, since there is within it the implication of illegitimacy and that the insurgent is an insurrectionist. Burman, "Insurgency," p. 21, rightly points out that "insurgency is a circuit of *reciprocal violence* (our italics), where the players are the state establishment and the challengers of the same." Pakem, *Insurgency in North East India*, p. 3, states that in his informal meetings with leaders of these movements they had never described themselves as "insurgents" but rather as patriots, freedom fighters, defenders of their people, and so on. "Insurgent" is therefore not a self-designation but a term generally applied by their opponents. A similar problem is raised by the use of the phrase "security forces." It is clear that sympathizers of insurgents (whether passive or active) do not regard the military, paramilitaries, and sometimes the civil police as contributing to their personal security, but rather as sources of institutional violence. The use of both these terms is very problematic. However, since this terminology seems to have established itself in the literature I shall use it for the purposes of this paper. For a fuller account of the causes of insurgency, the militarization of Manipur, and the widespread abuse of civil rights see John Parratt, *Wounded Land: Politics and Identity in Modern Manipur* (New Delhi: Mittal, 2005).

2. Christianity in Nagaland and Manipur

Protestant Christianity in these states is dominated by the Baptists, and was largely established by the American Baptists, who traditionally have a strongly evangelical and biblicist approach. Catholicism was introduced much later, but has grown in importance, largely due to its emphasis on educational work. The removal of foreign missionaries in the 1960s affected the Baptists more than the Catholics, who relied upon a large contingent of south Indian priests, mainly Silesians.

The earliest presence of missions in the northeast, both Catholic and Protestant, was almost incidental. By the early 1800s western missions were seeking an overland route into China, as access through the eastern sea coast of China was becoming more difficult. In pursuance of this aim the Baptists established a short-lived mission in Guwahati in 1829, and later a more permanent one further east at Sadiya. The first mission contact with the Naga tribes was in 1838, and the first Naga Christian community was established, by an Assamese evangelist, among the Ao subtribe in 1872. Thereafter other groups were gradually contacted, and Kohima (present capital of Nagaland) and Wokha became important centers for Christianity among the Angami Nagas. The other main tribal grouping, the Kukis, only began to convert to Christianity in the first decade of the twentieth century.

Manipur, as an independent princely state, was closed to missionaries until after the Anglo-Manipuri war of 1891. Subsequently very limited educational and medical mission work was permitted only in the hills (over which the British retained some control after the war), but was forbidden among the hinduized plains Meiteis. The first evangelism was carried out among the Tangkhul Nagas in Ukhrul, and subsequently at Kangpokpi (which became a center for Kuki Christianity).

Despite early reluctance, Christianity spread among both tribal groups. There was a substantial increase due to the so-called Manipur revival, which began in 1916. This actually began in the Chin (Lushai) Hills (the present Mizoram) and at first affected mainly the Kukis, but by the 1920s had spread to Manipuri Nagas. In the beginning there was some persecution of Christians by the traditionalists, and mutual suspicion between the Naga subgroups was only slowly broken down. Despite the acceptance of a common faith, the age-old antagonism between Naga and Kuki continues. While it is true, as Downs indicates,[9] that Christianity has been a unifying factor, it has

9. F. S. Downs, *The History of Christianity in India*, Vol. V, part 5, *Christianity in North*

nonetheless been singularly unsuccessful in eradicating completely the inter- and intra-tribal conflict.[10] The relationship between the evangelical Baptists of the Council of Baptist Churches in North East India and the Catholics has not been smooth.[11]

While figures are difficult to assess, there can be no doubt that Christianity has become the "official religion" (Downs) of Nagaland and Mizoram, and probably 80 percent of the population of these states would regard themselves as Christian. In Manipur most of the Naga and Kuki tribals, who make up around a third of the population of some two million, may also be regarded as Christian. There is also a small, but growing, interest in Christianity among the Meiteis. This may in part be a political, as well as a religious, protest against the Indian mainstream. However, Manipur, like other parts of the northeast, has been the recipient in recent years of a wholly counterproductive proliferation of fundamentalist splinter groups, usually financed from America, which has resulted in the emergence of a confusing (to the non-Christian) number of mini-churches.

3. Political Resistance

The area known as the Naga Hills (the present Nagaland minus the Tuenseng tract) was only loosely administered by the British. On the independence of India in 1947, Naga leaders made it clear that in their view the Naga people had never historically been part of India and that they did not wish to join the Indian Union. The Hydari agreement concluded between Sir Akbar Hydari, governor of Assam, and the Naga leaders recognized their right to develop separately during a ten-year period under the general superintendence of the governor of Assam, and that the final decision regarding union or independence would be made thereafter. The Indian government interpreted this to mean that after ten years full integration would be effected. Meantime, in August 1947, the National Nagaland Council (NNC) declared independence for the region, and held a plebiscite that gave absolute support for this declaration. India naturally rejected the plebiscite, and the Nagas then boycotted the

---

East India in the Nineteenth and Twentieth Centuries (Bangalore: Church History Association of India, 1992), p. 132.

10. For example, the Kuki-Naga massacres of the 1990s, and the in-fighting among different subgroups in the National Socialist Council of Nagaland: see Phanjoubam Tarapot, Bleeding Manipur (New Delhi: Har-Anand, 2003).

11. Indeed, D. Syiemlieh, A Brief History of the Catholic Church in Nagaland (Shillong: Vendrame Institute Publications, 1990), p. 75, claims that a persecution of Catholic Nagas was provoked by the largely Baptist NSCN underground.

Indian elections. Nehru paid a flying visit to both Nagaland and Manipur in 1953, but ignored the voice of the people in both states. Integration, masterminded by Sirdar Patel and V. P. Menon, was put into brutal effect. Repressive measures began in 1953. Three years later the Indian army occupied towns and villages, some civilians were shot, and their corpses were displayed publicly as a warning to insurgents. That same year the NNC set up its rival government. The Indian government gave some ground. The Tuenseng tract was joined to the Naga Hills in 1956 and the region given some autonomy. Nagaland became the first of the smaller northeastern regions to be granted statehood in 1963.

In 1972 the NNC and the "Federal Government of Nagaland" were declared unlawful. The Indian Government negotiated the Shillong Accord with moderates in 1975, and this caused a split within the Naga elite. The National Socialist Council of Nagaland (NSCN) was formed by a group of leaders (including Muivah, a Tangkhul Naga from Ukhrul district in Manipur) and went underground as a guerrilla organization. Attacks on Indian army and paramilitary personnel increased. In-fighting between the insurgent groups took place (often fueled by ethnic subdivisions). In 1980 Indian and Myanmar armies inflicted a severe defeat on the NSCN, but it subsequently regrouped and remains a powerful insurgent force.

Manipur, meanwhile, despite being able to trace its history as an independent kingdom back nearly two thousand years, and being the first state on the Indian subcontinent to hold full and free elections, was summarily annexed in 1949. It was to be 1972 before Mrs. Gandhi bowed to mounting pressure both within and outside Manipur to restore it to full statehood, but now within the Indian Union. Underground insurgent groups, whose origins reach back before 1947, re-emerged in the 1960s and remain a potent force. Some attempts, with varying degrees of success, have been made to bring together the chaotic mix of insurgency movements in both northeast India and Myanmar. The situation is however fraught with intra- and inter-ethnic rivalries, which have manifested themselves in periodic explosions of violence.

4. Abuses Committed by the Security Forces

It is not our purpose in this paper to detail the abuses of human rights that have been perpetrated under the cover of the Armed Forces Special Powers Act (AFSPA; see below), and in any case a full inventory of the atrocities committed by the military and paramilitary forces is not possible. Many acts go unreported, especially in rural areas and where victims have neither the education nor political understanding to report them, and in those cases where complaints are made there is hardly ever any redress. India's "closed door" policy towards the northeast also means that foreign journalists and human rights workers are kept out, and that reports which appear in the Indian press are often heavily sanitized. The local press reports on deaths, disappearances, abuses, and protests on a very regular basis, but often without editorial comment. Abuses are often directed not towards suspects but at innocent civilians, including women and juveniles. Civil rights workers have frequently been targeted in order to attempt to silence them. Meira Paibi, the Meitei women's movement devoted to passive protest against abuses, has often been met with physical violence on the part of the paramilitaries, even against pregnant and very elderly women. Detailed accounts of the worst abuses are therefore difficult to get access to. However, I shall refer subsequently to some of the more public examples to indicate the scale of structural violence. These are only a sample of an abuse that involves a continuous depressing catalogue of random shootings of civilians, deaths in custody, disappearances, detainings contrary even to AFSPA, rapes, arrests, and torture, all of which occur regularly.[12] What characterizes almost all cases is that they are simple acts of revenge visited upon an unarmed and non-violent civilian population for attacks on paramilitaries by insurgency groups. One has to ask whether it has become a policy to attempt to restrain insurgency by the abuse of non-combatants. This is simply, as an Amnesty International paper put it, a pattern of violence.

As Pradip Phanjoubam points out,[13] there are two levels of violence in situations such as obtain in Manipur. The higher is the disregard for basic human life on the part of those whose official role should be one of protection,

---

12. Sources: for a list of 147 acts of violence committed between February and June 1973 see the Minority Rights Group (MRG) report *India and the Nagas*, pp. 28-30; the Human Rights Forum, Manipur, paper on "Death of Civil Liberties and Democratic Rights in Manipur," Delhi, dated 20 November 1980, gives other early cases; Phanjoubam Tarapot, *Insurgency Movement in North-Eastern India* (New Delhi: Vikas Publishing House, 1993), pp. 147ff., gives a large number of cases in the 1980s; the statement of the United National Liberation Front (UNLF) to the Working Group on Indigenous Populations, Geneva, July/August 1996 gives further cases, including ten of custodial deaths; see also Interim Report (dated 26 Oct. 2000) of the Independent People's Inquiry Commission, Manipur, headed by H. Suresh (Bombay High Court Judge); and several papers of the Committee on Human Rights (COHR) including "Right to Life" (Imphal, Manipur State, 1997) and "The Killings Continue" (a report on the summary execution of civilians during 1997), also its National Seminar on Human Rights (Imphal, Manipur State, 1994). More recently, *Manipur Update* has begun to fully document abuses, and the journal of the Manipur Research Centre, *Orient Vision*, gives a checklist of main events.

13. Pradip Phanjoubam, "And the Pattern of Abuse," *Manipur Update* 1, no. 1 (1999): 7.

in the illegal detentions, the indiscriminate retaliatory shootings, and other forms of violent physical abuse. This is a structural, or institutional, violence sanctioned by AFSPA. The second level is less overt but just as real. This is the sense of unease that disrupts normal life, business, and social activities, in which "security" forces are seen as agents of an oppressive psychological intimidation and *insecurity*, which renders a truly human life all but impossible.

In 1980, following the deaths of two CRPF (Central Reserve Police Force) personnel in an insurgency attack, the CRPF conducted what the security forces euphemistically term a "sweep" or "combing" of villages. The inhabitants of Patsoi village, men and women of all ages, were forced to strip naked. Over fifty males (some as young as sixteen, others over sixty) were so severely beaten that a number were disfigured for life. Many were subjected to torture, causing three deaths, including one woman. All the livestock was slaughtered, and possessions were looted. Four years later, again after an attack on the CRPF, they retaliated by spraying bullets at a crowd watching a football match at Heirangthong in Imphal. Twenty-six spectators were killed.

The CRPF were involved in another massacre in January 1995. A group of insurgents fired on the CRPF in the RMC hospital in Imphal. The CRPF called in reinforcements, who arrived after the insurgents had fled. These began firing indiscriminately on hospital staff and bystanders. Of the nine who died, one was a medical student, another a cleaner, and six were auto rickshaw drivers. These were shot in two separate incidents. A Commission of Inquiry found that none of the victims were armed, two were shot after they had raised their hands, and all six rickshaw drivers were taken behind a building and shot at close range; further, that all shootings took place after the hostiles had fled, that non-Manipuris (i.e., Indians from outside the region) were escorted out unmolested, and that the CRPF had uttered the order "kill all the Manipuris." The official security forces' report, as is usual, claimed the civilians were killed in crossfire.

In April 1995 there was a massacre in the Nagaland capital Kohima. Incredible as this may seem, the Rastriya (National) Rifles mistook a tire burst in their own convoy for a bomb attack and began firing indiscriminately in the town. The Assam Rifles (another paramilitary body) and the CRPF, hearing the shooting, hastened to the scene and joined in. The firing from these security forces lasted for an hour, and resulted in the death of seven innocent civilians and the serious injury to over twenty others. The dead included two young girls (aged three and eight); seven other children were among the injured. Even mortars were used in this attack on a nonexistent enemy, though their use in civilian areas is strictly forbidden under army rules.

A more recent massacre took place at Tonsen in October 1999. This was again in retaliation for an earlier attack on the CRPF by insurgents, and once more the killings took place after the insurgents had fled the scene. CRPF forces then stopped a bus passing through the area, which contained thirty-seven polling officials for a local election (all of course unarmed). They were called out from the vehicle and shot. There were a number of deaths, and many were seriously wounded. Also killed were innocent bystanders, including women, and two men who were later dragged from a truck and shot at close range. The disturbances in Imphal as a result of the geographical extension of the ceasefire agreement with the Muivah faction of the NSCN (which was later rescinded) resulted, in June 2001, in another fifteen deaths and over two hundred injured.

The characteristic feature of all these cases (and they could be multiplied) is that they were not operations conducted against insurgents, but were waged against unarmed civilians, usually long after the insurgents had fled the scene. More seriously, these are attacks by a central security force, which (as we shall see) is unable to be brought to account for its actions.

The most infamous case, however, concerned the Assam Rifles at the Naga village of Oinam in the north Manipur hills. This is one of very few cases in the northeast to have been the subject of an Amnesty International report, based largely on the brave witness of Christian Manipuri Naga victims and human rights workers, despite extreme intimidation. Oinam is a very remote village, difficult of access especially in the monsoon season. In July 1982 there was a serious attack on a military post by the NSCN, in which some soldiers were killed and a large quantity of arms stolen. The response from the Assam Rifles was delayed. Indian official army reports called Operation Bluebird "a highly disciplined" response under Major-General P. L. Kukrety, the commanding officer of Manipur Sector. It was in reality anything but that, as the Manipur authorities — after being denied access to a part of their own state for a period — eventually found out. In the sweep fifteen civilians were killed in cold blood, four of them being over fifty. There was no respect even for the state authorities; one MLA (member of the state parliament) was arrested, and the minister of education's house was raided without warrant. In Phuba village twenty-six people were severely tortured, some sustaining permanent injury, and houses were demolished. At Phaibung Khullen a similar number were tortured. Oinam itself suffered the worst. When the state medical officer was permitted to visit the village late in July he found no one: all had been confined for several weeks either in schools or the church, or in the open air. Children, the elderly, and pregnant women were not spared; several women gave birth and lost children in these conditions. Numerous women were raped by the Assam Rifles (one young woman later committed suicide), and others were compelled to do forced labor. Many were subjected to torture to extract false confessions and to intimidate them from reporting the violence. Boys as young as fifteen were subjected to electric shock torture. Of the fifteen persons deliberately murdered, the official post mortems demonstrated that some had been shot at close range (some in the back) and others hanged. Oinam remains an appalling stain on the conscience of the world's largest democracy, but one that has consistently been denied by the military authorities, despite overwhelming evidence.

The military presence is massive. In Manipur, for example, (a state of around two million) there are ten army battalions (of roughly 1,000 men each). There are in addition large numbers of paramilitary forces. Nagaland, with a population of around a million, has a comparable military presence. Of the paramilitaries, the Central Reserve Police Force is probably the most hated, and has a reputation for arrogance and lack of discipline; they have been responsible for much of the brutalizing and killing of civilians. Among their other duties they often guard public buildings, but their inability to speak Manipuri, Nagamese, or English, and their general attitude, engenders mistrust on both sides. Besides these there are the Assam Rifles and (on the border) the Border Security Force. The presence of the security forces is felt in all areas of life. Markets and urban streets are patrolled by armed gun carriers as well as foot soldiers, and there is a pervasive sense of an armed presence which, despite its official role, engenders more suspicion and insecurity than confidence. Crucially, none of these bodies have any real training to control civil unrest; retaliation rather than confidence building is their usual response.

5. A Persecution of Christians?

The conflict between the Indian security forces and the insurgency groups in the northeast is sometimes portrayed as a persecution of a Christian minority in a country that, though professedly secular, is largely in its mainstream dominated by hinduized values. The high percentage of Christians in the northeast, as compared with all other parts of India except Kerala, does indeed on the surface make it look as though there are religious motives involved in the violence perpetrated on civilian populations. This view finds support in that the Delhi government has from time to time criticized the churches for being anti-Indian. Furthermore churches have often been targeted, and occupied by troops and paramilitaries, and even used as places of detention, torture, rape, and murder.

In reality, however, the situation is much more complex than this, and ethnicity plays as large a role in the equation as religion. In northeast India, like Myanmar, Thailand, and some other southeast Asian countries, Christianity was often adopted not by the mainstream of the population but by tribal peoples. Consequently alienation from the mainstream on the ground of ethnicity has tended to be reinforced by a second alienation on the ground of religion. At root the suppression and violation of human rights in northeast India is ethnic — it would not be mistaken to call it racial: religious difference has reinforced this.

Nevertheless, it is clear that the Naga insurgency movements in India, like the comparable Chin and Karen independence movements in Myanmar, do have to a degree a Christian ideological base. From the beginning Christianity was perceived as a cement that would bring together the various Naga subtribes. It was therefore a prominent element in their Naga identity in contrast to what was seen as neo-colonialism by Hindu India. It is significant that the Rev. Michael Scott, one of the members of the earlier abortive Peace Mission, was widely perceived as being the Nagas' spokesman. In the earlier period a substantial number of pastors joined the underground. The insurgents did not fight on Sundays unless attacked.[14] The slogan "Nagaland for Christ" was a recognized rallying cry, and to some extent still is. Overtly Christian elements have appeared in official statements. The Constitution of the Federal Government of Nagaland, while it guaranteed free profession and practice of any religion, declared that Christianity would be the religion of an independent Naga state. It was not averse to using religion as a propaganda tool either, when it claimed that the "Hindu government" of India had adopted a policy of stopping Nagas eating meat. In the earlier days of the movement volunteer gospel teams preached under armed guard (one might almost say gun in one hand, Bible in the other), and the conduct of the jungle camps was (and to some extent remains, like those in Myanmar) ordered by Christian spiritual activities. As with the non-Christian Meitei movements, the NSCN tended towards puritanical lifestyle, banning alcohol and drugs, and discouraging sexual immorality. Provision of social amenities, like schools and clinics, goes hand in hand with religious teaching. The NSCN operates not only in Nagaland itself, but recruits and has bases in neighboring states. The northern hill areas of Manipur have especially been the locations for Naga insurgents' bases and attacks on the security forces. The Meitei insurgency movements, of course, do not share this Christian factor. Religious protest in their case, such as it is, is tied up with a broad cultural renaissance, which began in the 1930s.

14. B. Horam, *Naga Insurgency* (New Delhi: Cosmo, 1988), pp. 76-77.

In one sense, of course, the question whether this is religious persecution or not is not the central issue. The violence of the region is essentially a matter of human rights, of the violent suppression of ethnic minorities by state power. This oppression is indeed to some extent random, at the hands of undisciplined troops and paramilitaries, often under officers who either turn a blind eye or are themselves co-perpetrators of violence. The fundamental issue, however, is not just one of random violence. It is rather that violence against civilians is underpinned by institutional means.

6. Structural (Institutional) Violence

The situation is a result not simply of the inherent sinfulness of individuals and groups, but because the political, legal, and social structures permit violence to go unchecked and indeed actively underpin it. Structural (or institutional) violence may be defined as a situation in which the political, social, and legal structures are such as to permit, or encourage, the suppression of ethnic, social, or religious minorities under the guise of keeping law and order within the state. There are at least three main aspects of structural violence in the northeastern region of India today. These are: first, the massive presence of so-called "security forces," which prevents the civilian state governments from functioning normally; second, the powerlessness of the law courts in the region to bring the security forces to account for abuses, which is exacerbated by procrastination and subservience to the political authority of the central courts; and, third, the virtual absence of any practical application of human rights agreements. The structure that underlies all these aspects is the Armed Forces Special Powers Act.[15]

The designation of Nagaland and Manipur along with other parts of the northeast as "disturbed areas" has effectively meant that they have been sub-

---

15. AFSPA was approved despite very strong opposition in Parliament (by members from several different regions of India) on the grounds that it violated fundamental human rights, that it gave what were in effect emergency powers to lower-ranking security personnel without the formal declaration of an emergency, and that it was specifically applied only in the northeastern region of India, despite there being equally "disturbed" areas elsewhere. One of the two Manipuri members of the Lower House in his speech against the bill gave examples of how the armed forces had already been guilty of rape and wanton occupation of churches. The equally draconian Terrorist and Disruptive Activities Act (TADA) was approved in 1985 and applied to a large number of states and Union territories. It was extended on four occasions, and a more severe version of the act is currently being considered. This act also violates several aspects of basic human rights.

ject to an undeclared state of emergency. This circumscribes not only the liberties of individual citizens, but it also seriously limits the freedom of the state governments. Successive governors of military or police background, and even more the military brigadiers who have overall control of security policy and personnel, have not infrequently acted against the state governments and at times accused them of inaction and even collusion with the insurgents. In effect, the state governments have had their teeth drawn and can exist only in uneasy subjection to a hostile central controlling presence. The same may be said of the due processes of law, for security personnel are not subject to normal restraints and cannot be charged under civil law for any acts, however heinous, claimed to have been carried out in the course of their duty. This situation has resulted from the application of the Armed Forces (Special Powers) Act to the northeast. The origins of this act go back to 1942: it was originally intended to enable the British to take action against internal subversion during the Second World War, and it applied throughout India. Like a number of other repressive colonial enactments, it was later used by an independent India to repress what it saw as dissent within its own borders, specifically in the northeastern region. In 1958 it was declared to apply to those areas designated as "disturbed" in all of the present seven states of the northeast, and at that time the Naga Hills and the Ukhrul District of Manipur were so designated. In 1970, 1975, and 1978 the designation "disturbed areas" was progressively extended over other divisions of Manipur, and in September 1980 the whole state was declared a "disturbed area." The act has remained in force throughout the states up to the present. The 1958 act (amended in 1972) goes much further than the 1942 British legislation. Crucially, it replaced the term "emergency" with "disturbed areas." Originally the status of "disturbed area" could only be declared by the particular state government concerned, but in 1972 this power was given to the central government. As important, however, was the fact that whereas the 1942 act gave special powers under the act only to those with the military rank of captain and above, the 1972 amendment extended this to "any commissioned officer, warrant officer, non-commissioned officer, or any of equivalent rank" (i.e., any soldier except the lowest private). These powers are in effect powers over life and death. They include the right "to fire upon or otherwise use force, even to the causing of death, on any person who is acting in contravention of any law"; to arrest without warrant anyone suspected of being about to commit an offense; to enter, search, and destroy any premises suspected of being used for storing arms; and in each case the soldier "may use for that purpose force as may be necessary" (AFSPA 1972 section 4). As we have seen, "no prosecution, suit or other legal proceeding shall be instituted, except with the previous sanction of central government against any person in respect of anything done or purported to be done in exercise of the powers conferred by this act" (AFSPA 1972 section 6).

Human rights organizations have been powerless to curtail these draconian powers. In 1980 the Human Rights Forum (Manipur) was formed in Delhi and submitted to the Supreme Court (under Public Interest Litigation Process) a petition challenging the legality of AFSPA. Two years later the Naga People's Movement for Human Rights submitted a similar petition. As is common in India, these disappeared down legal black holes, and the latter was not dealt with until November 1997. The Supreme Court ruling upheld the act as constitutional and broadly followed the government line that the act did not grant to the military powers that were excessive, though it did underline the responsibilities of the security forces (especially in surrendering any suspect to the civil police within twenty-four hours), and issued a series of "do's" and "don'ts." Such guidelines have little force and are not seldom ignored by the security personnel. The ruling failed to address the crucial issue, that what is essentially emergency legislation intended for times of war (and indeed applied throughout India during the wars with China and Pakistan) has been applied selectively to the northeast region for decades.

7. Christian Responses

A context of structural violence is, in Gustavo Gutiérrez's phrase, a sinful situation. As such it demands a theological response. This response will, of course, be partially shaped by the fact that a substantial number of those who suffer under this situation are themselves Christians, and there are indications that at the very least in some incidents the security authorities show contempt for churches and Christian spokespersons. However, Christians do not have the monopoly of suffering, and, as we have seen, the abuses are equally directed towards those, like the majority of Meiteis, who are not Christian. Overall the religious affiliation is only one factor; a much greater one is the contempt that is felt for the Mongoloid northeast as a whole. It is therefore fundamentally an ethnic or racial violence. But whatever the complexities of the situation, any theological response has to speak for all oppressed communities, not just the Christian ones.

While Christians as a whole might be agreed about the nature of a sinful situation they are rarely in agreement as to what to do about it. Sadly, theological discussion in the northeast has been constrained almost to the point of nonexistence, and structural violence has never been clearly on the theological agenda. One might characterize the widespread attitude as retreat into pietism and a concern with a non-political cultural theology. The only substantial tribal theology to appear from the northeast (and that, one has to say, fairly unoriginal) scarcely mentions the issue of oppression.[16] Even the book edited by S. K. Chatterji of the Christian Institute for the Study of Religion and Society (CISRS), which has been involved in political issues since its inception, contains only a few lines of pious hope for political education.[17] There are no doubt reasons for this. Tribal theology in the northeast is very undeveloped, and much of its thinking is derivative of the North American evangelical Baptist tradition.[18] Theological criticism of the government and security forces may also increase the perception of the church as anti-Indian. However, the nettle will have to be grasped sooner rather than later if the church is to have any relevance. A retreat into pietism and a purely cultural theology, coupled with a tacit acceptance of the political status quo, will not do much to address a situation of structural violence that has now operated for half a century.

Those who followed the South African theological debate on the violations of basic human rights resulting from apartheid will recall that the essence of the argument of the Kairos Document was that when a government puts in place unjust structures by legislation, backed by the law courts and the security forces, which violate basic human rights, it forfeits its legitimacy.[19] For basic human rights to life also have a theological underpinning, derived from the Christian doctrines of creation and redemption. In such circumstances Christians have the right, even the duty, to resist the illegitimate structures of government. In the South African situation the illegitimacy of government clearly applied to the whole state. In northeast India the position is somewhat different, for the Indian Constitution does in fact grant basic rights to all the population. It could then be argued that what is at stake here is not the illegitimacy of government as a whole, but of that specific legislation (i.e., AFSPA) which has created structural violence in the states of the northeast.

16. Takatemjen, *Studies on Theology and Naga Culture* (Delhi: ISPCK, 1998): only at the end of the book on p. 140 does he suggest the political situation is the place to start.

17. S. K. Chatterji, ed., *Society and Culture in North East India* (New Delhi: ISPCK, 1996).

18. However, evangelicals, even those at the more conservative end of the spectrum, are elsewhere taking a substantial role in seeking to analyze and grapple with political issues, and there is certainly nothing inherent in evangelicalism that makes it any less able than other theological stances to speak prophetically about political issues.

19. *Challenge to the Church: A Theological Comment on the Political Crisis in South Africa*, 5th ed. (Braamfontein and London: Kairos Theologians, CIIR, BCC, 1986), known as the Kairos Document.

There are, of course, those who would argue that the inclusion into India of both Nagaland (which was only loosely administered by the British) and Manipur (which was never fully administered by them) was a case of neo-colonial annexation. This position, which seems to me to be quite correct from a historical perspective, was the original rationale for the insurgency movements, most of which still seek complete independence. Against this must be weighed the question of whether it is not too late to turn the clock back to the pre-1947 situation, and also the practical issue of whether such an agenda is likely to succeed. While it seems to me there may be some theological justification for regarding such an armed struggle as a "just war," there is no realistic possibility of India's letting the smaller states go without appalling bloodshed (unless, of course, the Indian Union as a whole breaks up, as some more radical political scientists would argue). The most that can be expected is greater autonomy (as happened after a bloody and prolonged insurgency in Mizoram, also mainly Christian). The original vision of the NSCN of an independent Christian state of Nagaland (which, according to some, should be expanded by incorporating much of Manipur, Assam, and Arunachal Pradesh where there are substantial Naga populations) certainly will not do. Despite some gains, the Naga insurgency movements have by their actions forfeited much of the claim they had to be regarded as Christian protest movements.

If then the options of an apolitical quiescence and of armed revolution are difficult to defend on theological grounds, what is left? Three other approaches have been tried, those of peace initiatives, of legal constitutional challenge, and of civil disobedience.

Peace initiatives go back to the very earliest period after 1947. It was Naga Baptist ministers who urged the Indian government to set up a Peace Mission in the 1960s. They initiated another Peace Council in 1974, and have from time to time made other individual and collective attempts to broker a peace. None of these have succeeded, partly because of the church's inability to carry the more extreme radicals with them, partly because some Delhi-based politicians have accused Christian leaders of being secessionist. It has been a bitter tight rope for church leaders to walk.

8. Legal Challenges and Civil Right Movements

Legal challenges to structural violence have been mounted with great regularity, mainly by human rights organizations (which, of course, often include Christians) but also from time to time by church bodies. We have already alluded to the challenges to the legality of AFSPA in the Delhi High Court, but cases against the security forces have also been brought for specific incidents. The biggest problem, indeed the insuperable problem, here is that AFSPA specifically prevents any case being brought against any member of the forces while in pursuance of his duties unless this is approved by the central government. Since permission from the central government has never been granted, this in effect means that the security forces are above the civil law. Technically therefore any charges against the security forces, whether of murder, abduction, rape, or other forms of violence, can only be tried by court martial, to which civil lawyers cannot easily gain access. This seldom happens even when evidence is overwhelming. In the rare cases when it does occur no report is made public. The opportunities for redress against the armed forces are virtually nonexistent. The most the state governments can do is to order an inquiry. This they have frequently done, though more often than not such inquiries run into the sand or findings are not made public. In cases of detentions and disappearances courts have been asked to order a habeas corpus. This has sometimes produced results, though more often than not the security forces simply claim the detainee was released from their custody. In the many cases where the victims are later discovered murdered, responsibility is denied. Claims for compensation do sometimes succeed in the courts. After the Oinam atrocities, for example, the Naga People's Movement for Human Rights filed petitions against the Assam Rifles in the High Court in Guwahati and the court directed that detainees should be released and there should be reparations. Shortly thereafter the Manipur Baptist Convention's Women's Union filed on behalf of women who had been sexually assaulted and subjected to forced labor. Sometimes Christian women have appealed directly to the source of power, as when the Kohima Women's Baptist Assembly wrote to Mrs. Gandhi protesting against the rape of Naga girls by the 1st Maratha Battalion — an abuse that actually happened in a church. Other cases of a similar nature have been filed in state and High Courts. Compensation, when granted, is usually small, intimidation of witnesses is routine and often brutal, and heavy military presence in uniform at hearings is a further way to silence witnesses. It is to the credit of lawyers and civilians (many of them with little education) that such cases are sometimes won. By and large the legal option runs up against the fact that AFSPA effectively puts the security forces outside the law, however heinous their actions might be.

It is this perceived exclusion of civilian victims from recourse to the law where the security forces are concerned that more than anything else has led to widespread alienation from things "Indian," for rightly or wrongly the security forces are identified with the central government. Thus the spiral of violence is given another turn.

9. AFSPA and Human Rights Legislation

Civil rights groups protest at great risk to their safety. In Manipur these are mainly Meitei (therefore not predominantly Christian). Foremost among them have been the All Manipur Students' Union, Civilians Against Atrocities, and most effective of all the Meira Paibi. All these groups have been subjected to the banning of peaceful demonstrations, beatings and detentions, and occasional loss of life. It must be emphasized that there are movements elsewhere in India, especially in Delhi, that have taken up the need to restore human rights in the northeast.

India signed up to the UN agreement on Human Rights in 1991, and three years later stationed a Manipuri human rights representative in Imphal. However, his remit is entirely civil, since AFSPA explicitly excludes all security personnel from charges of human rights violations. India also signed the Vienna Declaration and Programme of Action (adopted by the 1993 Vienna World Conference on Human Rights). This committed signatories to "abrogate legislation leading to impunity for those responsible for grave violations of human rights . . . and to prosecute such violations, thereby providing a firm basis for the rule of law." When AFSPA has been subjected to scrutiny and severe criticism by UN committees on human rights, India has consistently claimed that AFSPA does not violate basic rights and that it is necessary for the peace of the country as a whole.

However, AFSPA does quite blatantly violate international conventions, including the Universal Declaration of Human Rights, the Convention on Economic and Cultural Rights, the International Covenant on Civil and Political Rights, the Convention Against Torture, the UN Code of Conduct for Law Enforcement Officials, the UN Body of Principles for Protection of All Persons Under Any Form of Detention, and the UN Principles on Effective Prevention and Investigation of Extra-legal and Summary Executions. Security forces have also frequently violated sections of the UN Convention on the Rights of the Child (1989).[20] It has also been pointed out that AFSPA violates

---

20. See my discussion of AFSPA in *Wounded Land*, pp. 146-60. The UN International Human Rights Committee (e.g., CCPR/C/79/Add.81 4th Aug. 1997) has leveled severe criticisms at India because of AFSPA, and has repeatedly called for security forces to be subject to civil law in cases of abuse of civilians.

sections of the Indian Constitution, especially articles 21 (on the right to life) and 22 (protection against arrest), as well as sections of the Indian Criminal Procedure Code.

10. A Theological Challenge

Human rights are a theological issue. As Jürgen Moltmann points out, after World War II it has been recognized that the way a country treats its people is not a matter only for that country itself but for all.[21] The excuse of "not interfering in internal affairs" is no longer a valid defense. The situation today in northeast India is sadly all too common in today's world despite the plethora of human rights agreements. This paper may not have looked very different if it had dealt with Myanmar, Sudan, or a dozen other countries where ethnic and religious human rights are being daily violated — except for the very important fact that India claims to be a democracy and has had a long tradition of protest against oppression.

Christians in northeast India have largely been left on their own in dealing with the structural violence of their region. I would suggest that this challenge now needs to be taken up at the national level, that is, within India, and also at the wider ecumenical level.

During the 1980s a bombshell was dropped upon the playground of the Indian theologians. The Sanskritic tradition of doing Christian theology in India, which indeed had had a long and remarkable history and had occupied some brilliant minds, found itself challenged to the point of being dismissed as irrelevant by the irruption of Dalit theology. The Sanskritic theological tradition is actually very little threat to the underlying Hindu culture of India: it uses Hindu concepts, largely obeys Hindu philosophical categories, and is eager for dialogue. Its disadvantage is that it is elitist and largely irrelevant to the majority of Christians, around 70 percent of whom do not belong to the upper castes. Dalit theology sharply rejected the Sanskritic approach. In the political power game Dalits also had been, largely against their will, incorporated into the Hindu system as a kind of fifth caste (hence were called by the Indian Constitution "scheduled castes"). Political and religious leaders (including Gandhi) argued strongly for keeping them within the overall socio-religious categories of Hinduism. Significantly, the Indian Constitution makes a similar implicit assumption about the tribals by calling them "scheduled tribes," and the fluidity between scheduled castes and

---

21. Jürgen Moltmann, *God for a Secular Society* (London: SCM Press, 1999), p. 119.

scheduled tribes in some Indian states is evident from census data. However, the tribal peoples of the northeast are different.[22] They have never been hinduized and have always been quite distinct from Hindu societies. Tribal theology can no more be absorbed by the Sanskritic "mainstream" of Indian theology than tribals themselves can be absorbed into the hinduized cultural mainstream. Nor, despite the common lot of oppression, can tribal theology be subsumed under Dalit theology.[23] A second radical shift in theological thinking in India is demanded, to recognize and indeed to celebrate the fact that a coherent and valid tribal theology will be manifestly different from both the Sanskritic and the Dalit traditions. But it must build on the long tradition that both have of political action — from those who like Brahmabandhav Upadhyaya at the beginning of the century became involved in the independence struggle, through to the Gandhian Christians, the CISRS, and now the Dalits. My own feeling, however, is that African theology, which is successfully beginning to marry the cultural with the political agenda, is a rather better mentor (though till now totally neglected) for tribal Christians than anything that has yet emerged from the subcontinent itself.

In the 1960s M. M. Thomas (who towards the end of his life became governor of Nagaland) edited a book entitled *Tribal Awakening*.[24] Since then there has been relatively little published evidence that this agenda has been taken seriously as far as the northeast is concerned, or that the debate between Christians in this region and the heartland of India has progressed very far — and this despite the large numbers of well-trained tribal Christian leaders. One has to ask whether the church in India — which shared the mainstream prejudice against Dalits — also shares the mainstream prejudice against the Mongoloid peoples of its northeast.

But there is also a wider ecumenical challenge. It seems to me that there is little active involvement by the churches elsewhere or by the WCC in bringing attention to structural violence against Christian minorities not only in northeastern India but also in Myanmar, where a similar situation obtains.[25]

---

22. This fact is recognized by Albert Minz, "Dalits and Tribals: A Search for Solidarity," in V. Devasahayam, ed., *Frontiers of Dalit Theology* (Delhi: ISPCK, 1997), pp. 130-58.

23. As some tribals in the Indian heartland seem to be in danger of doing: see, e.g., Nirmal Minz, "Dalit-Tribal: A Search for a Common Ideology," in James Massey, ed., *Indigenous People: Dalit Issues in Today's Theological Debate* (Delhi: ISPCK, 1994), pp. 134-42; also James Massey, *Minorities in a Democracy: The Indian Experience* (New Delhi: Manohar, 1999).

24. M. M. Thomas and R. W. Taylor, eds., *Tribal Awakening* (Bangalore: CSIRS, 1965).

25. I am reliably informed that a few years ago when a delegation of tribal Christians

Publicizing abuses is too often left to journalists and to human rights organizations, whose motives may be mixed, and who in any case hardly get direct access to the states of northeast India. The churches both locally and internationally have the greater responsibility.

The Christian faith is one of mutual sharing (1 Cor. 12:26, "If one member suffers, all suffer with it"). Moreover, the church cannot any longer, after the holocaust and the repeated cases of genocide in Asia and Africa since then, avoid its obligation to be in Bonhoeffer's phrase, a "church for others." Structural violence is not just a political issue, it is not even just a human rights issue: it is primarily a theological issue, in that it represents the sinful mutilation of the image of God in which human beings are created.

approached one of the directors of the WCC (who was himself an Indian) about the problems of the northeastern region, his response was dismissive.

Bibliography of Principal Secondary Sources

Aboagye-Mensah, Robert Kwasi. "Socio-Political Thinking of Karl Barth: Trinitarian and Incarnational Christology as the Ground for His Social Action and Its Implications for Us Today" (unpublished Ph.D. thesis, University of Aberdeen, 1984).

Abraham, K. C. "Globalization: A Gospel and Culture Perspective," *International Review of Mission* 85, no. 336 (Jan. 1996): 85-92.

Adogame, Afe. "African New Religious Movements in Europe," *Zeitschrift für Religionswissenschaft* 10 (2002): 33-49.

————. "Engaged in the Task of 'Cleansing' the World?: Aladura Churches in 20th Century Europe," in Klaus Koschorke, ed., *Transcontinental Links in the History of Non-Western Christianity* (Wiesbaden: Harrassowitz, 2002), pp. 73-86.

————. *Celestial Church of Christ: The Politics of Cultural Identity in a West African Prophetic-Charismatic Movement* (Frankfurt am Main: Peter Lang, 1999).

Afram, Alex. "African Christian Council, Hamburg, Germany," *International Review of Mission* 89, no. 354 (July 2000): 434-35.

[anon.] "African Universities: The Staff Dilemma," *West Africa* (29 May–4 June 1995): 843-44.

Ahmed, Akbar. *Islam, Globalization and Postmodernity* (London: Routledge, 1992).

Albrow, Martin. *The Global Age* (Palo Alto, CA: Stanford University Press, 1997).

Ambalavanar, D. J., ed. *The Gospel in the World: Essays in Honour of Bishop Kulandran* (Madras: Christian Literature Society, 1985).

Amoah, Elizabeth, and Mercy Oduyoye. "The Christ for African Women," in Virginia Fabella and Mercy Oduyoye, eds., *With Passion and Compassion: Third World Women Doing Theology* (Maryknoll, NY: Orbis Books, 1988), pp. 35-46.

Amonoo-Neizer, Eugene H. "Universities in Africa — The Need for Adaptation, Transformation, Reformation and Revitalization," *Higher Education Policy* 11, no. 4 (1998): 301-9.

Anderson, Gerald H., ed. *Biographical Dictionary of Christian Missions* (New York: Macmillan Reference, 1998).

Appadurai, A. *Modernity at Large: Cultural Dimensions of Globalization* (Minneapolis: University of Minnesota Press, 1996).

————. "Disjuncture and Difference in the Global Cultural Economy," in Mike Featherstone, ed., *Global Culture* (London: Sage, 1990), pp. 295-310.

————. "Globalization and the Research Imagination," *International Social Science Journal* 160 (June 1999): 229-38.

Appelbaum, Patricia. "The Legions of Good Will: The Religious Culture of Protestant Pacifism, 1918-1963" (unpublished Ph.D. thesis, Boston University, 2001).

Ariarajah, Wesley. *Hindus and Christians: A Century of Protestant Ecumenical Thought* (Grand Rapids: Eerdmans, 1991).

Arthur, John A. *Invisible Sojourners: African Immigrant Diaspora in the United States* (Westport, CT: Praeger Publishers, 2000).

Asamoah-Gyadu, Kwabena. "Renewal Within Christianity: A Historical and Theological Study of Some Current Developments Within Ghanaian Pentecostalism" (unpublished Ph.D. thesis, University of Birmingham, 2000).

————. "'Fireballs in Our Midst': West Africa's Burgeoning Charismatic Churches and the Pastoral Role of Women," *Mission Studies* 15-16, no. 296 (1998): 15-31.

Augé, Marc. *Non-Places: Introduction to an Anthropology of Supermodernity*, trans. from the French by John Howe (London: Verso, 1995).

Austin, Robert. "Armed Forces, Market Forces: Intellectuals and Higher Education in Chile, 1973-1993," *Latin American Perspectives* 24 (Sept. 1997): 26-58.

Awoniyi, Femi. "Video Film Uniting Africa," *African Courier* 6, no. 31 (April/May 2003): 9, 26.

Axford, Barrie. *The Global System: Economics, Politics and Culture* (New York: St. Martin's Press, 1995).

Axling, William. *Kagawa* (New York: Harper & Brothers, 1932).

Barber, Benjamin R. *Jihad vs. McWorld: How Globalism and Tribalism Are Reshaping the World* (New York: Ballantine, 1996).

Barratt, Thomas Ball. *When the Fire Fell, and An Outline of My Life* (Oslo: Alfons Hansen and Sonner, 1927).

Barrett, David. *Schism and Renewal in Africa: An Analysis of Six Thousand Contemporary Religious Movements* (Nairobi: Oxford University Press, 1968).

Barrett, David, and Todd Johnson, "Annual Statistical Table on Global Mission," *International Bulletin of Missionary Research* 23, no. 1 (Jan. 1999): 24-25.

Barrett, David B., George T. Kurian, and Todd M. Johnson, eds. *World Christian Encyclopedia: A Comprehensive Survey of Churches and Religions in the Modern World,* 2nd ed., 2 vols. (New York: Oxford University Press, 2001).

Barth, Fredrik. *Balinese Worlds* (Chicago: University of Chicago Press, 1993).

Bauman, Zygmunt. *Globalization: The Human Consequences* (Cambridge: Polity Press, 1998).

Bays, Daniel H. "The Growth of Independent Christianity in China, 1900-1937," in

Daniel H. Bays, ed., *Christianity in China, from the Eighteenth Century to the Present* (Stanford, CA: Stanford University Press, 1996).

―――. "Christianity in China: A Case Study of Indigenous Christianity: The Jesus Family, 1927-1952," in *Religion* (Journal of the Kansas School of Religion) 26, no. 1 (Oct. 1988): 1-3.

Bediako, Kwame. *Christianity in Africa: The Renewal of a Non-Western Religion* (Maryknoll, NY: Orbis Books, 1995).

―――. "The Significance of Modern African Christianity — A Manifesto," *Studies in World Christianity* 1, Part 1 (1995): 51-67.

―――. "Facing the Challenge: Africa in World Christianity in the 21st Century — A Vision of the African Christian Future," *Journal of African Christian Thought* 1, no. 1 (June 1998): 52-57.

―――. "Africa and Christianity on the Threshold of the Third Millennium: The Religious Dimension," *African Affairs* 99, no. 395 (April 2000): 303-23.

―――. "A Half Century of African Christian Thought: Pointers to Theology and Theological Education in the Next Half Century," *Journal of African Christian Thought* 3, no. 1 (June 2000): 5-11.

Beidelman, T. O. *Colonial Evangelism* (Bloomington: Indiana University Press, 1982).

Bell, G. K. A. *The Stockholm Conference 1925* (London: Oxford University Press, 1926).

Benne, Robert. *Quality with Soul: How Six Premier Colleges and Universities Keep Faith with Their Religious Traditions* (Grand Rapids: Eerdmans, 2001).

Berger, Peter. "Four Faces of Globalization," in P. O'Meara et al., eds., *Globalization and the Challenges of a New Century: A Reader* (Indianapolis: Indiana University Press, 2000), pp. 419-27.

―――. "Four Faces of Global Culture," *National Interest* 49 (Fall 1997): 23-29.

Berryman, Phillip. "Churches as Winners and Losers in the Network Society," *Journal of Interamerican Studies and World Affairs* 41, no. 4 (1999): 21-34.

Beyer, Peter. *Religion and Globalization* (London: Sage Publications, 1994).

―――. "Privatization and the Public Influence of Religion in Global Society," in Mike Featherstone, ed., *Global Culture: Nationalism, Globalization and Modernity* (London: Sage Publications, 1990), pp. 385-93.

Bhabha, Homi. *The Location of Culture* (London and New York: Routledge, 1994).

Bliese, Richard H. "Globalization," in K. Müller, T. Sundermeier, S. B. Bevans, and R. H. Bliese, eds., *Dictionary of Mission: Theology, History, Perspectives* (Maryknoll, NY: Orbis Books, 1998), pp. 172-78.

Bollag, Burton. "The New Latin: English Dominates in Academe," *Christian Higher Education,* 8 September 2000, p. A73.

Bourgault, Louise. "The Jim Bakker Show: The Programme, Its Viewers and Their Churches," *Journal of Communication and Religion* 11 (March 1988): 32-40.

Bowen, John. "Islamic Transformations: From Sufi Doctrine to Ritual Practice in Gayo Culture," in Rita Smith Kipp and Susan Rodgers, eds., *Indonesian Religions in Transition* (Tucson: University of Arizona Press, 1987), pp. 113-35.

Bowers, Joyce M. "Partnership and Missionary Personnel," *International Review of Mission* 86, no. 342 (July 1997): 248-60.

Boyd, Nancy. *Three Victorian Women Who Changed Their World* (New York: Oxford University Press, 1982).

Brecher, Jeremy, J. B. Childs, and J. Cutler, eds. *Global Visions: Beyond the New World Order* (Boston: South End Press, 1993).

Brouwer, S., P. Gifford, and S. D. Rose. *Exporting the American Gospel: Global Christian Fundamentalism* (New York: Routledge, 1996).

Browne, David. "Film, Movies and Meanings," in Clive Marsh and Gaye Ortiz, eds., *Explorations in Theology and Film* (Oxford: Blackwell Publishing, 1997), pp. 33-58.

Bulatao, Jaime. *Split-Level Christianity* (Quezon City: Ateneo de Manila University Press, 1966).

Burtchaell, James Tunstead. *The Dying of the Light: The Disengagement of Colleges and Universities from Their Christian Churches* (Grand Rapids: Eerdmans, 1999).

Busia, K. A. *Africa in Search of Democracy* (London: Routledge & Kegan Paul, 1967).

Cannell, Fenella. *Power and Intimacy in the Christian Philippines* (Manila: Ateneo de Manila University Press, 1999).

Carey, James. "A Cultural Approach in Communication," *Communication* 2 (1975): 1-22.

Casanova, José. "Globalizing Catholicism and the Return to a 'Universal Church,'" in Susanne Rudolph and James Piscatori, eds., *Transnational Religion and Fading States* (Boulder, CO: Westview Press, 1997), pp. 121-43.

Castles, S. and M. J. Miller. *The Age of Migration: International Population Movements in the Modern World* (New York: Guilford Press, 1998; 1st ed., 1993).

Castro, Emilio. "Editorial," *Ecumenical Review* 41, no. 1 (Jan. 1989): 1-3.

Chase-Dunn, Christopher. "Globalization: A World-System Perspective," *Journal of World-System Research* 5, no. 2 (1999): 165-85.

Chatfield, Charles. *For Peace and Justice: Pacifism in America, 1914-1941* (Knoxville: University of Tennessee Press, 1971).

Chatterji, S. K., ed. *Society and Culture in North East India* (New Delhi: ISPCK, 1996).

Clarke, A. K. *A History of the Cheltenham Ladies' College, 1853-1953* (London: Faber and Faber Ltd., n.d.)

Cohen, David. "The Worldwide Rise of Private Colleges," *Christian Higher Education*, 9 March 2001, p. A47.

Coleman, Simon. *The Globalisation of Charismatic Christianity* (Cambridge: Cambridge University Press, 2000).

Collins, Travis. "Missions and Churches in Partnership for Evangelism: A Study of the Declaration of Ibadan," *Missiology* 23, no. 3 (July 1995): 331-39.

Comaroff, Jean and John. *Of Revelation and Revolution: Christianity, Colonialism, and Consciousness in South Africa*, 2 vols. (Chicago: University of Chicago Press, 1991, 1997).

Comor, Edward. "The Role of Communication in Global Civil Society: Forces, Processes, Prospects," *International Studies Quarterly* (2001): 389-408.

Corbett, Charles Hodge. *Shantung Christian University* [*Cheeloo*] (New York: United Board for Christian Colleges in China, 1955).

Corbit, Nabban J. "Music as Prophecy in the African Church," *Christian Media* 7 (1993).

Cox, Harvey. *Fire from Heaven: The Rise of Pentecostal Spirituality and the Reshaping of Religion in the Twenty-First Century* (Cambridge, MA: Perseus Books, 1995).

Crabble, Richard. "The Role of Christian Media in Church and Society," *Christian Media* 2, no. 1 (1991).

Cracknell, Kenneth. *Justice, Courtesy, and Love: Theologians and Missionaries Encountering World Religions, 1846-1914* (London: Epworth Press, 1995).

Cummings, William K. "Private Education in East Asia," in William K. Cummings, ed., *The Challenge of Eastern Asian Education* (Albany: State University of New York Press, 1997), pp. 135-52.

Dake, Liu, Ma Fuzhen, and Shen Guomin. *The History of Japanese Invasion of Shandong* (Jinan: Shandong People's Press, 1990).

Davey, Andrew P. "Globalisation as Challenge and Opportunity in Urban Mission," *International Review of Mission* 88, no. 351 (Oct. 1999): 381-89.

David, Joel. *The National Pastime: Contemporary Cinema* (Pasig City, Philippines: Anvil Publishing Inc., 1990).

Davies, Christie. "David Martin: Sociologist of Religion and Humorist," in A. Walker and M. Percy, eds., *Restoring the Image* (Sheffield: Sheffield Academic Press, 2001), pp. 49-68.

Dayton, Donald W. "Yet Another Layer of the Onion; or Opening the Ecumenical Door to Let the Riffraff In," *Ecumenical Review* 40 (Jan. 1988): 87-110.

———. "The Search for the Historical Evangelicalism: George Marsden's History of Fuller Seminary as a Case Study," *Christian Scholar's Review* 23 (Sept. 1993): 12-33.

———. "Rejoinder to Historiography Discussion," *Christian Scholar's Review* 23 (Sept. 1993): 62-71.

De Soto, Hernando. *The Mystery of Capital: Why Capitalism Triumphs in the West and Fails Everywhere Else* (New York: Basic Books, 2000).

Devasahayam, D. M., and A. N. Sunarisanam, eds. *Rethinking Christianity in India* (Madras: Hogarth Press, 1938).

Douglas, Bronwen. "From Invisible Christians to Gothic Theatre: The Romance of the Millennial in Melanesian Anthropology," *Current Anthropology* 42, no. 5 (2001): 615-50.

Downs, F. S. *The History of Christianity in India.* Vol. V, part 5, *Christianity in North East India in the Nineteenth and Twentieth Centuries* (Bangalore: Church History Association of India, 1992).

Droogers, André. "Globalization and Pentecostal Success," in André Corten and Ruth Marshall-Fratani, eds., *Between Babel and Pentecost: Transnational Pente-*

costalism in Africa and Latin America (Bloomington and Indianapolis: Indiana University Press, 2001), pp. 41-61.

Dyer, Paul D. "The Use of Oral Communication Methods in Health Education, Evangelism and Christian Maturation" (unpublished D.Min. thesis, Bethel Theological Seminary, 1994).

Eddy, Sherwood. *A Century with Youth: A History of the Y.M.C.A. from 1844 to 1944* (New York: Association Press, 1944).

————. *Pathfinders of the World Missionary Crusade* (New York: Abingdon-Cokesbury Press, 1945).

Eliade, Mircea. *Patterns in Comparative Religion* (New York: The World Publishing Company, 1968).

Elphick, Richard. *Christianity in South Africa: A Political, Social, and Cultural History* (Berkeley: University of California Press, 1997).

Engel, J. F., and W. A. Dyrness. *Changing the Mind of Missions: Where Have We Gone Wrong?* (Downers Grove, IL: InterVarsity Press, 2000).

Eni, Emmanuel. *Delivered from the Powers of Darkness* (Ibadan: Scripture Union, 1987).

Escobar, Samuel. "The Global Scenario at the Turn of the Century," in W. Taylor, ed., *Global Missiology for the 21st Century: The Iguassu Dialogue* (Michigan: Baker Academic, 2000), pp. 23-46.

Esposito, John, and Michael Watson, eds. *Religion and Global Order* (Cardiff: University of Wales Press, 2000).

Essayas, Menkir. "Content and Context of Christian Communication," in Robert N. Kizito, ed., *Communication and Human Rights in Africa: Implications for Development* (World Association for Christian Communication — Africa Region Publication, 1992), pp. 79-102.

Featherstone, M., et al. *Global Modernities* (London: Sage Publications, 1995).

Fernandes, Rubem César. *Censo Institucional Evangélico CIN 1992: Primeiros Comentarios* (Rio de Janeiro: ISER, 1992).

Firth, O. M. J. "Globalization: A Christian Perspective on Economics," *Dialogue* (Colombo) 24 (1997): 101-24.

Fischer, Nicole. "Towards Reconciled Communities in Mission," *International Review of Mission* 79, no. 316 (Oct. 1990): 479-86.

Fishman, Joshua A. "Globalization at Work: The New Linguistic Order," *Foreign Policy* 113 (1998): 26-41.

————. "The Triumph of English," *The Economist*, 22 December 2001, pp. 65-67.

Fleming, Daniel J. *Whither Bound in Missions* (New York: Association Press, 1925).

Florini, Ann M., ed. *The Third Force: The Rise of Transnational Civil Society* (Washington, DC: Carnegie Endowment for International Peace, 2000).

Fosdick, Harry Emerson. *The Living of These Days: An Autobiography* (New York: Harper and Brothers, 1956).

————. *Chronicles of a Generation* (New York: Harper and Brothers, 1958).

Freston, Paul. "The Transnationalisation of Brazilian Pentecostalism: The Universal

Church of the Kingdom of God," in A. Corten and R. Fratani, eds., *Between Babel and Pentecost: Transnational Pentecostalism in Africa and Latin America* (London: Hurst, 2000), pp. 196-215.

———. *Evangelicals and Politics in Asia, Africa and Latin America* (Cambridge: Cambridge University Press, 2001).

Friedman, Jonathan. *Cultural Identity and Global Process* (London: Sage Publications, 1994).

Friedman, Thomas L. *The Lexus and the Olive Tree: Understanding Globalization* (New York: Farrar, Straus and Giroux, 1999).

Frykenberg, R. E., ed., *Pandita Ramabai's America: Conditions of Life in the United States* (Grand Rapids and Cambridge: Eerdmans, 2003).

Fukuyama, Francis. *The End of History and the Last Man* (London: Hamish Hamilton, 1992).

Gerloff, Roswith. "Religion, Culture and Resistance: The Significance of African Christian Communities in Europe," *Exchange* 3, no. 3 (2001): 276-89.

———. "Editorial," *International Review of Mission* 89, no. 354 (July 2000): 276-77.

Giddens, Anthony. *Runaway World: How Globalization Is Reshaping Our Lives* (New York: Routledge, 2000).

Gifford, Paul. *African Christianity: Its Public Role* (Bloomington: Indiana University Press, 1998).

Glüer, Winfried. *T. C. Chao's Thought* (Hong Kong: Christianity Literature Press, 1998).

Goethals, G. T. *The Electronic Golden Calf: Images, Religion and the Making of Meaning* (Cambridge, MA: Cowley, 1990).

Gowing, Peter G. "Frank Charles Laubach, 1884-1970: Apostle to the Silent Billion," in G. H. Anderson et al., eds., *Mission Legacies: Biographical Studies of Leaders of the Modern Missionary Movement* (Maryknoll, NY: Orbis Books, 1994), pp. 500-507.

Greider, William. *One World, Ready or Not: The Manic Logic of Global Capitalism* (New York: Simon and Schuster, 1997).

Guillén, Mauro F. "Is Globalization Civilizing, Destructive or Feeble? A Critique of Five Key Debates in the Social Science Literature," *Annual Review of Sociology* 27 (2001): 235-60.

Gutek, Gerald and Patricia. *Visiting Utopia Communities* (Columbia: University of South Carolina Press, 1998).

Hackett, R. "Charismatic/Pentecostal Appropriation of Media Technologies in Nigeria," *Journal of Religion in Africa* 28 (1998): 258-77.

———. "Women and New Religious Movements in Africa," in Ursula King, ed., *Religion and Gender* (Oxford: Blackwell, 1995), pp. 257-90.

Hallencreutz, Carl F. *Kraemer Toward Tambaram: A Study in Hendrik Kraemer's Missionary Approach* (Uppsala: Gleerup, 1966).

Hamilton, Malcolm. *Sociology and the World's Religions* (New York: St. Martin's Press, 1998).

Harding, Susan. "Convicted by the Holy Spirit: The Rhetoric of Fundamental Baptist Conversion," *American Ethnologist* 14, no. 1 (1987): 167-81.

Hardy, Dennis. *Alternative Communities in Nineteenth Century England* (London and New York: Longman, 1979).

Harper, Susan Billington. *In the Shadow of the Mahatma: Bishop V. S. Azariah and the Travails of Christianity in British India* (Grand Rapids: Eerdmans; Richmond, UK: Curzon, 2000).

————. "The Politics of Conversion: The Azariah-Gandhi Controversy over Christian Mission to the Depressed Classes in the 1930's," *Indo-British Review* 15, no. 1 (1988): 147-75.

Harr, John Ensor, and Peter J. Johnson. *The Rockefeller Century* (New York: Charles Scribner's Sons, 1988).

Harrison, M. Hunter. "The Study of the Relation Between Christianity and Other Religious Faiths: The Contribution of Eric J. Sharpe," in D. J. Ambalavanar, ed., *The Gospel in the World: Essays in Honour of Bishop Kulandran* (Madras: Christian Literature Society, 1985).

Hastings, Adrian. *A History of Christianity in Africa 1950-1975* (Cambridge: Cambridge University Press, 1979).

Haynes, Jeff. *Religion and Politics in Africa* (London: Zed Press, 1996).

Hefner, Robert W. "Of Faith and Commitment: Christian Conversion in Muslim Java," in Robert W. Hefner, ed., *Conversion to Christianity: Historical and Anthropological Perspectives on a Great Transformation* (Berkeley: University of California Press, 1993), pp. 99-125.

Hertz, Noreena. *The Silent Takeover: Global Capitalism and the Death of Democracy* (New York: The Free Press, 2001).

Hexham, Irving, and Karla Poewe. "Charismatic Churches in South Africa: A Critique of Criticisms and Problems of Bias," in Karla Poewe, ed., *Charismatic Christianity as a Global Culture* (Columbia: University of South Carolina Press, 1994), pp. 50-69.

Hobgood, Ben C. "History of Protestant Higher Education in the Democratic Republic of the Congo," *Lexington Theological Quarterly* 33 (Spring 1998): 23-38.

Hock, Klaus. "'Jesus Power — Super Power': On the Interaction Between Christian Fundamentalism and New Religious Movements in Africa," *Mission Studies* 12, no. 1 (1995): 56-70.

Honggang, Ma., ed. "An Introduction of a Burgeoning Chinese Christian Sect: The Jesus Family," *Xiejin* 7, no. 5 (16 Oct. 1948): 6-7.

Hoogvelt, A. *Globalization and the Postcolonial World: The New Political Economy of Development* (Baltimore: Johns Hopkins University Press, 1997).

Hoover, Stewart M. *Mass Media Religion: The Social Sources of the Electronic Church* (London: Sage Publications, 1988).

Hopkins, C. Howard. *John R. Mott, 1865-1955* (Grand Rapids: Eerdmans, 1979).

Horam, B. *Naga Insurgency* (New Delhi: Cosmo, 1988).

Howell, Brian. "At Home in the World: Philippine Baptists and the Creation of Context" (unpublished Ph.D. thesis, Washington University, St. Louis, 2002).

Hunt, Stephan. "'A Church for All Nations': The Redeemed Christian Church of God," *Pneuma* 24, no. 2 (Fall 2002): 185-204.

Huntington, Samuel. *The Clash of Civilizations and the Remaking of World Order* (London: Touchstone, 1998).

Hurtado, Larry W. *One God, One Lord: Early Christian Devotion and Ancient Jewish Monotheism,* 2nd ed. (Edinburgh: T. & T. Clark, 1998).

Hutchison, William R. *Errand to the World: American Protestant Thought and Foreign Missions* (Chicago: University of Chicago Press, 1987).

Jassy, Marie France P. "Women in the Independent Churches," *Risk* 7, no. 3 (1971): 46-49.

Jathanna, O. V. *The Decisiveness of the Christ-Event and the Universality of Christianity in a World of Religious Plurality: With Special Reference to Hendrik Kraemer and Alfred George Hogg as well as to William Ernest Hocking and Pandipeddi Chenchiah* (Bern: Peter Lang, 1981).

Jenkins, Philip. *The Next Christendom: The Coming of Global Christianity* (New York: Oxford University Press, 2002).

Jongeneel, Jan A. B. "European-Continental Perceptions and Critiques of British and American Protestant Missions," *Exchange* 30, no. 2 (April 2001): 103-24.

Juergensmeyer, Mark. *The New Cold War? Religious Nationalism Confronts the Secular State* (Berkeley: University of California Press, 1993).

Jules-Rosette, Benetta. "Cultural Ambivalence and Ceremonial Leadership: The Role of Women in Africa's New Religious Movements," in John C. B. and Ellen Low Webster, eds., *The Church and Women in the Third World* (Philadelphia: Westminster Press, 1985), pp. 88-104.

Kabasélé, François. "Christ as Chief," in Robert J. Schreiter, ed., *Faces of Jesus in Africa* (Maryknoll, NY: Orbis Books, 1991), pp. 103-15.

Kairos Document. *Challenge to the Church: A Theological Comment on the Political Crisis in South Africa,* 5th ed. (Braamfontein and London: Kairos Theologians, CIIR, BCC, 1986).

Kalu, Ogbu U. "Estranged Bedfellows: The Demonization of the Aladura in African Pentecostal Rhetoric," *Missionalia* 28, no. 2/3 (2000): 121-42.

―――. Review of *African Christianity: Its Public Role, International Bulletin of Missionary Research* 24, no. 1 (Jan. 2000): 36.

―――. *Power, Poverty and Prayer: The Challenges of Poverty and Pluralism in African Christianity, 1960-1996* (New York: Peter Lang, 2000).

―――. "Preserving a Worldview: Pentecostalism in the African Maps of the Universe," *Pneuma* 24, no. 2 (Fall 2002): 110-37.

Kammerer, A. "Customs and Christian Conversion Among Akha Highlanders of Burma and Thailand," *American Ethnologist* 17, no. 2 (1990): 277-91.

Kaplan, Robert. "The Coming Anarchy," in Patrick O'Meara et al., eds., *Globalization and the Challenges of a New Century: A Reader* (Indianapolis: Indiana University Press, 2000), pp. 34-60.

Keller, Rosemary, gen. ed. *Methodist Women, a World Sisterhood. A History of the World Federation of Methodist Women 1923-1986* (N.p.: The World Federation of Methodist Women, n.d.).

Keohane, Robert, and Joseph S. Nye, Jr. "Globalization: What's New? What's Not? (And So What?)," *Foreign Policy* (Spring 2000): 104-19.

Khilnani, Sunil. *The Idea of India* (London: Hamish Hamilton, 1997).

Khor, Martin. "Global Economy and the Third World," in J. Mander and E. Goldsmith, eds., *The Case Against the Global Economy and for a Turn Towards the Local* (San Francisco: Sierra Book Clubs, 1996), pp. 47-59.

King, Richard. *Orientalism and Religion* (London: Routledge, 1999).

Kipp, Rita Smith. "Conversion by Affiliation: The History of the Karo Batak Protestant Church," *American Ethnologist* 22, no. 4 (1995): 868-82.

Kirk, Andrew. *What Is Mission? Theological Explorations* (Minneapolis: Fortress Press, 1999).

Klapper, Joseph T. *The Effects of Mass Communication* (New York: Free Press, 1960).

Klaus, Byron D. "Pentecostalism as a Global Culture: An Introductory Overview," in M. W. Dempster et al., eds., *The Globalization of Pentecostalism: A Religion Made to Travel* (Irvine, CA: Regnum Books International, 1999), pp. 127-30.

Kosambi, Meera, ed., *Pandita Ramabai Through Her Own Words: Selected Works* (New Delhi: Oxford University Press, 2000).

Kraemer, Hendrik. *The Christian Message in a Non-Christian World* (London: Edinburgh House Press, 1938).

Kuehl, William, and Lynne K. Dunn. *Keeping the Covenant: American Internationalists and the League of Nations, 1920-1939* (Kent, OH: Kent State University Press, 1997).

Kuma, Afua. *Jesus of the Deep Forest: Prayers and Praises of Afua,* trans. Jon Kirby (Accra: Asempa Publishers, 1981).

Landes, David S. *The Wealth and Poverty of Nations: Why Some Are So Rich and Some So Poor* (New York: W. W. Norton & Company, 1999).

Lester, Toby. "Oh, Gods!," *Atlantic Monthly,* February 2002, pp. 37-45.

Levy, Daniel C. "Latin America's Private Universities: How Successful Are They?" *Comparative Education Review* 29 (Nov. 1985): 440-59.

Lewis, Donald M. "Globalization: The Problem of Definition and Future Areas of Historical Inquiry," in Mark Hutchinson and Ogbu Kalu, eds., *A Global Faith: Essays on Evangelicalism and Globalization* (Sydney: Centre for the Study of Australian Christianity, 1998), pp. 26-46.

Lewis, Todd V. "Charisma and Media Evangelists: An Explanation and Model of Communication Influence," *The Southern Communication Journal* 54 (1988): 95-111.

Lipschutz, R. D., with J. Mayer. *Global Civil Society and Global Environmental Governance* (Albany: State University of New York Press, 1996).

Litonjua, M. D. "Global Capitalism: The New Context of Christian Social Ethics," *Theology Today* 56 (July 1999): 210-28.

Longfield, Bradley J. *The Presbyterian Controversy: Fundamentalists, Modernists, and Moderates* (New York: Oxford University Press, 1991).

Ludwig, Frieder. "Nigerian Christian Initiatives in Great Britain. The African Churches Mission in Liverpool and the Aladura Churches in London Compared: Six Theses," paper read at conference on "The Significance of the African Religious Diaspora in Europe," University of Leeds, 8-11 September 1997.

————. "Tambaram: The West African Experience," *Journal of Religion in Africa* 31, no. 1 (2001): 49-91.

Lynn, Richard, and Tatu Vanhanen. *IQ and the Wealth of Nations* (Westport, CT, and London: Praeger, 2002).

Lyon, David. "Wheels Within Wheels: Glocalisation and Contemporary Religion," in M. Hutchinson and O. U. Kalu, eds., *A Global Faith: Essays on Evangelicalism and Globalization* (Sydney: Centre for the Study of Australian Christianity, 1998), pp. 47-68.

————. *Jesus in Disneyland* (Cambridge: Polity Press, 2000).

MacNicol, N. *The Story of Pandita Ramabai: A Builder of Modern India* (Calcutta: Association Press, 1926).

Maggay, Melba A. *Filipino Religious Consciousness* (Quezon City: Institute for Studies in Asian Church and Culture, 1999).

Maher, Ian. "Liberation in *Awakenings*," in Clive Marsh and Gaye W. Ortiz, eds., *Explorations in Theology and Film* (Oxford: Blackwell Publishers, 1997), pp. 97-113.

Malcolm, Teresa. "Meeting Deplores Globalization," *National Catholic Reporter* 34, no. 24 (April 1998): 9.

Maluleke, Tinyiko Sam. "North-South Partnerships — The Evangelical Presbyterian Church in South Africa and the Département Missionnaire in Lausanne," *International Review of Mission* 83, no. 328 (Jan. 1994): 93-100.

Manikam, Rajah B. "The Effect of the War on the Missionary Task of the Church in India," *International Review of Mission* 36, no. 142 (April 1947): 175-90.

Marsden, George. "History of Fuller Seminary as a Case Study," *Christian Scholar's Review* 23 (Sept. 1993): 12-33.

Marshall, Paul, ed. *Religious Freedom in the World* (Nashville: Broadman and Holman, 2000).

Marshall, Ruth. "God Is Not a Democrat: Pentecostalism and Democratization in Nigeria," in Paul Gifford, ed., *The Christian Churches and the Democratisation of Africa* (Leiden: E. J. Brill, 1995), pp. 239-60.

Marshall-Fratani, Ruth. "Mediating the Global and Local in Nigerian Pentecostalism," *Journal of Religion in Africa* 28, no. 3 (1998): 278-315.

Martin, David. *Tongues of Fire: The Explosion of Protestantism in Latin America* (Oxford: Basil Blackwell, 1990).

————. "Evangelical Expansion in Global Society," in Donald M. Lewis, ed., *Chris-*

tianity Reborn: The Global Expansion of Evangelicalism in the Twentieth Century (Grand Rapids and Cambridge: Eerdmans, 2004), pp. 273-94.

—————. *Pentecostalism: The World Their Parish* (Oxford: Blackwell, 2002).

Marty, Martin E., and R. Scott Appleby, eds. *Fundamentalisms and the State* (Chicago: University of Chicago Press, 1993).

Mason, David E. *Frank C. Laubach, Teacher of Millions* (Minneapolis: T. S. Denison & Co., 1967).

Massey, James. *Minorities in a Democracy: The Indian Experience* (New Delhi: Manohar, 1999).

Matties, George. "Religion and Films: Capturing the Imagination," *Religion and Film* 2, no. 3 (1998): 156-88.

Maxwell, David. "In Defence of African Creativity," *Journal of Religion in Africa* 30, no. 4 (2000): 468-81.

—————. "Christianity Without Frontiers: Shona Missionaries and Transnational Pentecostalism in Africa," in David Maxwell, ed., with Ingrid Lawrie, *Christianity and the African Imagination: Essays in Honour of Adrian Hastings* (Leiden: E. J. Brill, 2002), pp. 295-332.

Mayer, Ann Elizabeth. *Islam and Human Rights* (Boulder, CO: Westview Press, 1999).

McCann, Dennis P. "Catholic Social Teaching in an Era of Economic Globalization: A Resource for Business Ethics," *Business Ethics Quarterly* 7 (March 1997): 57-70.

McGee, Gary B. "'Latter Rain' Falling in the East: Early-Twentieth-Century Pentecostalism in India and the Debate over Speaking in Tongues," *Church History* 68, no. 3 (Sept. 1999): 648-65.

McGrath, Alister E. *The Future of Christianity* (Oxford: Blackwell, 2002).

McLuhan, Marshall, and B. Powers. *The Global Village: Transformation in World, Life and Media in the Twenty-First Century* (Oxford: Oxford University Press, 1989).

McQuail, Denis. *Mass Communication Theory: An Introduction,* 3rd ed. (London: Sage Publications, 1994).

Mengisteab, Kidane. *Globalization and Autocentricity in Africa's Development in the 21st Century* (Lawrenceville, NJ: Africa World Press, Inc., 1996).

Menon, V. P. *The Integration of the Indian States* (Hyderabad: Orient Longman, 1956).

Meyer, Birgit. "Make a Complete Break with the Past," *Journal of Religion in Africa* 28, no. 3 (1998): 316-49.

Minz, Albert. "Dalits and Tribals: A Search for Solidarity," in V. Devasahayam, ed., *Frontiers of Dalit Theology* (Delhi: ISPCK, 1997), pp. 130-58.

Minz, Nirmal. "Dalit-Tribal: A Search for Common Ideology," in James Massey, ed., *Indigenous People: Dalits: Dalit Issues in Today's Theological Debate* (Delhi: ISPCK, 1998), pp. 134-42.

Mittelman, James H. *The Globalization Syndrome: Transformation and Resistance* (Princeton: Princeton University Press, 2000).

—————. *Globalization: Critical Reflections* (Boulder, CO: Lynne Rienner, 1996).

Moltmann, Jürgen. *God for a Secular Society* (London: SCM Press, 1999).

Moreau, A. Scott, ed. *Evangelical Dictionary of World Missions* (Grand Rapids: Baker, 2000).

Morsy, Zaghoul, and Philip G. Altbach, eds. *Higher Education in an International Perspective: Critical Issues,* International Bureau of Education Studies on Education 3 (New York and London: Garland Publishing, 1996).

Mukarji, D. "Gospel and the Search for Identity and Community," *International Review of Mission* 85, no. 336 (Jan. 1996): 25-34.

Mumper, Sharon. "An Indonesian Leader Speaks to the West, an Interview with Chris Marantika," *Evangelical Missions Quarterly* 22 (Jan. 1986): 6-11.

Nadler, L. B., Jeffrey L. Courtright, and Marjorie Keeshan Nadler. "Why Do People Give Money to Televangelists? A Pentecostal Development Explanation," *Journal of Communication and Religion* 19, no. 2 (1996): 47-58.

Nandi, Jack M. O. "The Jerusalem Church of Christ: A Historical and Theological Analysis" (unpublished M.A. thesis, University of Nairobi, 1993).

Newbigin, Lesslie. "A Sermon Preached at the Thanksgiving Service for the Fiftieth Anniversary of the Tambaram Conference of the International Missionary Council," *International Review of Mission* 78, no. 307 (July 1988): 325-31.

Ng, Peter Tze Ming. "Secularisation or Modernisation: Teaching Christianity in China Since the 1920s," *Studies in World Christianity* 5, no. 1 (1999): 1-17.

Noll, Mark A. "Who Would Have Thought?" *Books & Culture* 7 (Nov./Dec. 2001): 21.

Nutt, Rick L. *The Whole Gospel for the Whole World: Sherwood Eddy and American Protestant Mission* (Macon, GA: Mercer University Press, 1997).

Ohmae, Kenichi. *The Borderless World* (New York: Harper Business, 1990).

Omenyo, Cephas N. *Pentecost Outside Pentecostalism: A Study of the Development of Charismatic Renewal in the Mainline Churches in Ghana* (Zoetermeer: Boekencentrum, 2002).

Onyango, Maurice. "Churches of the Poor: African Independent Churches," *Wajibu* 2 (1997): 6-8.

Ositelu, Rufus. "Missio Africana! The Role of an African Instituted Church in the Mission Debate," *International Review of Mission* 89, no. 354 (July 2000): 384-86.

Pace, Enzo. "Religião e Globalização," in Pedro Ari Oro and Carlos Alberto Steil, eds., *Globalização e Religião* (Petrópolis: Vozes, 1997), pp. 25-42.

Padwick, John. "Towards a Change in Spirituality? Working in Development with Kenyan Spirit Churches," in D. Shenk, ed., *Working in Partnership with African Churches* (Elkhart, IN: Mission Focus, 1991).

Pakem, B., ed. *Insurgency in North East India* (New Delhi: Omsons, 1997).

Parker, Michael. *The Kingdom of Character: The Student Volunteer Movement for Foreign Missions (1886-1926)* (Lanham, MD: ASM and University Press of America, 1998).

Parratt, John. *Wounded Land: Politics and Identity in Modern Manipur* (New Delhi: Mittal, 2005).

Parratt, S. N. Arambam, and J. Parratt. "Reclaiming the Gods: A Neo-Traditional Protest Movement in Manipur," *Archiv Orientální* 67 (1999): 241-48.

Parry, Tony. "West Yorkshire African Caribbean Council of Churches, England," *International Review of Mission* 89, no. 354 (July 2000): 436-37.

Patrinos, Harry Anthony. "The Privatization of Higher Education in Colombia: Effects on Quality and Equity," *Higher Education* 20, no. 2 (1990): 161-73.

Peel, J. D. Y. *Aladura: A Religious Movement Among the Yoruba* (London: Oxford University Press, 1968).

Perraton, Jonathan. "Review Article: The Global Economy — Myths and Realities," *Cambridge Journal of Economics* 25 (2001): 669-84.

Phanjoubam, Pradip. "And the Pattern of Abuse," *Manipur Update* 1, no. 1 (1999): 7.

Phillipson, Robert. "English for Globalization or for the World's People?" *International Review of Education* 47 (July 2001): 185-200.

Pobee, John S. *Toward an African Theology* (Nashville: Abingdon, 1979).

———. *Kwame Nkrumah and the Church in Ghana, 1949-1966* (Accra: Asempa Publishers, 1988).

———. *Exploring Afro-Christology* (Frankfurt: Peter Lang, 1992).

———. *West Africa: Christ Would Be an African Too,* Gospel and Cultures Pamphlet 9 (Geneva: WCC Publications, 1996).

Poewe, Karla, ed. *Charismatic Christianity as a Global Culture* (Columbia: University of South Carolina Press, 1994).

Rafael, Vicente. *Contracting Colonialism: Translation and Christian Conversion in Tagalog Society under Spanish Colonial Rule* (Durham, NC: Duke University Press, 1993).

Ramachandra, Vinoth. "The Honor of Listening: Indispensable for Mission," *Evangelical Missions Quarterly* 30 (Oct. 1994): 404-9.

Rees, D. Vaughan. *The 'Jesus Family' in Communist China* (London: Paternoster Press, 1976).

Repp, Martin. "For a Moratorium on the Word 'Partnership,'" *The Japan Christian Review* 64 (1998): 28-34.

Rickett, Daniel. "Developmental Partnering," *Evangelical Missions Quarterly* 34 (Oct. 1998): 438-45.

Riis, Ole. "Modes of Religious Pluralism Under Conditions of Globalisation," *Journal on Multicultural Societies* 1, no. 1 (1999): 21-34.

Robert, Dana. "The Methodist Struggle over Higher Education in Fuzhou, China, 1877-1883," *Methodist History* 34 (April 1996): 173-89.

———. *American Women in Mission: A Social History of Their Thought and Practice* (Macon, GA: Mercer University Press, 1997).

———. "Shifting Southward: Global Christianity Since 1945," *International Bulletin of Missionary Research* 24, no. 2 (April 2000): 50-58.

Roberts, Jon H., and James Turner. *The Sacred and the Secular University* (Princeton: Princeton University Press, 2000).

Robertson, Roland. "The Sacred and the World System," in Philip E. Hammond, ed.,

The Sacred in a Secular Age: Toward Revision in the Scientific Study of Religion (Berkeley: University of California Press, 1985), pp. 347-58.

———. "Church-State Relations and the World-System," in R. Robertson and T. Robbins, eds., *Church-State Relations: Tensions and Transitions* (New Brunswick: Transaction Books, 1987), pp. 39-52.

———. "Globalization and Societal Modernization: A Note on Japan and Japanese Religion," *Sociological Analysis* 47 (1987): 35-42.

———. "Religion and the Global Field," *Social Compass* 41, no. 1 (1994): 121-35.

———. *Globalization: Social Theory and Global Culture* (London: Sage Publications, 1996).

———. "The Globalization Paradigm: Thinking Globally," in Peter Beyer, ed., *Religion im Prozeß der Globalisierung* (Würzburg: Ergon Verlag, 2001), pp. 3-22.

Robinson, Simon. "The Lord's Business," *Time* (Europe) 155 (7 Feb. 2000); see online reference, www.time.com/time/europe/magazine/2000/27/christian.

Russell, Susan D., and Clark E. Cunningham, eds. *Changing Lives, Changing Rites: Ritual and Social Dynamics in Philippine and Indonesian Uplands* (Ann Arbor: University of Michigan Press, 1989).

Ruthven, Malise. *Islam: A Very Short Introduction* (Oxford: Oxford University Press, 1997).

Saha, Lawrence J. "Universities and National Development: Issues and Problems in Developing Countries," in Zaghloul Morsy and Philip G. Altbach, eds., *Higher Education in an International Perspective: Critical Issues*, International Bureau of Education Studies on Education, vol. 3 (New York and London: Garland Publishing, Inc., 1996), pp. 80-89.

Samita, Zachariah W. *Christian Crusades in Nairobi: An Analysis of Social-Religious Factors Underlying Their Upsurge* (Addis Ababa: OSSREA, 1998).

Samuel, Vinay. "Keynote Address: Evangelical Response to Globalization: An Asian Perspective," *Transformation* 16 (Jan. 1999): 4-7.

Samuel, Vinay, and Chris Sugden. "Mission Agencies as Multinationals," *International Bulletin of Missionary Research* 7 (Oct. 1983): 152-55.

Sanajaoba, Naorem, ed. *Manipur Past and Present: The Heritage and Ordeals of a Civilization,* 3 vols. (Delhi: Mittal Publications, 1988-1995).

Sanneh, Lamin. *Translating the Message: The Missionary Impact on Culture* (Maryknoll, NY: Orbis Books, 1989).

———. *Encountering the West: Christianity and the Global Cultural Process* (Maryknoll, NY: Orbis Books, 1993).

———. *Whose Religion Is Christianity? The Gospel Beyond the West* (Grand Rapids: Eerdmans, 2003).

Sarin, V. I. K. *India's North East in Flames* (New Delhi: Vikas, 1980).

Sarpong, Peter K. "Asante Christology," *Studia Missionalia* 45 (1996): 189-205.

Saul, J. S., and C. Leys. "Sub-Saharan Africa in Global Capitalism," *Monthly Review* 51, no. 3 (July/Aug. 1999): 13-30.

Scott, Bruce. "The Great Divide in the Global Village," *Foreign Affairs* 80, no. 1 (Jan./ Feb. 2001): 160-77.

Seabury, Ruth Isabel. *Daughter of Africa* (Boston: Pilgrim Press, 1945).

Segato, Rita Laura. "Formações de Diversidade: Nação e Opções Religiosas no Contexto da Globalização," in Pedro Ari Oro and Carlos Alberto Steil, eds., *Globalização e Religião* (Petrópolis: Vozes, 1997), pp. 219-48.

Sengupta, Padmini. *Pandita Ramabai Saraswati: Her Life and Work* (London: Asia Publishing House, 1970).

Shah, A. B., ed. *The Letters and Correspondence of Pandita Ramabai,* compiled by Sister Geraldine (Bombay: Maharashtra State Board for Literature and Culture, 1977).

Shenk, Wilbert R. "The Origins and Evolution of the Three-Selfs in Relation to China," *International Bulletin of Missionary Research* 14 (Jan. 1990): 28-35.

Sherman, Mary Antoinette Brown. "The University in Modern Africa: Toward the Twenty-First Century," *Journal of Higher Education* 61 (July/August 1990): 363-85.

Sherwood, Marika. *Pastor Daniel Ekarte and the African Churches Mission Liverpool 1931-1964* (London: Savannah Press, 1994).

Showalter, Nathan D. *The End of a Crusade: The Student Volunteer Movement for Foreign Missions and the Great War* (Lanham, MD: Scarecrow Press, 1998).

Sider, Ronald J. *Rich Christians in an Age of Hunger: Moving from Affluence to Generosity* (Nashville: Word Publishing, 1997).

Siewert, J. A., and E. G. Valdez, eds. *Mission Handbook* (Monrovia, CA: MARC Publications, 1997).

Sitory, T. Valentino. "Rainbow in a Fallen World: Diversity and Unity in Christian Higher Education in Asia Today," in *Rainbow in a Fallen World: Diversity and Unity in Christian Higher Education Today,* proceedings of a conference sponsored by the International Council for the Promotion of Christian Higher Education, Lusaka, Zambia, 29 July–5 August 1987 (Sioux Center, IA: Dordt College Press, 1990), pp. 137-52.

Sloan, Douglas. *Faith and Knowledge: Mainline Protestantism and American Higher Education* (Louisville: Westminster John Knox Press, 1994).

Smith, Donald E. *India as a Secular State* (Princeton: Princeton University Press, 1963).

Smith, Dwight P. "Slaying the Dragons of Self-Interest: Making International Partnership Work," *Evangelical Missions Quarterly* 28 (Jan. 1992): 18-23.

Smith, C. Stanley. *The Development of Protestant Theological Education in China in the Light of the History of the Education of the Clergy in Europe and America,* part 2 (Shanghai: Kelly and Walsh, Ltd., 1941).

Son, Bong-Ho. "Christian Higher Education Where Christians Are a Minority — in Respect to Its Curriculum," in *Rainbow in a Fallen World: Diversity and Unity in Christian Higher Education Today,* proceedings of a conference sponsored by the International Council for the Promotion of Christian Higher Education,

Lusaka, Zambia, 29 July–5 August 1987 (Sioux Center, IA: Dordt College Press, 1990), pp. 157-63.

Srivastava, Dhirendra K. *Religious Freedom in India: A Historical and Constitutional Study* (New Delhi: Deep & Deep Publications, 1982).

Stackhouse, Max L. "Globalization, Faith and Theological Education," *Theological Education* 35 (Spring 1999): 67-77.

Stark, Rodney. "Efforts to Christianize Europe, 400-2000," *Journal of Contemporary Religion* 16, no. 1 (2001): 105-23.

Steadman, Roger H., et al., eds. *The Advertisers Guide 2002* (Nairobi: Steadman Associates, 2000).

Steedly, Mary Margaret. "The Importance of Proper Names: Language and 'National' Identity in Colonial Karoland," *American Ethnologist* 23, no. 3 (1996): 447-75.

Stinton, Diane. *Jesus of Africa: Voices of Contemporary African Christology* (Maryknoll, NY: Orbis Books, 2004).

Stromberg, Peter. *Language and Self-Transformation: The Study of the Christian Conversion Narrative* (Cambridge: Cambridge University Press, 1993).

Sundkler, Bengt G. M. *Bantu Prophets in South Africa* (London: Oxford University Press, 1961).

Syiemlieh, D. *A Brief History of the Catholic Church in Nagaland* (Shillong: Vendrame Institute Publications, 1990).

Takatemjen, *Studies on Theology and Naga Culture* (Delhi: ISPCK, 1998).

Tapp, Nicholas. "The Impact of Missionary Christianity upon Marginalized Ethnic Minorities: The Case of the Hmong," *Journal of Southeast Asian Studies* 20 (1989): 70-95.

Tarapot, Phanjoubam. *Bleeding Manipur* (New Delhi: Har-Anand, 2003).

———. *Insurgency Movement in North-Eastern India* (New Delhi: Vikas Publishing House, 1993).

Tatlow, Tissington. *The Story of the Student Christian Movement of Great Britain and Ireland* (London: Student Christian Movement Press, 1933).

Taylor, Richard W. "E. Stanley Jones, 1884-1973: Following the Christ of the Indian Road," in G. Anderson et al., eds., *Mission Legacies: Biographical Studies of Leaders of the Modern Missionary Movement* (Maryknoll, NY: Orbis, 1994), pp. 339-47.

Taylor, William D. "Lessons in Partnership," *Evangelical Missions Quarterly* 31 (Oct. 1995): 406-15.

Ter Haar, Gerrie. "Strangers in the Promised Land: African Christians in Europe," *Exchange* 24, no. 1 (February 1995): 1-33.

———. *Halfway to Paradise: African Christians in Europe* (Cardiff: Cardiff Academic Press, 1998).

Thelle, Notto R. "Karl Ludvig Reichelt, 1877-1952: Christian Pilgrim of Tao Fong Shan," in Gerald H. Anderson et al., eds., *Mission Legacies: Biographical Studies of Leaders of the Modern Missionary Movement* (Maryknoll, NY: Orbis Books, 1994), pp. 216-24.

Thomas, M. M., and R. W. Taylor, eds. *Tribal Awakening* (Bangalore: CSIRS, 1965).

Thompson, Grahame. "Introduction: Situating Globalization," *International Social Science Journal* 160 (June 1999): 139-52.

Thorogood, Bernard. "Sharing Resources in Mission," *International Review of Mission* 76, no. 304 (Oct. 1987): 441-51.

Thurow, Lester. *The Future of Capitalism: How Today's Economic Forces Shape Tomorrow's World* (New York: Penguin Books, 1996).

Tilak, Jandhyala B. G. "The Privatization of Higher Education," *Prospects* 21, no. 3 (1991): 227-39.

Tomlinson, John. *Globalization and Culture* (Chicago: University of Chicago Press, 1999).

Trahair, Richard C. S. *Utopias and Utopians: A Historical Dictionary* (London and Chicago: Fitzroy Dearborn Publishers, 1999).

Trinidad, Ruben F. "Nicolas Zamora and the IEMELEF Church," in Anne C. Kwantes, ed., *Chapters in Philippine Church History* (Colorado Springs: International Academic Publishers, Ltd., 2002), pp. 203-24.

Turner, Harold. "The Contribution of Studies on Religion in Africa to Western Religious Studies," in M. E. Glasswell and E. W. Fasholé-Luke, eds., *New Testament Christianity for Africa and the World* (London: SPCK, 1974), pp. 169-78.

————. *The Life and Faith of the Church of the Lord Aladura*, 2 vols. (London: Oxford University Press, 1967).

Useem, Andrea. "In East Africa, New Private Colleges Fill a Growing Gap Between Supply and Demand," *Christian Higher Education*, 10 September 1999, p. A65.

Van Engen, Charles, et al. *The Good News of the Kingdom: Mission Theology for the Third Millennium* (Maryknoll, NY: Orbis Books, 1993).

Vanter, David. "Globalization and the Cultural Effects of the World-Economy in a Semi-Periphery: The Emergence of African Indigenous Churches in South Africa," *Journal of World-Systems Research* [http://csf.colorado.edu/wsystems/jwsr.html] 5 (1999): 105-26.

Verghese, B. G. *India's Northeast Resurgent: Ethnicity, Insurgency, Governance, Development*, 2nd ed. (New Delhi: Konark, 1997).

Vernooij, Joop. "Winti in Suriname," *Mission Studies* 20, no. 1 (2003): 140-59.

Viswanathan, Gauri. *Outside the Fold: Conversion, Modernity and Belief* (Princeton: Princeton University Press, 1998).

Wacker, Grant. *Heaven Below: Early Pentecostals and American Culture* (Cambridge, MA: Harvard University Press, 2001).

Wagner, C. Peter. "Mission and Church in Four Worlds," in *Church/Mission Tensions Today*, ed. C. Peter Wagner (Chicago: Moody Press, 1972), pp. 215-32.

Wallerstein, Immanuel. *The Modern World-System* (New York: Academic Press, 1974).

Walls, Andrew F. "Towards Understanding Africa's Place in Christian History," in J. S. Pobee, ed., *Religion in a Pluralistic Society* (Leiden: E. J. Brill, 1976), pp. 180-89.

————. "The Christian Tradition in Today's World," in Frank Whaling, ed., *Religion* in *Today's World: The Religious Situation of the World from 1945 to the Present Day* (Edinburgh: T. & T. Clark, 1987), pp. 76-109.

————. *The Missionary Movement in Christian History: Studies in the Transmission of Faith* (Maryknoll, NY: Orbis Books, 1996).

————. "African Christianity in the History of Religions," in Andrew F. Walls, *The Cross-Cultural Process in Christian History* (Maryknoll, NY: Orbis Books, 2002), pp. 116-35.

————. "Africa in Christian History: Retrospect and Prospect," in Andrew F. Walls, *The Cross-Cultural Process in Christian History* (Maryknoll, NY: Orbis Books, 2002), pp. 85-115.

————. "Eusebius Tries Again: Reconceiving the Study of Christian History," *International Bulletin of Missionary Research* 24, no. 3 (July 2000): 105-11.

————. "Christian Scholarship in Africa in the Twenty-First Century," *Journal of African Christian Thought* 4, no. 2 (Dec. 2001): 44-52.

————. "Theology Is Moving South: Where Christian Growth and Fruitful Questions Are," *Trust* (New Year, 2003): 14-19.

Walsh, Michael. "Catholicism and International Relations: Papal Interventionism," in J. L. Esposito and M. Watson, eds., *Religion and Global Order* (Cardiff: University of Wales Press, 2000), pp. 100-118.

Warner, R. Stephen. *New Wine in Old Wineskins: Evangelicals and Liberals in a Small-Town Church* (Berkeley: University of California Press, 1987).

Waruta, Douglas W. "Who Is Jesus Christ for Africans Today? Prophet, Priest, Potentate," in J. N. K. Mugambi and Laurenti Magesa, eds., *Jesus in African Christianity: Experimentation and Diversity in African Christology* (Nairobi: Acton Publishers, 1989).

Waters, Malcolm. *Globalization* (London: Routledge, 1995).

Weber, Max. *Ancient Judaism* (New York: Free Press, 1952).

————. *The Protestant Ethic and the Spirit of Capitalism* (London: Unwin, 1985).

Webster, John C. B. *The Dalit Christians: A History* (Delhi: ISPCK, 1992).

Weeks, Priscilla. "Post-Colonial Challenges to Grand Theory," *Human Organization* 49, no. 3 (1990): 236-44.

Wilson, Bryan. *Religious Sects: A Sociological Study* (London: Weidenfeld & Nicolson, 1970).

Wilson, Everett A. "They Crossed the Red Sea, Didn't They? Critical History and Pentecostal Beginnings," in Murray W. Dempster et al., eds., *The Globalization of Pentecostalism: A Religion Made to Travel* (Irvine, CA: Regnum Books International, 1999), pp. 85-115.

Wilson, Stan Le Roy. *Mass Media, Mass Culture: An Introduction* (New York: McGraw-Hill, 1993).

Wolfe, Alan. "The Opening of the Evangelical Mind," *Atlantic Monthly,* October 2000, pp. 55-76.

Woodhead, Linda, and Paul Heelas, eds. *Religion in Modern Times* (Oxford: Blackwell, 2000).

Woodward, Kenneth L. "The Changing Face of the Church: How the Explosion of Christianity in Developing Nations Is Transforming the World's Largest Religion," *Newsweek*, 16 April 2001, pp. 46-52.

Wu, Silas H. *Dora Yu and Christian Revival in Twentieth-Century China* (Boston: Pishon River Publishers, 2002).

Yao, Kevin Xiyi. *The Fundamentalist Movement Among Protestant Missionaries in China, 1920-1937* (Lanham, MD: University Press of America, 2003).

Yates, Timothy. *Christian Mission in the Twentieth Century* (Cambridge: Cambridge University Press, 1994).

Yeh, Wen-Hsin. *The Alienated Academy: Culture and Politics in Republican China, 1919-1937* (Cambridge, MA: Council on East Asian Studies/Harvard University, 1990).

Zha, Shijie, "Shandong 'Yesu Jiating' de Jingji Xingtai Chutan, 1927-1942" [the economic activities of the 'Jesus Family' in Shandong, 1927-1942], *Guoli Taiwan daxue lishi xuexi xuebao* 15 (1990).

Index